D1732108

IMAGINING THE ROMAN EMPEROR

How was the Roman emperor viewed by his subjects? How strongly did their perception of his role shape his behaviour? Adopting a fresh approach, Panayiotis Christoforou focusses on the emperor from the perspective of his subjects across the Roman empire. Stress lies on the imagination: the emperor was who he seemed, or was imagined, to be. Through various vignettes employing a wide range of sources, Christoforou analyses the emperor through the concerns and expectations of his subjects, which range from intercessory justice to fears of the monstrosities associated with absolute power. The book posits that mythical and fictional stories about the Roman emperor form the substance of what people thought about him, which underlines their importance for the historical and political discourse that formed around him as a figure. The emperor emerges as an ambiguous figure. Loved and hated, feared and revered, he was an object of contradiction and curiosity.

PANAYIOTIS CHRISTOFOROU is Departmental Lecturer in the Faculty of Classics, University of Oxford, and at Oriel and Jesus Colleges.

IMAGINING THE ROMAN EMPEROR

Perceptions of Rulers in the High Empire

PANAYIOTIS CHRISTOFOROU

University of Oxford

CAMBRIDGE
UNIVERSITY PRESS

Shaftesbury Road, Cambridge CB2 8EA, United Kingdom

One Liberty Plaza, 20th Floor, New York, NY 10006, USA

477 Williamstown Road, Port Melbourne, VIC 3207, Australia

314–321, 3rd Floor, Plot 3, Splendor Forum, Jasola District Centre,
New Delhi – 110025, India

103 Penang Road, #05–06/07, Visioncrest Commercial, Singapore 238467

Cambridge University Press is part of Cambridge University Press & Assessment,
a department of the University of Cambridge.

We share the University's mission to contribute to society through the pursuit of
education, learning and research at the highest international levels of excellence.

www.cambridge.org
Information on this title: www.cambridge.org/9781009362498

DOI: 10.1017/9781009362504

First published 2023

A catalogue record for this publication is available from the British Library.

A Cataloging-in-Publication data record for this book is available from the Library of Congress.

ISBN 978-1-009-36249-8 Hardback

Contents

Preface: in omnibus varius – *A Multifaceted Emperor* *page* ix
Acknowledgements xiii
List of Abbreviations xv

Introduction: An Imagined Emperor 1

1 A History of the Roman Emperor 6
 1.1 Talking about the Emperor and Finding the 'Popular' Voice in the
   Conversation 8
 1.2 The Emperor Historiographically and Constitutionally 28
 1.3 The Emperor As a Series of Paradoxes 58

2 The Emperor As an Arbiter of Justice 62
 2.1 *Iustitia* and *aequitas*? 'Virtues' and the Evidence for Justice 65
 2.2 Statues of the Emperor in the Roman World 73
 2.3 Fictional Encounters of Justice in Literature 83

3 The Generosity of the Roman Emperor 99
 3.1 *Benefacta laudare*: Generosity in Roman Imperial Politics 99
 3.2 How to Become Emperor: A Digression on the Succession 102
 3.3 Exhibiting Generosity through the Next Generation: Heirs
   and Benefactors 115
 3.4 Generosity As *princeps* 120

4 Wonder Tales 131
 4.1 Paradoxography and Empire: Where *thaumata* and *miracula* Are 134
 4.2 The Emperor of Wonder at Rome 142
 4.3 The Emperor As Wonder and Monster 149

5 Wisdom and Wit: Making Fun of the Emperor 160
 5.1 Public and Hidden Transcripts in Imperial Humour 160
 5.2 Collapsing the 'Good' and 'Bad' Emperor Binary 166
 5.3 Laughing with an Elephant and the Dangers of Making Fun
   of an Emperor 168

6   Living in an Age of Gold, or the Emperor As a Temporal Figure 179
    6.1 The Emperor through Time   179
    6.2 An Imperial Present of Gold and Iron   185
    6.3 Imperial Past: Memory, History, and Remembering the Roman
         Emperor   203
    6.4 Imperial Futures: Impersonations, Resurrections, and the Afterlife
         of an Emperor   224

    Coda: The Worlds of the Roman Emperor   233

References   238
Index   265

τοῖς ἀγαπητοῖς μου γονεῦσι

Preface: in omnibus varius – *A Multifaceted Emperor*

This book is founded on the study of the emperor in his world and how the inhabitants of the Roman empire understood this larger-than-life figure. The common strand that runs through this book can be formulated as follows. The Roman emperor seems to be a set of binaries, which makes him seem contradictory. Take two possible vignettes of the Roman emperor: the passive emperor responding to petitions, which on the face of it seems logistically challenging, and the emperor as a single godly figure and the focus of cult, given the variety of cultic activities that were associated with the emperor and his family across the empire. These vignettes become difficult to reconcile into a single figure. The binaries include the status of the emperor as a political figure within the Roman state: a *princeps* amongst *cives*, though the responsibility and power he wielded were in fact supreme, blurring the lines between his person and the *res publica*. The emperor was a man and a god, statuses which are hard to separate; the emperor was both placed above the laws and lived according to them; and the position of emperor was imbued with an authority and power that made it unassailable, though the history of this period is littered with instances of the contested legitimacy of any given *princeps*. The emperor could be seen to be radically free from coercion and uniquely shackled with the responsibilities of being the moral exemplar of the Roman world. More profoundly, such an assumption has the Roman emperor both appear to be a supreme commander in the mould of illustrious *summi viri* of the past and described as a slave, in the company of lesser entities as seen by Roman social sensibilities: slaves, freedmen, women, and bandits as well as freaks and monsters – all of which reveal anxieties about the power associated with the emperor himself. These binaries, and how they collapse into a single person, form the subject of this book.

These binaries cannot be separated from each other entirely, as they describe a nominally single entity, the Roman emperor. The fact that they are embodied in a single person should suggest similarities in any given theme conceptually, which supplies a great deal of information about the thought-world of the inhabitants of the Roman empire (i.e. the conceptual assumptions and ideas that inform how these people understood the world around them). Instead of accentuating the contradictions and 'problems' inherent in this interpretation, the point that I am arguing here appreciates the inconsistencies *as* inconsistencies rather than attempting to explain them away.

Indeed, inconsistency and 'incompleteness' are endemic in the position that comes from its foundation. Augustus never packaged a 'complete' emperor, with a title, constitutional formalisation, or a set of particular duties. Rather than seeing the age of Augustus as a 'half-baked' principate, the principate was never complete at all: much was left to ambiguity and expectation.[1] It is because of this incompleteness, then, that the emperor could occupy all his roles simultaneously. To put it in a more 'political' and 'legal' way, the position that Augustus held seemed to be cobbled together from various magisterial and religious roles, yet those titles never added up to embody a complete and definable position. That 'extra' portion in itself was volatile and subjective, namely the clout or charisma a leader held.[2] In this way, any single term or single power to describe the nature of the emperor would be by definition reductive and particular to that context, which in turn suggests that the emperor was meant to be jagged, incomplete, and more than the sum of his parts. Imagination then can run wild on the various roles that he could fulfil, grounded in both 'reality' and 'fiction'.

A career could be spent exploring the various binaries and boundaries at play within the person of the emperor.[3] However, there can be a historical explanation for why this form of autocracy developed in this manner, which has to do with the form of *res publica* that Augustus laid down, based as it was on the politics of consensus and cooperation. I also discuss trends and examples that illustrate the 'doubleness' of the Roman emperor.[4] I do not pretend to be comprehensive in my treatment

---

[1] Drinkwater (2019: 12); Drinkwater (2013). [2] Ando (2000).

[3] For a recent attempt, see Hekster (2023), esp. 1–22.

[4] I borrow this concept from Greensmith (2020: 49–51), who notices an aspect of doubleness in Greek culture in the Roman empire that reflects on the tensions in cultural and intellectual life in the Greek east. In the context of the reception of Homer in the third century, the idea of engaging in the 'poetics of the interval' suggests a longing to supply meaning to gaps of knowledge, whilst also appreciating the existence of the gap itself. Such a reading speaks well to the idea of the Roman emperorship, to which his subjects supplied much imagination to the 'interval' between the realities of his power and the expectations placed on the position, along the several axes I have enumerated here. The emperor becomes a temporal figure, imbued with different meanings as you observe him. Hence the 'ambiguities' and 'doubleness' of his reception.

of the Roman emperor in the first two centuries AD. A holistic treatment of the Roman emperor that treats his manifestations across time and space in the Roman empire would be a feat of collaboration, which would necessarily include scholars of different disciplines. What I seek is a blueprint of enquiry.

Heisenberg's uncertainty principle, to fashion a metaphor from physics, illustrates the understanding of the Roman emperor outlined in this book. To describe the principle, it is impossible to determine both the momentum and the position of a particle with high precision at the same time. Observing one phenomenon (say momentum) with high precision means that you cannot observe the other (the position) with high precision. Accordingly, there is a gap in measurable knowledge when considering an object. I believe this principle can be applied to the Roman emperor. To observe one aspect of the emperor, such as his status as a godlike figure, may throw light on his position in between human and divine affairs, but doing so may obscure how the emperor was considered a human political office. This is but one tension that can be observed with respect to the emperorship, which makes the position a multifaceted one, subject to the measurement we choose to quantify at any given time.

The focus of this book is on the position of the emperor and how he was conceived by his subjects. Such an activity may prove to demystify the Roman emperorship, particularly along two axes: First, to prove that the Roman emperor was a politically resonant figure across the empire, and not just in the juridical and constitutional context of the city itself, or even amongst the citizen population across the empire. By definition, the Roman emperor had to be understandable and approachable in different contexts, which led to the multifaceted nature of his office. Second, to show that the processes of legitimation and criticism are in some part comparable to different forms of autocracies in human history, and that by appreciating the differences and similarities in those vastly different contexts of time and space, we may come to an understanding of how monarchies form and replicate themselves. Such an activity is the argument of Duindam's book *Dynasties* and Bartlett's *Blood Dynasty*, and the Roman emperor should be seen within that continuum, rather than exceptionally idiosyncratic.[5]

This book was written throughout much of the decade of the 2010s, and the argument gestated particularly after the times of Brexit, the rise of

---

[5] Duindam (2016); Bartlett (2020).

Trumpism, and the SARS CoV-2 pandemic. Much of what happened during these times helped sharpen my interest in how people respond to crisis and perceived political upheaval, as well as the volatility of information as seen through social media and the Internet. The difficulties of discerning truth from falsehood have come to the forefront in our times, making my chosen project one of pertinent interest. In many ways, my book serves to vindicate the importance of fictionality to the study of history, as it is those responses to fears and imagination that can help inform political and social interactivity.

Acknowledgements

This book was a labour of love for many years, both before and after my doctorate. Its completion would not have been possible without the encouragement and support of friends and family alike. First mention goes to my wife and confidant, Philippa Christoforou, who has read through many versions of this work and has listened to me go on about the Roman emperor for many years now. None of what I have written here would have been possible without her love and steadfastness, particularly through lean times and heavy teaching loads. Any success in my life has been because of her. To my parents, Andreas and Jacqueline, and my sister, Nasia, to all of whom this book is dedicated, I thank them for the encouragement, prayers, and reminders that history has been my calling since I was very young.

Pride of place goes to my doctoral supervisor, Nicholas Purcell, who turned me to this ambitious project, kept me focussed on the task, and opened my mind to both the grand themes and the small nuances of history. The book would not have been possible without him, and I continue to learn from his suggestions and help. I thank my doctoral viva examiners, Professor Teresa Morgan and Professor Olivier Hekster, for the invaluable aid at the start of my career and the helpful suggestions as to how to push the project forward. Warm thanks to Michael Sharp, Natasha Burton, and Linsey Hague for their hard work and help getting the book ready for publication.

I also thank those who have entrusted me with employment since I finished my doctorate: Beate Dignas, Alfonso Moreno, Felix Budelmann, Barney Taylor, Ed Bispham, Lisa Kallet, Bill Allan, Bruno Currie, Juliane Kerkkhecker, Luca Castagnioli, Armand D'Angour and Georgy Kantor as well as the communities at Magdalen, Brasenose, Exeter, University, St John's, Oriel and Jesus Colleges for their vibrant scholarly environments. Many thanks especially to Georgy, who kindly read and commented on drafts of this book. The countless discussions

I have had with those colleagues and in those places have enriched the book no end. Special thanks go to St John's College and Dr Matthew Nicholls – the support received for research grants and a dedicated space to write the book during the global pandemic made it possible to complete this work.

Friends made during these times have been steadfast and fundamental to my thinking as an academic. To Jim Matarazzo, for the love, support, and encouragement. To Lukas Payne, for the logical foundation to my work, the endless jokes, and the enriching friendship throughout the years. To Benjamin Stevens, for steadfast friendship, support, and help with the knottiness of English. To Bram ten Berge, who has meticulously read and commented on my work and continues to be a close collaborator and friend. To Samson Kambalu, who always challenges assumptions and makes me think critically about both form and content. I hope he might find some of his inspiration and the *nyau* in these pages. To Daniel Robinson, for the encouragement and the willingness to listen to my ideas over countless cups of coffee and dinners. To Talitha Kearey, for being the best colleague I could ask for, an even better friend, and a formidable scholar. To Karolina Sekita, for the undying support, encouragement, and the confidence to pursue topics in Greek history. And to Emma Greensmith, whose brilliant scholarship, love, and immeasurable support have helped me improve and appreciate my own accomplishments and abilities. Her keen eye for form and detail will inform my pedagogy and scholarship well into the future, and her careful attention to drafts of my work have immeasurably improved the outcome; in short, this book would not be possible without you. Here is to many more years as part of your team. There are also many others who have helped along the way that are too numerous to name, including all my students throughout the years. All of you believed in my capabilities when I could not and for that I am eternally grateful.

Final words go to my family, both present and past: Georgia, Michalis, Panayiotis, Jo, Chris, Sandy, La'akea, Manuel Alberto Quijano, and Maria Italia. Owing to time and long distances, much of life has been spent away from you and home. The sacrifices made by my parents and my family have made my life and career possible, and I hope that this book is a testament to my gratitude. The final dedication goes to my θεία Μάρω, who passed away near the end of my doctoral work. In lieu of the hoped-for celebration on the completion of my toils, I pour libations in remembrance of her; αἰωνία ἡ μνήμη.

Abbreviations

Abbreviations of ancient authors follow the conventions in the *Oxford Classical Dictionary*, fourth edition. For the journal abbreviations, I have followed *L'année philologique*. All papyri are cited according to the latest version of the *Checklist of Editions of Greek, Latin, Demotic and Coptic Papyri, Ostraca and Tablets*, published online (http://library.duke.edu/rubenstein/scriptorium/papyrus/texts/clist.html).

Acta = Musurillo, H. 1961. *Acta Alexandrinorum*. Leipzig.

AE = *L'année epigraphique*.

ANRW = Temporini, H. and W. Haase (eds.). 1972. *Aufstieg und Niedergang der römischen Welt. Geschichte und Kultur Roms im Spiegel der neueren Forschung*. Berlin and New York.

APM = Musurillo, H. 1954. *Acts of the Pagan Martyrs*. Oxford.

BGU = *Aegyptische Urkunden aus den Königlichen (later Staatlichen) Museen zu Berlin, Griechische Urkunden*. Berlin.

CAH [2] = *The Cambridge Ancient History*, 2nd ed., 14 vols. Cambridge.

CIL = *Corpus inscriptionum Latinarum*. Berlin.

Corinth 8.2 = West, A. B. 1931. *Corinth, VIII.2, Latin Inscriptions*. Cambridge, MA.

Dig. = Mommsen, T., P. Krueger and A. Watson (eds.). 1985. *The Digest of Justinian*. Philadelphia.

DPR = Mommsen, T. 1889–96. *Le droit public romain*, 7 vols., trans. P. F. Girard. Paris.

EJ = Ehrehberg, V. and A. H. M. Jones (eds.). 1976. *Documents Illustrating the Reigns of Augustus and Tiberius*, 2nd ed. Oxford.

I.Assos = Merkelbach, R. (ed.). 1976. *Die Inschriften von Assos*. IGSK Band 4. Bonn.

I.Sardis = Buckler, W. H. and D. M. Robinson (eds.). 1932. *Sardis, VII: Greek and Latin Inscriptions*. Leiden.

IG = *Inscriptiones Graecae*. Berlin.

IGR = R. Cagnat (ed.). 1901–27. *Inscriptiones Graecae ad res Romanas pertinentes.* Paris.

ILAfr = Cagnat, R., L. Chatelain, and A. Merlin. 1923. *Inscriptions latines d'Afrique (Tripolitaine, Tunisie, Maroc).* Paris.

ILLPRON = Hainzmann, M. and P. Schubert. 1986–. *Inscriptionum lapidarium Latinarum provinciae Norici usque ad annum MCMLXXXIV repertarum indices.* Berlin.

ILS = Dessau, H. 1892–1916. *Inscriptiones Latinae selectae,* 3 vols. Berlin.

Inscr. Ital. 13.2 = Degrassi, A. (ed.). 1963. *Inscriptiones Italiae Academiae Italicae Consociatae ediderunt. Volumen XIII, Fasciculus II, Fasti anni Numani et Iuliani.* Rome.

Liddell and Scott, *Greek–English Lexicon,* 9th ed., rev. H. Stuart Jones (1925–40); suppl. By E. A. Barber and others (1968).

LTUR = Steinby, E. M. (ed.). 1993–9. *Lexicon Topographicum Urbis Romae,* 6 vols., Rome.

OCD[3] = Hornblower, S. and A. Spawforth. 2003. *Oxford Classical Dictionary,* 3rd ed. Oxford.

Orac. Sib. = *Oracula Sibyllina.* Cited in Gauger, J.-D. (ed.). 1998. *Sibyllinische Weissagungen.* Düsseldorf.

PIR[2] = Groag, E., A. Stein, and L. Petersen et al. (eds.). 1930–. *Prosopographia Imperii Romani saec. I. II. III,* 2nd ed. Leipzig.

RGDA = *Res gestae divi Augusti.*

Roman Statutes = Crawford, M. H. (ed.). 1996. *Roman Statutes* (BICS Suppl. 64). London.

Ruggiero, *Diz. Epigr.* = de Ruggiero, E. (ed.). 1886–1997. *Dizionario epigrafico di antichità romane.* Rome.

SCPP = *Senatus Consultum de Pisone Patre,* text, translation and commentary from J. B. Lott. 2012. *Death and Dynasty in Early Imperial Rome.* Cambridge.

SEG = *Supplementum Epigraphicum Graecum.* Leiden.

Sherk, *RDGE* = Sherk, R. K. 1969. *Roman Documents from the Greek East: Senatus Consulta and Epistulae to the Age of Augustus.* Baltimore, MD.

Smallwood, *Gaius* = Smallwood, E. M. 1967. *Documents Illustrating the Principates of Gaius, Claudius and Nero.* Cambridge.

StR = Mommsen, T. 1887–8. *Römisches Straatsrecht,* 3rd ed., 3 vols. Leipzig.

SVF = von Arnim, H. F. A. and M. Adler (eds.). *Stoicorum veterum fragmenta,* 4 vols. Leipzig.

Syll.[3] = Dittenberger, W. 1915–24. *Sylloge inscriptionum Graecarum*, 3rd ed. Leipzig.

TLG = *Thesaurus Linguae Graecae.*

TLL = *Thesaurus Linguae Latinae.*

TS = *Tabula siarensis*, text, translation, and commentary from J. B. Lott. 2012. *Death and Dynasty in Early Imperial Rome*. Cambridge.

An Imagined Emperor

Aurea secura cum pace renascitur aetas . . .

A Golden age with an assured peace is reborn . . .[1]

. . . sed legibus omne reductis
ius aderit, moremque fori vultumque priorem
reddet et afflictum melior deus auferet aevum.

> . . . yet, with laws being restored as a whole, justice will arrive, and a better god will remove the age of misery and restore the customs of the forum and its former appearance.[2]

The opening epigraph is from Calpurnius Siculus' first *eclogue*, here recounting the prophecy of Faunus inscribed on a beech tree. It is found by Corydon and Oryntus in their effort to escape the sun in late summer.[3] The inscription describes the coming of a new golden age, precipitated by a young emperor who will restore peace and order, to the joy of the people, and bring back a time of plenty and life without care, just as the poets had described.[4] In many ways, it captures the essence of several themes that will be explored in this book, which is a study of the perception and reception of the Roman emperor from the perspective of his subjects. These are timelessness, comparability, and liminality, which can be explained as follows. The temporal dimension involves the continual existence of the emperorship, in the sense of the idea of the permanence of the emperor, which gave him a timeless quality. This brings us to comparability, which invites the judgement and scrutiny of different emperors from the perspective of his subjects within the rubric of what it means to be an emperor – a conversation that is continually being augmented with the advent of new emperors and the reinterpretation of previous ones. Finally, his liminality

---

[1] Calp. *Ecl.* 1.42–6. All translations are my own, loosely adapted from the Loeb translations in the first instance, with exceptions noted throughout the book.
[2] Calp. *Ecl.* 1.71–3.   [3] Cf. Wiseman (1982: 57).   [4] For more on these themes, see Chapter 6.

I

is due to the emperor being caught between several different roles and worlds that are inherent to the nature of the position. Depending on context, the emperor can be perceived to be *basileus*, responding to petitions from his subjects, and also the first amongst equals in Rome.[5] He could be a paragon of moral rectitude, distant from the vicissitudes of luxury, but also seen in the company of freaks, engaging in depravity.[6] He could also be godly, standing between humanity and the divine; a bringer of peace and plenty to the world; a harbinger of a new golden age; but also a *Saturnalicius princeps*, a figure who brings about ruin and chaos.[7]

As a precursor, all these themes are present in Calpurnius Siculus. The lack of specificity in the allusions to any singular emperor points to the malleability of the themes and images with which he is elaborating.[8] Indeed, the strength of the argument that the *iuvenis* described throughout this poem as clearly being a reference to Nero was challenged by Champlin a few decades ago, who argued for a third-century date and the young man actually being Alexander Severus.[9] This precipitated a scholarly firestorm involving several classicists, commencing with a strong rejection of Champlin in order to bolster the Neronian date.[10] However, the terms of these debates concerning the historical and literary references apparent in Calpurnius Siculus, alongside analyses of his metre, syntax, and prosody, fall beyond the scope of this book. Perhaps the key point to argue takes its cue from Horsfall's agnosticism in the dating of the poems, namely concerning the timelessness of its themes.[11] In other words, the references above could refer to a specific emperor, yet they are framed in such a way that they can be disputed. Temporal wavering is at play here, brought into relief by the mythological references, which places the discourse of what it means to be an emperor outside of time. As this book will show, this developing conversation scrutinised the idea of the emperor throughout the period in question, namely the first two and a half centuries of our era, allowing for comparison to occur between different emperors and different contexts.

---

[5] Millar (1977: 3, 11).   [6] Dench (2005: 279–92).

[7] Dench (2005: 280); Dickison (1977: 634–47).   [8] Cf. Horsfall (1997: 166).

[9] Champlin (1978), esp. 98–100.

[10] For a comprehensive account of this debate, see Martin (1996: 34–5, n. 4). For the first reactions, see Townend (1980: 166–74), Mayer (1980: 175–6), and Wiseman (1982: 57–67). For Champlin's response, see Champlin (1986: 104–12), alongside aid from Armstrong (1986: 113–36), for a more literary and metrical analysis of the poet's work that preferred a later date. For a sceptical appraisal of the earlier date, see Baldwin (1995a: 157–67) and Horsfall (1997: 166–95).

[11] Horsfall (1997: 192–5). Cf. Potter (1994: 141) for a similar argument with respect to the emperors in the Sibylline Oracles.

Indeed, this is also observable in the quotation in the epigraph, which involves a judgement on the suitability of different emperors in their ability to ensure the peace and prosperity of the empire. Not only does the new emperor bring the return of a golden age, but he does so at the expense of the previous emperor and his age of oppression. Accordingly, there is an inherent comparability between different emperors. Furthermore, the debate highlights the importance of the emperor within the conceptual framework of how the world works; it is the emperor who is responsible and culpable for the good and the bad. The hope for a *melior deus*, who would ensure peace and prosperity in the world, was met with the fear that he would fall short of the mark. Not only does this god remove the previous age of affliction; he also creates an age of law and justice, which can be observed through the political life of the Roman people. Such are the peculiarities of the Roman monarchy that it could allow godly metaphors yet also stress and foster political and civic life. The idea that there would be a 'better god' highlights the extraordinary scrutiny placed on the position and conduct of the Roman emperor and indeed the different roles he had to fulfil.[12]

This theme of the liminality of the emperor is one that runs throughout this book and often involves the expectation or understanding of the emperor as someone who occupies a space between the real and the imaginary – seemingly contradictory and inexplicable. Such was the impression of the Roman emperor on the *imaginaire*. The contradictory roles of the emperor can be argued to be extremes, part and parcel of the spectrum of opinions concerning what made an emperor 'good' or 'bad', which seem separable and distinct. However, when the lens becomes less focussed on encompassing the position of the emperor, these roles become less easily delineated. Hence the liminality: all these roles contribute to how the emperor was perceived by his subjects in the Roman empire, and therefore it permeates the discourse concerning the emperor. This means that we often get a contradictory view of the emperor, one that cannot be easily defined or explained. A goal of this book is to appreciate the cracks and fissures that populate the thought-world of the Roman emperor, in order to appreciate the different roles the emperor had to fulfil and also to see the differing perspectives of these roles, particularly from a wider, inclusive perspective.

Though this book cannot be exhaustive, a comparative look at different sources, including iconographic, papyrological, literary, and epigraphical material, revealed several interesting points which aggregated to provide an

---

[12] See Chapter 1.1 on the paradoxes of the Roman emperorship.

alternative perspective of the Roman emperor in his world. It is alternative in the sense that I attempt to flip the picture and observe the idea of the emperorship from the perspective of his subjects rather than attempt to assess outward representations of the position.[13] Reception, rather than representation projected outwards, is the key difference here.[14] Also, the book does not outline or explain the nature of Roman imperial administration, which includes the senatorial, equestrian, and freedmen officials who ran the day-to-day business of the Roman empire.[15] It is this choice of lens and focus that reveals different impressions of the emperor.

Indeed, these impressions seem to confirm the subjectivity and volatility of the position. It is subjective in that it seemed ideologically incumbent to the success of an emperor to be challengeable. In other words, there is the idea that the emperor was dependent on the consent of his subjects in order to rule. This involves the corollary that he could lose his power. This in turn evokes Weber's schema of charismatic authority, which brings us to volatility. The emperor's authority is volatile in both the vastly different and contradictory imaginations of the emperor, encompassing both what was hoped and feared in his conduct and the instability of the system that resisted a smooth succession of one emperor to the next. In terms of the historical impact, it means that the system had a failsafe: if an emperor proved to be unsuitable for the position, he could be removed, but not to the destruction of the system itself. This meant that what people thought about him *mattered*, thus meaning that what people thought about the emperor and talked about was important to the political, social, religious, and cultural life of the empire. Moreover, whether these impressions of the Roman emperor were strictly *true* misses the point of the discourse. Conversations about the emperor need not to have been true to have had an impact on the historical, social, and cultural context of the Roman empire. Once rumour and stories are promulgated, they become historical entities in their own right which reveal the reception of an emperor in the Roman world. Such is the murky world of talk about the Roman emperor that must be appreciated.

This thought-world about the emperor was a moving target, constantly evolving through time and space. In other words, the expectations and fears about the Roman emperor were added to by both real and imagined perceptions of him and his actions, made more and more complex by new

---

[13] Cf. further discussion in Chapter 1.1.

[14] For projected images and messages of emperors in portraiture and representation, see Hekster (2023: 45–69).

[15] For provincial administration, see Lintott (1993) and Davenport (2019).

examples being set alongside reassessment of the old. All this has essential implications for the sort of emperor that was imagined, giving a different perspective than a legal or administrative delineation of the office and his duties. It importantly suggests an emperor with a larger-than-life role, which transcended time and space, as hinted at in the passages of Calpurnius Siculus in the opening epigraph. To reiterate, this means that the emperor had more liminal and celestial aspects. His position made it necessary for him to be seen as a mediator between worlds, taking on different guises in different contexts, which meant that he had to be perceived to be solving a wide variety of problems, from the banal to the fantastical.

The book is split into thematic chapters and each one deals with the duties and expectations placed on the emperor. Chapter 1 serves as an introduction to the relevant themes concerning the power of the Roman emperor and how to approach our evidence from the perspective of his subjects. The chapter first deals with how anecdotal evidence and fiction are crucial to accessing the thought-world of the emperor's subjects and how they viewed the Roman emperorship. Second, I discuss the history and historiography of the Roman emperor and explore different vignettes of the emperor that reveal the position's multifaceted nature, which can be explained through its peculiar constitutional makeup. The chapters that follow are divided thematically and recount different 'topics of conversation' within the discourse about the emperor, each of which describes aspects of a thought-world about him. Such topics include the emperor as an arbiter of justice (Chapter 2), a supreme benefactor (Chapter 3), a curator of marvels (Chapter 4), and a subject of humour and derision (Chapter 5). The sixth and final chapter concerns the legacy and afterlife of the emperor, including the impression of the timelessness of the position, which was in constant dialogue with itself.

I hope that the breadth of topics and evidence discussed will weave a thought-provoking tapestry of the different and various perceptions of the Roman emperor. Accordingly, this book opens up the emperor to understandings of continuity and comparison, not in the sense of fixity or an unchanging impression but rather how different emperors from different contexts could be conceptually compared and contrasted to each other. It also creates a study concerning how an autocratic ruler was understood and perceived by his subjects, both revealing the weight of expectation and the difficulty of being an emperor and highlighting the resonance of the emperor as an idea for comparison with different periods of history.

CHAPTER I

A History of the Roman Emperor

What will be argued in this chapter and this book concerns the multivalence of the Roman emperor that was *baked into* the constitutionality of the position and which contributed to its perception as a many-sided figure. Furthermore, this multivalence was a feature of the position as developed from Augustus onwards. I do not mean that Augustus had *planned* the emperorship to develop as it did but rather that the slippery nature of the position Augustus created, especially with respect to its definition and its powers, was a theme that remained centuries afterwards. The peculiar mix of constitutionally sanctioned powers that were derived from the political culture of the Roman republic and the charismatic authority of *Imperator Caesar* contributed to this problem of definition that resonated into the future. The unusual and confusing constitutional make-up of the Roman emperor, therefore, contributed to wide-ranging interpretations of his position and his duties across the empire. This can be no better seen than in a letter to Marcus Aurelius by Fronto in the second century AD, in which the role of the emperor is outlined:

> Nam Caesarum est in senatu quae e re sunt suadere, populum de plerisque negotiis in concione appellare, ius iniustum corrigere, per orbem terrae litteras missitare, reges exterarum gentium compellare, sociorum culpas edictis coercere, benefacta laudare, seditiosos compescere, feroces territare. Omnia ista profecto verbis sunt ac litteris agenda.

> For it falls to a Caesar to carry by persuasion necessary measures in the Senate, to address the people in public assembly on many matters, to correct the injustices of the law, to dispatch rescripts throughout the world, to take foreign kings to task, to control by edicts crimes among the allies, to praise their services, to supress the rebellious and to cow the proud. All of this must be done through the dispatch of speech and letters.[1]

---

[1] Fronto, *De eloquentia* 1.5; cf. Philostr. *Letters of Apollonius of Tyana* 21.

Jagged and seemingly contradictory, the Roman emperor here fulfils many roles at once. Taken together, that a single figure is expected to fulfil these expectations should be put under historical scrutiny, not least given that the first roles that are outlined in the passage have to do with political life in the city of Rome itself. This *political* role of the Roman emperor can be easy to sideline, given the default interpretation of the Roman emperorship as an absolute monarchy. This political function will be treated in Section 1.2, but it is important to state that whereas the autocratic nature of the Roman emperor should not be underestimated, he still had to live within the constraints of a republican tradition that informed political life in Rome itself. The emperor's power becomes more acute across the empire, where the monarchical character of a Roman magistrate and his *imperium* come into play. That this enormous power could bleed into the Roman emperor's function within the city itself as we move towards the second century AD is not in question. What *should* be stressed is the ideological function of the Roman emperor as a mediator within the political life of Rome, which involved the public activities of senatorial meetings, assemblies, and judicial hearings. Empty or cynical as we may be about this pageantry and show, that there was an expectation to carry out these functions informs the ideology of both the Roman principate and the position of the emperor itself. Projection is key, therefore, especially in the communicative role of the emperor through speech acts and letter-writing. Though Fronto, as Marcus Aurelius' Latin tutor, stresses his own importance in the passage, this technology for the conveyance of opinion and ideology was crucial.[2] These points will be discussed further with respect to the *Lex de imperio Vespasiani* and the emperor's relationship to the law.[3] Still, it is notable that they appear here in Fronto's list of an emperor's duties.

The emperor's position as described in this passage is an active one, at least with respect to speech, campaigning, and writing. The emperor must cow the proud and crush rebellions, as well as send letters across the empire and receive embassies. Images of responsiveness, accessibility, and justice are all alluded to in this passage. Furthermore, there seems to be a tension in the passage between these duties of the emperor – between those of response and suggestion and those of force and compulsion. One phrase has distinct resonance in these lines: in the Latin, it is *feroces territare*, which means to

[2] Lavan (2018: 282–4) for the recent debate on self-fashioning in letter-writing, and Noreña (2007: 261–72) and Woolf (2015: 136–7).
[3] See Section 1.2.6; cf. Buongiorno (2012: 524–5).

frighten the savage with a frequentative verb to suggest sustained and intense action, a reference to the martial role of the emperor and the suppression of revolt and resistance both within and outside the empire. It does seem to intensify other clauses in the passage, particularly *reges exterarum gentium compellare, sociorum culpas edictis coercere* and *seditiosos compescere*. To have *benefacta laudare* sandwiched in between these more harrowing images of the emperor should draw attention to the juxtapositions of these different duties and thus the difficulty of maintaining an equilibrium between the variant potential images and duties of a Roman emperor.

This is an effective passage to illustrate the enigma that is the position and the variant expectations placed on the role.[4] The nature of the position, its ideology, its power, and from where it derives its authority are all difficult problems in its historical understanding. The emperor occupies different roles simultaneously and can perceivably switch between them. Depending on context, and building upon the images provided by Fronto in his list, the emperor can be perceived to be a king, responding to petitions from his subjects, and also the first amongst equals in Rome.[5] He could be a paragon of moral rectitude, distant from the vicissitudes of luxury, but also seen in the company of monsters, engaging in depravity.[6] He could be the bringer of peace and plenty to the world, a harbinger of a new golden age, but also a figure that brings about ruin and chaos.[7] All these variant images of the emperor contribute to the understanding of the emperor and his functions across the empire, which encompasses both the real and the imagined. The section that follows first deals with how to access the imagination about the Roman emperor, before moving on to discuss the emperor's constitutional position and how it has been interpreted through time.

1.1 Talking about the Emperor and Finding the 'Popular' Voice in the Conversation

But no power, no empire, can hope to exist for long unless it wins the assent and trust of the majority of its subjects, and the question that this lecture aims at answering is, 'What did the common people under the Empire expect of their rulers, and how were they satisfied?' It is no good simply referring the inquirer to such treatises as Seneca *On Clemency*, Dio Chrysostom *On Kingship*, or the younger Pliny's

---

[4] This subject has a long bibliography. For various understandings of the Roman emperor and his enigmatic role, see Millar (1977); Ando (2000); Noreña (2011), esp. 56–7, 318–20; Tuori (2016), esp. 192–5; Desmond (2020: 11–12, 32–3, 105–7).
[5] Millar (1977: 3, 11).   [6] Dench (2005: 279–92).   [7] Dench (2005: 280).

Panegyric on Trajan. Instructive these treatises are, and useful . . . but they have one common fault: with their elegance and sophistication, their almost painfully literary quality, they can have reached and influenced only a small circle, whereas we are concerned with the ordinary people, 'What did the farmer in Gaul, the corn-shipper in Africa, the shopkeeper in Syria, expect?'[8]

At the Raleigh Lecture on History in 1937, M. P. Charlesworth showed his interest in the attitudes of subjects towards the empire and asked the question of what they expected from the emperor, and what they thought about him – an interesting question, which is fraught with difficulties and pitfalls. Charlesworth himself seems to disavow the literary production of the upper echelons of society, noticing that their learning and social position would inform their opinions about the *princeps*. Yet Charlesworth's solution to his enquiry was to explore the 'propagandic' output of the centre, which included observing imperial coinage, arguing for both the purposeful propagation of an imperial idea or image and its unproblematic reception by a wider population.[9] In other words, Charlesworth's method was to extrapolate popular opinion on the emperor from evidence of his actions and images, which included media that could be interpreted as having been disseminated by the government.[10] This approach to the understanding of ideology and image dissemination in the empire has had a large impact on the historiography of the Roman empire.[11]

   This approach is altered here. The endeavour is to find popular voices in the evidence we do have, which might range from subliterary texts such as the *Acta Alexandrinorum* to Tacitus and Suetonius. The point is to appreciate the potential for a multiplicity of voices that reflect *conversations* about the emperor, which involves a dialogue between participants in a public transcript. As such, any evidence can be included insofar as it reflects wider concerns and shows an interest in what people say about the emperor, all of which may reveal discord and disagreement. The existence of that tension suggests the multiplicity of an emperor's reception, which enriches our understanding of an emperor's thought-world, or what he was thought to be. This is the approach of Hekster in his monograph *Emperors and Ancestors*, who chooses to concentrate on archaeological and numismatic

---

[8] Charlesworth (1937: 5).   [9] Charlesworth (1937: 12–13).
[10] Noreña (2001: 147): 'each coin minted at Rome was an official document and as such represented an official expression of the emperor and his regime'.
[11] Ando (2000), esp. 19–48; Flaig (2019); Syme (1939: 448–75); Noreña (2001: 146–68); Noreña (2011, esp. 1–26); Nutton (1978: 209–20); Rogers (1991); Veyne (2002); Wallace-Hadrill (1981b); Winterling (2009: 9–33); Zanker (1988), esp. 3; Hekster (2022).

evidence first, with literary sources coming in as contrast.[12] My approach flips this equation and focusses on written sources whilst using art historical and numismatic material as contrast. The balance is calibrated this way because (1) speech acts are important as social interactions and opinions that formulate what an emperor is expected to be and (2) such dialogues are observable in iconographical evidence, too, and thus such evidence acts as an important foil. In all, reactions and impressions are fundamental. Another volume may be needed to explore the variety of potential evidence that could be brought to bear. However, the purpose here is to find tensions in all sorts of evidence, which might reveal the expectations placed on the emperor, which will be treated in a thematic way, and what the variety of opinions might be in those themes.

Before commencing with the difficulties of this subject, it is important to outline the underlying premise of this book, which has been a theme running through the first part of this chapter. As highlighted by Charlesworth in the section epigraph, the idea that the imperial regime and its power were derived from the *consensus* of different constituencies has been important to the understanding of the Roman government in the early principate.[13] The corollary of this premise is that the dialogue that existed between emperor and subject was important to this idea of consensus and that people's opinions of the emperor *mattered*. Who those participants were in that conversation is a fundamental matter of discussion. That said, the emperor was a transcendental figure who appeared across the empire, meaning that he was not only a *princeps* in the city but variously a supreme magistrate, *hegemon*, *basileus*, or even *theos* across the Roman world. It is through these different roles that we can reconstruct the tapestry of opinions that surrounded the idea of emperorship.

The distinction that needs to be drawn here concerns how those opinions mattered, too. Looking for the *political* impact of opinions on the actions and history of the regime would be a chimera, as such an interpretation would presume a large degree of political agency resting with the silent masses of the Roman empire, suggesting that this was the sort of discourse that could make or break an emperor. Also, such a reading would put far too much onus on the impact of political upheaval, which may suggest that the

---

[12] Hekster (2015: 36–7).

[13] Cf. Noreña (2011: 7): 'With these influential collectivities the emperor was in constant dialogue, both real and symbolic, interacting with each in a highly prescribed manner calculated to elicit the public displays of consensus, or "acceptance", upon which imperial legitimacy ultimately rested.' Cf. Weber (1978: 1114–15) on charismatic authority, whence the kernel of these ideas is derived; see also Flaig (2019).

only time wider opinions about the emperor mattered was in the context of violent overthrow. This would go too far. My interest is to explore the variety of impressions about the emperor that include times of crisis and normality. My goal is summarised in an alteration of Millar's famous dictum: whilst it is true that 'the emperor was what the emperor did',[14] it is also apparent that 'the emperor was what the emperor *seemed*'.[15]

The purpose of this short section is to outline, problematise, and discuss the various analytical issues that arise from attempting to observe and record what people thought about the emperor. It focusses on problems of interpretation and the attempt to read the opinions of a wider population in the evidence. This seeming paradox reveals the tension between the constructed world in which the discourse of interaction between people and *princeps* operates and the actual world that it alludes to.[16] Such is the difficulty of finding that line between the reality and a mirage. Depending on the cynicism of the author, the ability to read the 'real' situation behind the vignette can be variable and problematic. However, the substance of talk and discourse about the emperor in the contexts described, for instance at the imperial court or the circus, is in itself an abstract phenomenon that *represents* opinion rather than giving a *real* breakdown of what people thought about the emperor.[17] That is lost to history and perhaps not as important as the constructed images about the emperor, fashioned by his subjects. The act of the recording of such material about what people said about the emperor points to the modes in which the emperor was discussed and understood, which could open a window into the discourse about the emperor, which is useful *even in* falsehood.[18] What should be admissible in the history of understanding the Roman emperor follows.

1.1.1 Remembering the Roman People

How do we access the opinions and thoughts of a wider population in the empire about the emperor?[19] Unpacking the question, as well as the problem of sources, poses more questions than at first meet the eye.

---

[14] Millar (1977: 6).

[15] Cf. Laurence and Paterson (1999: 183): 'Millar has taught us that the emperor was what the emperor did; this paper explores the proposition that the emperor was also what the emperor *said*.' Cf. Potter (1994: 99) and Hekster (2015: 1) for variations on this theme.

[16] For example, see Beard (2014: 140) on the tension between the literary representation and the 'social reality' of laughter between emperor and subject.

[17] I owe this point to my discussion with Professor A. Wallace-Hadrill.

[18] Cf. an articulation of this argument in Christoforou (2021), using the example of Philo and his *legatio ad Gaium*.

[19] Cf. Beard (2014: 4) on this problem with accessing how Romans laughed.

12 A History of the Roman Emperor

What is meant by a 'wider population'? Is 'public opinion', or even the opinions of that wider population in the empire, accessible? How do we approach the evidence of potentially 'popular' opinion in our 'elite' sources? Can such a binary opposition of 'elite' and 'non-elite' perspectives be easily delineated? Are some sources of evidence better than others? This section can serve as a beginning to tackling these difficult issues and to find new perspectives.

First, the issue of a wider population. A persistent interest for Roman historians in the past few decades is the assessment of how 'democratic' political life in the city of Rome was, particularly with respect to the politics of the mid-to-late Republic. The work of numerous scholars has gone back and forth on the level of political power that the *populus Romanus* and the *plebs* held,[20] particularly with respect to voting rights and the force of the popular assemblies at Rome.[21] Though many scholars err on the side of hierarchy and stress the political power of the senatorial aristocracy, there is much scope for seeing political power being held by the *populus*, both ideologically and concretely, particularly in terms of their numbers and voting patterns. Such reconsiderations might defy expectations of client-ship, geographical restrictions, and socio-economic pressures that have been important in previous scholarship that has understood the power of the *populus Romanus* as restricted.[22] In the end, the picture of popular participation in Roman politics is far more complex than it had been thought and has thus become a fundamental topic of study. Part of this 'popular turn' encompasses several important themes and complexities that run throughout republican history: the widening of the citizenship to foreigners and manumitted slaves, including the historical punctures of the Social War; the role of census rank in political hierarchies; and the contestations of the late Republic involving questions of the role of the

---

[20] Gaius 1.3: *plebs autem a populo eo distat, quod populi appellatione universi cives significantur, connumeratis et patriciis; plebis autem appellatione sine patriciis ceteri cives significantur* (The *plebs*, however, are distinct from the people: by the appellation 'populus' the whole citizen body is meant, with the patricians also considered in that number. By the name 'plebs', the remaining citizens without the patricians are meant). A wide designation of people meaning variously the citizens across the empire. Cf. Ando (1999: 28–9), for the fashioning of new hierarchies as citizens spread across the empire geographically, and Lavan (2020), on the slipperiness of the terms *Romani* and *Rhomaioi*. Cf. Lavan (2016) for the proportion of citizens in the population across the empire.

[21] A select bibliography of the scholarship follows: Millar (1998); Hall (1998); Morstein-Marx (2004); Yakobson (2010); Wiseman (2009); Jehne (1995); Gruen (1974: 47–82); Mouritsen (2017); Hölkeskamp (2010); Feig Vishnia (2012); Nicolet (1980); Morstein-Marx (2021: 3–7).

[22] On the flexibility of public opinion and groups of opinion in the *populus Romanus*, see Rosillo-López (2017: 155–94); for the volatility of political life and voting patterns, see Yakobson (1992); Rafferty (2021: 139–50); cf. Rosenblitt (2016).

state in matters such as land reform and the remit of magistrates. To put it another way, what were the opinions of the *populus Romanus* (and its sections) on pertinent political issues of the late Republic? How might they have changed towards the middle of the first century BC? In the end, asking the question of their political role and power has pushed us closer to constructing answers to those queries.

When we reach the age of the principate and the coming of autocracy, one might assume that the age of popular politics had ended and that one-man rule made political life redundant in the city.[23] Yet the question of what their role in political life is remains important to ask. The *populus Romanus* remained the 'sovereign' body of the Roman state into late antiquity, giving weight to the idea that the emperor remained accountable to them.[24] As Flaig has argued in *Den Kaiser herausfordern*, such account-ability was manifested in an imperial *Akzeptanzsystem*, whereby the emperor needed to cultivate his 'acceptance' amongst important constitu-encies across the Roman empire or else he could suffer usurpation and deposition.[25] In his estimation, such constituencies included the *plebs* in the city of Rome and the citizen soldiers stationed in legions across the empire. As such, the problem with the view of a lack of popular involve-ment in imperial politics is twofold. First, there is an assumption that the only way political pressure can be asserted is through *institutional* means, thus giving a sense of legal legitimacy – a process that indeed did wane throughout the principate and became more perfunctory into the second century AD.[26] The issue with this interpretation is that it reads politics in a manner too strict: there are ways to outline and exert political opinion outside 'official' channels, which might include protest and violence, both of which were far from absent from the nominally more free age of the Republic.

Second, the emperor was *required* to operate in both official and unoffi-cial capacities, meaning that his encounter with the wider citizenry may be both routine and ad hoc. With respect to the Roman people, such activities meant engaging in speeches and assembly voting in an official capacity (with Fronto, Pliny, and the *Lex de Imperio*) *and* also appearing at the

---

[23] See Courrier (2014: 607–13) for an excellent outlining of the scholarship and the 'apolitical' age of the first century AD; Brunt (1977: 95). Cf. Yavetz (1969: 3–5); Millar (1977: 301–2, 368); De Ste. Croix (1981: 384–6); cf. Tac. *Ann.* 1.15, which seems to have an outsized role in modern perceptions of popular participation in electoral life, on which see Coarelli (2001: 39) and Courrier (2014: 630).

[24] See pp. 53–58; cf. Courrier (2014: 480).   [25] Flaig (2019).

[26] At least this remains the scholarly consensus, which will need updating given the scholarship on popular politics in the late Republic; cf. Wiseman (2009: 236). For the political power of the *plebs* in this age, see Courrier (2014) and Kröss (2017).

theatre and games, subject to the scrutiny and view of the population and often also to their rhythmic chanting and shouting.[27] In reality, these contexts suggest that the line between the formal and the informal was blurry, boiling down to a question of accessibility of the emperor to the needs and concerns of the *populus Romanus* at Rome. Such a dynamic was put forward by Griffin, who noted that the street corner, the arena, and the theatre were all spaces in which the *plebs urbana* were to be found.[28] However, the alteration to the argument here is not to dismiss such spaces as unimportant;[29] rather, it is to assert that these spaces mattered politically as well and should be read in concert with the 'official' capacities of the *populus Romanus* in their assemblies, even if their voting and legislative roles became more and more perfunctory into the second century. One example will suffice in this context that contains an ambiguous case between these categories. In the aftermath of the death of Germanicus, and in the context of the internment of his ashes in the Mausoleum of Augustus, Agrippina the Elder is shown as an object of devotion on the part of the Roman people:

> plena urbis itinera, conlucentes per campum Martis faces. illic miles cum armis, sine insignibus magistratus, populus per tribus concidisse rem publicam, nihil spei reliquum clamitabant, promptius apertiusque quam ut meminisse imperitantium crederes. nihil tamen Tiberium magis penetravit quam studia hominum accensa in Agrippinam, cum decus patriae, solum Augusti sanguinem, unicum antiquitatis specimen appellarent versique ad caelum ac deos integram illi subolem ac superstitem iniquorum precarentur.

> The streets of the city were full, and torches shone through the Campus Martius. There, the soldiers with their weapons, the magistrates without their insignia, and the people in their tribes cried out that the *res publica* had fallen with no hope remaining, doing so too visibly and openly for you to believe that they remembered their rulers. Indeed, nothing pierced Tiberius more than the zeal of the people that burned for Agrippina, since they called her the glory of the fatherland, the sole blood of Augustus, the singular example of a bygone age, and turning towards the sky and gods they prayed that her progeny be kept safe and preserved against enemies.[30]

---

[27] Courrier (2014: 613–39) for evidence and discussion of collective political action in the principate. See Aldrete (2003), Rouéche (1984), and Courrier (2014: 652) for acclamations.

[28] Griffin (1991); Courrier (2014) for a comprehensive outlining of these more ad hoc encounters with the emperor. For the difficulty with defining the *plebs urbana*, see Kröss (2017: 61–3).

[29] Griffin (1991: 40–1): 'Lampoons and grumbling at street corners, or rather in the large and convenient gathering places in which the poorer inhabitants of a Mediterranean city spend most of their time, were hardly a serious threat.'

[30] Tac. *Ann.* 3.4.

The most important takeaway for our purposes here is the official and unofficial dynamics at play. The people engage in shouting acclamations towards Agrippina with seeming spontaneity and comparable to other evidence of large congregations of people shouting slogans or titles.[31] Importantly, though, the suggestion here is that the *populus Romanus* appear in their 'tribes' in the Campus Martius, suggesting their organisation along the lines of the *comitia tributa*. Indeed, in a lacunose section of the *Tabula Siarensis*, which is a bronze inscription found in Spain that preserves the *senatus consultum* that outlines the honours given to Germanicus Caesar after his death, the *tribus urbanae et [rusticae . . .]* are praised for their zeal and honours given to Germanicus, which corroborates their assembly in Tacitus.[32] The passage also underlines an important relationship between the *domus Augusta* and the *populus*, presented here by Tacitus as the focalised perspective of the people: in this context, there is a connection between the safety and the health of the *princeps* and his family, which is an ideological cornerstone to their relationship (though here concentrated on Germanicus, Agrippina, and her offspring, at the expense of Tiberius).[33] Though Tacitus might use this example as evidence for growing enmity and infighting within the household, the appearance of the people here suggests that their opinion mattered on questions concerning imperial politics and an emperor's legitimacy.

In any event, this episode suggests that the emperor and his milieu were subject to scrutiny and direct communication by the Roman people, an ideologically significant point which might suggest why such focalised examples are recorded. The emperor had to be seen as challengeable and criticisable. Indeed, the rich evidence we have of these encounters might allow us to access more than an 'official' or 'public' transcript to think critically about what different sections of society thought about the Roman emperor.

Before discussing how to access different potential transcripts and viewpoints, a problem still remains on definitions and the hierarchies incumbent in the Roman world. In short, 'wider population' and the *plebs Romana/ populus Romanus* are not synonyms, particularly given that Roman enfranchisement ranged between 18 per cent and 33 per cent of the total population of the Roman empire up to the *constitutio Antoniniana* of AD 212.[34] Such

---

[31] Cf. Suet. *Cal.* 6.1; cf. Courrier (2014: 652–7).

[32] *TS* ll. 154–60. For more on the *Tabula Siarensis* and its context, see Lott (2012: 46).

[33] Cf. *TS* ll. 154–60 and *SCPP* ll. 472–5, for the contextually relevant presentation of the people concerned with the 'safety' of the *domus*. Cf. Tac. *Ann.* 2.41.

[34] Lavan (2016, 2019). Another study might explore the implications of a lower estimate of citizens in the Roman empire and the dynamics of social relationships both locally within communities and

a statement, however, does not throw the baby out with the bath water. The idea that the emperor was subject to the scrutiny of the *populus Romanus* is an important factor of his reception. Therefore, this relationship should prompt the pursuit of similar relationships across the Roman empire, including those outside the more restrictive category of citizens (though a large group), which suggests that the role of the emperor was to be not only a mediator within and between an elite but a figure that engaged with individuals and groups both within and beyond the purview of Roman power.[35]

In truth, the emperor was a transcendent figure in the social hierarchy. In Geza Alföldy's description of the Roman imperial society as a pyramid, the emperor stands atop the structure, with the rest of society beneath.[36] Though such a model in a reductive sense can be called schematic, vertical links between the separations in society transcend boundaries. Such a model has the emperor as a central figure who maintains relationships with individuals and groups within social hierarchies. In other words, the emperor both is a part of the hierarchy, serving to validate privileged individuals and communities through honours and benefaction, and stands apart from that hierarchy, in that he is seen as an intercessory figure who was accessible to different individuals and groups.[37]

This category described here can be refined by observing the 'proximity' to the figure of the emperor himself, in which different sections of society at different levels had relationships and contacts with the Roman emperor, including members of the imperial family, the senatorial elite and its members, and down through society to enslaved people. Such a proximity might be better seen as conceptual rather than geographical, since the emperor may cultivate close relationships with groups both near and far and closer or farther in social standing. In the end, the Roman citizen body, which can be taken to include the *plebs*, citizens, and citizen communities across the empire, as well as the citizen soldiery, are only a few threads of the complex political and social tapestry of the Roman world. However proximate individuals and groups were to the emperor, the reception of the emperor seems to be an activity that they shared and in which they attempted to make sense of his position and duties in their world.

---

translocally between communities in the Roman empire. As an example, see Cébeillac-Gervasoni and Lamoine (2003).
[35] Nicolet (1991); Dench (2018); Millar (1977), esp. 363–464.   [36] Alföldy (1985: 94).
[37] Lendon (1997).

1.1.2 *'Public' Opinion and Transcripts*

How might we access different transcripts? Where might we find the material? One way may be to attempt to access 'public opinion'. Following Habermas' work on the eighteenth century, public opinion came to mean the rational and enlightened 'outcome of common and public reflection on the foundations of the social order'.[38] Therefore, in the modern age, public opinion has been important in understanding democratic societies, with a particular interest in gauging the position or standing of individuals and groups in society on topics pertaining to government and its actions.[39] This understanding is seemingly wedded to its modern context: a scientific study of the breakdown of voting or poll data on relevant issues.[40] An essential question is whether this concept can be retrojected into premodern societies, where such data is lacking.[41] As Kuhn has argued on the issue of 'public opinion' in classical studies, a problem lies in whether scholars agree that public opinion exists or not.[42] In his seminal work *Bread and Circuses*, Veyne argued that the idea of finding public opinion on the emperor was problematic:

> The emperor's name was spoken with respect, but people did not have political opinions and political discussion was unknown ... The thousands of graffiti and painted inscriptions to be read on the walls of Pompeii surprise us, for there is not a single one that we should call political – only repetitions of 'Long Live the Emperor' (*Augusto Feliciter*). The emperor is not politics ...[43]

In Veyne's estimation, even the medium that had access to 'thoughts on the street', the graffiti in Pompeii – a manifestation of a 'political discussion' – was markedly apolitical when it came to the question of the emperor.[44] As Malik has articulated more recently, we can indeed find evidence of 'political' humour on the walls of Pompeii through the graffito *Cucuta ab ra[t]ioni[b]us| Neronis Augusti*, or 'Hemlock, the accountant of Nero Augustus'.[45] Such an inscription displayed the ability of the emperor to 'take a joke' and gives the impression of a thought-world where poison might be used to enrich the imperial coffers.[46] More

---

[38] Habermas (1989), p. 96 for quotation, who also discusses the etymology of opinion. Cf. Kuhn (2012: 13–14) on Habermas' contextually specific thoughts on *öffentlich meinung*.

[39] Benson (1967: 523–4); cf. Kuhn (2012: 11–13).   [40] Back (1988: 279, 283–4).

[41] Kuhn (2012: 13, 15).   [42] Kuhn (2012: 15).   [43] Veyne (1990: 296).

[44] See Franklin (2001: 108).

[45] *CIL* 4.8075 = *AE* (1962) 133. See Malik (2019: 785–7), for the pun between Cicuta/Cucuta, with the former being the spelling for the poison. Beard (2008: 50–1); cf. Purcell (1999: 183). For horror and humour associated with account-taking, cf. Suet. *Cal.* 29.2.

[46] Malik (2019: 788).

importantly, though, this evidence points to a public dynamic that allowed space for such humour to circulate and be recognised as such and that works particularly well at a local political level, where the butt of the joke may be directed at the political elite who would not want the attention of the imperial court.[47] In any event, the emperor here is part of political discourse.

Thus, Veyne's statement would be a rather narrow view of what could constitute 'public opinion', which for Veyne does not include the expressions of 'submission' and loyalty towards the emperor but rather the opinions of senators, 'the narrow ruling class who had knowledge of public business and public events, represented a sort of public opinion'.[48] As Kuhn rightly points out, such a view of public opinion is indebted to Enlightenment conceptions of rational thought and criticism on politics, as described by Habermas.[49] This is a restrictive framework both in its purview of what was involved in the political arena and in that it curtails its participants to (subjectively) rational people. It disregards the more bizarre and unusual interpretations of the Roman emperor, which were a part of the discourse about who the emperor was and how he seemed to be, as is illustrated by Mr Poison in Pompeii.[50] The conceit of this work is therefore not about reconstructing poll data, or assuming that politics had died in this age, but rather about exploring the spaces in which conversations about the Roman emperor occurred.

After outlining what might constitute 'public opinion(s)', the question of how we might find the evidence of such opinions comes into sharp focus. On the one hand, one could stress multiplicity and diversity as the most important factors.[51] However, a common issue at stake is how to access the opinions of those rendered silent by time and history.[52] The argument that our sources come from an urban male, elite perspective is a truism often stated and rarely challenged: it is cited often with chagrin that we have a tiny percentage of the total literary output of antiquity and that it comes 'entirely (from) the work of an elite of birth, wealth, and education'.[53] Nonetheless, the so-called elusive quarry has been mined by numerous scholars in an attempt to appreciate and reconstruct

---

[47] Malik (2019: 789–91), for a compelling argument on how the joke might work at the expense of P. Paquius Proculus.

[48] Veyne (1990: 295).   [49] Kuhn (2012: 14–15).

[50] For instance, see Chapter 5 on the more bizarre and wondrous associations.

[51] Hopkins (1978a: 216).

[52] Cf. Padilla Peralta (2020: 155–9) for a discussion of how categories of knowledge were obliterated by Roman power, termed here 'epistemicide'. Cf. Johnston (2017: 282).

[53] Beard (2014: 4).

a subaltern voice.[54] Before engaging with the methods utilised by these scholars, there is a distinction that needs to be made here. The studies that have explored these methods of analysis have had the expressed wish to ascertain and determine popular, as opposed to elite, *culture*, with the attempt to regain information about a large proportion of people whose story has been lost to history or at best badly (mis)represented in the evidence.[55] This book focusses on the figure of the Roman emperor, a figure of prominence in the cultural production of the Roman empire who had an interest in recording and discussing what people said and thought about him.[56] In other words, the contention here is that while *elite* voices may be prominent, they were not hermetically sealed from the rest of society and in fact may reflect wider concerns focalised around the encounters of the emperor with members of society across the Roman world.

One potential point of access is to study the discrepancies in power relationships between the dominant and subordinate in society to appreciate the nature of the discourse in public in the face of power and the corresponding discourse in clandestine confines.[57] This methodology takes its cue from Scott on discrepant power relations in Southeast Asia and his understanding of social interaction between these groups. He creates a model of three modes of speech that describe the interaction between the subordinate and the dominant.[58] The first is the *public transcript*, which is a façade put in place by the subordinate classes that mirrors the ideology and concerns of the dominant class, thus maintaining and affirming the social order:

> That the poor should dissemble in the face of power is hardly an occasion for surprise. Dissimulation is the characteristic and necessary pose of subordinate classes everywhere most of the time – a fact that makes those rare and threatening moments when the pose is abandoned all the more remarkable. No close account of the life of subordinate classes can fail to distinguish between what is said 'backstage' and what may be safely declared openly.[59]

---

[54] Horsfall (2003: 20–3); Morgan (2007: 3–4); Toner (2009: 5–7); Kurke (2011: 3); Forsdyke (2012: 16–18); Beard (2014: 4).
[55] Cf. Horsfall (2003: 26); Purcell (1994: 644).   [56] Cf. Purcell (1999: 183).
[57] Forsdyke (2012: 6–18). Cf. Ahl (1984), on the intricate 'art of safe criticism', and Roller (2001).
[58] Cf. Burke (1978: 23–4): This model of different transcripts has its parallels in Peter Burke's utilisation of the social anthropologist Robert Redfield's model of the Great Tradition and the Little Tradition, where the former is the closed, elite discourse and the latter is popular. The similarity lies in the existence of different vernaculars that had varying degrees of overlap, meaning that seemingly distinct social groups nevertheless have a shared culture.
[59] Scott (1985: 284); cf. Scott (1990: 4, n.7).

Second, and in opposition, is the *hidden transcript*, which is what the lower classes say about the higher classes behind closed doors:

> Every subordinate group creates, out of its ordeal, a 'hidden transcript' that represents a critique of power spoken behind the back of the dominant. The powerful, for their part, also develop a hidden transcript representing the practices and claims of their rule that cannot be openly avowed. A comparison of the hidden transcript of the weak with that of the powerful and of both hidden transcripts to the public transcript of power relations offers a substantially new way of understanding resistance to domination.[60]

The third is a mix between the two, a *transcript* that is purposefully ambiguous and misleading in order to confuse and hide a group's true opinions – a transcript that could include 'rumor, gossip, folktales, songs, gestures, jokes, and theater of the powerless as vehicles by which, among other things, they insinuate a critique of power while hiding behind anonymity or behind innocuous understandings of their conduct'.[61] In other words, focussing on such material, often anecdotal and seemingly fictitious, is in fact fundamental in writing a history of different transcripts of the emperor.

A key point of Scott's paradigm is how discrepant power relations affect the nature and content of the discourse between the subordinate and the dominant. In different contexts, different opinions on the emperor *could* be expressed, and some which may seem contradictory to each other may hide alternative meanings to what is being openly said. However, this should not be taken too far, for the paradigm can be problematised as follows. One issue is the identification of 'subordinate' and 'dominant'. It would perhaps be easy to use this opposition in correspondence with the seemingly straightforward dichotomy of 'elite' and 'non-elite'.[62]

However, the negotiation of power relations in the Roman world was much more complex and complicated further by the existence of the emperor in the social framework.[63] This can be observed in an illuminating passage in Epictetus' *On Freedom*, which deserves quoting in full:

> ταῦτα ἄν τις ἀκούσῃ δισύπατος, ἄν μὲν προσθῇς ὅτι 'ἀλλὰ σύ γε σοφὸς εἶ, οὐδὲν πρὸς σὲ ταῦτα,' συγγνώσεταί σοι. ἄν δ' αὐτῷ τὰς ἀληθείας εἴπῃς ὅτι

---

[60] Scott (1990: xii).
[61] Scott (1990: xiii, 19); cf. Forsdyke (2012: 40–1), for a discussion on this idea.
[62] Cf. Toner (2009: 5–6).
[63] Shaw (1982: 30–3, 36–7), esp. fig. 2, for Shaw's interesting schema on social relations in the Roman empire.

'τῶν τρὶς πεπραμένων οὐδὲν διαφέρεις πρὸς τὸ μὴ καὶ αὐτὸς δοῦλος εἶναι,' τί ἄλλο ἢ πληγάς σε δεῖ προσδοκᾶν; 'πῶς γάρ,' φησίν, 'ἐγὼ δοῦλός εἰμι; ὁ πατὴρ ἐλεύθερος, ἡ μήτηρ ἐλευθέρα, οὗ ὠνὴν οὐδεὶς ἔχει· ἀλλὰ καὶ συγκλητικός εἰμι καὶ Καίσαρος φίλος καὶ ὑπάτευκα καὶ δούλους πολλοὺς ἔχω.' 'Πρῶτον μέν, ὦ βέλτιστε συγκλητικέ, τάχα σου καὶ ὁ πατὴρ τὴν αὐτὴν δουλείαν δοῦλος ἦν καὶ ἡ μήτηρ καὶ ὁ πάππος καὶ ἐφεξῆς πάντες οἱ πρόγονοι. Εἰ δὲ δὴ καὶ τὰ μάλιστα ἦσαν ἐλεύθεροι, τί τοῦτο πρὸς σέ; τί γάρ, εἰ ἐκεῖνοι μὲν γενναῖοι ἦσαν, σὺ δ' ἀγεννής; ἐκεῖνοι μὲν ἄφοβοι, σὺ δὲ δειλός; ἐκεῖνοι μὲν ἐγκρατεῖς, σὺ δ' ἀκόλαστος; καὶ τί, φησί, τοῦτο πρὸς τὸ δοῦλον εἶναι; — οὐδέν σοι φαίνεται εἶναι τὸ ἄκοντά τι ποιεῖν, τὸ ἀναγκαζόμενον, τὸ στένοντα πρὸς τὸ δοῦλον εἶναι;' — 'τοῦτο μὲν ἔστω,' φησίν. 'ἀλλὰ τίς με δύναται ἀναγκάσαι, εἰ μὴ ὁ πάντων κύριος Καῖσαρ;' — 'οὐκοῦν ἕνα μὲν δεσπότην σαυτοῦ καὶ σὺ αὐτὸς ὡμολόγησας. ὅτι δὲ πάντων, ὡς λέγεις, κοινός ἐστιν, μηδέν σε τοῦτο παραμυθείσθω, ἀλλὰ γίγνωσκε, ὅτι ἐκ μεγάλης οἰκίας δοῦλος εἶ. Οὕτως καὶ Νικοπολῖται ἐπιβοᾶν εἰώθασι "νὴ τὴν Καίσαρος τύχην, ἐλεύθεροί ἐσμεν."'[64]

If a certain individual, twice consul, heard this, he will agree with you if you respond, 'But *you* are a wise man, these things do not apply to you'. But if you responded to him truthfully that 'You do not differ at all to slaves sold three times, with respect to being a slave', what else but beatings do you expect? 'How, indeed,' he says 'am I a slave? My father was free, my mother was free; no one has a sale contract of me. But I am also a senator and a friend of Caesar, I have been consul, and I own many slaves.' 'First of all, most excellent senator, perhaps like you, your father was also a slave in the same servitude, and your mother and grandfather and all of your ancestors all the way down. And even if they were free to the greatest extent, what is this fact to you? For what, if they were noble, and you were common? If they were fearless, and you a coward? If they were calm and collected, and you unruly?' And what, he says, does this have to do with being a slave? Does not the act of doing something that is involuntary, forced on you and pitiful seem to you related to being a slave? 'That is indeed the case', he says. 'But who is able to compel me, save for the lord of all, Caesar?' So surely you have one master as you yourself have admitted. That, however, he is a common master of all, as you say, in no way should be a comfort to you, but know that you are a slave in one great house. Thus the Nicopolitans are also accustomed to shout 'By the fortune of Caesar, we are free!'

It is a dialogue between a senator and Epictetus, an ex-slave. The senator challenges the statement that he is no different than a thrice-sold slave

---

[64] Arr. *Epict. Diss.* 4.1.6–13. Cf. Philo, *Leg.* 119, who creates a similar comparison between slavery and being subject to a despotic emperor in particular: 'For what would be a more burdensome evil for a slave than a hostile master? Subjects of the emperor are slaves.' Τί γὰρ ἂν εἴη δούλῳ βαρύτερον κακὸν ἢ δεσπότης ἐχθρός; δοῦλοι δὲ αὐτοκράτορος οἱ ὑπήκοοι. For discourses of servitude, see Lavan (2013).

by underlining his status as an ex-consul, a freeborn person, and some-one who owns slaves himself.[65] Philosophically, Epictetus is distinguish-ing between the idea of liberty as a social and political category and the idea of freedom from being compelled, particularly compelled by an emotional reaction to a given situation.[66] In this passage, we are tantal-isingly close to a dialogue between different members of society, imagined between a Roman senator and a man of much lower rank, liable to beating, and perhaps Epictetus himself, a freedman who had been a slave of the prominent freedman of Nero, Epaphroditus.[67] Such a unique perspective deserves to be stressed: having been a slave himself at Rome, within the remit of the *familia Caesaris*, Epictetus had close proximity to the emperor; his philosophical training involved inter-actions with Musonius Rufus and took him to Nicopolis after Domitian's ban on philosophers in Rome in AD 95, which saw him open his philosophical school in Augustus' victory city near Actium.[68] As such, Epictetus' position was interstitial: he came from a background of servitude, which never left him, and he remained close to the halls of imperial power and its elite.[69] Such proximity is reflected by Epictetus' discussions of the position of the emperor relative to society, often citing the dangers of being close to the *princeps*.[70]

In giving us the underlying truth of what it means to be free according to his philosophical system, Epictetus conjures a fundamental vignette of the emperor for our purposes that has repercussions on his relationship with his subjects. In this designation, the existence of the emperor redefined power relationships across the empire, which created uncer-tainties and discrepancies between social groups.[71] Put alternatively, proximity to the Roman emperor and his power transcended the hier-archies of status in the Roman world, which in turn allowed individuals and groups to gain favour by establishing a relationship with the emperor directly. Status dissonance, therefore, is the observable phenomenon that fuelled keen commentary by senators such as Tacitus and Pliny, where

---

[65] Millar (1965: 144); cf. Starr (1949: 25–6). Cf. Arr. *Epict. Diss.* 4.1.45–48.
[66] Long (2002: 27, 197), for a discussion of Arr. *Epict. Diss.*   [67] Long (2002: 10–12).
[68] Gell. *NA* 2.18.10.
[69] Cf. Long (2002: 38–40), for the connection between Epictetus and his student, Arrian, the Bithynian historian famous for his *Anabasis* of Alexander of Macedon and also a Roman senator.
[70] Starr (1949: 24–5); Millar (1965: 143–4); Millar (1977: 78); Arr. *Epict. Diss.* 1.2.19–24; 2.14.18; 4.1.45–48; 4.13.5.
[71] Cf. MacLean (2018: 104–30), esp. 106, and *CIL* 10.6093 for a study of the social dynamics of the emperor's *liberti* with the rest of society. Tac. *Ann.* 3.36, on the use of the image of the emperor as protection against legal reprimand from the higher orders. Cf. Price (1984b: 191–4).

the realities of power and the pageantries of political performance were in tension.[72] The existence of the emperor created such a dynamic that simultaneously maintained social hierarchies, as seen in the imperial governmental structure filled with the senatorial and equestrian orders, yet broke those hierarchies through the gravity of a position that factored in intercession and favour. Through the words of Epictetus, we can reconstruct a thought-world that had Caesar equated to a power of compulsion; and in the shouts of the Nicopolitans, his fortune ensures their freedom, accentuating his position as *kyrios* of all.[73] In this manner, we are close to descriptions of discrepant power relationships between the emperor and his subjects.

This passage puts Scott's paradigm into perspective: discrepant power relationships could be felt by those considered to be 'elite' actors in the Roman empire, suggesting that they could fulfil the 'subordinate' group in Scott's model, which further suggests that they themselves could engage in a 'hidden transcript'. Put differently, given the higher powerful position of the Roman emperor with respect to (for instance) the senatorial class, the discourse they engaged in could be argued to have had 'hidden' components: criticisms and true sentiment concealed with various techniques.[74] Thus, it becomes problematic to delineate where an 'elite' transcript ends and where a 'non-elite' one begins, since what we have transmitted to us is a shared phenomenon. However, such bleeding of categories is only an issue if one insists on a stark polarity between elite/non-elite. I argue that experiences of the emperor, and the conversations about him, were experienced by different people and groups up and down the social scale, all of which contributes to our image of the emperor.[75] In other words, lines between groups are blurred in the experience of the emperor's power, which suggests similarities in discourse on the emperor between the 'low' and the 'high', including the spectrum of resistance to compliance.[76]

---

[72] On status dissonance, see Bodel (2016); cf., for example, Tac. *Hist.* 4.1–10, for the dynamics surrounding the *lex de imperio Vespasiani* and the famous 'Pallas' letters, Plin. *Ep.* 7.14, 8.6, cf. 4.22, and Mauricus. Pageantry is an important motif of the emperor's constitutionality.

[73] Cf. Dickey (2001: 6–7).

[74] Ahl (1984), for this very phenomenon of what he calls the 'art of safe criticism'.

[75] Purcell (1999: 183).

[76] One debate that necessarily falls beyond the scope here is the debate on 'Romanisation', on which see Dench (2018: 3–17), Johnston (2017), and esp. Bénabou (1976). Examples of 'resistances' to the emperor will be discussed, given that the emperor was a symbol of Roman power. See Chapters 4 and 5.

1.1.3   The Usefulness of Anecdotes

At this juncture, the question of evidence becomes pertinent. In short, the nature of our evidence tends towards the anecdotal: instances of interaction between emperor and groups/individuals are episodic in nature, appearing as snapshots in time and often unmoored from their contexts.[77] Fictionality also presents an obvious problem for an ancient historian: if our anecdotal stories about emperors are fictional, how can we excavate the historical truth from these accounts? Such a phenomenon is compounded by the existence of autocracy, under which salacious stories about unpopular rulers could circulate. Biography and historiography begin to look alike, and stories across our period start to look similar to each other.[78] However, what may seem to be an insurmountable problem of synchronic evidence depends on what *sort* of question you ask of the evidence at hand. As a short answer to this issue, such evidence is problematic if one is set to excavate the 'true' character or personality of an emperor or a ruler; it ceases to be problematic if these stories are taken to be part of the thought-world about the emperorship in general or of a given emperor in particular. Thus, the source of the truth value is recalibrated.[79] The issues at stake are nicely illustrated by the following thoughts of Yavetz:

> It should be said that from the outset that of course Augustus' *dicta* must be taken with a grain of salt . . . For our purposes, however, it does not matter whether Augustus actually said certain things . . . It is with Augustus' public image that we are concerned. From this point of view, his *dicta* and *apophthegmata* are of primary importance. They reveal very interesting character traits, which, in my opinion, are undoubtedly his.[80]

Contradictions arise with the statement, for Yavetz at first rightly stressed that these anecdotes would have travelled through many media before reaching the surviving text and that they reflect sayings that were attributable to that person in the context of the discourse. However, disregarding these caveats, and returning to the idea that in the end *real* nuggets of

---

[77] Morgan (2007: 236–9): 'An event which is supposed to have happened once in the past has universal relevance.'

[78] On the generalisation of history under the principate, see Pelling (1997); Syme (1980); Bowersock (1994); and pp. 179–182.

[79] Cf. Makhlaiuk (2020: 229), for similar thoughts on a similar set of interesting material, in this case imperial nicknames.

[80] Yavetz (1990: 31–2). This is quoted as such in Laurence and Paterson (1999: 186), where Yavetz's argument is subject to scrutiny of his final point: that Augustus' character was somehow salvageable from these stories and sayings. However, cf. Yavetz (1990: 28), for a more balanced view on what these sources reveal about personality.

information about the emperor's personality remain, undermines the carefully analysed issues with the evidence at hand. For example, note the following passage from the *Historia Augusta*, where the author lists the personality traits of Hadrian:

> idem severus laetus, comis gravis, lascivus cunctator, tenax liberalis, simula-
> tor <dissimulator>, saevus clemens, et semper in omnibus varius.

> As a person he was at the same time serious and happy, friendly and burdensome, playful and a procrastinator, stingy and generous, veiled, cruel and merciful, and always in all things changeable.[81]

This set of contradictions tells us little about Hadrian's personality, suggesting how obscure, and perhaps diversionary, this information could be and is particularly frustrating *if* the only goal is to build an accurate interpretation of Hadrian's character.

Such a focus on authenticity has therefore been a stumbling block for scholarship. In an article about the problematic use of anecdotes in modern history in order to gain 'social, economic, and administrative details',[82] Saller gives the following possibilities of reconstructing the 'reality' behind the story since it was divorced from its context:

> The details in an anecdote could reflect any one of four 'realities': an accurate reproduction of the details of the time of the original story, anachronistic accretions grafted on at some unknown point during the transmission, accretions by our literary source reflecting the author's own times, or accretions by our literary source reflecting what the author envis-
> aged the period of the anecdote to be like.[83]

These points are valid, particularly if one wants to reconstruct the real context of the events. However, discussing the discourse and stories that surround the emperor in the early principate is a different matter. In this sense, *authenticity* is not an issue, as the substance of discourse does not have to be true per se, for it is more important that these stories were circulating and reflecting ideological concerns. Indeed, Saller suggests that the value in anecdotes lies in attitudes and ideology and that they reflect general character traits that were expected of a *princeps*, in actions as well as in words. This concern with exemplarity is common in ancient historiography and particularly flourishes with respect to the principate.[84] In other words, the truth of these anecdotes lies not in their content but rather in

---

[81] HA, *Hadr.* 14.   [82] Saller (1980: 69).   [83] Saller (1980: 80–1).

[84] Saller (1980: 82). For more on this interest in *exempla*, see Roller (2001), on aristocratic responses under one-man rule, and Roller (2018), on the genre of exemplary literature.

the thought-world they convey.[85] Their importance should not be under-estimated, as stated by Purcell:

> Those stories, *fabulae*, are integral to the working of the Roman system, and so is the paradox that their subject should be precisely the more covert behaviour of the rulers. What we are seeing in all of this is the most distinctive feature of the early principate: the intimate involvement of ordinary people in the construction and definition of the image of the emperor, his role, and his family.[86]

Thus, their fictionality conveys anxieties about and interests in the truth behind the veils of an emperor's family and so *are* the substance of what the emperor is seen to be.

However, the activity of isolating and privileging the fictional in stories about the emperor should not be used to discount their historical value as reflections of discourse, which is an unfortunate by-product of rehabilitating the images of 'bad' emperors. A pertinent example is Tiberius. In a series of articles written since 2008, Champlin has steadily and carefully analysed several stories and anecdotes about Tiberius.[87] For the most part, his focus has been on exposing their fictionality and hostility towards the second *princeps*, finding parallels for those stories in world literature.[88] Similar to Yavetz, he effectively shows the difficulty of stressing certain evidence over others to create a comfortable, non-contradictory reconstruction of an emperor's character, showing us that there were indeed different images of Tiberius in our evidence, not all of which are negative.[89] Furthermore, and more particular to Champlin, the existence of comparable stories and the inconsistencies of their morals suggest that these anecdotes tended to be generalising, given that they could be found in folk tales throughout history, and that their dark and fictional characteristics suggest a hostile hand. Champlin advocates for a healthy scepticism of the image of Tiberius the Monster: 'Tales of power gravitate

---

[85] Saller (1980: 73, 82), with Plin. *Ep.* 9.33.1: *Incidi in materiam veram sed simillimam fictae dignamque isto laetissimo, altissimo planeque poetico ingenio; incidi autem, dum super cenam varia miracula hinc inde referuntur. Magna auctori fides. Tametsi quid poetae cum fide? Is tamen auctor, cui bene vel historiam scripturus credidisses* (I've happened upon a subject of truth, though it resembles fiction very closely, and is worthy of your most abundant, lofty and obvious poetical genius. Indeed, I came upon it whilst having dinner, when various wondrous matters were being discussed. The author inspires great trustworthiness – that said, what do poets have to do with trust? – However, this author you could in fact trust if he were to write a history). Cf. Morgan (2007: 4–8), for the usefulness of fable in reconstructing popular ethics in the ancient world.
[86] Purcell (1999: 183).   [87] Champlin (2008, 2012, 2015a, 2015b).   [88] Champlin (2008).
[89] Champlin (2008: 418).

naturally to a princeps: the cumulative effect of these monarchical stereotypes must be to cast doubt on the historical truth of any single item.'[90]

On most of these points there is little disagreement here. However, the interest moves towards what happens after we accept that this anecdotal material about Tiberius, or indeed about any emperor, is mostly fictional. The question now becomes one of exploring *why* Tiberius was thought of in such a fabulous manner, whether negatively or positively. The discussion thus far has concentrated on the sort of history that is possible from anecdotal material and the proximity of the Roman emperor to fabulous stories. In this light, the answer to the question of Tiberius and fiction is not to reject them as spurious stories with little historical relevance. While the historical truth in their content might be slim, their relevance lies in what these stories *reflect* about the reception of emperorship. These stories, then, tantalisingly point to a discourse about the emperor that attempted to understand him through fable and fiction. By this token, imperial historiography and biography are spliced with seemingly fictional stories because that seems to be a way in which to conceptualise the emperorship.

Making such an assumption allows for more evidence to be admissible as potential vignettes of the thought-world about the Roman emperor, which might include imperial historiography, biography, legal texts, subliterary writings found in papyri, and more patently 'fictional' accounts found in poetry and fable.[91] In such evidence, we might observe the emperor Tiberius and a busybody attempting to gain imperial favour; another story with Augustus trying a case; yet other evidence showing Hadrian producing *sententiae* in bilingual teaching materials; *acta* depicting ambassadorial encounters between Alexandrian dignitaries and the emperor; the appearance of the emperor in humorous encounters in Macrobius' *Saturnalia*; and his apparition in the dreams of Artemidorus' *Oneirocritica*.[92] If taken with Scott's paradigm, the interest of such literature in power relations between emperor and subject opens up a world where a 'hidden transcript' was being discussed, thus establishing the literature's historical value.

As a final example, observe the anecdote about Hadrian and the old woman, which Millar used on the first page of his *Emperor in the Roman*

---

[90] Champlin (2008: 413–14); cf. Champlin (2015b: 295).
[91] Morgan (2007: 4–8); cf. Kugelmeier (2019: 261–2), for a more pessimistic view.
[92] Phaed. 2.5; *ardaliones* seems to be a derogatory term for a court busybody. Cf. Mart. 2.7.7; 4.78.9. Cf. Henderson (2001: 10–13). Cf. Champlin (2008: 417); Phaed. 3.10. Cf. Henderson (2001: 38–41); Phaed. 1.30; Morgan (2007: 57–63).

World.[93] When the woman asked for the emperor's time and the latter declined, she made the famous retort: καὶ μὴ βασίλευε (Don't rule then!).[94] Parallels of the same story made Millar question its authenticity.[95] However, the existence of such parallels should not be taken as irrelevant to the context of understanding what the emperor did. Indeed, Millar's use of the anecdote was to illustrate a wider theme in the duties of the Roman emperor, namely the importance of 'petition and response' in the inter-action between subject and emperor. Thus, the truth value of the anecdote does not reside in whether it actually happened but in what it conveys about the perceptions of the respective roles of emperor and subject in society. Why such bold discourse directed at the emperor was allowed rests in the political and legal role of his position. The next section outlines this argument and the challenges that an autocratic figure who defies simple designation, let alone the title 'king', have posed for historians since antiquity.

1.2   The Emperor Historiographically and Constitutionally

1.2.1   *The Outline of a Problem*

The power of the Roman emperor is notoriously difficult to define. In modern scholarship, there has been a reticence in describing the enormous discretionary and invasive power of the emperor in monarchic or 'kingly' terms. The reality of the emperor's power was such that he could do what he thought was necessary, creating the paradox of autocratic power that could not be seen to be monarchic.[96] This is most readily observable in the titles, names, and descriptors of power ascribed to the emperorship, which were numerous and of varying importance. Given that emperors had names, titles, and offices that were not necessarily coterminous with their reigns, no specific title could in fact encompass his power and duties. The fascinating nature of the emperor's power – outside the constraints of

---

[93] Millar (1977: 3).   [94] Dio 69.6.3.

[95] Millar (1977: 4). Millar spends time discussing the potential purpose of these stories in Plutarch but then argues that the conceptions evoked by the author 'imposed themselves firmly and concretely on the real life and routine of the emperor'. For alternative versions of this story that were all produced under the high empire, if on different topics, see Plut. *Mor.* 179 C–D; Plut. *Vit. Demetr.* 42. The story about Antipater is quoted in Stobaeus: Stob. *Flor.* 3.13.48. All three stories have the exact same ending retort. Cf. Champlin (2008: 414).

[96] The historiography of the Roman emperor is immense. The great tension of the 1970s in the debate between Millar and Hopkins created a disagreement on Millar (1977); Dench (2018).

legality and the Roman constitution and yet ideologically informed and supported by them – has only heightened its multiplicity.[97]

This multiplicity has posed a challenge to scholarly attempts to understand the position from the early principate and beyond, at least in terms of a simple explanation about its constitutional and extraconstitutional makeup. For instance, Theodor Mommsen argued that every principate began and died with each *princeps*, stating that there was no continuity.[98] In the legal and constitutional framework of Mommsen's *Römisches Staatsrecht*, the emperor was much the same as another magistrate, imbued with *imperium* and with a temporal limit (i.e. the death of the emperor). In contradistinction to a magistracy, though, the emperorship did not have a single title under which its duties and powers could be summarised, as 'consul' or 'praetor' did.

Along these lines, attempts to ascribe a catch-all phrase to the emperor's position and power have eluded modern scholars, at least when it comes to summarising the emperorship and explaining it to students and wider audiences, where brevity and simplicity are paramount. The problem of definition is caused, in large part, by the many, often ambiguous, terms the Romans themselves used to describe imperial power and its holders: Augustus, Caesar, and *princeps*, amongst others, not to mention the Greek versions of such titles.[99] When such terms are transposed into English and other languages, they typically take on a wider meaning than their Latin originals: the word 'emperor' is especially significant in this respect.[100] Descriptors of power have been numerous, all with varying contours of meaning and application. In particular, since the discovery of the correct term that filled the lacuna in chapter 34 of the *Res gestae divi Augusti*, there has been increasing consensus that the term *auctoritas* comes closest to describing Augustus' extraconstitutional power.[101] The pre-eminent *auctoritas* that Augustus held in comparison to his senatorial colleagues was sufficient to explain his overt superiority in a world where legally and

---

[97] Cf. Hekster (2017), on the 'constraints of tradition' that inform the particularities of the imperial position, and Hekster (2023: 4–17), for an introduction to the multiplicity of the emperorship through time.

[98] *StR* II 749–50.   [99] Béranger (1953).

[100] *Imperator* originally meant 'general' and was an honorific title given to successful generals by their troops. It was used as a *praenomen* by the young Octavian and became one of the usual titles of future emperors into late antiquity, entering into the Romance languages and English to designate the sovereign ruler of an empire, a much wider meaning than its Latin root.

[101] Furedi (2013: 60–2): 'The Romans themselves used the term in an expansive sense in order to make sense of a variety of different relationships and experiences. This was a politically contested and protean term that could be harnessed to assist a variety of projects. However, despite its multiple usages, *auctoritas* represented a claim to influence, respect, and esteem.'

constitutionally the power of his various offices was no greater than that of any other magistrate. Augustus, then, made the ideology of his position contingent and deferential by definition, evinced in the various titles he refused and accepted.[102] More recently, Rowe, for instance, has sought to defy the scholarly consensus on the term *auctoritas*: he argues that we need to be cautious about stretching political terms to encompass the whole power of the emperorship rather than a more contextual reading that stresses Augustus' pre-eminence at that point, even though this call has been met with scepticism.[103] In the end, the Roman emperorship, with its many descriptors, defies ascription to a single, hold-all term – a fact which is counter-intuitively bolstered by the fact that *auctoritas* also evades simple definition, as do several Latin words of, about, and describing power (*imperium, dominatio, potestas, maiestas, dignitas*, and so on). Perhaps this was the point: that the emperor's power could be described in several different ways, with varying connotations being added alongside the term used in each context. This statement, however, does not mean that *auctoritas* is not an important modern tool with which to understand the power of the emperor but rather it suggests that a multifaceted approach is necessary.

More recently, Alison Cooley has challenged the model of a 'constitutional' implementation of a system that can be called 'the Principate'. In short, the planned institutionalisation of a constitutional framework from the 'Augustan Principate' onwards is a mirage, created to describe Augustus' impact on the *res publica*. Such schematic interpretations become brittle once one focusses on particular contexts and 'principates', thus eliding the particular mix of legal and charismatic contributions that made up the legitimacy of a particular emperor. Cooley's sharp focus on the Augustan and Tiberian era has reiterated more systematically the impression of earlier scholars regarding the difficulty of assigning a hold-all term to describe the position Augustus and Tiberius held in its entirety. Alternatively, Cooley emphasises a much more receptive and extraconstitutional basis for Augustus' pre-eminence and position: building on previous scholarship, she shows that the term *statio* was the primary contemporary term used to describe the position Augustus held and Tiberius inherited, citing evidence including Velleius Paterculus and the *Senatus consultum de Pisone patre*.[104] This euphemistically military

---

[102] *RGDA* 34; cf. Freudenburg (2014: 1–9); Rich (2012).
[103] Rowe (2013); cf. Galinsky (2015a), for an effective rebuttal and the efficacy of *auctoritas* to conceptualise Augustus' principate.
[104] Hereafter, the *SCPP*; Cooley (2019: 76–8); cf. Matthews (2010: 70–1); Vell. Pat. 2.124.2; Gell. *NA* 15.7.3; *SCPP* 126–30; Val. Max. 2.1.8, 2.2.6; *statio* is noted before the publication of the *SCPP* in

descriptor evokes a guard on duty, which 'fits nicely with descriptions of the princeps as protector and saviour of the *res publica*' – resonant themes for future emperors as well.[105] Perhaps the most important takeaway from Cooley's article is her stress on flexibility, elegantly described as Augustus' principate rather than 'the Augustan Principate' and thus underlining contingency and charisma as important facets of legitimation as much as legal definitions and the conferral of a bundle of powers.

More on the direct analysis on appropriate terms and on fundamental texts will follow in Sections 1.2.2–1.2.5. One point should be stressed at this juncture: what seems to be occurring in modern scholarship is a consensus that stresses the emperor's 'true' power as being extraconstitutional, that is, not conforming totally to the Latin vocabulary of power with which it was described. This process of legitimation would be fashioned from an emperor's charismatic authority rather than any magistracy he held during his reign. However, what our goal should be is to reconcile the seemingly unbridgeable chasm between image and reality. To stress magisterial power over image, for instance, would only produce an incomplete understanding of the ideology and function of the Roman emperorship. Put plainly, for the Roman emperor to be the Roman emperor, rather than just another magistrate or a king, he must fulfil the role as a Roman magistrate, priest, general, senator, citizen, and more *as well as* his role as a figure who wielded supreme and intercessory power. The existence of one does not preclude the existence of the other. To describe the emperorship in an unbalanced way would be to describe a different political system. In essence, the critique that follows of both our ancient evidence and our scholarly approaches will be informed by this assumption.

Importantly, this argument can be approached via two distinct roads, though they intertwine in reaching the end goal. One focusses solely on the available evidence at hand, and thus is uncontaminated by imported assumptions and expectations of other monarchical systems. The second takes a comparative approach, which sees the Roman emperorship as an example of autocratic government that can be studied in contrast to other examples in world history. The first approach was taken by the magisterial study of Millar, which consciously refrained from engaging with socio-logical models of autocratic government. This empirical method sought to appreciate the evidence per se. Subsequently, the evidence would be

---

1996 by Levick (1999: 57), whose book was originally published in 1976. Cf. Béranger (1973: 153–63); cf. Jacques, Scheid, and Lepelley (1990: 1–46), for an excellent summary on the emperor's constellation of powers. See Pani (1997: 237–270) for a good summary on the principate and *statio*.
[105] Cooley (2019: 78).

divided thematically into the administrative roles of the emperor and his relationship with individuals, institutions, and communities across the empire. Thus, by the collection of a vast amount of material, Millar recreated what the emperor was through his observable activities. What was revealed was a passive emperor who responded to petitions and requests – an administrator whose daily activities were tied up in the work of running a vast empire.

On the face of it, this approach seemed to pay little heed to the symbolic role of the emperor, the constitutional niceties of the position, or the more fantastic and fictitious stories that populate the historical record. Indeed, some of these criticisms were levied by Hopkins in the review 'Rules of Evidence', which strongly disagreed with Millar's approach, precisely because Millar disavowed a sociological or comparative approach, not to mention the lack of attention given to the imperial cult. Though this debate is now more than forty years old, its disagreements were recently revived by Beard in a *Times Literary Supplement* article, which elicited responses from colleagues.[106] In some senses, the terms of the debate have remained similar: a disagreement over what to privilege in the record and how to describe and conceptualise the Roman emperor, which often comes down to attention and approach. In short, the solution to this impasse is to stress a holistic approach, which considers that both these seemingly polarised sides are fundamental to understanding the emperor. In other words, the multifaceted nature of the Roman emperorship means that a wide-ranging approach is needed that pays attention to both the vast array of evidence available and its context and also asks questions about the symbolic and paradoxical aspects of the emperorship. Furthermore, this supposed polarity collapses when other themes are considered, which could include topics as wide as the administration of imperial estates, through iconographical studies of imperial portraiture, to local iterations of the imperial cult across the empire.[107]

Despite these self-consciously alternative stances, they share the same end goal: to understand what the Roman emperor was and how his position was understood. These different approaches are not irreconcilable, as you can reach one through the other. The brilliance of Millar's approach was that it created an empirical model of understanding the Roman emperor, and the importance of Hopkins' statements was that they recentred the significance of ideology in understanding what the emperor

---

[106] Hopkins (1978b); Beard (2020).
[107] See Hekster (2022), for such an approach to the emperorship in iconography.

was. Both were fundamental to taking the Roman emperor as a category and theme worthy of study, rather than tessellating the history according to reign and period. The emperor is worth studying as an office as well as any individual ruler with their own personality.

1.2.2　On the Constitutionality of the Roman Emperor

The ideological function of the emperorship, caught between its autocratic characteristics and a republican mould, influenced how it was perceived and understood, which manifested in numerous themes in our historical record. As noted in Section 1.2.1, scholarship has assessed the balance between an autocratic understanding of the Roman emperor and one that respected the political culture in which it operated.[108] This book seeks to reconcile these seemingly disparate strands of scholarship but also to stand apart from them. The ambiguities of and difficulties in describing the position of the Roman emperor contain these issues at their heart, which simultaneously appreciates both the autocratic and the constitutional expectations placed on the position. I also take the assumption that the nature of imperial ideology affected how the emperor would be understood by a wider population across the empire, which therefore forms fundamental foregrounding to the remainder of this book.

As noted in Section 1.1, there is a conscious decision here to view the Roman emperor from the bottom up rather than the top down.[109] Roman political ideology was based on expectations placed on, and scrutiny of, an elite and an ideology that was based on the sovereignty of the *populus Romanus*.[110] Such underlying values would suggest that what people thought about the emperor was in fact *fundamental* to the functioning of the system. These values, therefore, would explain the importance of how the emperor seemed, as this impression was the substance of politics. In other words, much of the themes discussed in this book highlight how ideological expectations of the emperor filtered into perceptions of his role from the perspective of his subjects.

Such ideological expectations also have a temporal component, which involves the longevity of the Roman emperorship as an office that reaches

---

[108] Hekster (2017, 2022), for recent overviews. The Roman emperor has been a subject of scrutiny for a long time in different fields of study: see Kaldellis (2015); Flaig (2019); Omissi (2018); Cornwell (2017: 20–3); Levick (2010: 309); Morell et al. (2019). For the Roman emperor as a subject in political philosophy, see Desmond (2020: 104–5); Hegel (2004: 314); Agamben (1998).
[109] Kaldellis (2015: 3).　　[110] Cf. Morstein-Marx (2021: 3–7), for a precis of this debate.

well beyond the disintegration of the Roman empire.[111] The Roman emperorship was in constant dialogue with its past, present, and future as it moved through time, which is directly connected to the hazy definition Augustus gave the position at its inception. Put another way, the actions of emperors, and perceptions thereof, would recast examples set by previous emperors, alter the perceptions of the sitting emperor, and open up a powerful potential for future emperors to act within that mould. Though contexts and political configurations changed as we move into late antiquity, this transcript of imperial action remained, which allowed for subsequent iterations of the Roman emperor to draw from it for inspiration for their own imperial political cultures.[112]

Our discussion now turns to the building blocks of the position of the Roman emperor, with the ambiguities and tensions already discussed in mind as we focus in on various powers and duties the position of 'emperor' held at any given moment of its existence. Such a discussion involves the list of duties included in Fronto's advice, discussed in the introduction to Chapter 1, which reveals the *dialogic* character of an emperor's job: speech acts and writing were thus fundamental, which put forth an image of the emperor at work.[113] Part of this process is the *response*, not in this case of the emperor being a passive recipient of requests, though this was proven by Millar to be an important part of the equation. Rather, it is the response of other sides of the conversation, which might be occupied by tradition, law, the senate, the Roman people, and communities across the empire. The imagination and expectations of these sets of ideas and groups created the spaces in which the emperor operated.[114] The fact that there were so many different things that the emperor had to converse with goes some way to explain how multifaceted the position came to be. Simply put, the emperor was not only what he did but also what he was imagined to be.

Such interstitial spaces are notably present in what can be termed the 'constitutional' description of the Roman emperor, which are variously the emperor's position with respect to the state and the law. Here, the definitions and interpretations of the emperor's *imperium*, *potestas*, and *auctoritas* move into focus: from where each of these are derived and their respective relationships to other *imperia*, *potestates*, and *auctoritates* that existed in the *res publica* as well as the aspects of the emperorship that were left unspoken and undefined. Such tensions are observable in the examples

---

[111] I discuss the emperor as a temporal figure in Chapter 6; cf. Christoforou (2021: 88).
[112] For examples of this thinking in Byzantine studies, see Kaldellis (2015) and Kruse (2019).
[113] Millar (1977).　　[114] Cf. Lenski (2016: 6–12), on the 'composite' Constantine.

discussed here: the nature of the Augustan settlements and the provisions under the *Lex de imperio Vespasiani*. Rather than being an exhaustive account of the history of either political context, or indeed a full analysis of the various offices and terms of power that an emperor could collect through the course of his reign, the point here is to illustrate the nature of his power and its inherent contradictions. This phenomenon can be boiled down to the embedding of supreme power within a Roman framework informed by law and custom.

Depending on the level of granularity, the discussion at any given point of the principate of the political nature of the emperorship could be endless, which might include a history of a certain legal term or magisterial power (such as *maiestas* or *imperium maius*), prompting due attention to the precedents and developments of those categories from the republic. There is a wealth of scholarship on such topics, and I do not seek to supersede it through the systematic collection and analysis of such terms: this activity deserves focussed attention.[115] Instead, I will map the thought-world about the Roman emperor that placed him at the crossroads between undefined extraconstitutional power and political institutions, offices, and customs. Such placement necessitates deft negotiation, making the analysis of his power at any given point challenging. The Roman emperor, thus, was more than the sum of his parts and yet needed those parts to operate in the political culture of the world he inhabited. However, we need not place these two realms in opposition with each other, as if the constitutional description of the emperor was somehow hermetically sealed off from the informal world of his power. Such a distinction misreads the dynamics of the compromise between the emperor and the state from the Augustan age onwards. Rather, it is the informal way of expressing constitutional settle-ments and the importance of more informal arrangements that supplement the legal and political magistracies and duties that are a necessary part of understanding the emperor. The emperor is affirmed informally in consti-tutional arenas, such as seen in *leges de imperio*, of which we have the *Lex de imperio Vespasiani* as a crowning example.[116] Such conscious ambiguity in the political sphere can go some way to explain the multifaceted nature of the position's reception through time. As such, an appreciation of the constitutional underpinning of the principate will form the bedrock of the more fictional and bizarre fears of, and expectations placed on, the emperor in the second half of this book.

---

[115] See Noreña (2011) as an example and Christoforou (2021) for my own foray into this world.
[116] On the *lex* and its precedents, see Buongiorno (2012: 518–20).

1.2.3   Auctoritas

The Augustan 'settlements', as they are called, are a complex process of religious, legal, and political changes to the *res publica* that were stretched out over the long primacy of Octavian/Augustus, with each episode adding precedents and wrinkles to the relationship between the *princeps* and the state. These are not restricted to the political and legal arrangements, such as the length and size of Augustus' provincial command, the nature of his *imperium*, and the granting of political powers without accompanying magistracies (sc. *tribunicia potestas*), but also involve legislation known as his moral reforms, religious and social initiatives, and building programmes that altered the fabric of Rome and its rituals. The nuances and changes across time are too numerous to chart here, though there is a wealth of scholarship that engages in deep exegeses of the available evidence.[117] The purpose here is to focus on a couple of examples that reflect the supremacy of the emperor within a political and legal framework, with it being described in Roman political vocabulary, and yet also that reflect the same supremacy being predicated on a more ineffable and ill-defined status outside the state apparatus. This section is not about intention, that is, whether Augustus or his political milieu intended for his *statio* to have this mix, whether the different calibrations and additions throughout Augustus' long life were planned or inevitable, or when we can date and define the nature of the emperor's *imperium*. The result remains the same: the primacy of Augustus was embedded within the political framework of the *res publica*, with rules to be followed and expectations to be fulfilled.[118]

Particular consideration will be given to the concept of *auctoritas* and how the term figured in Augustus' own description of his position, particularly in the process of the 'first' settlement in 28–27 BC.

> In consulatu sexto et septimo, postquam bella civilia exstinxeram, per consensum universorum potens rerum omnium, rem publicam ex mea potestate in senatus populique Romani arbitrium transtuli. Quo pro merito meo senatus consulto Augustus appellatus sum et laureis postes aedium mearum vestiti publice coronaque civica super ianuam meam fixa est et clupeus aureus in curia Iulia positus, quem mihi senatum populumque Romanum dare virtutis clementiaeque et iustitiae et pietatis caussa testatum est per eius clupei inscriptionem. Post id tempus auctoritate omnibus

---

[117] Eck, Schneider, & Takács (2003); Hurlet and Mineo (2009: 75–99); Levick (2010: 68–99); Vervaet (2014: 252–75); Griffin (1991: 24–32); cf. Buongiorno (2012: 519), for *comitia ob tribunicia potestatem*.
[118] Hekster (2017).

praesti, potestatis autem nihilo amplius habui quam ceteri qui mihi quoque in magistratu conlegae fuerunt.

> In my sixth and seventh consulships, after I had extinguished the civil wars, through universal consent I held power over all matters, I transferred the state from my power to the control of the Senate and People of Rome. For this service I was named Augustus by senatorial decree, and the doorposts of my house were adorned publicly with laurels, and a civic crown was fastened above my doorway, and a golden shield was places in the Julian senate house, which the Senate and People of Rome gave me on account of valour, clemency, justice and piety, which is testified through an inscription on that shield. After that time I excelled everyone in authority, but I held no more power than others who were my colleagues in a magistracy.[119]

Behind these words lies the complex negotiations that were taking place between Caesar's heir and the Roman community after the triumviral period and several years of civil war, which involve the annulment of unjust laws enacted in the triumviral period and the organisation of the provinces – a process that spanned two years.[120] Augustus' statements concentrate on the publicly transacted relationship between himself and the Senate and People of Rome: such a reading is evinced by mention of a *senatus consultum*, the laurels adorning Augustus' threshold, and the civic crown above the doorway. In other words, we are in the political world of appearances here as much as we are in a legal and constitutional one.[121] As such, Augustus' pre-eminent *auctoritas* should be read in that light, particularly given its informal nature and how it was dependent on an individual's perceived elevated position within the state.[122] Rather than being *the* byword for Augustus' conception of the principate, in essence what we have is a description using contemporary political vocabulary, which attempted to explain Augustus' position within the state, both formally and informally.[123] Such a reading allows for different terms to be used in different contexts, which illuminates the multifaceted nature of imperial nomenclature.[124] This reading also allows us to appreciate the transaction of power and its display. *Auctoritas* is important insofar as it describes Augustus' extralegal clout, but it needs to work together with the *potestas* of the magistracies unmentioned, the *imperium*

---

[119] *RGDA* 34 trans. adapted from Cooley (2009).

[120] For a full account of the history behind the first settlement, see Rich (2012), esp. 63, 65–6, and 78, for the development of the 'emergency' throughout Augustus' primacy thereafter; cf. Rich and Williams (1999); Cowan (2019: 29–45).

[121] Cowan (2019: 31).   [122] Balsdon (1960: 43–4); cf. Rowe (2013: 3–9).

[123] In response to Rowe (2013: 2).   [124] Cooley (2019).

he received from his consular command, and the honorific language that stresses Augustus' merit. In other words, Augustus had won the republican game of honours that would cement his position as the *princeps civitatis*, but this could only work if publicly transacted in the language of republican honorifics.

The point here is not to delineate when Augustus held *auctoritas* alone and did not hold magisterial *potestas* that was de facto greater than other magistrates in the state, or what the specific function of Augustus' *auctoritas* was in the context of 28/27 BC.[125] *Auctoritas* works well in this period as an 'informal' acceptance of overall care and leadership, read alongside the granting of a large provincial command for the purpose of pacification,[126] supplying a qualified interpretation of Cassius Dio's account that acknowledges the chronological inaccuracies of the historian.[127] Rather, the longer-term point should be stressed here, which sees a tension between formal and informal powers – a statement that works for many points of Augustus' principate as well as the reigns of future emperors. Indeed, this tension of the retention of monarchical power in a republican guise, noticed by Dio and acknowledged even in a deeply contextual reading, is an enduring legacy of the Augustan settlements, intended or not.[128]

Focus should return to the question of estimation within the semantic implications of the term *auctoritas*. A key phrase in this passage that helps our interpretation is *consensus universorum*. As noted in Section 1.2.1, Mommsen's understanding of the principate was founded on the sovereignty of the people,[129] which meant that the *princeps* was no different than a magistrate, elevated to supreme office, with constitutional restrictions on his power.[130] Accordingly, the principate was different from what can be understood as an absolute monarchy; it was by the consent of constituents of the Roman empire that the emperor owed his position.[131] *Consensus universorum*, then, is an important ideological aspect of the Roman

---

[125] Rich (2012: 41, 63–4).
[126] Rich (2012: 56–7); Vervaet (2014), 254–6, for Augustus' *summum imperium auspiciumque*, 270–2, for Vervaet's argument of its 'permanence'.
[127] Rich (2012: 51–2), with Dio 53.2.6–22.5. Cf. Suet. *Aug.* 28.2.
[128] Rich (2012: 66): 'By these arrangements, as Dio saw so clearly, Augustus ensured the continuance of his monarchical power while cloaking it in a republican guise.'
[129] *StR* II 749–50 = *DPR* V 6–7. The reference here is to the *populus Romanus*. See Ando (1999: 14). Cf. Cic. *Rep.* 1.39; cf. Gaius, 1.3. What constituted the *populus Romanus*, and the difference with the *plebs Romana* and indeed other collectives across the empire, will be discussed in Section 1.2.
[130] *StR* II 749–50 = *DPR* V 6–7.
[131] *StR* II 844 = *DPR* V 116. Cf. Veyne (2002: 6). Cf. *StR* II 1132–3 = *DPR* V 445–6. The *consensus universorum* is a wider body of support than the *populus Romanus*, which would stretch Mommsen's model. Cf. Flaig (2011: 77).

principate and is reflected in numerous sources,[132] and notably used by Augustus.[133] His power, therefore, was claimed to be sanctioned by universal consent. This is further reflected in the legal tradition. Ulpian wrote that:

> quod principi placuit, legis habet vigorem: utpote cum lege regia, quae de imperio eius lata est, populus ei et in eum omne suum imperium et potestatem conferat.

> That which pleases the princeps has the force of law. This is because, with the *lex regia*, which was carried concerning his *imperium*, the people transfer to him their entire *imperium* and *potestas*.[134]

The emperor's powers were given to him by the people, even if his power was discretionary and wide-ranging.[135] Such a reading not only stresses the importance of the people's sovereignty in the Roman state but also places enormous weight on the ability of the princeps to fulfil his role and live up to the trust placed in him.

This argument brings us back to *auctoritas* itself.[136] *Auctoritas* is a distinct concept to the holding of military or political office, and the power that comes with it, which in Latin is described by the words *potestas* and *imperium*.[137] To have *auctoritas* encompassed ideas of having the necessary clout to initiate and inspire in relation to other actors and institutions in Roman society.[138] Moreover, within its semantic usage is a sense of ratification, including *auctoritas patrum*, in contexts of the senate approving the legislation from public assemblies.[139] The term carried force in contexts of power and jurisdiction and entailed the moral prestige of its holder.[140] It had

---

[132] See pp. 102–109 on the idea of 'acceptance'; cf. Hammond (1959: 10, 24, n. 44–8). Cf. Plin. *Pan.* 10.1; cf. Val. Max. 1. *pr.*

[133] Aug. *RGDA* 34. Cf. *StR* II 844 = *DPR* V 116. For further on consensus, see Ando (2000) and Lobur (2008).

[134] *Dig.* 1.4.1.pr. = Ulp. *Inst.* 1. Cf. Schulz (1945), for problems with the text and alternative interpretations.

[135] Straumann (2016: 246–7). Cf. Brunt (1977: 107–8).

[136] Wirszubski (1950: 116–17). See Hurlet (2020: 172–3) for a definition.

[137] Drogula (2007: 422–7); Magdelain (1947: 49); Wirszubski (1950: 109–23).

[138] Cf. Furedi (2013: 60–2). Furedi quotes Dio to bolster his point about *auctoritas*, within Dio's discussion of the Senate's *auctoritas*: Dio 55.3.5: 'But it was affected as *auctoritas*, in order that their decision would be clear. Such is the force of this term made manifest. For to translate it each time into Greek is impossible'; 'ἀλλὰ αὐκτώριτας ἐγίγνετο, ὅπως φανερὸν τὸ βούλημα αὐτῶν ᾖ. Τοιοῦτον γάρ τι ἡ δύναμις τοῦ ὀνόματος τούτου δηλοῖ· ἑλληνίσαι γὰρ αὐτὸ καθάπαξ ἀδύνατόν ἐστι.'

[139] Magdelain (1990: 392, 402), for a discussion of the development of the term *auctoritas* and its association with the Senate.

[140] Magdelain (1990: 403): 'Bientôt, il s'étendit aussi au prestige moral des prudents et des hommes éminents.'

the aspect of more personal qualities that involved high moral character, in a figure whose words and deeds carried more weight.[141]

In essence, *auctoritas* was difficult to define as it was based on estimation, seemingly giving its holder unparalleled abilities to influence, which then makes *auctoritas* the crucial component in autocracy.[142] However, this difficulty is a red herring, as it pits 'supra-legal' and official power against each other unnecessarily. Though there is disagreement on the derivation and meaning of Augustus' *auctoritas* at *Res gestae* 34.3, the recent exchange between Rowe and Galinsky has revealed a fundamental overlap.[143] The strength in Rowe's argument stresses that *potestas* was equal to others rather than having surpassed all in *auctoritas*.[144] For Rowe, 'it is an affirmation that he conformed to collegiality'.[145] In this sense, Rowe is reiterating the legal and constitutional aspects of Augustus' position, which allows for the deferential attitude of Augustus' regime to the institutions and hierarchies of the republic.[146] Though Galinsky prefers seeing *auctoritas* as wide-ranging as the term implies, the point he makes is that *auctoritas* is used in a transactional sense of the influence and impact that Augustus actually had, rather than an abstract notion of his unbridled power.[147] In my view, *auctoritas* is effective because it is exercised in a political arena that guarantees the ideological goals of peace, prosperity, and concord. Deference and collegiality sit together with influence and prestige, not in opposition.[148]

Indeed, such an argument works in negative examples. The unsavoury idea of proscription comes to mind here, with a particular case being Varro Murena, who was implicated in a conspiracy after the problematic trial of Marcus Primus. To enumerate the issues would fall beyond the scope of this book, but suffice it to say that Augustus' actions were justified by his assertion that it was in 'the interest of the state', which was safeguarded by his *auctoritas*, which is wielded in a public context.[149] Both the symbolic

---

[141] Cf. Magdelain (1947: 112): 'Autorité personnelle ou autorité légale, selon la forme de la constitution, mais, dans tous les cas, autorité dont la mission était, par le jeu d'une sagesse providentielle, d'assurer le bien commun.'

[142] Wirszubski (1950: 116).

[143] Rowe (2013: 1–15). Cf. Galinsky (2015a: 244–9), for a rebuttal of Rowe's arguments.

[144] Rowe (2013: 9).   [145] Rowe (2013: 15). Cf. Wallace-Hadrill (1982a: 32–48).

[146] Vervaet (2014: 286). Cf. Hurlet (2001). Rowe (2013: 3–4). Hurlet (2020: 174–5), for a fair appreciation of Rowe's arguments.

[147] Galinsky (2015a: 249).

[148] Rowe (2013: 6–9). Cf. Hurlet (2020: 185–6), for a full discussion of the malleability of *auctoritas* and Roman political terminology.

[149] Dio 54.3.3: Augustus replied 'τὸ δημόσιον'. On Primus and Varro, see Levick (1975: 156–63), esp. 161 on this issue. Cf. Strabo 14.5.4, in the context of this trial on Athenaeus of Tarsus and a roof falling on his head, both actual and metaphorical. Many thanks to Georgy Kantor for pointing out the relevance of this passage to me.

and constitutional aspects of the emperor's power were ideologically important to the position.

1.2.4   Leges et iura p.R. restituit

A particularly important example of these dynamics between Augustus' powers and the state within the process of the first settlement is the famous *leges et iura* coin.[150] This *aureus*, struck in 28 BC, depicts Octavian on both the obverse and the reverse: he is shown wearing a laurel wreath under the legend IMP CAESAR DIVI F COS VI, which dates the coin to his sixth consulship.[151] Notably, the reverse depicts Octavian seated on a curule chair, togate and holding a scroll, which likely represents the edicts by which he abrogated the illegal laws of the triumviral period.[152] The reverse legend reads LEGES ET IURA P.R. RESTITVIT, which scholars have translated differently given disagreement on whether *populus Romanus* should be in the genitive or dative: 'Imperator Caesar, son of the divine (Julius Caesar), consul for the sixth time, (he) restored statutes and laws of (or "to") the Roman People.'[153] Even if we accept Mantovani's assertion that the dative would be too explicit and discourteous, implying that Octavian had conquered the Roman people,[154] there is a sense of transaction at play here, making it challenging to think away a discrepant and unequal relationship between Augustus and the state thereafter. Indeed, this reading is implied in analyses of the *Res gestae* and informs many scholarly interpretations of Augustus' pre-eminent *auctoritas* and position in the state.[155] Yet legal deference should be read in the depiction at the same time as Augustus' autocratic posturing.[156]

The coin elucidates how the first settlement was a process that ran across Augustus' sixth and seventh consulships, as Augustus himself summarised

---

[150] *CM* 1995.4–1.1. For a full analysis of the coin and its context, see Rich and Williams (1999); Mantovani (2008: 5–11), for interpretation of the legend on the reverse. Cf. Abdy and Harling (2005: 175), for a second example of the coin. Cf. Cowan (2019: 29–31), for a summary of recent scholarship on the coin. For an image, see the British Museum website (Museum no. 1995-0401-1): www.britishmuseum.org/collection/object/C_1995-0401-1.

[151] Rich and Williams (1999: 169–75), for similar coins, esp. the PAX cistophori of Ephesus, 13 *RIC* 476 = *RPC* 2203; Mantovani (2008: 6), for a discussion of Octavian's title. Cf. Rowan (2019: 126).

[152] Rich and Williams (1999: 182–3, 197), with Tac. *Ann.* 3.281–2 and Dio 53.2.5. Mantovani (2008: 11).

[153] For a pithy summary of the debate and different interpretations, see Rich (2012: 91–2). Cf. Levick (2010: 69); cf. Mantovani (2008: 24–7).

[154] Mantovani (2008: 30), for the emphatic point that the Roman people would not be described as conquered. Cf. Rich (2012: 92).

[155] Rich (2012: 93), for the parallel with the *Res gestae*.

[156] *Pace* Abdy and Harling (2005: 175), which is rather matter-of-fact about the 'constitutional facade'.

in *Res gestae* 34.1, and alludes to the transfer of power to the *arbitrium senatus populique Romani*. The process and its reception would have been complex, which involves questions of Augustus' relationship with political institutions and the law.[157] *Leges et iura* have been read as a typical phrase that denotes both private and criminal legal norms in an objective sense, rather than the subjective sense of 'rights' in English.[158] The words *leges et iura* could also point to a world without tyranny, used to convince that the abuse of legal norms was at an end and that Augustus was engaged in a long-term project of recalibrating the *res publica* and his role within it.[159] In all, the legend proves two conjoined points. First, that the law and civic cooperation were the outwardly stated aims of the state after 28 BC and, second, that Augustus himself was instrumental in their construction. As such, we have the common ingredients of the active roles of the individual *princeps* and the Roman community in the performance of consensus.

Such a reading is made more intricate if we consider the depiction of Octavian himself on the coin. If the togate Octavian is in fact a representation of a statue, which both depicted the annulment edict and commemorated a corresponding *senatus consultum*, we have the necessary ingredients for consensus-building activities in a public forum.[160] Even without the statue, the image of Octavian in civilian dress gesturing a transfer of power accentuates both the act of restoring the force of the law and his singular importance to the *res publica*, in a similar form as the inscription.[161] Following Mantovani's observation, the depiction of Octavian on both sides of the coin illustrates the conceit of an autocratic government monopolising the full potential of representation that a coin can provide.[162] While this statement is correct, the coin (as with other evidence of Augustus and his reforms) attempts to have it both ways: to represent conciliatory and civil politics of cooperation and consensus *and* to underline Augustus' exceptional and indispensable role in that

---

[157] Cowan (2019: 37–42), for the idea of 'competing' interpretations of the first settlement.
[158] Mantovani (2008: 13–22), for evidence of the use of *leges et iura* in literature, quotation on 22: 'ossia adotta una forma tipica e solenne per designare le norme giuridiche – essenzialmente di diritto privato e criminale –, il diritto romano in senso oggettivo.' Rich and Williams (1999: 187–90), for a wider reading of the measures encompassed under the phrase.
[159] Cowan (2019: 34, 44).
[160] Rich and Williams (1999: 187); Rich (2012: 94–5, n. 15), citing Schäfer (1989: 128–30, 238–41), for sculptural evidence depicting magistrates with curule chair and *scrinium*; cf. Kuttner (1995: 53–4), for the connection between coinage and honorific statues.
[161] Cowan (2019: 42–4), for the question of 'restoration', with Vell. Pat. 2.89.1–6.
[162] Mantovani (2008: 51).

consensus. Such activities publicly proclaimed that Augustus and the *res publica* are inextricably linked.

1.2.5   The Constraints of Expectation

Such themes are replicated in other evidence, not only from Augustus' later reign, when the calibrations of the first settlement had changed but also under the rule of future emperors. In these examples, the dynamics are similar, even if there are nuances and differences in historical contexts. Of course, there are different arenas for these 'constraints' to appear.[163] In particular, the military prowess of the Roman emperor was always an expectation placed on the position, not least because the emperor was a supreme magistrate imbued with *imperium*, which is the power to command troops, but also because many emperors, including Augustus himself, achieved their power through military conflict and strength.[164] My interest throughout this chapter is on the *political ideology and language* that legitimised emperors, whether they came to power through civil war, coups, or dynastic succession.[165] Put another way, though the arenas and expectations might have developed from Augustus through the high empire and the Severan age into late antiquity, there was a necessary step in Roman political culture to legitimise that force through legal and political routes. The political language is similar and based around themes of collective reconciliation, cooperation, and consensus, even if the spectre of military intervention or coercion is ever present.[166]

An illustrative example of this dynamic is the acceptance of the title of *pater patriae* by Augustus in 2 BC.[167] Here is how it is rendered in the *Res gestae*:

> Tertium decimum consulatum cum gerebam, senatus et equester ordo populusque Romanus universus appelavit me Patrem Patriae idque in vestibuli aedium mearum inscribendum, et in curia et in foro Aug. sub quadrigis, quae mihi ex s.c. positae sunt, decrevit.

---

[163] Hekster (2023: 106–32), for a discussion of these roles.

[164] See Hekster (2023: 106–30), for the importance of military legitimacy to the Roman emperorship from Augustus into late antiquity. For the importance of the military to legitimation in the early empire, see Ash (1999) with Tacitus' *Histories*, esp. Tac. *Hist.* 4.1–11. See Flaig (2019), for the interaction of political and military legitimacy through acceptance.

[165] For the tension between dynastic power and the politics of the state, see Hekster (2015) and esp. Madsen (2016).

[166] For more, see Lobur (2008), esp. 12–36. Cf. Rosenblitt (2016).

[167] For recent discussions, see Courrier (2014: 717–8) and Russell (2019: 327).

> As I was holding my thirteenth consulship, the senate, equestrian order, and the entire Roman people named me Father of the Fatherland and decreed that (the name) should be inscribed in the entrance to my house, in the senate house, and in the August Forum under the chariot, which were placed there for me by senatorial decree.[168]

Questions of the *domus Augusta* and the importance of the family to politics and political functions across the empire will be discussed in subsequent chapters. However, one point should be made here. There is a blurring of the distinction between public and private in this passage, which is alluded to not only by Augustus' acceptance of the title *pater patriae*, which contains the idea that his fatherhood extended across the Roman citizen body,[169] but also by the fact that it was commemorated in both (nominally) private and public spaces by public acclamation and decree.[170] Thus, blurriness and doubleness are part of the ideological equation.

The theme of doubleness continues in questions about consensus and cooperation in this passage, which simultaneously outlines the public importance of different sectors of society, and the centrality of Augustus, as seen twenty-six years earlier with the first settlement. As pointed out by Russell, the performance of consensus in their constituent parts (senate, equestrian order, and people) is an essential factor, as it accentuates unanimity.[171] The fuller version of this anecdote as it appears in Suetonius gives us a picture of the desired consensus within the state:

> Patris patriae cognomen uniuersi repentino maximoque consensu detulerunt ei, prima plebs legatione Antium missa, dein quia non recipiebat ineunti Romae spectacula frequens et laureata, mox in curia senatus, neque decreto neque adclamatione sed per Valerium Messalam is mandantibus cunctis: 'quod bonum', inquit, 'faustumque sit tibi domuique tuae, Caesar Auguste! sic enim nos perpetuam felicitatem rei p. et †laeta huic† precari existimamus: senatus te consentiens cum populo R. consalutat patriae patrem'.

> Everyone (i.e. whole body of citizens) offered to him the title '*pater patriae*' by sudden and total consent. The plebs went first, sending a delegation to Antium. Then they asked again, because he had not accepted it, on entering the theatre at Rome, which the plebs filled wearing laurel wreaths. Shortly

---

[168] *RGDA* 35.

[169] For a fuller treatment of Augustus' fatherly role and the blurring of public and private space in the Augustan age, see Severy (2003), esp. 158–80.

[170] See Dio 55.12.5 for Augustus' house as a 'public' space, which mentions Augustus' role as pontifex maximus. Cf. Severy (2003: 99–101). For nuances of public and private space in the republic, see Russell (2016), esp. 191 for the collapsing of public and private space into the person of Augustus himself.

[171] Russell (2019: 327).

after, the senate offered the title in the senate house, not through a decree or acclamation but through Valerius Messala. With the approbation of all, he said, 'May fortune and favour be with you and your house, Augustus Caesar! For we reckon that we pray for the perpetual prosperity for the *res publica* and the happiness for this city. The senate, in agreement with the people of Rome salute you 'Father of the Fatherland'.[172]

Of note here are the performative refusals to accept the title from a delegation of the *plebs* (presumably in an official capacity as the 'People' of Rome) and more informally in a crowded theatre. Rather than reading this episode of Augustus as spurning the *plebs* in favour of the legitimating stamp of the Senate, the point of the delay is to allow for the whole state to proclaim Augustus univocally 'Father of the Country', as heard through the reported speech of Messala.[173] In other words, the scope of universality is increased at each step, with more constituent parts adding their voice to the unanimity, as suggested more circumspectly in the *Res gestae*. Augustus himself accentuates the theme of universal consent (*hunc consensum uestrum*) and the importance of future approbation. The legitimacy of his position required the future public performance of consensus, with the active participation of the senate and the people of Rome.[174] The themes of unanimity and the image of the different institutions of the *res publica* coming together as one body to elevate an extraordinary individual are all present here, which linked the importance of the individual to the future prosperity of the *res publica*.[175] As before, there are constraints of expectation in this relationship, which encompasses a tradition of political, religious, social, and legal norms, the responsibility of Augustus in his *statio*,[176] and the idea of a lifelong and continued testing and performance.[177]

Nor does this particular theme fall away in discussions thereafter on the performance of legitimacy for Roman emperors. It is striking that the attention to conciliatory politics and performativity remains an integral

---

[172] Suet. *Aug.* 58.1–2.

[173] Russell (2019: 328). Cf. Ando (2000: 160–8), for affected consensus rituals involving the senate.

[174] For more on the idea of 'acceptance', see pp. 102–109; Flaig (2019).

[175] These are the dynamics at the first imperial succession in Tac. *Ann.* 1.7–14. The ideology of consensus and the figure of the individual are seen at 1.12.2 in the words of Asinius Gallus: *unum esse rei publicae corpus atque unius animo regendum*. For this fraught episode, see Woodman (1998).

[176] Cf. *SCPP* ll 446–7: *omnem spem futuram paternae pro r(e) p(ublica) stationis in uno repos[i]ta<m>*. The paternal guardpost that Tiberius holds mirrors that of his father; see Cooley (2019).

[177] Cf. Suet. *Aug.* 99.1: for the performativity of the position, see the apocryphal penultimate words of Augustus: ἐπεὶ δὲ †ΤΙΑΧΟΙ† καλῶς τὸ παίγνιον, |δότε κρότον καὶ πάντες ἡμᾶς μετὰ χαρᾶς προπέμψατε. (Since the play had been done well, give us applause and all of you send us away with well wishes.) Kaster (2016: 129–30), for the textual problems of this quotation. I thank Emma Greensmith for pointing out the appropriateness of this passage.

cog in vastly different contexts separated by centuries. Two further examples will suffice here: one from Pliny and the other from Symmachus. Pliny's *Panegyricus*, which grew out of his *actio gratiarum* delivered in AD 100 on the assumption of his suffect consulship and subsequently published and dedicated to the emperor Trajan.[178] Throughout Pliny's speech, there are suggestive comments on the expectations of the social and political role of the emperor through a series of images of good conduct on the part of the emperor.[179] Thus, a sense of reciprocity exists between emperor and subject, *princeps* and fellow citizen, which acknowledges both the exceptional place of the emperor and the importance of political life in the *res publica*. In a passage on the nominations of candidates for magistracies,[180] Pliny comments on the conduct of Trajan:

> Contigit ergo oculis nostris antiqua facies, princeps aequatus candidatis, et simul stantis intueri parem accipientibus honorem qui dabat. Quod factum tuum a cuncto senatu quam vera acclamatione celebratum est: "Tanto maior, tanto augustior"! Nam cui nihil ad augendum fastigium superest, hic uno modo crescere potest, si se ipse summittat securus magnitudinis suae. Neque enim ab ullo periculo fortuna principum longius abest quam humilitatis.

> The ancient form of procedure has touched our eyes: a *princeps* equal to the candidates, and at the same time regarding him equal in standing to those receiving the honour which he confers. That action of yours, which is celebrated by the whole senate as a true honorific: So much the greater; so much the more August. For when a man can no longer improve on his supreme position, the only way he can rise still higher is by stepping down, confident in his greatness. There is nothing the fortune of *principes* has less to fear than the risk of being brought too low.[181]

In Pliny's words, Trajan's position is even more elevated through deference and humility. The only way that his 'rank' can increase is through the estimation of senators and others alike.[182] In these words, too, there is a sense of social pressure placed on the emperor, which importantly were

---

[178] Radice (1968: 166).

[179] Cf. pp. 6–8; cf. Plin. *Pan.* 2.3–4, where Trajan is likened to a citizen and a parent rather than a tyrant or lord.

[180] On this process, and how formal or technical the emperor's power in elections was, see Flach (1976: 200); Levick (1967: 228–30), where Levick nails the need for nuance in the political roles of the emperor: 'His activities were flexible and this was to his advantage: a prudent opportunist like Augustus would avoid being imprisoned in over-refined and invidious *potestates*.' Cf. Courrier (2014: 631).

[181] Plin. *Pan.* 71.3–6.

[182] Cf. Wallace-Hadrill (1982a: 42), where Wallace-Hadrill sees a similar dynamic under the term *ciuilitas*, which 'aptly evokes the behaviour of a ruler who is still a citizen in a society of citizens, where the freedom and standing of the individual citizen is protected by the law, not the whim of an autocrat'.

not always perceived to have been fulfilled, as evinced by Pliny's description of the previous age under Domitian, a leitmotif in the *Panegyric*.[183] The success of the community is directly proportional to that of the emperor and his expected conduct, which, as Pliny notes just after the quoted passage, was not always the case.[184] In this example concerning candidature and elections, Pliny reiterates the wider ideological point of consensus and cooperation.

An example also presents itself from the late empire. Though it is strictly outside the period discussed in this book, it reflects a common theme that runs through Roman political legitimation, and well worth Roman historians of previous periods paying due attention to, though we find ourselves in a different world, with different imperial centres and different military and political organisations.[185]

Quintus Aurelius Symmachus was an influential senator in the late Roman empire and orator and composer of several speeches and letters during the second half of the fourth century AD.[186] In his fourth *oratio* on behalf of his father, Symmachus takes the opportunity to give thanks for his father's consulship by commending the relationship between senate and emperor – a relationship Gratian was attempting to reconcile at that time.[187]

> Quam raro huic rei publicae, patres conscripti, tales principes contigerunt, qui idem vellent, idem statuerent quod senatus ... at nunc idem principes nostri quod proceres volunt. unum corpus est rei publicae adque ideo maxime viget ...
>
> How rare is it in this *res publica*, conscript fathers, that such *principes* come to be: those who desire the same and institute the same decrees as the senate ... and now our *principes* wish the same as our leading men, The body of the *res publica* is one and thus it is greatly strong.[188]

The different political context and the succession crisis of the time suggest that these words carry important ideological weight; the conscious

---

[183] E.g. Plin. *Pan.* 69.7; cf. Tac. *Agr.* 3.1. Cf. Whitton (2015), for Pliny's artful juxtaposition between the Trajanic and Domitianic ages, as seen through the recounting of his career. Cf. Flower (2006: 236, 261–70).

[184] Plin. *Pan.* 72.2–3. cf. Tuori 2016: 174–5, 188, for the importance of *exempla* in fashioning the expectations placed on emperors.

[185] Cf. Kruse (2019: 10–15), for a refashioning of Roman identity through a conscious dialogue with the past.

[186] Sogno (2006: 17–25), for Symmachus' career under Valentinian I and Gratian. Kelly (2013a: 261). Omissi (2018), for a general history of politics, legitimacy, and panegyric in the third and fourth centuries AD.

[187] For the argument of a political crisis in the aftermath of Valentinian I's death, see Kelly (2013b: 377–97), esp. 393 for the consulship of Avianius Symmachus.

[188] Symm. *Or.* 4.5–6.

transposition of political vocabulary from the early principate suggests its ideological importance. Indeed, the rest of this speech and the *pro Trygetio* are littered with allusions to the political life of the late republic and early empire.[189] These words are cut from the same ideological cloth as those used in the early principate, which suggests a level of expectation about the nature of the relationship between the emperor and the political institutions of the state, along with a tension between expectation and reality.[190] It also suggests the importance of the examples of the early principate to the processes of political legitimation in the late empire, which shows a conscious desire to engage in a dialogue with the past about the emperor's position.[191] The point here is not to argue that the principate and the late empire are the same but rather to illustrate the power of the ideological kernel, which seems present across different political and social contexts and bears similarity to the political and social dynamics observed under Augustus. Accordingly, the pursuit of consensus and the volatility in that pursuit become features of the system, which affects the perception of the Roman emperor and his efficacy.

1.2.6   The Law and the Emperor

The dichotomies in Sections 1.2.3–1.2.5 are observable through questions about the emperor's relationship with the law. Given the importance of 'constitutionality' in both the understanding of the formation of the Roman principate and the legal and narrative evidence of the emperor acting as an adjudicator, it should not be a surprise that the emperor and the law have received due attention in scholarship, insofar as charting what the emperor was through the legal actions he carried out or exploring the formal origins of his jurisdictional capacities in the offices he held.[192] However, the point here is not to align with a 'functionalist' or 'formalist' approach to the emperor's duties with respect to the law. Rather, it is to explore what the ideological expectations were in, and the ideological implications of, placing the emperor in a position between absolute judicial discretion and the expectation to conform to legal customs and constraints.

---

[189] Cf. Symm. *Or.* 5.3. Sogno (2006: 23–4).

[190] Wytzes (1977: 180), who notices similar arguments in Symmachus and the *Res gestae*.

[191] For a stress on this sort of continuity that can bridge the divides between the early empire and late antiquity, see Hekster (2023: 10).

[192] See Tuori (2016: 5–7) for an overview of both approaches, with special emphasis on Millar (1977: 6–7) and Honoré (1994: 12–31), who provides an overview of the evidence of emperor as 'judge', and 33–48 for the system of rescripts.

In this sense, my view of the emperor's relationship to the law is one of a dialogue not only between the emperor and the law but also between the emperor and his subjects. Here, the thought-world of the legal emperor was mapped as we move deeper into the principate.[193]

More on this topic will be discussed in Chapter 3. However, it is important to explore here the tension between the idea that the emperor was released from the law (*legibus solutus*) but chose to abide by it (*legibus vivere*).[194] This tension was seen in Section 1.2.3 with the quotation by Ulpian, who notes that whatever pleases the emperor has the force of law, whilst noting that that discretionary power was ultimately derived from the Roman people.[195]

Still, it is an open-ended statement that suggests that the emperor, as the principal lawgiver, was above the law because his opinion was law.[196] As Plisecka rightly notes about the open-ended nature of imperial judicial oversight, 'it can be assumed that the normative impact of any imperial enactment employed in the legal practice is independent of the form and relies exclusively on the authority (*auctoritas*) of the lawgiver'.[197] This is corroborated by Ulpian himself with the dictum:

> quodcumque igitur imperator per epistulam et subscriptionem statuit vel cognoscens decrevit vel de plano interlocutus est vel edicto praecepit, legem esse constat.[198]

> Indeed, whatever the emperor establishes through letter and rescript, decrees in judicial investigations, or speaks on level ground or carries through edict, stands as law.

Therefore, the law could be made through any medium that the emperor chose, including even outside the setting of a tribunal (*de plano*).[199] That said, Ulpian argues that this had to be within the bounds of utility.[200] This

---

[193] See Tuori (2016: 7) for an argument I support totally: 'Far from being a mere reflection of the imperial role, this dialogue and the actions of the emperors as part of it were integral in shaping and formulating imperial adjudication by creating custom, hopes, and expectations.'

[194] For the issue of dating when the emperor was above the law, Wirszubski (1950: 130–6). Cf. Tuori (2016: 11).

[195] See Section 1.1.1. Cf. Tuori (2016: 282–3) for the Severan context of Ulpian's statement.

[196] Cf. Brunt (1977: 108, 110).

[197] For the implications of imperial subscriptions and ἀποκρίματα being distinguished, as well as the evidence of emperors making legally binding announcements in the field (which is to say that any pronouncement made by the emperor was legally binding), see Plisecka (2019: 304–5).

[198] *Dig.* 1.4.1.1 = Ulp. *Inst.* 1; cf. *Dig.* 1.2.12 = Pompom. *Encheiridion* 1; cf. Gaius. 1.5. cf. Honoré (1994: 33) for definitions.

[199] Plisecka (2019: 287–8).

[200] *Dig* 1.4.2. = Ulp. *De Fidecommissis* 4: *In rebus novis constituendis evidens esse utilitas debet, ut recedatur ab eo iure, quod diu aequum visum est.* See, however, *Dig.* 48.18.18.10 = Paulus, *Sent.* 5: *Custodiae non solum pro tribunali, sed et de plano audiri possunt atque damnari.*

indicates a legal distinction between *planum* and *tribunal*, which needed clarification despite the ability to try and convict prisoners in either setting. Literally, a *tribunal* was a raised platform from which a magistrate could pronounce official judicial decisions and a *planum* denoted the opposite in terms of location, 'at ground level'. That the emperor's power would extend explicitly to both should indicate his wide-ranging judicial powers, which included 'official' and 'unofficial' contexts, enhancing the ambivalence of the imperial position and also extending it to different, extra-judiciary settings.[201] By the same token, the context of *de plano* is both magisterial and more 'informal', suggesting a more accessible encounter between petitioners and the emperor in many potentially different contexts; and it also suggests open and clear decisions being made in a public political setting, thus placing expectations and norms on the conduct of imperial justice.[202] In this sense, the tension concerning the emperor's legal role is observable between the seemingly arbitrary and wide-ranging power of the emperor and the specific and often political locations in which that power was exercised.[203]

Such a status granted the emperor enormous legal oversight, but it did not necessarily equate to the emperor being above the law. However, it was the case, as stated by Ulpian in his commentary on the Julian and Papian laws, that *princeps legibus solutus est* (the *princeps* is absolved from the laws).[204] Now, this statement might be more specific, intended to restrict the emperor's exemption to the marriage laws, and not necessarily anywhere else.[205] That being said, there is other evidence that refers to this special dispensation for the emperor. In his explanation of the office of emperor and its powers, Dio states the following:

Λέλυνται γὰρ δὴ τῶν νόμων, ὡς αὐτὰ τὰ Λατίνα ῥήματα λέγει· τοῦτ' ἔστιν ἐλεύθεροι ἀπὸ πάσης ἀναγκαίας νομίσεώς εἰσι καὶ οὐδενὶ τῶν γεγραμμένων ἐνέχονται.[206]

---

[201] See Braund (1993: 224–5).

[202] Dolganov (2018: 177–8) and Plisecka (2019: 295, n. 42). Such an attention to location and openness is evoked in another use of the term starting from the republican period, which appears in clauses that stress publication in open places that can easily be read at ground level: cf. *lex Acilia repetundarum* (*Roman Statutes*, n. 1: 65–111) *lex municipii Malacitani* (*CIL* II, 1964) *lex Irnitana* (Wolf 2011) and a letter by Commodus to Chersonesus Taurica (*CIL* III 13750 = *AE* (1893) 126 = *AE* (2003) 28).

[203] Cf. Herz (2020: 116–17), for the complex self-fashioning of authoritative precedent and deference to the political status quo under Alexander Severus.

[204] *Dig* 1.3.31. = Ulp. 13 *ad l. Iul. et Pap.*   [205] Brunt (1977: 108); cf. *StR* II 751 = *DPR* V 8–9.

[206] Dio. 53.18.1. Λατίνα ῥήματα merits note as it suggests Dio had first-hand knowledge of the Latin text or phrase. There seem to be close similarities between what Dio states and what the jurists say (cf. *Inst. Iust.* 2.17.8; *Cod. Iust.* 6.23.3. However, it would be hard to state definitively that Dio's

For they are absolved from the law, as said in the Latin phrases themselves. This means that they are freed from all obligations of law and are held by no statutes.

This is reiterated again later in the same book:

πάσης αὐτὸν τῆς τῶν νόμων ἀνάγκης ἀπήλλαξαν, ἵν᾽, ὥσπερ εἴρηταί μοι, καὶ αὐτοτελὴς ὄντως καὶ αὐτοκράτωρ καὶ ἑαυτοῦ καὶ τῶν νόμων πάντα τε ὅσα βούλοιτο ποιοίη καὶ πάνθ᾽ ὅσα ἀβουλοίη μὴ πράττῃ.

They absolved him (sc. Augustus) from all obligation to the law, as I have already stated, so that he might be truly independent and have complete control over both himself and the laws; that he could do everything that he wished and not do anything that he did not wish.[207]

Dio's *interpretatio Graeca* of the emperor's powers was an attempt to explain to his audience an aspect of the imperial regime as it should be configured, namely that the emperor was above the law so that he might do what he wished and refrain from doing that which he did not wish.[208] Moreover, Dio here is fashioning a deft analysis of the imperial position that transcends the historical context of the late first century BC, noting the tension between the enormous power emperors held in contrast to the republican names the state still used, choosing to accentuate the monarchical element of the principate.[209]

The optative mood is key here, and it remained as a potential for emperors thereafter, for the action of exercising powers above the law *could* happen rather than *did* happen willy-nilly.[210] Furthermore, the phrase has precedent in Greek philosophical thought. In the fragmentary treatise *On Laws*, Chrysippus discusses the Stoic theory on the pre-eminence of natural law over all:

ὁ νόμος πάντων ἐστὶ βασιλεὺς θείων τε καὶ ἀνθρωπίνων πραγμάτων· δεῖ δὲ αὐτὸν προστάτην τε εἶναι τῶν καλῶν καὶ τῶν αἰσχρῶν καὶ ἄρχοντα καὶ ἡγεμόνα, καὶ κατὰ τοῦτο κανόνα τε εἶναι δικαίων καὶ ἀδίκων καὶ τῶν φύσει

---

source would directly be the contemporary legal texts. What can be said is that the passage is Dio's interpretation of the Latin phrase as he had understood it, whatever that source may have been; cf. Dio 53.19.6 for his claim of wide knowledge and the different sources for his evidence. Cf. Millar (1964a: 34–8). Cf. Plisecka (2019) for Latin and Greek in legal enactments; cf. Mitchell (2016: 684) for local Greek interpretations of official documents in Latin.

[207] Dio 53.28.2.

[208] Compare this discretion to the anecdote of Vedius Pollio, his man-eating *muraenae*, and Augustus' reaction in Sen. *De Ira*, 3.40.2., discussed on pp. 155–156. Cf. Madsen (2016: 146–8) for Dio's positive view of Augustus' one-man rule, and 154–8 for the problem of *dynasteia* under the Severans, all of which are crucial to Dio's own historical context, and that the imperial state was not run as it should have been.

[209] Dio 53.17.11.   [210] See Section 1.2.2.

πολιτικῶν ζῴων προστατικὸν μὲν ὧν ποιητέον, ἀπαγορευτικὸν δὲ ὧν οὐ
ποιητέον.

> The law is king of all human and divine affairs. It is necessary that it is the
> protector of both good and bad, as a ruler and leader, and accordingly be the
> rule of the just and unjust, and be guardian of political animals by nature on
> what must be done, and be prohibitory on what must not be done.[211]

The antithesis at the end of the sentence, with the law allowing emperors
to do what they should, and also prohibiting them from doing what they
should not, is quite similar to Dio's *sententia*. However, there are important distinctions. In Chrysippus, the implication is that the natural law
remains above all, which would imply that the monarch would be
subordinate to it.[212] In contrast, Dio's emperor is absolved from law.
This paradox can be solved by suggesting that the *nomos* that Dio is
discussing here is human law, or the laws of the state, meaning that the
emperor's use of discretion corresponds to right reason and the natural
law itself that allows him to decide what to do and what not do, which is
compatible with Stoic thought.[213] Moreover, the specific 'to not do what
he did not wish' also seems to refer to *anupeuthunos archē*, the idea that
monarchy was 'unchecked rule', meaning that the monarch could refuse
to be accountable.[214] This suggests that the emperor's powers were
limitless. Needless to say, the reality of the situation was more complicated, which has been discussed.[215] To return to Dio's interpretation, the
desired historiographic effect was one of comparison and similarity across
the history of the Roman principate, what Pelling described as 'general-
izability': 'This taste for generalizabilty is a feature of Dio the
historian ... the man who is interested in the way imperial history as
a whole ticks.'[216]

   Despite problems with Dio's chronology of the early principate, Dio's
interest in generalisation is important in understanding the paradoxical
relationship between the emperor and the law. Brunt argued that Dio was
incorrect in pushing this absolution too far back to 24 BC and that it was
rather a reflection of the reality that the emperor was *legibus solutus* in the

---

[211] *Dig.* 1.3.2 = *SVF* III. F. 314 = Marcinanus *Inst.* 1; Murray (1971: 220). Cf. Brouwer (2015: 63–6) for the
background of this idea through stoic philosophy.
[212] Murray (1971: 221).   [213] Murray (1971: 221).
[214] Murray (1971: 216–17), on the idea of *anupeuthunos archē* in Greek philosophy. Cf. Dio Chrys.
Or. 3.43.
[215] Murray (1971: 276–8).
[216] Pelling (1997: 143). Cf. Pelling (1983: 223). For more on this idea of comparison over different
periods of history, see pp. 26–27.

Severan period, with the implication that Augustus had no such dispensation that Dio had stated.[217] This still does not entirely explain away the issue of the emperor's supreme power, which had manifestly existed quite early on, as hinted by Ovid (*res est publica Caesar*)[218] and Seneca (*Caesari ... omnia licent*).[219] The issue for Brunt was to find the source of the emperor's immunity from the laws and whether an origin date can be deduced.[220] Though the study of origins can in fact be important, isolating a particular date does not do justice to the *dynamics* of the ideology at work, in which the supreme power of the Roman emperor and the institutions and laws of the state had to coexist. Such a reading is essential in helping us understand the various competing clauses of the *Lex de imperio Vespasiani*.[221]

Brunt suggested that the origin of the opinion of jurists such as Ulpian was in the famous 'clause VI' of the *Lex de imperio Vespasiani*:

> utique quaecunque ex usu rei publicae maiestateque divinarum | humanarum publicarum privatarumque rerum esse | censebit, ei agere facere ius potestasque sit, ita uti divo Aug(usto), Tiberioque Iulio Caesari Aug(usto), | Tiberioque Claudio Caesari Aug(usto) Germanico fuit.

> and that whatever he reckons to be according to the custom of the *res publica* and the 'greaterness' of divine and human, public and private matters, let there be right and power for him to undertake and to do, just as there was for the divine Augustus, Tiberius Iulius Caesar Augustus, and Tiberius Claudius Caesar Augustus Germanicus.[222]

This clause gave Vespasian the right to act in a way he saw fit for the matters of the state, which extended to its dignity in human, divine, public, and private affairs – an unlimited scope that was based on the emperor's discretion. Further, this right allegedly went back to Augustus himself. However, Brunt was reluctant to date it back to Augustus and Tiberius, due to their scrupulous attention to Republican sensitivities,[223] and prefers the date AD 37, when Gaius became *princeps*.[224] Brunt's reluctance presents a conundrum: if modern historians are unwilling to accept the absolute nature of the emperor's power from the time of Augustus, at what moment

---

[217] Brunt (1977: 109). Cf. *StR* II 752 = *DPR* V 10. Cf. Millar (1964a: 96).   [218] Ov. *Tr.* 4.4.15.

[219] Sen. *ad Polyb.* 7.2. Cf. the discussion of Augustus' settlements: see pp. 36–42.

[220] For a summary of the evidence of *leges de imperio* with analysis of the *Lex de imperio Vespasiani* itself, see Buongiorno (2012: 518–21).

[221] For a clear and concise analysis of the *Lex* and previous scholarship on the document, see Tuori (2016: 169–77).

[222] *CIL* 6.930 = *ILS* 244 = 1996: 579, ll. 17–21, with trans. adapted; Brunt (1977: 103). Cf. Flaig (2019: 559).

[223] Cf. Wallace-Hadrill (1982a: 32–48).   [224] Brunt (1977: 114–15).

did the emperor's powers become truly absolute?[225] In the end, we may not be able to answer this question with precision, for evasiveness of definition remained a persistent aspect of the emperor's power. This is reflected in the general ambiguities of the display and perception of an emperor's power during the early principate; imperial society was wrestling with transgressions of meaning, rank, and status in the reconfiguration of the world around the orbit of the new autocracy.[226] The problem with any attempt to carefully date the collection of powers into the emperorship is that it entails a restrictive view of what those powers were. The presence of ambiguities and contradictions are the point and a feature of the system.

This spectre of contradiction can be seen in clause VI, which can be seen to make the rest of the law effectively redundant.[227] If the emperor had all the powers to do what he saw fit, why did the document need to spell out the various duties and modes of conduct of the emperor with respect to the senate and people of Rome?

Before analysing the document and the above-mentioned tensions in more detail, it is important to see the emperor's powers in light of a more recent interpretation, which argues that this *bricolage* becomes a feature of the process of legitimation under the principate. In an article on the constitutionalism in Rome, Ando has argued for the importance of this marriage between the looming reality of the emperor's power and the 'observation of constitutional niceties' traced back to the republican era.[228] Ando explores three principal ways in which the monarchy was legitimised through a simultaneous attention to, and avoidance of, true legal and constitutional procedure: the prorogation of magistracies (i.e. the attainment of a power of a magistracy without the procedure of an election),[229] the evocation of the principle of the sovereignty of the Roman people in order to

---

[225] Cf. Matthews (2010: 69–70), for a reading that supposes that the consular *relatio* at Tiberius' succession was to ask him to take on Augustus' *statio* (Tac. *Ann.* 1.13.4). Such a reading acknowledges both the fact that Tiberius already possessed the imperial power by legislation and that Augustus' position was also conceived as informally described and inheritable. Many thanks to the anonymous reader for the relevance of this point.

[226] This has recently been expertly outlined in an Oxford Philological Society talk by Nicholas Purcell, titled 'The Princess and the Procurator', which outlines the examples of the transgressions in society and the anxieties about their positions.

[227] Tuori (2016: 172), for the important point that the law 'simultaneously gives a blanket authorisation but prohibits actions that are unprecedented'.

[228] Ando (2013: 920); it is important to note that Ando seems to suggest that the close attention to constitutional practice and the ingenious ways the Romans devised to bypass that practice were features that become prominent under the principate, though he does concede that attention to these matters becomes apparent when the republican system started experiencing convulsions in the second century BC.

[229] Ando (2013: 922–4).

override constitutional impasses,[230] and the bypassing of the strict procedure that governed the bodies of state such as the Senate and *comitia* in enactments made by the emperor, giving those enactments the same status *just as if* procedure had been followed to the letter.[231] In other words, Rome used the language and practice of republican law and politics to abrogate the previous system with its intricacies, pitfalls, and checks, as well as to establish a new one that maintained a monarchical element at its core and that simultaneously overrides all of those intricacies.

This view on the 'constitutionalism' of the principate can go a long way in helping us describe the nature of the system and understand the seemingly contradictory sentiments in the *Lex de imperio Vespasiani*. Ando is spot on when he ascribes this practice to a Roman thought-world that saw the principate as part of the continuum of political practice before its creation:

> Constitutionalism became an important feature of Roman historical and political self-consciousness under the Principate because it enabled them to understand the history of their community from the late second century B.C.E., if not before, straight through to the Principate within a single interpretive framework.[232]

Accordingly, this framework is far more useful than using the metaphor of an empty screen of legal niceties covering an autocracy beneath. The negotiation and reconfiguration of the political world was even more complex and intricate, even if there is a strong temptation to interpret it as an autocratic sham. It is almost impossible to separate the seemingly 'true' nature of the absolute autocratic power of the *princeps* from the interpretive framework it was couched in.[233]

These tensions are patent in the whole of the *Lex de imperio Vespasiani*, which moves between paying close attention to 'constitutionalism' and strict procedure, as well as granting the emperor overriding powers that would place him above the law and outside the observance of such constitutional procedure in the first place.[234] In another clause (III), where the relationship between the Senate and the emperor is discussed,

---

[230] Ando (2013: 924–7). Cf. Straumann (2016), esp. 119–26, on the idea of popular sovereignty as a fundamental aspect of constitutional thought at Rome, and 245–7 on its transformation under the principate to legitimise the emperor's powers.

[231] Ando (2013: 927–31).   [232] Ando (2013: 92).

[233] See Caballos Rufino (2021: 313) for an example of the new *senatus consultum* of 14 AD found in Spain, which contains such deft negation between Tiberius and the senate in the immediate context after his succession.

[234] This paradox is well delineated in Ando (2013: 930–1), analysing clauses IV and VIII of the document.

we read that the emperor is allowed to convene the senate when he sees it fit and necessary. The results of such meetings would hold the same force just as if the senate had been declared and held according to statute:

> utique cum ex voluntate auctoritateve iussu mandatuve eius | praesenteve eo senatus habebitur, omnium rerum ius perinde | habeatur seruetur, ac si e lege senatus edictus esset habereturque.

> and that when the senate shall be convened according to his wish or authority, by his order or mandate or in his presence, the law in all matters should be maintained and observed, as if the senate had been summoned and was being convened according to statute.[235]

The language here suggests that the emperor could act through the authority of the senate without having to abide too strictly to the procedure of calling the senate into session. However, in the previous clause (II), the rights of previous emperors to convene the senate, to make and refer motions, and to call for *senatus consulta* are given to Vespasian as well, which are all aspects of procedure that the subsequent clauses seem to allow him to bypass. Both clauses taken together suggest that both the ability to use constitutional procedure *and* the ability to bypass it are essential parts of the system.[236]

My argument follows Ando's, though with a slightly modified reading of the full dynamics in question. As Ando argues in his analysis of clause III:

> [This clause establishes] that actions taken by the emperor in the future or the past will retroactively be understood as having occurred other than as they did, namely, as having occurred through those procedures by which sovereign power had once been legitimately exercised ... [I]n return for Vespasian's conceding to the Senate the right to pass such a law – in return, in other words, for Vespasian's acknowledging the Senate to be the final repository of authority within the state – the Senate allows that all his actions will be held legal exactly as if they had been conducted according to strict procedure.[237]

Pushing this argument further, Vespasian is engaging in a process of compromise and gives attention to constitutionalism. Tradition and the conduct of political life in the city of Rome are seen as fundamental and are thus celebrated in the bronze monument that is this *lex*.[238] In other words, both the ability to bypass procedure at will *and* the willingness to subordinate oneself to that procedure are the nature of the principate. Accordingly, the concession of the authority to the Senate and people of Rome was a process

---

[235] *CIL* 6.930 = *ILS* 244 = 1996 ll. 7–9, with trans. adapted from Lewis & Reinhold (1990: 11–13), accessed online at https://droitromain.univ-grenoble-alpes.fr/Anglica/vespas_Lewis.htm.
[236] Cf. Tuori (2016: 176–7).   [237] Ando (2013: 930–1).   [238] Cf. Tuori (2016: 177).

that continued after the enactment of this *lex de imperio*, which balanced the tension between exercising the sweeping powers the law conferred and the affirmation of where those powers were ultimately derived from.

This principle seems evident in the perceived accountability of the emperor with respect to the law, which held that even though the emperor was absolved from the laws, he lived according to them.[239] In line with a developing anxiety of the Severans to connect themselves to the past, both dynastically and legally,[240] what we have is another variation on the theme of imperial power contingent upon the precedent of the emperorship, which involved a deference to the expectations of the role and the political infrastructure it inhabited.[241] For example, in Justinian's *Institutes*, Severus and Caracalla are quoted concerning inheritance under defective wills.[242] A similar opinion was expressed by Alexander Severus.[243] Of note here is the juxtaposition between what was allowed and what was proper for an emperor. On one side, the emperor was perfectly capable of exploiting his personal exemptions from the law,[244] as cited by each Severan emperor.

On the other, the repetition of *legibus vivere*, 'to live according to the laws', is an interesting phrase to use to describe the relationship between the emperor and the law.[245] This seemingly innocuous term *legibus vivere* has largely escaped scrutiny in the legal commentaries. However, it does not take long to find parallels, particularly in philosophy. Similar phraseology appears in Cicero, where the thoughts on how to live from the Academic/Peripatetic and Stoic schools are contrasted, with the latter resembling the sentiment we have in the legal texts to live according to nature's law.[246] Moreover, it points to parallels in Greek thought, with an example being from Plato that living according to laws is necessary to differentiate between humans and wild animals.[247] Finally, living 'according to the laws' appears in views differentiating between legitimate kingship and tyranny.

---

[239] Cf. Tuori (2016: 290).   [240] Herz (2020: 105); Tuori (2016: 290); Hekster (2015: 209–21).

[241] Cf. pp. 31–35.

[242] *Inst. Iust.* 2.17.8: *secundum haec divi quoque Severus et Antoninus saepissime rescripserunt: 'licet enim,'* inquiunt, *'legibus soluti sumus, attamen legibus vivimus'.* (Following this, the divine Severus and Antoninus also wrote most frequently: 'Though it is allowed (they said) that we are absolved from the laws, nonetheless we live according to them.')

[243] *Cod. Iust.* 6.23.3. cf. Dio. 53.18.1.   [244] cf. *StR* II 750–752 = *DPR* V 7–9.

[245] For example, Xen. *Mem.* 4. 6. 12. See Mitchell (2013: 129–43) for the constitutionality of ruling according to the laws in archaic and classical Greece, with accompanying evidence. Cf. Wirszubski (1950: 133–4); Millar (1977: 3–4); cf. Béranger (1953: 154); cf. Braund (2009: 24–7) for a short discussion of kingship in Greek literature.

[246] Cic. *Leg.* 1.56.

[247] Pl. *Leg.* 874e. Cf. Murray (1971: 276–7) for the principle as applied in Hellenistic kingship, rarely enacted in practice.

Despite the exemption, then, the emperors here are displayed as not having exploited advantages in private law but as living by the laws and living by the example of what the proper conduct of the imperial office should be.[248] This can also be observed in a statement made by Pliny in the *Panegyricus* that he was hearing and learning for the first time that the emperor was not above the laws but the laws above the emperor.[249] All of this evidence suggests both a choice and an obligation. The reality was that the emperor was above the law through his pre-eminence. However, it was also essential for emperors to exhibit restraint and *be seen to choose* to subject themselves to the law.[250]

Throughout this section, focus has been on the difficulty of describing the emperor, which is connected to the ambiguous way he was understood in his constitutional role – a theme that continued in different contexts across the first two centuries of the existence of the emperorship. Without placing stress on one side over the other, an emperor's appearance and conduct mattered, even if his power was theoretically absolute.[251] This tension, which manifested itself in different contexts and discussions about the emperor's position in politics and society, can help us explain the importance of how the emperor seemed when acting in his office. The variety of contexts that this tension appears in also points to the multifaceted nature of the emperorship, which sees the emperor cast in different and seemingly contradictory roles. Such a multifaceted nature might explain the breadth of different interpretations that emperors have received in scholarship in the past. In the end, the point of this section was to highlight how the constitutionality of the emperor, and its ancient and modern interpretations, has revealed a jagged and seemingly contradictory figure, fulfilling many roles at once.

1.3   The Emperor As a Series of Paradoxes

The purpose of this chapter can be boiled down as follows. The Roman emperor and his role in the politics, culture, and society of the Roman empire can be understood through the series of relationships that he

---

[248] Ideologically, that the emperor and his family lived by example is important. One is brought to think of Julia's misbehaviour under Augustus and the reported consternation it brought. Suet. *Aug.* 65. Cf. Tac. *Ann.* 3.12.1–2, where Tiberius argues that he is not to abuse the power of his role to settle private scores in the context of Cn. Piso's trial and the death of Germanicus.

[249] Plin. *Pan.* 65.1: *quod ego nunc primum audio, nunc primum disco, non est 'princeps super leges', sed 'leges super principem.* Cf Sen. *ad Polyb.* 7.2. Cf. Dio 69.20.4, where Hadrian states that Antoninus Pius had been reared according to the laws 'κατὰ τοὺς νόμους'.

[250] Cf. Brunt (1977: 109); cf. Herz (2020: 106).

[251] Wallace-Hadrill (1982a: 40). Cf. Charlesworth (1939: 1–10); cf. *StR* II 750 = *DPR* V. 7.

participated in and cultivated and the perceptions that come from those interactions. Both the world that Millar and Hopkins described, and indeed the world of Fronto, can be seen in such social interactivity. These descriptions taken together reveal the tension between the emperor's roles, which are often paradoxical and confusing. However, the worlds that Millar and Hopkins set up in antagonistic contrast to each other should in fact be seen together, meaning that the emperor is both what he did and what he was imagined to be. Both are part of the dialectical world of interactions and relationships, with the emperor as a major participant in this conversation. Importantly, though, he is not the sole participant in the conversation, particularly on what he may or may not control about what people thought and said about him. As such, imagination lies at the other side of the equation, too, in the presentation of the emperor's interlocutors, which could range from the senate and the people of Rome to provincial communities from Irni to Oenoanda and Britain to Mesopotamia. What we are delving into is the politics of show and display, where how one is perceived is fundamental and in fact informs how one operates and acts in the Roman world.

Such a statement could apply to several themes of interest, and I hope to visit these spaces in the future in greater depth, particularly the perceptions of Greek and Roman identities and their encounter with Roman power in the communities and literatures of the Greek east.[252] Concentrating on the Roman emperor, however, reveals the tensions of perception incumbent in the position. This chapter has outlined how such tension manifested in the constitutional role of the Roman emperor and his relationship to the law; the political and social restraints placed on the emperor in his interaction with the institutions and constituencies of the Roman *res publica*; and how attempts at understanding and calibrating the Roman emperor in scholarship have revealed often starkly different views of what the emperor was, ranging from tyranny to a constitutionally restrained magistrate. At the same time, the tensions are also seen in the range of relationships the emperor cultivated, both with abstract concepts such as the 'law' and with individuals and communities across the empire. It is within these spaces that the tensions that we can observe in his political and constitutional roles were transacted and tested.

---

[252] The beginnings of such work can be seen in Christoforou (2021). Inspiration for a self-conscious performance of identity in literature owes itself to Greensmith (2018: 261–2) and Greensmith (2020).

In this way, we should not be surprised to see the emperor cast in vastly different roles that often do not line up and that reveal a paradoxical reception of the figure from the perspective of his subjects. As a corollary, the often fictional representations of the emperor, manifested in stories that seem too good to be true, reveal an important facet of the discourse surrounding the emperor. Stories and fables were employed in attempts to make sense of such a powerful figure, with the added tensions that come with this particular manifestation of autocratic rule: the emperor enjoyed autocratic power as *princeps* and *primus inter pares*, to cite but one paradox amongst several that straddle human and divine affairs.

In all, the existence of such a paradoxical figure reveals a fascinating dialogue, which describes a world of mutual perception between emperor and subject. What matters in this dialogue is what is seen in such mutual observations, which reflects fears and expectations that are important facets of public opinion. Indeed, such a tension is what Wintrobe described as the 'Dictator's Dilemma', through the lens of the 'dictator'. The problem faced by those in absolute power is the inability to know the minds of their subjects:[253]

> The dilemma is … a paradox: As the dictator's power over his or her subjects increases, his or her problem appears to become larger. The more threatened they are by the ruler, the more the subjects will be afraid to speak ill of or to do anything which might conceivably displease him or her … The greater the dictator's power, the more reason he or she has to be afraid … The problem is *two-sided* … As much as dictators want to be loved, the subjects want them to believe that they are loved, for only then are the people safe from them. If they can make their dictator believe that they truly worship (or even that they support) him or her, then he or she need not fear them; and if in turn the ruler does not fear them, they need not fear him or her.[254]

This paradox reveals a similar issue that Scott discussed in his system of different transcripts. It points to an elaborate game that involved emperor and subject, entailing the discourse that existed between and about them. It also finds a direct parallel in the appearance of emperors and potential heirs

---

[253] See Wintrobe (1998: 20–2); cf. Back (1988: 283).

[254] Wintrobe (1998: 22). See Morgan (2015: 86–9) for a similar discussion on the difficulty of building 'trust' in relationships between ruler and ruled in understandings of both 'good' kingship and tyranny, with a particular citation of a negative example in Seneca's *De clementia*, 1.26.1. Also compare with *De clementia*, 1.26.2, and the trepidation of the people once cruelty has taken its toll. Cf. Davenport (2021).

going incognito – dressing up to find out what others truly think about them, such as Germanicus did amongst his troops in Germany.[255] Accordingly, smoke and mirrors are a fundamental part of the discourse, heightening the probability of masking and falsehoods. The paradox reveals a danger in such discourse, with the possibility of it being fatal to both sides. Such fear of death and putting on appearances should not, however, be dismissed as screens and shams and thus be seen as useless to history. Instead, such stories are fundamental to understanding the intricate interactions between emperor and subject.

The 'Dictator's Dilemma' also suggests an interest in power dynamics, which subordinates Wintrobe's 'dictator' through the fear of negative opinion being held by the emperor's subjects. This rejigs the nature of absolute power, revealing the precariousness of being a ruler and giving his subjects the ability to criticise him. In this sense, it is a marrying of Scott's paradigm of a hidden transcript and Flaig's *Akzeptanz* thesis, in that there was an importance placed on how the emperor was perceived. However, one should not place this within a totalitarian framework, with binary oppositions between the benevolent and tyrannical or the good and bad. Rather, it reveals a spectrum of opinion that constantly scrutinised and criticised the emperor for his conduct, which in turn shows a deep curiosity about his position in the world. From this assumption, we can construct a picture of what inhabitants of the Roman empire thought about the emperor.

---

[255] Tac. *Ann.* 2.13; cf. Suet. *Ner.* 26, Dio 61.9.2, and Plin. *NH.* 13.126, for evidence of Nero's masquerading, and Dio 54.35.3, for Augustus'. Cf. Jasnow (2015) for analysis.

CHAPTER 2

The Emperor As an Arbiter of Justice

The first major vignette concerning the Roman emperor is his role as a dispenser of justice. A major image of Augustus and his successors was a healthy and respectful relationship with the law, which involved a seemingly enigmatic relationship between the emperor as a supreme judge and a legal system rooted in the constitutional framework of the Roman state.[1] Moreover, the emperor was simultaneously above the law and lived according to it, making his position conceptually difficult and challenging to describe.[2] In this sense, we can observe a figure that had the discretionary power to legislate and make pronouncements on legal matters yet was constrained by expectation and the legal codes of the world in which he operated.[3] This enigma is worth interrogating further, as it is within such a tension that different perspectives of the role of the emperor in the world can be found.

The emperor was the mediator who had to solve disputes, in that he had the power to enact and override statutes. With this came expectations of fairness and civility being placed on him to find solutions to social and legal problems. The development of judicial procedure, particularly with respect to civil law and the formation of the new system known in scholarship as *cognitio extra ordinem*, meant that governors and emperors were given the right to adjudicate over cases in the first instance or hear appeals outside of the old formulary system, which was a two-pronged process that involved a magistrate appointing a judge to hear the case.[4] In short, this system put the onus on a magistrate or emperor to act as a judge, which thus places

---

[1] See Tuori (2016: 4) for a good summary of the legal system and the centrality of the Roman emperor.
[2] See Section 1.2.6, with Tuori (2016: 11).
[3] The legal world of the Roman empire was tessellated and local, allowing for different jurisdictions to hold sway according to context. For discussion and bibliography, see Czajkowski et al. (2020); Kantor (2013, 2015, 2020).
[4] For an introduction to the development of this procedure, see Rüfner (2016: 260–2); cf. Butti (1982: 35–9, 54–7), on the emperor as a place of appeal. Cf. Berger (1953: 394). This new judicial procedure slowly overtook the old one during the principate.

great expectations on them to adjudicate fairly and equitably. The key here is perception: the emperor was a judge who could intercede through a single-phase procedure and in the appeals process, which manifested itself in perceptions of the emperor as a guarantor of fair adjudication in images and vignettes in evidence, including numismatics, epigraphy, papyri, and literature.

However, given that we are in a world of perception, the spectrum of potential impressions of the emperor as a judge is wide. The image of the emperor as a judge is jagged and inconsistent, which fits well with the argument outlined in this book thus far. Tuori argues for the doubleness of the emperor as a judge: 'the irreconcilable differences between the idealized portrayals of emperors adjudicating and the images of abuses of power by the same emperors . . . in effect, the image of the emperor in the historiography of the Principate is twofold: an ideal ruler who is wise and equitable, and an insane monster engaging in arbitrary acts of terror.' Tuori rightly notes that the role of the judge is essential in both sides of the equation.[5] The purpose of this chapter is to tease out these discrepancies and inconsistencies in our evidence to reconstruct the thought-world of the emperor as a mediator, judge, and arbitrary ruler.

In line with what I argued in Chapter 1, my modification of this description of the emperor and the dispensation of justice is that this tension need not be problematic or overly stark, in that the 'irreconcilable differences' reflect a thought-world of fear and expectation concerning the arbitrary role of the Roman emperor and the ways in which people came to understand the range of the emperor's powers. In other words, there seems to be a projected image of an emperor as a broker of justice that straddles several binaries at the same time. Not only does this image include the tension between the emperor's unlimited power and an adherence to 'republicanism', which focusses on what the emperor's relationship to the law was and how the paradox between his absolute power and the *res publica* was reconciled.[6] There were also expectations that derived from a legal and exemplary tradition that became more and more rich with each new emperor, which made emperors attentive to the precedents they would set with the decisions they made; there were sets of ideas rooted in analogy and examples from the past, which need not have been solely Roman,[7] used to make sense of the

---

[5] Tuori (2016: 127).   [6] See Section 1.2.1.

[7] Cf. Tuori (2016: 9). This point is especially important in a period where the catalogues of understanding encompassed the Mediterranean basin and beyond at the height of the Roman empire. The question becomes whether we can excavate these different epistemologies for understanding monarchical power. For tantalising impressions from Egypt, see Herklotz (2007).

arbitrary power of the emperor that might look like other forms of power; and there were stories, often seemingly too good to be true, that variously cast the emperor as a good judge or a monster. In this manner, the emperor was in dialogue with the past *and* the future of his position *as well as* between the transactional and legal world he inhabited (rescripts, letters, edicts); furthermore, a rich fictional and mythical culture and literature were used to understand the emperor, which accordingly fashioned sets of vignettes that made the emperor fictional himself. Such a revelation need not worry the historian. The emperor was both a temporal and an imagined figure – we should *expect* him to be present in these different spaces. What we have are different transcripts that exist together, which present the emperor as both a fair judge and an arbitrary tyrant.

My understanding of 'justice' in this chapter is more widespread than a focus on legal cases and the courtroom. In any event, the emperor's judicial power transcended the tribunal and followed him at Rome and in the provinces; it also formed an important part of the dialogue between the emperor and his subjects. As such, the focus will remain trained on the side of perception and reception rather than on projections of justice on imperial media, save where they reflect wider concerns about the question of fairness and justice.[8] Though it does encompass the procedural side of the law, involving the active formulation and creation of the law by the emperor (including the institutions of the Roman state), my focus remains on the ideological side. How was the emperor perceived in terms of justice and fairness? Can we observe the nature of his relationship with subjects of different backgrounds across the empire, including slaves? How might we reconcile the competing images of the just emperor and the cruel emperor?

The following discussion is divided as follows. First, I briefly discuss the problematic definition of justice and its Latin equivalents, reiterating the importance of flexibility in finding the location of justice in ideological understandings of the Roman emperorship, which shows the emperor as being fair and upholding equity. Here, too, will be a discussion of the different media such ideas of justice might appear on, including coinage. Second, and building upon the question of evidence, the focus moves towards descriptions of judicial encounters between emperors and subjects, starting with the evidence of imperial statuary as places of asylum before moving on to different genres of literature to find vignettes of the emperor acting as judge, which include Artemidorus' *Oneirocritica*, the *Acta*

---

[8] Cf. Hekster (2020).

Alexandrinorum, the *Hermeneumata Pseudodositheana*, and encounters of emperors and brigands in imperial historiography.

2.1   *Iustitia* and *aequitas?* 'Virtues' and the Evidence for Justice

The focus of much of this chapter not only involves the emperor's role as an arbiter of justice but also revolves around the fears and expectations of his subjects, which are concepts more nebulous and slippery than what can be encompassed under singular terms in Latin or indeed in English. As such, 'justice' in this chapter counts as a shorthand to describe judicial encounters between emperors and subjects, which may or may not convey real-world judicial contexts or legal backgrounds in their strict contexts. Such is the substance of an ideological understanding of the Roman emperor. In short, this conceptual framework will at times break with the terminology, particularly the language of 'virtue', that has thus far informed our understanding of the Roman emperor. The argument in this section is that words such as *aequalitas*, *dikaiosynē* in Greek, can be interpreted as the principle of equity, which has broad implications for understanding the idea of justice and the emperor's place in that world. Again, the emperor's judicial role meant that he was seen as a dispenser of justice as well as giving the impression of fairness. I argue that we can see this theme in coinage and particularly in provincial coinage in the Greek east.

Such an argument builds upon important work done on the 'canon of virtues' in the last forty years. Wallace-Hadrill problematised the 'set canon of virtues' forty years ago, when he showed that there was no consistent set of virtuous terms that were promulgated, that the canon was not necessarily equal to the ἀρεταί of Greek philosophical precedent, and that virtuous terms often changed as the Roman principate progressed deeper into our era.[9] Wallace-Hadrill went further and saw a tension between different modes of understanding an emperor's virtues, which would only be elided and distorted by a strict reliance on a canonical view of a set of particular virtues. In other words, context mattered to understand the stress of terminology.[10]

In a similar vein, Noreña has shown the wide variety of these terms that appear in different media from the ancient world, including literature,

---

[9] For the discussion on this, see Wallace-Hadrill (1981b: 299–319); cf. Ryberg (1966: 238) and Weinstock (1971: 228–59) on the *clupeus virtutis*.
[10] Wallace-Hadrill (1981b: 318).

panegyric, inscriptions, and coinage.[11] In constructing an 'ethical profile' of the Roman emperor, he stressed the interest in the personal characteristics of an emperor, both real and imagined.[12] His model charts a terminology of virtues that was most used by the government in the projection of its power, which conglomerated to form a 'coherent semantic and ideological system'.[13] The goal here is slightly different. Noreña sought to reconstruct centralised projections of powers and virtues and how the provincial aristocracy in the Roman west responded.[14]   The purpose here is to problematise strict categories and terminologies of virtue and examples of justice that might transcend the semantic ranges of the terms found on official projections of power.[15] The difficulties of appreciating the various virtues and vices that litter our sources in both Greek and Latin should not be underestimated: indeed, many of these specific 'virtues' have not received the attention that they deserve.[16] What should be stated is that these concepts are slippery at best and often elide into each other.[17]

From a different perspective, problematising the 'canon' and breaking its terminology is a similar problem that we encountered before with the debate on *auctoritas* and other Latin terms of power that litter our evidence and histories of the emperorship: trying to assign all the emperor's power under a singular term, whether understood as 'constitutional' or 'informal', is liable to oversimplification or inflexibility. In reality, it was a conscious combination between what might be seen as 'constitutional' powers being employed and described in informal ways, and vice versa, that existed from the inception of the principate. Putting too much weight on one side of the equation risks misunderstanding the nature of the Roman emperorship.

---

[11] Noreña (2001: 146–68); Noreña (2011).   [12] Noreña (2011: 56).   [13] Noreña (2011: 57).

[14] Noreña (2011: 245–76), for his study of honorific inscriptions from the Roman west and their use of similar titles and terms to honour the emperor in a way that constructed a dialogue between the centre and the periphery in how to honour the Roman emperor. It should be stated that his argument does not push a 'top-down' view of the honorific system but a local engagement in the imperial system that in turn stood to reinforce social hierarchies and helped legitimise local regimes. For a summary of this argument, see 271–3, 318–19.

[15] Cf. Hekster (2015: 1) for a similar argument.

[16] For an example of the diversity of terminology, see Noreña (2011: 37–8) and 63–100 for his taxonomy of virtues as depicted on coinage. Wallace-Hadrill (1981b: 298–323), esp. 300–6. Cf. Béranger (1953) for a discussion on the different virtues that contributed to the ideology of the principate. Cf. Classen (1991); cf. Charlesworth (1937: 10–17); cf. Fears (1981: 841–5, n. 67), for a bibliography of works for various virtues, including *aequitas, iustitia, aeternitas, clementia, concordia, felicitas, fides, hones, libertas, liberalitas, moderatio, pax, pietas, providentia, salus, spes,* and *virtus.* Cf. Morgan (2007: 10–11). Cf. Morgan (2015) on *fides* and Hekster (2020) on *iustitia.*

[17] See, for example, Noreña (2011: 64) for discussions on *aequitas* and collocations with similar terms, such as *temperantia, fortitudo,* and *prudentia.* Similar analyses are done for *pietas* (71–2), *virtus* (80), and *liberalitas* (84–5). For a different perspective, see Morgan (2007: 191–206), for a popular language of morality, which outlines a different taxonomy of ethics.

What we have again, then, is a problem of being too binary in separating 'formal' and 'informal' descriptions of the emperor's power and his duties. Such binary thinking translates into over-focussing on the ethical vocabulary of 'virtues', which is commonly seen in describing the Roman emperor and his qualities.[18]

That said, focussing on the terminology *itself* is not a red herring; rather, the problem lies with an overly strict understanding of terms such as *aequitas, pietas, virtus, liberalitas,* and *providentia*, amongst others, that appear on imperial coinage, from which Noreña has identified the 'official taxonomy of imperial character' and a 'canon of virtues'. As rightly noted by Noreña, focussed analysis of the 'conceptual and expressive schemas in which these types were embedded' is fundamental to finding the wider discourse that gave meaning to these terms in context.[19] Such a 'taxonomy' gives us categories of description to work with, from which we can build a wider world where related images and ideas can be connected.

The point made here, though, is one of perspective. Rather than taking the perspective of the imperial regime and mint (i.e. what are the virtues and terms that are chosen to be projected), these terms here are viewed from the perspective of the emperor's subjects, which allows for conceptual bleeding between different images and terms and makes the assumption that ideas of justice are not hermetically sealed off from the emperor's duties outside of a strictly legal environment. This is not to eschew the terminology of virtue but rather to appreciate how the semantic range of terms such as *aequitas* and *iustitia* can be conveyed without the overt use of those terms in the conversation; it is a question of ideas as well as taxonomy.

Thus, an itinerary has been charted that uses the terminology of virtue as a springboard into wider ideological conceptions of the emperor's role. The next step is to find such terminology on imperial iconographic media that pertain to the concept of 'justice', with a particular focus on coinage. In a recent article on the depiction of justice (or lack thereof) on imperial media, Hekster applies a method that involves analysing images of the emperor dispensing justice in statuary, monumental reliefs or coinage either in the presence of a *capsa* (the deposit box for legal enactments), the holding of a scroll, or sitting on a curule chair. Given the rarity of the relevant material, Hekster has made a case for justice not translating to imperial media, including monumental architecture (where the evidence seems to convey an emperor's power rather than depict him in

---

[18] Noreña (2011: 37–62).   [19] Noreña (2011: 63).

a jurisdictional role) and numismatic evidence (where depictions of the emperor dispensing justice appear rarely).[20] My discussion here will focus on the latter form of evidence and the disjunct between the terminology of virtue and the iconography on the coins.

A cornerstone of Hekster's argument rests on the work of Noreña on two types of the *uirtutis* coinage that pertain to 'justice': *iustitia* and *aequitas*. The lack of *iustitia* on virtue denarii was striking: only 2 per cent of that subset of imperial coinage depicted *iustitia*, which meant it could not be counted as one of the 'core' values.[21] Alternatively, *aequitas* features more regularly, appearing in 24 per cent of the virtue silver coinage.[22] In this schema, *aequitas* emerges as one of the core virtues. Denoting symmetry, balance or evenness in weighing, ground level or spirit, *aequitas* took on the meaning of fairness in judicial contexts, particularly with respect to a personal quality of the judge to adjudicate fairly.[23] However, scholarly consensus has followed the argument that *aequitas* on imperial coinage has a far narrower semantic range: equilibrium or balance in weights, which suggests fairness in the administration of the imperial mint.[24] This argument rests on the depiction of *aequitas* on coinage as a female personification holding a rod or cornucopia and a pair of scales.[25] As such, *aequitas* appears on imperial coinage to instil the intrinsic value of the coin and thus the authority of its ultimate issuer, the emperor. Compellingly, the inverse correlation of debasement and the frequency of *aequitas* types suggest an attentiveness of the imperial mint to the intrinsic value of its silver coinage, suggesting that public display of this virtue was meant to align with monetary value.[26] In other words, when the silver content of the coins decreased through the second into the third centuries AD, so did the appearance of *aequitas*.[27] This narrow meaning, however, cannot encompass every example of the depiction of justice or the appearance of the terms *aequitas* and *dikaiosynē* in our record. Such a definition of *aequitas* is not the whole story when we dig further into its semantics and into evidence in different contexts.

Still, the view that its use is connected to the fairness in the running of the imperial mint is pervasive. In such a reading, *aequitas* does not count as

---

[20] Hekster (2020: 254–8).   [21] Noreña (2011: 62); cf. Hekster (2020: 253).
[22] Noreña (2011: 60–2).
[23] Noreña (2011: 63–4), with relevant literary evidence for the semantic range of *aequitas*.
[24] Noreña (2011: 67).   [25] Noreña (2011: 66, n. 103). E.g. *RIC* I 744.
[26] Noreña (2011: 70). Cf. Elkins (2017: 93–5), for a short summary on the scholarly debate on *aequitas*.
[27] Noreña (2011: 68–70), for a quantitative analysis of the relationship between the frequency of *aequitas* types and the debasement of silver coinage, with figs. 2.1–2.2.

a manifestation of justice on imperial iconography, which includes its representation as a standing or sitting female figure holding scales. Indeed, Hekster pushes this argument further when discussing the provincial coinage of the Greek east, where the equivalent to *aequitas* is *dikaiosynē* in Greek. As he notes, a search with the parameters of *dikaiosynē* on Roman Provincial Coinage Online has yielded 301 types, with the majority coming from the Alexandrian mint.[28] Though such numbers hardly represent a ubiquitous depiction of justice on provincial coinage, there are still types spanning across the eastern Roman empire from Alexandria to the Balkans, dating from Augustus into the third century, that depict *dikaiosynē* on coins, which needs some explanation.[29]

The first point to make is about semantics. The Greek term *dikaiosynē* has clear overlap with the Latin term *aequitas*, with the more common usage of the term aligning more closely with the general meaning of 'justice' and 'fairness', whether in judicial contexts or just actions in relationships.[30] *Aequitas*, too, encompasses 'equity' and 'fairness' in jurisprudence and thus is connected conceptually to the wider semantic range of justice.[31] Both terms are therefore firmly placed in a judicial context. Furthermore, though *dikaiosynē* is represented on coinage as a female personification, often with cornucopia but always with scales, the Greek legend ΔΙΚΑΙΟΣΥΝΗ on the reverse accompanying the figure is more rare, appearing in sixteen entries only, mostly from Alexandria dating from Nero to Antoninus Pius, with two types from Ephesus under Hadrian (*RPC* III 2080) and Gordian III (*RPC* VII.1 37 2).[32] Do such depictions evoke *aequitas* in terms of the fair administration of the mint, or is the semantic range more standard in those contexts? Does it matter that the legend ΔΙΚΑΙΟΣΥΝΗ appears only sparingly? Indeed, depending on context, different ranges of meaning could be evoked by the depiction of *aequitas* on coinage, such as the more literary meaning of 'fairness' under Nerva.[33]

Such points emerge when analysing certain examples of *dikaiosynē* coins. A full quantitative discussion of all types across the Greek east is not possible here, so the discussion will be restricted to *dikaiosynē* types from Prymnessos

---

[28] Hekster (2020: 258, n. 42). See Roman Provincial Coinage (RPC) Online (https://rpc.ashmus.ox.ac.uk) with *dikaiosynē* in the search parameters.

[29] For the point of small numbers of *dikaiosyne* types, see Hekster (2020: 258).

[30] *LSJ* s.v. δικαιοσύνη, with Thgn. 147. Cf. Thom (2009: 319–20). Cf. Wallace-Hadrill (1981a: 28), for a brisk discussion of *dikaiosynē* as fairness in measuring.

[31] *TLL* 1.1015.38–1016.32, esp. 1015.65–7, for its application to civil law, with citations. Cf. Jördens (2020: 28) on *aequum*.

[32] See Roman Provincial Coinage (RPC) online (https://rpc.ashmus.ox.ac.uk) with δικαιοσύνη in the search parameters.

[33] Elkins (2017: 103).

in Phrygia. Outside Alexandria, Prymnessian coinage depicts *dikaiosynē* from the time of Augustus into the third century.[34] Though not accompanied by a legend on the reverse, *dikaiosynē* appears seated or standing, holding scales and often two ears of corn (e.g. *RPC* I 319 9).[35] Indeed, the image of the scales alone on the reverse also appears in certain types, thus evoking the iconography accompanying *dikaiosynē* (e.g. *RPC* I 3210 from the reign of Nero). As such, *dikaiosynē* in Prymnessos predates the appearance of *aequitas* on imperial coinage, with similar though not identical iconography. Her prominence can be explained by the fact that *dikaiosynē* was the most prominent goddess of Prymnessos, thus underlining her importance to local identity. As Mitchell argues: 'The ears of corn show that the Prymnessians believed that the goddess watched over their crops and guaranteed their harvests . . . but her name shows clearly that her roots lay in rural sanctuaries where *Hosion* and *Dikaion*, *Hosia*, and the other Phrygian gods of justice presided over the dealings of peasant villagers'.[36] By tapping into this particular thought-world of justice in a local Phrygian context, we can observe a rich tapestry of meanings that both align and break with the depiction of justice in different contexts. Such readings can be delineated as follows: the multifaceted meaning of *dikaiosynē* in Prymnessos comes from her importance as the chief deity in the polis, with a connection to agricultural prosperity and wider understandings of justice and fairness in Phrygia.[37] Moreover, there is a local/Roman dynamic, as the choice to depict *dikaiosynē* expresses an aspect of Prymnessian identity in the relationship between a local elite, as local magistrates are named on the coinage, and Roman authority, as evoked through the heads of emperors depicted on the obverse of coins. Such images point to expectations of fairness and justice that had local significance projected onto Roman power, of which the emperor was the chief symbol. Thus, local imagery that has its own semantic range must sit with wider ideas of *aequitas* coinage, which would at the very least blur singular and hermetically sealed meanings of 'justice' across the Roman empire.

Where does this leave us with respect to justice? First, though there are good points made about the lack of justice-related themes in imperial

---

[34] See Roman Provincial Coinage (RPC) online (https://rpc.ashmus.ox.ac.uk) with prymnessos dikaiosyne in the search parameters, which yields twenty-four entries with high-quality images.

[35] See *RPC* I, 3199, Roman Provincial Coinage (RPC) Online (https://rpc.ashmus.ox.ac.uk/coins/1/3199).

[36] Mitchell (1993: ii, 18). Cf. Levick (2013: 52). For an introduction to law and jurisdiction in Phrygia, see Kantor (2013).

[37] Nollé (1989: 658–9), for the argument that *dikaiosynē* here evoked distributive justice.

iconography, including on imperial and provincial coinages, more granularity is required in discussing these different types in context. As noted, the
coinage at Prymnessos suggests a long-standing and local attachment to
dikaiosynē. Moreover, identity and local politics were arenas of contestation
and projection, where local elites competed for primacy and favour with
Roman power and important choices were made with respect to
monumentality.[38] Through this dialogue with Rome on provincial coinage,
we can observe projections of local identity that are deemed important and
privileged in the wider currency of social exchange in the Roman empire *and*
a reflection of expectations placed on Roman authorities in reply. We can
therefore observe what local communities expected of Rome. We must
modify our parameters, pay attention to local idiosyncrasies, look for 'justice'
in different contexts, and realise the spectrum of understandings of justice, as
well as expectations placed on its supreme dispenser, the Roman emperor.

Second, there is the question of genre and arguments *ex silentio*. The
interest in themes of justice is clear in subliterary texts, including translation handbooks, historical fiction of ambassadorial encounters, and anecdotes of justice in imperial biography and historiography. Moreover, as will
be discussed further Section 2.2, in legal codes, interactions between people
and images of the emperor are important points of contact between rulers
and the ruled. As such, any potential place of encounter, whether on an
imperial itinerary of an emperor or indeed in front of an image of the
emperor, might count as a potential judicial encounter.

Such is the implication of a gold bust of Septimius Severus from
Plotinopolis in Thrace. Found in 1965 by the Greek Army (the context
of the excavation was not recorded), the bust would have been melted
down if it had not been for the intervention of officers, which shows the
precariousness and rarity of such objects.[39] The bust depicts Septimius
Severus, bearded and wearing a cuirass, and is 28.4 cm high and survives
almost intact.[40] Formed hollow, the bust was made to be portable and

---

[38] Howgego (2005: 14–15). For an excellent discussion on this process in the Roman west, see Johnston
(2017). See Revell (2009), esp. chap. 3. Cf. Zuiderhoek (2009). Cf. Elkins (2017: 100), for the idea of
'visual panegyric' in coinage, projecting ideals on the Roman emperor.

[39] de Pury-Gysel (2019: 313). Cf. Hekster (2023: 58–9) on the materiality of portraiture and the
existence of imperial portraits in precious metal and other expensive material. Cf. *SEG* 21.509 ll.
57–60 = Oliver (1989: 4065, 409: n. 196) for Marcus Aurelius and Commodus approving bronze
portraits of their likenesses being carried in at festivals in Athens. De Pury-Gysel has high-quality
images of the bust. Cf. 'Gold Bust of Severus', Wikipedia Commons, https://commons
.wikimedia.org/wiki/Category:Gold_Bust_of_Septimius_Severus.

[40] De Pury-Gysel (2019: 315–16), for full description and measurements, and 319–20, for the rarity of
such objects; cf. de Pury-Gysel (2017: 24–33).

potentially to be displayed in different contexts – such as an *imago* used in the contexts of the imperial cult, carried by an *imaginifer* in the Roman army, and as an effigy displayed in the presence of a magistrate.[41] De Pury-Gysel noted these contexts, with the important literary parallel found for the third category in Pliny the Younger, when as governor of Bithynia Pontus he encountered Christians and used the effigy of Trajan to encourage them to supplicate to the gods and the emperor.[42] To this should be added the scene in Tacitus between Cn. Domitius Corbulo and Tiridates, in the context of the agreement that Nero would crown Tiridates king of Armenia in Rome: 'it was then agreed that Tiridates place his kingly insignia before the bust of Caesar, not to be taken back again unless from the hand of Nero' (*tum placuit Tiridaten ponere apud effigiem Caesaris insigne regium nec nisi manu Neronis resumere*).[43] The effigy of the emperor becomes a symbol of his power and a proxy of his presence, which evinces the power of his image in the context of *imperium*-holding magistrates performing their duties.

Moreover, such contexts need not be mutually exclusive. When delegations arrived at Rome in AD 22 to petition the senate to maintain their rights of asylum at various sanctuaries across the Greek east, Tacitus mentions a petition from the Cretan delegation to uphold asylum of an image of the divine Augustus (*petere et Cretenses simulacro divi Augusti*).[44] Such evidence suggests several notable points. First, that the initiative of asylum for this *imago* was transacted on a local and provincial level, rather than from the centre. Such a statement is not new in understanding the imperial cult, but it leads on to an important further assertion. Second, such agency suggests a thought-world where the Cretans considered the image of Augustus to be both religiously significant and a manifestation of protection, for which they engaged in a dialogue with the Roman senate to guarantee the claim. Accordingly, we have a dialectical relationship with the emperor as a subject, which importantly contains many aspects of social life, including diplomacy, the politics of recognition, religious practices, and, significant for this chapter, expectations of judicial intercession. Though we do not know the context or location of this *imago*, the representation need not have explicitly conjured up the imagery and taxonomy of judicial practices as delineated by Hekster. Yet intercessory justice appears in this context, where we see the connection of religious, political, and judicial matters.

---

[41] De Pury-Gysel (2019: 319–27).   [42] Plin. *Ep.* 10.96.5.   [43] Tac. *Ann.* 15.29.
[44] Kantiréa (2014: 428), for analysis of the specific Cretan examples and the other *asyla* in Tacitus.

As noted by de Pury-Gysel in the analysis of Severus' bust, the *imago* 'thus presupposes a visible object that is effectively the embodiment of supreme authority, guaranteeing its legitimacy and thereby also legitimizing the local representatives of this authority'.[45] Accordingly, this rare evidence of a portrait in precious metal, combined with other evidence of *imagines*, gives us an opportunity to reconstruct potential encounters between people and judicial authority, bringing us close to a world of iconography and visual representation with the theme of justice. In this case, the emperor is acting as a mediator through his image, as a symbol of the power of his office and the guarantor of the power and mediation being transacted by the governors who carry such images.

The point to stress here is one of complexity. The context and uses of such *imagines* need not be strictly judicial, even though in many cases such images in precious metal would accompany a promagistrate, which makes their presence in judicial cases likely. Their status as symbols of power could also carry the possibility of intercession, which is to say the expectation of 'justice' understood broadly. Such is the implication of seeking asylum at the statues of emperors, a legal question of interest to our understanding of justice under the emperor, briefly alluded to with the example from Crete.

2.2 Statues of the Emperor in the Roman World

The ubiquity of statuary across the Roman empire should not be underestimated, as well as the variety of potential responses to its existence.[46] As noted by Hellström and Russell, statuary formed 'an imperial *koine*, a shared visual language of power largely developed under Augustus but modified during the centuries by new elements and juxtapositions', and it came in different shapes, sizes, and locations, both official and unofficial.[47] The taxonomy of statues in the Roman world was variegated too. On the face of it, statues enjoyed a carefully delineated semantic world in Greek and Latin, with differences in meanings and usages of terms such as *statua*, *imago*, and *simulacrum* in Latin and *agalma* and *andrias* in Greek.[48] However, Stewart argues that, though there were differences in terminology, particularly

---

[45] De Pury-Gysel (2019: 318).

[46] For an excellent summary, see Revell (2009: 80–109); Stewart (2003: 125–8); cf. Hellström and Russell (2020: 1–3). Cf. Tac. *Ann.* 2.53.

[47] Hellström and Russell (2020: 2).

[48] Stewart (2003: 20–8, 186–7), and esp. 206 for the blurriness between the sacred and the profane. For an example of an *andrias* set up to Hadrian, though he is then described as 'one of the Gods' (ἕνα μὲν τοῦ ἐν θεοῖς Ἀδριανοῦ), see *SEG* XI 492 and Cortés (2017: 112–13).

between statues that depict gods and those that depict humans, there was still haziness in these different categories, with degrees of overlap and synonymity:

> But these were expectations rather than clear-cut and consistent religious beliefs or compelling normative values. The language of the cult image arose from social practice rather than conceptual distinctions. Even among the painstakingly precise taxonomies of Roman law, the religious status of a statue was not always clear, or at least, the terms were sufficiently vague as to elude modern scholarship.[49]

This conundrum as presented is pertinent to the study of the emperor and his images. Given that the emperor had many roles that were consciously in-between polarities, such as human and divine affairs, vagueness becomes fundamental to the encounter of the emperor in the world.[50]

The dialectic of the encounter between emperor and subjects in statuary is often evoked with the following anecdote from Fronto:

> Scis ut in omnibus argentariis, mensulis, perguleis, taberneis, protecteis, vestibulis, fenestris usquequaque, ubique imagines vestrae sint volgo propositae, male illae quidem pictae pleraeque et crassa, lutea immo, Minerva fictae sculptaeve.

> You know that in all banks, moneychangers, stalls, inns, overhangs, entrances, windows, everywhere and anywhere, your images are put up for public view, though they are badly drawn and the majority are fashioned and sculpted with sloppy, or rather poor skill.[51]

The various representations of Marcus Aurelius that he encounters 'anywhere and everywhere' in the streets are described by Fronto as being incorrect yet still evoking the similarity, symbol, and representation of the imperial person. Though not accurate, these images were recognisable as *being* the emperor, which suggests the malleability of the emperor's image and the importance of projection and expectation placed on the idea of the

---

[49] Stewart (2003: 190).

[50] Ando (2000: 237): 'the ability of portraits to demand veneration, as it were, made them active forces within local affairs. They were instruments of power, they became powerful and animate in their own right.' Stewart (2003 170): 'Perhaps most importantly the cult of the emperors with their temples and sanctuaries, altars and statues was, like some of the other statuary dedications considered above, a centripetal cult, serving to reinforce long-distance relationships with the absent emperor or the imperial house and thereby also emphasizing the distance and the difference.' Cf. Hellström and Russell (2020: 4–8).

[51] Fronto. *Ad M. Caes.* 4.12.6; cf. Suet. *Titus.* 4.1 and Apul., *Apol.* 85.2. Cf. Ando (2000: 232–9) for a different examination of the power and ubiquity of the imperial image. Cf. Hellström and Russell (2020: 6).

emperorship. We are left with a general impression of greyness, uncertainty, and contradiction in the thoughts of the wider population about how the emperor looked. Indeed, the potential for various encounters and perceptions seems endless, so the focus here will be on the phenomenon of asylum-seeking at imperial statuary, which entails the theme of justice at its core.[52]

Another famous example that is framed similarly comes from Arrian. At the beginning of the *Periplus of the Black Sea*, in Trapezus in north-east Anatolia, Arrian describes a statue of the emperor Hadrian that was not good or had any resemblance to him, with the result being a request for its replacement:

> ὁ μὲν γὰρ ἀνδριὰς ἕστηκεν ὁ σός, τῷ μὲν σχήματι ἡδέως – ἀποδείκνυσιν γὰρ τὴν θάλατταν –, τὴν δὲ ἐργασίαν οὔτε ὅμοιός σοι οὔτε ἄλλως καλός· ὥστε πέμψον ἀνδριάντα ἄξιον ἐπονομάζεσθαι σὸν ἐν τῷ αὐτῷ τούτῳ σχήματι· τὸ γὰρ χωρίον ἐπιτηδειότατον ἐς μνήμην αἰώνιον.

> And while your statue is erected in a manner that is pleasing – for it looks out to the sea – the work neither resembles you nor is beautiful in any other way. Thus I have sent for a statue that is worthy to be named after you in the same fashion as before. For the place most suitable for eternal remembrance.[53]

As with Fronto, this passage has the perspective of a figure with a degree of proximity to the Roman emperor and thus shows the push-and-pull of the dissemination of the imperial image. This push-and-pull entails the local fashioning of an emperor's image and the direct intercession of Arrian, the governor of the province, which suggests that this dialogue had several participating interlocutors, with the reception and interpretation of the emperor's image at its centre. As noted by Hellström and Russell on this case: 'The emperor was neither author nor primary audience, but a means of triangulating a relationship between the city and Arrian and himself.'[54] Relationships are key in this interpretation, and particularly those that might have not had the emperor directly in mind. What we have is a snapshot of a vernacular of honours that underlines the importance of the benefactor who set up the statue and Trapezus as a city in Pontus and the Roman empire more widely. In this vernacular, the vocabulary (or

---

[52] Bauman (1974: 82–92); Hopkins (1978a: 221–5). For a more recent treatment of this rich subject, see Tuori (2016), esp. 1–18.
[53] Arr. *Peripl. M. Eux.* 1.3–4. Cf. Oliver (1989: n. 170), for a letter for Marcus Aurelius and Lucius Verus on the mutability and preservation of silver *imagines* of emperors.
[54] Hellström and Russell (2020: 9).

imagery) of the Roman emperor becomes an indispensable topic of conversation between and within communities.[55] Arrian is also representing his own closeness to the emperor through his ability to notice the level of quality and similarity in a statue, thus performing his own position in an imperial hierarchy, as he does in his historical works where he shows his ability to synthesise different accounts and underline his expertise as a historian and epistemologist.[56] Accordingly, the emperor's power tessellates outwards across the empire, negotiating relationships between the emperor and his governor and within society at large.

Finally, time and place are subjects of importance in this passage.[57] Both his action of restoration and its mention in the *Periplus* make the monument and its description eternal. The vectors of performance not only stretch out to encompass those different relationships as mentioned before but also become resonant symbols that could stretch into the future, creating their own relationships along the way and adding further complexities to the social dynamics across the Roman empire. Such a dynamic not only works in the transactional world of euergetism, and with it the expectations for future benefactions in the political economy of the polis. The Roman emperor also, along with his pictorial presence, represents a form of assurance into the future, which conveys honour into the future.[58] Thus, there was a conscious layering of precedent and a concern for the future from the perspectives of Hadrian, Arrian, and the Trapezians.[59] Performativity can be found at all levels, which shows how the idea of the emperor could resonate in different contexts, at many points outside his strict control or purview, and in particular how a statue could function as a node of interactivity.

This proposition can roughly be divided into two categories. First is the problem of desecration of an image, and thus the potential charges of *maiestas*. The title in the *Digest* that concerns the *Lex Iulia Maiestatis* has numerous excerpts concerning statues of the emperor which describe the possible problems of interpretation in legal cases when damage is inflicted upon an image of the Roman emperor.[60] For instance, whereas the excerpt from Scaevola's *Regulae* states that those who melt 'rejected' statues are not

---

[55] Hellström and Russell (2020: 9): 'they (sc. Trapezians) were signalling their imperial connection to their peers and neighbours.'

[56] Leon (2021: 24–32).   [57] For more on the emperor as a figure who transcends time, see Chapter 6.

[58] Cf. Hellström (2020: 163–5) and Rose (1997: 7), for a discussion of dynamics of benefaction into the future.

[59] Note the curious story of Domitian's statue on the *cliuus capitolinus* as mentioned in Procop. *Anecdota* 8.15–20.

[60] *Dig.* 48.4; cf. Bauman (1974: 82–5).

liable under the law of *maiestas*,[61] Venuleius Saturninus states in his *De iudiciis publiciis* that melting already-'consecrated' statues or images, or any similar action, would result in liability.[62] Therefore, there is a problem of consistency between these pronouncements, for the line between what could be argued as 'rejected' or 'consecrated' would have been subjective, not to mention whether or not the case would have been prosecuted at all.[63] Such a problem seems apparent in the early days of *maiestas* trials under Tiberius, where the emperor rejected a case against L. Ennius, who was accused of melting a silver statue of Tiberius.[64] In this passage, Tacitus is interested in exploring the problematic power dynamics between emperor and senate in this period, as well as questions over jurisdiction, which are wider questions on the nature of the principate than strictly about the status of an imperial image. Nonetheless, the example is pertinent as it suggests a level of discretion that was necessary in these cases in whether to prosecute, thus heightening the uncertainty.

This problem can be seen further in a rescript of Septimius Severus and Caracalla, included in the same title of the *Digest*: *nec qui lapide iactato incerto fortuito statuam attigerit, crimen maiestatis commisit* (nor does he, who hits a statue by chance with a stone thrown without aim, commit the crime of *maiestas*).[65] Again, there is subjectivity to this ruling, as the believability of the stone being thrown indeterminately and happening to strike a statue of the emperor is at least questionable, meaning that it could be completely discretionary whether such cases were tried. In essence, it highlights the potential problems that could arise from the interaction between representations of the emperor and people across the empire.

Statues are symbols of contention, as observable in the historical and biographical evidence. The evidence does not make it obvious if these instances were tried and resulted in execution. However, the dynamics of *maiestas* and its origins are not the focus here but rather the phenomenon of imperial images as a location of contention in society. Similar to the legal

---

[61] *Dig.* 48.4.4.1 = Scaevola *Reg.* 4.

[62] *Dig.* 48.4.6 = Venuleius Saturninus *de iudic. publ.* 2: *Qui statuas aut imagines imperatoris iam consecratas conflaverint aliudve quid simile admiserint, lege iulia maiestatis tenentur.* ('Those who have melted down the statues or images of the emperor that were already consecrated, or who commits another act in a similar way, are liable under the *Lex Iulia Maiestatis*.')

[63] Cf. Bauman (1974: 84) and Plin. *Ep.* 10.81.2, concerning the charges against the orator Dio Chrysostom for placing a statue of Trajan near the sepulchre of his wife and son. Trajan (*Ep.*, 10.82) rejects the suit to allay the fears of men and not create a precedent. The implication is that such a case could have been taken up if it were not for Trajan's intervention. Thus, there were many potential permutations from such cases.

[64] Tac. *Ann.* 3.70. Cf. Bauman (1974: 82–3).   [65] *Dig.* 48.4.5.1 = Marcianus *Reg.* 5.

evidence discussed earlier in this section, Suetonius provides the potential cases that could be seen as *maiestas* in his narrative of Tiberius' life, where a man is said to have replaced the head of a statue of Augustus with another. Suetonius then includes what might seem to be absurd examples of 'capital' crimes committed near an imperial image: *circa Augusti simulacrum seruum cecidisse, uestimenta mutasse, nummo vel anulo effigiem impressam latrinae aut lupanari intulisse* (to beat a slave near a representation of Augustus, to change clothes, or to take in a coin or ring with an imprinted image to a public toilet or brothel).[66] Thus, problems could abound from improper conduct with imperial images. Earlier in the *Tiberius*, Suetonius reports that the people of Nemausus in Transalpine Gaul toppled Tiberius' images and busts during his exile on Rhodes.[67] In the *Nero*, the emperor's statues were altered with props and critical inscriptions remarking on his decreasing popularity.[68] In the *Galba*, an omen that predicted the end of the Julio-Claudians had the heads of statues struck down.[69] In Plutarch's *Galba*, scenes of public frustration and violence in the civil war year occur alongside fallen statues of Nero, where Spiculus the gladiator is killed.[70] In Dio, there is a case that is comparable to the list Suetonius provides: indeed, a certain woman was tried and executed since she undressed in front of his (sc. Domitian) image.[71] In the *Historia Augusta*, the author describes the fall of Commodus' regime as the 'casting down' of his statues.[72] The *Life of Caracalla* contained anecdotes with a Suetonian twist which include a young *eques* who took a coin with the emperor's image into a brothel, was imprisoned, and escaped execution after the death of the emperor; an example of men being condemned for urinating near the statues and images of the *princeps*; and those who removed garlands from the statues of emperors as a way to prevent malaria.[73] In a final example from the *Historia Augusta*, Elagabalus orders his

---

[66] Suet. *Tib.* 58; cf. Tac. *Ann.* 1.74: Granius Marcellus, proconsul of Bithynia, is being tried for the charges of placing his statue above that of the imperial family and replacing the head of Augustus with Tiberius on another statue.

[67] Suet. *Tib.* 13.1.

[68] Suet. *Ner.* 45.2. Cf. Suet. *Dom.* 13.2, for another example of a quip placed on an imperial monument.

[69] Suet. *Galb.* 1.

[70] Plut. *Galb.* 8.7. Cf. Plut. *Galb.* 22.4 and 26.7, where statues of Galba are overthrown by soldiers. Cf. *Dig.* 48.4.7.4 = Modestinus, *Pand.* 12., which states that any violations of images or statues are more serious when perpetrated by soldiers.

[71] Dio 67.12.2: γυνὴ γάρ τις ὅτι ἀπεδύσατο ἐναντίον εἰκόνος αὐτοῦ ἐκρίθη τε καὶ ἀπώλετο. Cf. Dio 68.1.1.

[72] HA, *Pert.* 6.3. Cf. Gleason (2011: 49), for a discussion of Commodus' fall, and Dio 74(73).2.1 in particular, where the senate and the people wanted to cast down his images. Cf. Barry (2008: 222–46), for the evidence of collective violence and the mutilation of bodies during the ritual executions at the *Scalae Gemoniae* at Rome.

[73] Dio 78(77).16.5; HA, *M. Ant.* 5.7.

men to smear mud over Alexander Severus' name on his statues at the Praetorian camp at Rome, which was an example of Elagabalus' efforts to defame his heir: he also ordered that the names on Alexander Severus' statues in the camps be covered in mud, as was customarily done to tyrants.[74] This matter-of-fact description suggests a normality of either reverential or destructive actions towards symbols of the emperor's image. Despite the differences, all these stories contain the focal point of the Roman emperor's image at their core, with the correlation being that these ubiquitous images were locations of social cohesion and conflict, used in a myriad of ways to express opinion, allegiance, and disparagement towards the emperor.

The second category of potential encounter concerns the use of these statues as refuges or asylums.[75] The *Digest* includes excerpts concerning the status of statues and images of the emperor, particularly the use of these as sources of protection or places of refuge.[76] The opinions of the jurists can be split into two groups, which take different stances on the validity of taking refuge at an imperial statue. Ulpian describes the duties of governors in cases of maltreatment of slaves at the hands of their masters. It is within this context that Ulpian provides an example from a rescript of Antoninus Pius which involved the fleeing of slaves to an imperial statue due to alleged brutal treatment:

> Dominorum quidem potestatem in suos servos illibatam esse oportet nec cuiquam hominum ius suum detrahi: sed dominorum interest, ne auxilium contra saevitiam vel famem vel intolerabilem iniuriam denegetur his qui iuste deprecantur. ideoque cognosce de querellis eorum, qui ex familia Iulii Sabini *ad statuam confugerunt*, et si vel durius habitos quam aequum est vel infami iniuria affectos cognoveris, veniri iube ita, ut in potestate domini non revertantur. qui si meae constitutioni fraudem fecerit, sciet me admissum severius exsecuturum.

> It is necessary that the power of masters over their slaves is left unhindered, and that no man has his right taken away from him. But it is important for masters not to deny aid against cruelty, hunger or intolerable injury to those who justly ask for intercession. For that reason, be mindful of the complaints of those from the household of Julius Sabinus who fled to a statue, and if you either find that they have been kept more harshly than is just or wronged by scandalous harm, order that they be sent away, so that they

[74] HA, *Heliogab.* 13.7: *misit qui et in castris statuarum eius titulos luto tegeret, ut fieri solet de tyrannis.*
[75] Bauman (1974: 85–92).
[76] *Dig.* 1.6.2 = Ulp. *de off. procons.* 8; *Dig.* 1.12.1.1 = Ulp. *de off. praef. urb.* 1; *Dig.* 21.1.17.12 = Ulp. *ad ed. aedil. curul.* 1; *Dig.* 47.10.38 = Scaevola *Reg.* 4.; *Dig.* 48.19.28.7 = Callistratus *de cogni.* 6.

cannot return to the power of their master. If he breaks my pronouncements, let him know that I will punish this transgression more severely.[77]

Here, the ability for slaves to appeal to Caesar by seeking refuge at a statue
can be observed, even if we acknowledge that the masters' ownership was
upheld.[78] As Hopkins rightly pointed out, Antoninus Pius was very
careful to admonish cruelty while at the same time reiterating the
power of slave-owners over their slaves.[79] This could be developed further
to comment on the ambiguous role of the emperor as a mediator between
different groups in society and being seen and expected to rule in favour
or against people and groups in society according to the appropriate
context. What we have, then, is a social dynamic that placed the emperor
at the centre of the interaction between masters and slaves.[80] Thus,
steering a 'delicate course' could actually be the perception of support
for one group over another, leaving a polarised impression of the
emperor's conduct in terms of law and justice.[81] Moreover, it brings
into relief the potential actors in this particular legal interaction: not
only masters and the slaves but also magistrates and the emperor himself.
They had to navigate the intricacies and ambiguities of these cases that
revolved around the contested legal space that an imperial image or statue
created, which was a novel and abundant locus of interaction between
different sections of society. This meant that the emperor was not only
the mediator who had to solve disputes, in that he had the power to enact
and override statutes, with expectations of fairness and civility being
placed on him in order to find solutions to social and legal problems;
he was also the reason such interactions could occur in the first place.
Depending on perspective, he could be seen as both the problem and the
solution to this issue, no doubt at least to the chagrin of slave-owners. In
the end, this created a disjunctive picture of the emperor, allowing him to
be cast into different roles in the minds of his subjects.

   Therefore, it should not be surprising that the second group of opinions
concerning images and asylum would restrict the inviolability of that
refuge. An excerpt from the jurist Callistratus outlines how it is prohibited

---

[77] *Dig.* 1.6.2 = Ulp. *de off. procons.* 8; cf. *Dig.* 1.12.1.1 – Ulp. *de off. praef. urb.* 1., on the similar duties of
   the prefect at Rome. Compare with Sen. *Clem.* 1.18.2: *servis ad statuam licet confugere* (It is permitted
   for slaves to seek refuge at statues). Cf. *Dig.* 21.1.17.12 = Ulp. *Ad ed. aedil. Curul.* 1, which includes the
   opinion that slaves who flee to statues should not be seen as fugitives; cf. Hopkins (1978a: 222).
[78] Hopkins (1978a: 222–4).   [79] Hopkins (1978a: 222).
[80] The multivalency of potential legal cases was enormous, as shown in Millar (1977: 507–49).
[81] Cf. Section 2.1.

to seek sanctuary at an emperor's image when there is the intent to injure another person:

> Ad statuas confugere vel imagines principum in iniuriam alterius prohi-
> bitum est. cum enim leges omnibus hominibus aequaliter securitatem
> tribuant, merito visum est in iniuriam potius alterius quam sui defen-
> sionis gratia ad statuas vel imagines principum confugere: nisi si quis ex
> vinculis vel custodia detentus a potentioribus ad huiusmodi praesidium
> confugerit: his enim venia tribuenda est. ne autem ad statuas vel
> imagines quis confugiat, senatus censuit: eumque, qui imaginem caesaris
> in invidiam alterius praetulisset, in vincula publica coerceri divus Pius
> rescripsit.[82]

> It is forbidden to seek refuge at the statues or images of emperors in the case
> of harm to another. Since the laws provide safety equally to all men, it is
> rightly seen that seeking refuge at statues or images of emperors is done for
> the sake of harming another rather than in self-defence, unless someone who
> is detained by those more powerful flees from their bondage and restraint to
> this type of refuge. To those people this favour must be granted. However,
> the senate decided that no one should seek refuge at statues or images: and,
> as Antoninus Pius ruled, he who carries before him an image of Caesar to the
> detriment of another should be kept in public prison.

This excerpt provides an interesting case, as it conflates what can be seen as two separate ordinances into one.[83] One concerns the seeking of sanctuary at a statue to incite injury and the other the use of portable images to do the same.[84] The differences are slight enough that confusion could occur, since both cite the end result being the incitation of some sort, either using an image as refuge after insulting someone or using an image as protection in an act of provocation. However, instead of stressing the conclusion that the law made the seeking of sanctuary at imperial images restrictive, thereby suggesting that most rulings went against the refugee, it should be stated that it proves the status of these statues as places of contention between different groups in society, leading to intricate and complex legal issues, with the emperor as its focal point.

A striking example of such an interaction is the case of Annia Rufilla in AD 21, as written by Tacitus. Her actions were described as part of

---

[82] *Dig.* 48.19.28.7 = Callistratus *de cogni.* 6.   [83] Bauman (1974: 88).

[84] Cf. *Dig.* 47.10.38 = Scaevola *Reg.* 4., which cites a *senatus consultum* that prohibited the carrying of a statue of the emperor for use at the detriment of others. Cf. Bauman (1974: 87–9), for more on the intricacies of this passage.

a growing tendency for those of a lower station to provoke the *boni* in society by grasping an *imago Caesaris*:

> incedebat enim deterrimo cuique licentia impune probra et invidiam in bonos excitandi arrepta imagine Caesaris: libertique etiam ac servi, patrono vel domino cum voces, cum manus intentarent, ultro metuebantur.

> All the worst individuals had been overcome by a form of licence whereby their stirring up of abuse and resentment against good people was accomplished with impunity, since at the same time they were grasping an image of Caesar; and even freedmen and slaves were dreaded on their part when they raised their voices and hands against patron or master.

Such an episode suggests a change in the social dynamics through the existence of the emperor and his image.[85] Tacitus underlines the upheaval that the existence of the emperorship placed on social hierarchies, providing us with the specific case of Gaius Cestius and Rufilla, who hurled abuse at the senate and then sought protection from an *effiges imperatoris*.[86] In light of such occurrences, Cestius himself sought refuge in appealing to Drusus the Younger for aid, since he argued the laws effectively had been overturned and become useless.[87] The result was that Drusus set an example by convicting and imprisoning Rufilla.[88] The early date of this example may point to the specific context of the problem, namely a struggle to understand fully the implications of autocratic rule in the early principate, with different sectors of society attempting to find their position within the power dynamic.

More specifically, the excerpt from Callistratus suggests that such cases remained problematic into the second century.[89] Thus, the idea that the emperor was a source of law and justice seems to be a widespread idea.[90] Utilising Scott's paradigm, what Rufilla was emboldened to do was to expose a 'hidden transcript': subversive opinions about one more dominant in comparison to her in society, in this case Cestius and his senatorial *milieu*.[91] This was possible due to the altering power dynamics in society introduced by the emperor and his image. Within this understanding, the imperial image, and by proxy the emperor, would be seen as a protector of her opinions and thoughts, shielding her from potential reprimand and

---

[85] Tac. *Ann.* 3.36.1, trans. adapted from Woodman (2004).   [86] Tac. *Ann.* 3.36.3.
[87] Tac. *Ann.* 3.36.2–4: *abolitas legs et funditus versas.*   [88] Tac. *Ann.* 3.36.4.
[89] *Dig.* 48.19.28.7 = Callistratus *de cogni.* 6.
[90] Cf. Bauman (1974: 91), for further examples on the issue of asylum. Of particular note is Philostr. *VA.* 1.15., for a magistrate in Aspendos clinging to a statue of Tiberius during a food riot.
[91] See Section 1.1.3; Scott (1985, 1990).

litigation from others in society. Accordingly, the emperor and his image were thus a pressure valve, adding to the idea that they were locations of social cohesion and conflict, where problems of justice could be negotiated. Furthermore, Cestius' actions indicate that recourse to the emperor was similarly employed by the 'elite' and that their position below the Roman emperor allowed for the existence of their own 'hidden transcript' considering his power. The existence of multiple transcripts with no simple dichotomous 'elite' and 'sub-elite' division shows the intricate complexity of Roman society and the precarious position of the Roman emperor within it. In terms of perceptions of the Roman emperor with respect to justice, it meant that he could be seen as a protector and a feared arbiter by his subjects, to the extent that images of the emperor could be used as places of asylum and refuge by slaves.

2.3   Fictional Encounters of Justice in Literature

Importantly, the encounters of justice appear in more unusual genres of literature, which fall outside canonical historical and literary works. One such example is Artemidorus' *Oneirocritica*, a book of dream interpretations written in the second or third century AD.[92] There are a few dreams he describes in his work that involve the Roman emperor, particularly concerning civil cases.[93] In such examples, Artemidorus provides analysis of different types of dreams, supplemented by an exemplary passage, with specific references to cases and petitions involving the emperor. In a recent analysis of the emperor in Artemidorus, Thonemann notes that representations, rather than actual encounters with the emperor, appear most frequently, which suits our discussion of expectations and ideas of justice thus far.[94] The impression of the emperor that we do receive from Artemidorus is well-articulated by Thonemann and deserves quoting:

> It is abundantly clear that 'the emperor' as a single, actually existing individual hardly impinged on the world of Artemidorus and his readers

---

[92] On Artemidorus and the study of dreams, see Bowersock (1994: 77–98), Price (1986: 3–37), and more recently Thonemann (2020) on the concerns of Artemidorus, the profession of dream interpretation and its connection to scientific inquiry, and the difficulty of analysing the ancient conceptions of dream applicability. Price places Artemidorus within his intellectual *milieu*, with a particular concentration on his interest in predictive dreams and what can empirically be said about the future from their interpretation. Cf. in particular Artemidorus' distinction between ἐνύπνια ὄνειροι, Artem. 1.1; Price (1986: 10–12); Bowersock (1994: 80).

[93] Cf. Millar (1977: 528). Cf. Artem. 2.30 on a different theme that involves an emperor, concerning dreams of being the emperor, and what it means for different people.

[94] Thonemann (2020: 201–2); cf. Artem. 2.20.2.

at all. There is no sign that Artemidorus knew or cared much about emperors' roles as generals or as legislators; nor did he see one emperor as differing very much from any other.[95]

The only adjustment of such an interpretation is the sense that this image of the emperor is disappointing to the historian. On the contrary, Artemidorus is fundamental to our understanding of the perception of the emperorship, in this case in the Greek east, in that it depicts the emperor as an intercessory figure, a source of justice, and as a manifestation of imperial power. It need not worry us that there is nothing particularly specific about emperors (or rather individual emperors); the nebulous and hazy impression of the emperor and his intercessory power reveals a fascinating thought-world of expectations of justice and fears of retribution that have much more to do with what the emperor represents rather than the reality of any individual himself. It is the idea of the emperor that matters in this case. In Artemidorus, then, the emperor is a timeless figure: the stories about him lend weight to comparison with other forms of kingship and transcend narrow historical contexts.

This view is borne out in the following examples. The first refers to a dream about receiving something from the mouth of the emperor, resulting in favour for the receiver, using the example of a Chrysippus of Corinth, who dreamt that he received two teeth from the emperor's mouth, which resulted in him winning two cases in which the emperor was the judge.[96] The second example involves a Cilician who petitioned the emperor for his brother's inheritance but dreamt that he sheared half a sheep but was unable to get the remaining wool before he woke up. This resulted in the false expectation of receiving half of the inheritance, when it transpired that he would receive nothing.[97] The third example warns against untrustworthy etymologies, with the story being a dream about

---

[95] Thonemann (2020: 204).

[96] Artem. 4.31: Ὅ τι ἂν ἐκ τοῦ στόματος δῷ ὁ βασιλεύς, δι' ἀποφάσεως ὠφελήσει τὸν λαβόντα. Χρύσιππος ὁ Κορίνθιος ἐκ τοῦ στόματος τοῦ βασιλέως δύο λαβὼν ὀδόντας μιᾷ ἡμέρᾳ δυσὶν ἀποφάσεσιν ἐπὶ τοῦ βασιλέως δικαζόμενος ἐνίκησεν (Whatever the emperor might give you from his mouth, it will benefit the recipient through decision. Chrysippus the Corinthian received two teeth from the mouth of the emperor. On a single day, he won two judgements upon pleading his case in front of the emperor). Cf. Dio 65(66).1.3, where Nero loses a tooth in Vespasian's dream, meaning that he would become emperor.

[97] Artem. 4.51: Ὁ Κίλιξ ἀδελφοῦ κλῆρον ἀπὸ τοῦ βασιλέως αἰτῶν ἔδοξε πρόβατον κείρειν μέχρις ἡμισείας, καὶ τοῦ πόκου λαβεῖν [τὸ πλεῖστον] τὸ περισσὸν οὐ δυνάμενος διυπνίσθη. Καὶ προσδοκία μὲν ἦν αὐτῷ τὸ ἥμισυ τοῦ κλήρου λήψεσθαι, ἔλαβε δὲ οὐδέν (A Cilician who petitioned the emperor for his brother's inheritance dreamt that he had sheared only half a sheep and had not been able to collect the rest of the wool before he woke up. Though his expectation was that he would receive half of the inheritance, he in fact received nothing.)

someone called Νίκων (Nikōn, literally 'Victor') helping an attorney with a case before the emperor. He thought that this was a propitious sign for the result of the case, but Nikōn had lost a judgement previously, which in turn was the correct premonition for a defeat.[98] A final example highlights the intercessory power of the emperor:

Ἔδοξέ τις ναύκληρος ἐν Μακάρων νήσοις εἶναι καὶ ὑπὸ τῶν ἡρώων κατέχεσθαι, ἔπειτα ἐλθόντα τὸν Ἀγαμέμνονα ἀπολῦσαι αὐτόν. Ἀγγαρείᾳ περιπεσὼν ὑπὸ τῶν ἐπιτρόπων τοῦ αὐτοκράτορος κατεσχέθη, ἔπειτα ἐντυχὼν τῷ βασιλεῖ ἀφείθη τῆς ἀγγαρείας.

A certain merchant sailor thought that he was on the Isles of the Blest and was being held forcibly by heroes. Afterwards Agamemnon came and set him free. He, forcibly taken into public service, was held by imperial procurators. Afterwards, having met with the emperor, he was released from that service.[99]

Thus, the dream of Agamemnon releasing the ship-captain from the bonds of the heroes in the Isles of the Blest translated into the emperor releasing him from his liturgy and the custody of the imperial procurators. These no doubt apocryphal stories stretch credibility, but they reach a world of mentalities that connects imagination with the emperor. They show a conceptual connection between expectations and fears about justice manifested in dreams and their perceived correlation to reality.

A brief excursus is necessary: mention of procurators and other imperial officials being superseded by appeal to the emperor is an important theme in the study of the perception of the emperor's justice, just as it might be between other imperial officials.[100] An important example of this comes in the form of petitions from peasants and villagers across the empire.[101] One

---

[98] Artem. 4.80: Μέμνησο δὲ ὅτι εὐφήμων ὀνομάτων ἄπιστοι αἱ ἐτυμολογίαι, ἐὰν μὴ καὶ τὰ καθ᾿ ὧν τέτακται τὰ ὀνόματα εἰς ταὐτὸ ῥέπῃ. Οἷον Παῦλος ὁ νομικὸς δίκην ἔχων ἐπὶ τοῦ αὐτοκράτορος ἔδοξεν αὐτῷ συναγορεύειν Νίκωνά τινα καλούμενον. Ἦν δὲ οὗτος ὁ Νίκων πάλαι ποτὲ ἐπὶ τοῦ αὐτοκράτορος δίκην ἡττημένος. Καὶ ὁ μὲν Παῦλος τῷ ὀνόματι μόνῳ προσεῖχεν, ἦν δὲ αὐτῷ καταδίκης σημαντικὸς ὁ ὄνειρος ὀρθῶς καὶ κατὰ λόγον, ὅτι ἦν ὁ Νίκων λελειμμένος. (Remember that etymologies of nice words are untrustworthy, unless the matter that is set up alongside the words is inclined in the same manner. For instance, Paul, a lawyer who was having a trial in front of the emperor thought that a certain man called 'Nikōn' (Victor) was collaborating on the case. However, it was this Nikon who once long before lost a case in front of the emperor. However, Paul only paid attention to his name, when the correct and logical significance of the dream was that the sentence went against him, since Nikōn had lost.)

[99] Artem. 5.16. Cf. Millar (1977: 499). This fits into a wider theme of petition for exemption from civic duties, or liturgies, in the Greek world: see Millar (1977: 499–502); Dmitriev (2005); Zuiderhoek (2009).

[100] For the importance of procurators to imperial administration, see Davenport (2019), esp. 179–83.

[101] See Millar (1977: 246–7, 542–3) for examples of this sort of interaction. Millar creates a connection between the communities on imperial estates and villages of unknown status,

example is a fragmentary inscription from near Vaga in Africa (Béja, Tunisia) dated to AD 181, in which peasants complain of the excessive demands placed upon them and ask for the intercession of the emperor,[102] which is comparable to another from the imperial estate *saltus Burutianus*, with similar language.[103] It seems that repeated complaints to the emperors by the tenants against the procurators go unheeded, resulting in a *subscriptio* from Commodus, which restated the rule that the procurators follow his commands.[104] Despite the curtness of the reply, it indicates a similar theme to the inscription from Vaga: that recourse to the emperor was conceivable for complaints towards imperial officials, even from peasants or tenants in the imperial estates. Thus, there is a correlation between expectations and fears in this epigraphical material and the dreams that Artemidorus compiled. They indicate the liminal presence of the Roman emperor between the conduct of legal and petitionary procedure and the imagination of just outcomes.

Similar contours of hope for success can be seen in the *Hadriani Sententiae*. These are curious documents from the early third century, preserved with bilingual word lists from the ancient world, which were called *Hermeneumata*. They are themselves bilingual texts that preserve legal pronouncements of the emperor Hadrian, meant to be a teaching aid for language learning.[105] Scholars have been mostly reticent in using them as a historical source, preferring to see them as fictitious wise judgements of a later date and therefore providing little if no representative material for the conduct and execution of Hadrian's judicial activities.[106] However,

---

sending petitions to the emperor as complaints of exploitation. Cf. Abbott and Johnson (1926: nos. 139, 141–4), for examples of petitions from imperial estates. For a newer edition and more comprehensive look at these inscriptions, see Hauken (1998), especially with additions to the dossier of related inscriptions of petitions/responses from similar communities; cf. Philo, *Leg.* 161, for evidence of Tiberius ensuring the just conduct of his subordinates, with reference to their relations with the Jews.

[102] *CIL* 8.14428 A, ll. 12–13; cf. Hauken (1998: 31–3) for transcription, suggestions for the lacunae, and commentary; Millar (1977: 542).

[103] Millar (1977: 246); *CIL* 8.10570 = *CIL* 8.14464 = *ILS* 6870, iii; For transcription, translation, and commentary, see Hauken (1998: 2, 8–10) for the following transcriptions: *[Quae res co]mpulit nos m[i]serrimos homi\|[nes iam rur]sum divinae providentiae | [tuae supli]care. et ideo rogamus sa| cratissime Imp. subvenias* (This affair forces us wretched men once more to supplicate for your divine wisdom. And therefore, we request, most sacred emperor, that you aid us).

[104] *ILS* 6870, iv. Cf. *IGBulg* IV 2236 = *IGR* I 674 = *Syll.*³ 888 = *CIL* III Suppl. 12336 = *SEG* 44.660, the third-century inscription including the petition from Skaptopara in Thrace, with a similarly curt imperial reply.

[105] Lewis (1991: 267–80); Dickey (2012: 28); Millar (1977: 532).

[106] Dickey (2012: 28). Cf. Lewis (1991: 269–70), for a scholar named A. Arthur Schiller's attempt to rehabilitate these texts as representative of hearings before the emperor. Of note is the papyrus *SB* 6.9526 = *P. Col.* 6.123 (cited by Lewis 1991: 273), which gives us evidence of *apokrimata* resembling the *Hadriani sententiae*. The papyrus is available online: http://papyri.info/ddbdp/p.col;6;Apokri

their form and content can instead be used as evidence for the idea of the Roman emperor as an arbiter of justice – we find ourselves in a similar world to Artemidorus. Here, questions about whether they represent a reality of the procedure of imperial judgement are secondary to the descriptions of interactions between emperor and subject and what they can reveal about the concerns in the imagination of what could be expected from the Roman emperor in this juridical context. These *sententiae* include actors from different sectors of society, including soldiers, freedmen, an owner of *tabernae*, and parents, involving cases on a wide array of topics, such as the request of military appointment and *congiaria*, to requests from parents to force their children to take care of them.[107] In these *Sententiae*, Hadrian does not always grant the wishes of the petitioner but also refuses them. This suggests a perception that the emperor was not an indiscriminate giver. Furthermore, there is a continual juxtaposition between the different potential reactions of the emperor, from sympathy and benevolence to reprimand and cruelty. An example of the former would be No. 12 in the *Sententiae*, which gives a story about a father who had lost his sons to the military and feared for their safety from any action *extra ordinem*. Hadrian allays his fears by saying that they serve in peacetime (*Ne quid timeas; in pace enim militant*). He asks Hadrian to allow him to be a servant to them, and Hadrian responds by making him a centurion.[108] An example of the latter would be No. 15, in which Hadrian details the punishments for parricide:

> Fit quaedam lex eiusmodi omnibus hominibus, uti qui parricidium fecisset, publice in culleum missus consueretur cum vipera et simia et gallo et cane, impiis animalibus impius homo, et in plaustrum iunctum nigris bovis deportaretur ad mare et in profundum mitteretur; ostenderunt exemplum poenae, ut magis timeant.[109]

> Let there be a law of this manner for all men, that he who commits parricide, should publicly be sent away and sewn in a sack, with a snake, ape, cockerel, and dog, a wicked man with wicked animals, and then be deported to the

---

mata. Cf. Tuori (2016: 209–71), for Hadrian as an ideal judge in the literature, and 238–9 for the development of the relationship between the emperor and the law under Hadrian.

[107] Citations of the *Sententiae* come from the recent Teubner edition by Giuseppe Flammini, called *Hermeneumata Pseudodositheana Leidensia* under the third book, and are separated by case, from nos. 1–15 (pp. 67–77, or 3.1716–1960). See 1 = 3.1747–1759 for the soldier, 2 = 3.1760–1771 for the ex-slave-owner asking for his lost freedman's *congiarium* (see Lewis 1991: 274–5, for further analysis), 7 = 3.1814–1827 on the *tabernae* owner and the freedmen who run them, 3 = 3.1772–1781, 10 = 3.1856–1878, 11 = 3.1879–1895, 12 = 3.1896–1914, 13 = 3.1915–1926, for petitions from parents on different matters.

[108] *Hadriani sententiae* 12 = 3.1896–1914.   [109] *Hadriani sententiae* 15 = 3.1946–1959.

sea, tied to a cart fastened to black bulls, and sent into the deep. They have displayed the example of punishment, so that they might fear more keenly.

The punishment for parricide of being tied in a sack with an assortment of dangerous animals, taken by cart, and then thrown into the sea is couched in tradition, as an excerpt of Modestinus in the *Digest* indicates.[110] It is interesting that a description of such a punishment would appear in the bilingual teaching tradition, as it suggests a certain banality; such knowledge was seemingly common. It perhaps is what it tells us, an *exemplum poenae*, employed for fear.[111] The imagination of the emperor's status as an arbiter of justice thus straddles the potential for benevolence and the potential for punishment.[112]

In a similar vein are the *Acta Alexandrinorum*, and similar types of literature, such as the Acts of the Apostles and Philo's *Legatio ad Gaium*.[113] The so-called *Acta Alexandrinorum*, or the Acts of the Pagan Martyrs, are fictionalised accounts of Alexandrian embassies to Rome, where they face the Roman emperors and their Alexandrian Jewish antagonists. They attempt to evoke sympathy for the Alexandrians against an unsympathetic emperor, unfavourably depicted as siding with the Jewish community.[114] Importantly, there is a strand of consistency in the narrative across these crucial documents, for our purposes in the depiction of the emperor, as argued by Harker.[115] Exchanges are hostile, and the emperor is often perceived as tyrannical, regardless of which emperor is being

---

[110] *Dig.* 48.9.9pr = Modestinus *Pand.* 12: *Poena parricidii more maiorum haec instituta est, ut parricida virgis sanguineis verberatus deinde culleo insuatur cum cane, gallo gallinaceo et vipera et simia: deinde in mare profundum culleus iactatur. hoc ita, si mare proximum sit: alioquin bestiis obicitur secundum divi Hadriani constitutionem* (The penalty of parricide according to the custom of our ancestors is here instituted that the parricide is to be beaten by bloody rods and then enclosed in a sack with a dog, cockerel, snake, and ape: then the sack is to be thrown into the depths of the sea. It is thus, if the sea is nearby: otherwise, he is to be thrown to the beasts, following the order of the divine Hadrian). The Hadrianic embellishment of the law is a seemingly interesting parallel; for further evidence of such punishment: Cic. *Ros. Am.* 70, Cic. *Inv. Rhet.* 2.149, and Suet. *Aug.* 33.1, for an example of Augustus showing his diligence for justice by not sewing up a parricide in the sack.

[111] Cf. Coleman (1990: 70–3), esp. 72, for the parallel of the emperor as patron of 'fatal charades': spectacles of death in the arena meant to solidify the emperor as 'the authority of the supreme purveyor of justice'. See Chapter 4.

[112] Alongside these *sententiae* should be viewed the *Hadrianus* in the important Montserrat Codex, a late fourth-century-AD collection of a variety of texts in both Greek and Latin, including Cicero's *In Catilinam* I–II. The *Hadrianus* has a similarly sententious presentation of Hadrian, which are potentially rhetorical training exercises in the form of διήγημα or *narratio*, and includes scenes of justice and liberality. These longer stories provide a similar image of Hadrian as a just ruler. See Berg (2018: 107) for a description of the codex, 27 for the connection to the *Hadriani sententiae*, and 136–9 for analysis of its fourth-century context. See p. 189.

[113] Cf. Harker (2008: 32–4, 141–73). Harker also provides a recently updated list of *acta* literature preserved on papyrus (179–211).

[114] Harker (2008: 1).   [115] Harker (2008: 91, 43).

portrayed.[116] Selected examples have been chosen to exhibit the different representations of the Roman emperor and the potential perceptions of his role as a judge in these hostile accounts.

First are the so-called *Acta Isidori*, preserved on different papyri of different provenances,[117] which are accounts of the trial of Isidorus, a gymnasiarch of Alexandria, within the context of embassies to the emperor Claudius by the Alexandrian Greeks and Jewish community.[118] The less fragmentary column ii. of recension A reveals the scene of an encounter in some gardens ([ἐν τοῖς] λιανοῖς κήποις) in the presence of King Agrippa, twenty senators (sixteen of whom were of consular rank), and certain *matronae* at the court.[119] The conversation begins with a plea from Isidorus to Claudius for a hearing: κύριέ μου Καῖσαρ, τῶν γονά[των σου δέομαι] | ἀκοῦσαί μου τὰ πονοῦν[τα τῇ πατρίδι.] | ὁ αὐτοκράτωρ· μερίσω σο[ι ταύτην τὴν] | ἡμέραν (My lord Caesar, I am begging you on my knees to listen to the sufferings of my homeland. The emperor: I will grant you this day).[120] However, in column iii, the exchange had changed to hostility and insult, with Claudius accusing Isidorus of killing many of his friends and Isidorus arguing that it was on the orders of the then emperor Gaius that he had done so and that he would do the same again.[121] Thereafter are exchanges of insults of low birth: Claudius asks Isidorus if he was the son of a musician, to which Isidorus states that he is neither a slave nor a musician's son but a 'gymnasiarch of the great city of Alexandria' (διασήμου πόλεως [Ἀ]λεξαν[δρ]εί[ας] γυμνασίαρχος) and ends by calling Claudius the son of Salome, a member of the Herodian dynasty of Judaea.[122]

---

[116] The richness of the record is well explained by Harker (2008: 31–47, 48–98). For the papyri used in this section, the number assigned by Musurillo in both the Oxford and the Teubner editions of the texts will be used, alongside the corresponding papyrus collection publication number when first cited.

[117] For the complex information on provenance, date, and different published textual editions, see Musurillo (1954: 117–18) and Harker (2008: 187–9), under *APM* 4.A = Chrest.Wilck 14 = *C.Pap.Jud.* II 156A, 156d (cols i–ii: *BGU* 511 + col. iii: *P.Cair.Cat* 10448, *APM* 4.B = *P. Lond.* Inv. 2785 = *C.Pap.Jud.* II 156b, and *APM* 4.C = *P. Berol.* 8877 = *C.Pap.Jud.* II 156c.

[118] On the embassies and trials, see Harker (2008: 39–44). On the historical context of embassies from Alexandria to Gaius and Claudius, see Harker (2008: 9–31). On Isidorus and his contemporaries, see Philo *Flacc.* 18–21, 135–7, Musurillo (1954: 98) and Harker (2008: 15).

[119] *APM* 4.A.ii.4–8. Cf. Tuori (2016: 152–4), for analysis of this text and Claudius as a judge. Cf. *C.Pap, Jud.* II 153, 14–29, for a far more conciliatory reception from Claudius of the Alexandrian delegation.

[120] *APM* 4.A.ii.11–13; cf. *APM* 4.B.i.6–9.

[121] *APM* 4.A.iii.5–6: βασιλέως ἤκουσα τοῦ τότε | [ἐπ]ιτάξαντος. καὶ σὺ λέγε τίνος θέλεις | [κα] τηγορήσω (I listened to the orders of the then emperor. So you tell me who you wish and I will accuse them).

[122] *APM* 4.A.iii. 7–12: For Salome, part of the Herodian dynasty of Judaea, see Musurillo (1954: 128–30) and Kokkinos (1993: 177–92), esp. 191 n. 64, who reckons the accusation may have meant her daughter Berenike I.

The scene ends with Lampon, another Alexandrian delegate, calling Claudius deranged, leading to the order of their execution.[123] The impression is that Claudius did not give them the day for the hearing but quickly condemned them to death, being represented as unfairly biased towards the Jewish people.[124]

Comparisons to the historical context, which include the famous letter of Claudius to the Alexandrians calling for a calming of civil strife in the city and asking both communities to respect each other, have yielded a more balanced view of Claudius' conduct with regards to the Alexandrian problem.[125] Importantly, Claudius does not apparently take any one side over the other and both maintains a conciliatory tone and threatens that the Jewish community should respect his ruling, lest they feel his wrath, evoking a similar principle to Fronto's advice in *De eloquentia*, which was to praise the allies and suppress the rebellious:

> ἁπλῶς δὲ προσαγορεύωι ὅτι ἂν μὴ καταπαύσηται τὴν ὀλέθριον ὀργὴν ταύτην κατ' ἀλλήλων αὐθάδιον ἐγβιασθήσομαι δῖξαι ὑόν ἐστιν ἡγεμὼν φιλάνθρωπος εἰς ὀργὴν δικαίαν μεταβεβλημένος ... εἰ δὲ μή, πάντα τρόπον αὐτοὺς ἐπεξελεύσομαι καθάπερ κοινήν τεινα τῆς οἰκουμένης νόσον ἐξεγείροντας.

> I tell you simply that if you do not cease this destructive and stubborn anger against each other, I shall be forced to show you what a benevolent princeps is like when he is turned to just anger ... if you do not, I will pursue those who have risen up just like a common illness across the inhabited world.[126]

Thus, the impression of the emperor here is different from the one given by the *Acta Alexandrinorum*, a problem of great difficulty when attempting to reconstruct historical reality and the nature of Claudius' actions towards Alexandria from the *Acta*. However, the *Acta Isidori*, as preserved, date from much later, to the late second or early third century, and present a more stylised view of these trials in front of the Roman emperor. This is not to discount the problem of historicity and the pursuit of historical evidence from this material but to use them for a different purpose: the

---

[123] *APM* 4.A.iii.14–17: 'τί γὰρ ἄλλο ἔχομεν ἢ παρα[φ]ρονοῦντι βασιλεῖ τόπον διδόναι (What else do we have left than giving way to a deranged emperor).

[124] Cf. *APM* 4.B.i.17–18: κύριέ μου Καῖσαρ | τί [μέλει σοι ὑπὲρ Ἀγρίπ]που Ἰουδαίου τριωβολείου; (My lord Caesar, why do you bother with the three-obol Jew Agrippa?). Cf. *APM* 4.C.ii.23–24: κ]αὶ ὅλην τὴν οἰκουμένην [θέλουσι | ταράσ]σειν (they also wish to encourage unrest across the whole inhabited world) as other examples of anti-Jewish sentiment. Cf. Harker (2008: 43).

[125] *P.Lond.*6.1912 = *Sel.Pap.*II.212 (http://papyri.info/ddbdp/p.lond;6;1912). Cf. Harker (2008: 10–24), for a deeper analysis of the historical context.

[126] *P. Lond.* 6.1912, ll. 78–82, 98–100 = *Sel.Pap.*II.212 (I produce the Greek as written on the papyrus). Cf. Dench (2018: 105–6). Cf. Fronto, *De eloquentia* 1.5.

exploration of the perception of the Roman emperor from alternative perspectives gives different and contradictory impressions of his reception, which suggests that, despite projections from the emperor himself, the reception of his actions was more varied and precarious. Moreover, the *Acta* contribute to the discourse about the emperor, which is a historical phenomenon in its own right, as it frames how people thought about him. In the *Acta Isidori*, the emperor Claudius is portrayed as a tyrant, prejudicially predisposed against the Alexandrians, and therefore the definition of an unjust ruler.[127]

Once compared to similar examples in the *Acta Alexandrinorum* and parallel forms of literature, such a polarised view of the Roman emperor is not surprising, despite any apparent disjunct between the 'reality' and the 'representation'. For example, the representation of Trajan in the *Acta Hermaisci* reflects a similar picture to the one constructed of Claudius in the *Acta Isidori*.[128] In this case, the delegations from both the Greeks and the Jews of Alexandria appear at the emperor's court. There is an immediate juxtaposition between how the envoys from the different communities were treated. The Jewish delegation was greeted most cordially (ὁ δὲ Καῖσαρ εὐμενέστατα αὐ|τους ἠσπ[άσ]ατο – Caesar welcomed them most kindly)[129] but the Greeks coldly, with an accusation of misconduct towards the Jews: Ὁ δὲ οὐκ ἀπηντή|σατο, ἀλλ᾽ [εἶ]πεν· χαιρετίζετέ με ὡς ἄξιοι τυγ|χάνοντ[ες] τοῦ χαίρειν, τοιαῦτα χαλεπὰ τολ|μήσαντε[ς] Ἰουδαίοις; (He, though, did not receive them kindly, but said: you greet me as though you are worthy of a welcome, yet you dare to do such harsh deeds to the Jews?).[130] Thus, the proceedings are presented as rigged from the start. In comparison, the account of an embassy to Caligula, where Philo describes the cold conduct of the emperor towards the Jewish delegation, is comparable in fashion to the treatment of the Alexandrian Greeks in the *Acta*. Philo states that in greeting the emperor the Jewish delegation was cordial, bowing their heads in respect and saluting him as Imperator Augustus:

σαρκάζων γὰρ ἅμα καὶ σεσηρώς, 'ὑμεῖς,' εἶπεν, 'ἐστὲ οἱ θεομισεῖς, οἱ θεὸν μὴ νομίζοντες εἶναί με, τὸν ἤδη παρὰ πᾶσι τοῖς ἄλλοις ἀνωμολογημένον, ἀλλὰ

---

[127] Harker (2008: 43).
[128] *APM* 8 = *P.Oxy.*1242. Cf. Harker (2008: 189), for the information on the papyrus.
[129] *APM* 8.ii.30–1.
[130] *APM* 8, col. ii, 34–7. Cf. Musurillo (1954: 162), who argues for the falseness of this vignette and Trajan's strong record on justice (cf. Dio 68.6.2, 5.3). Rather, it is important to acknowledge the possibility of a less favourable representation, shown here, that fits into the general theme of the *Acta*.

τὸν ἀκατονόμαστον ὑμῖν;' . . . πόσης εὐθὺς ἀνεπλήσθησαν ἡδονῆς οἱ τῆς
ἐναντίας μερίδος πρέσβεις, ἤδη κατωρθωκέναι διὰ τῆς πρώτης
ἀναφθέγξεως Γαΐου τὴν πρεσβείαν νομίζοντες·

For he said, mockingly and at the same time with a grin, 'you are the god-haters, those who do not think that I am a god, though I am already acknowledged by all others as one, though not named by you?' . . . How quickly the ambassadors of the opposing side filled with great pleasure, assuming that they had already succeeded in their embassy at the first utterance of Gaius.[131]

Gaius is shown as being predisposed towards disliking the Jewish delegation. The ironic mentions of clemency and humanity by Philo, and the questions of Gaius, indicate the presented unfairness of the emperor in this situation.[132] There is the spectre of competition in this excerpt from Philo and an expectation that the emperor should be a fair mediator in these proceedings, even if he did not fulfil this role in the presented situation. Thus, we can see the contours of favour and disfavour that fomented competition between individuals and communities, transacted, both in reality and in imagination, in front of the emperor.

One might argue that these representations of 'bad' emperors, in both the *Acta* literature and Philo, indicate the existence of a healthy and continued opposition to the Roman empire and that they represent an affirmation of dissent towards the Roman order in Alexandria.[133] As a symbol and prime instigator of Roman power structures and knowledge, it is not surprising that the emperor becomes the focus of contestation.[134] More pessimistically, that resistance is understood through the person of the emperor himself suggests that thought-worlds of resistance are mapped onto the contours of Roman power itself and thus cannot be separated from them, which hints at the success of Roman hegemony and selective 'epistemicide'.[135] Put more bluntly, you cannot imagine yourself outside of a Roman framework.[136] Nonetheless, within these stories, the emperor

---

[131] Philo, *Leg.* 352–3, and 361–3, where the hostility of Gaius continues and he makes fun of the Jews for not eating pork, much to the amusement of the Alexandrian Greek delegation; see Hammond (1959: 32–3) for his analysis of this situation. Cf. Niehoff (2018) and Christoforou (2021) for Philo's posturing.

[132] Philo, *Leg.* 352: 'ὁ δὲ οὕτως ἐπιεικῶς καὶ φιλανθρώπως.'

[133] Cf. Harker (2008: 8, 174). Cf. MacMullen (1966: 84–90), for this interpretation of the *Acta Alexandrinorum*.

[134] For contours of resistance and response, see Dench (2018: 105–33); Mattingly (2011), and Padilla Peralta (2020).

[135] Padilla Peralta (2020: 175). For a more optimistic view, see Johnston (2017).

[136] Cf. Giusti (2016), for a similar argument on the all-encompassing nature of Augustan ideology.

remains the conceptual centre of power and justice in the world, or the location where problems, dissent, and competition can be discussed and debated. For our purposes, such activity evinced an engagement in the discourse of expectations and fears about the Roman emperor, all along the spectrum of resistance and collaboration.

Such subtlety can be seen in comparisons between emperors in the *acta*. In the *Acta Isidori*, Isidorus reveals to Claudius his loyalty to the previous emperor and promises to do the same for him.[137] Earlier in the *Legatio ad Gaium*, Philo engages in lengthy comparisons with both Tiberius and Augustus, including their respective treatment of the Jewish people, and laudatory descriptions of their reigns, thus providing a juxtaposition to the present age of Gaius.[138] Furthermore, the *Acta Appiani*, another example of *acta*-related literature, records a heated exchange between the emperor Commodus and an Appian, another gymnasiarch and ambassador from Alexandria:[139]

αὐτοκράτωρ εἶπεν·|νῦν οὐκ οἶδας τίνι [λα]λεῖς; | Ἀππιανός· ἐπίσταμαι· Ἀπ [πι]ανὸς τυράννῳ. | αὐτοκράτωρ [οὔκ,] ἀλλὰ βασιλεῖ. Ἀππια|νός· τοῦτο μὴ λέγε· τῷ γὰρ θεῷ Ἀντωνείνῳ [τ]ῷ π[ατ]ρί σου ἔπρεπε αὐτοκρατορεύειν.

The emperor said: Now do you not know to whom you are speaking? Appian: I know well. Appian (speaks) to a tyrant. The emperor: No, but a king. Appian: Do not say this, it was fitting for your father the divine Antoninus to be a ruler.[140]

The dialogue continues to list the good qualities of Marcus Aurelius – his philosophy, his lack of avarice, and his love of goodness – and then Commodus' opposite qualities of tyranny, dishonesty, and crudeness.[141] Thus, Appian compares and contrasts the fitness of each to the emperorship, with the result being that Commodus did not meet his requirements.[142] In his conclusion, Harker argued that the *Acta Alexandrinorum* were less about anti-Roman feeling in Alexandria and more about the exhibition of Hellenic identity in the city at the expense of other ethnic and political groups.[143] This may be the case, but the open criticism of the emperor within these stories requires separate comment. The fact that other forms of literature shared this

---

[137] *APM* A.iii. 5–6.
[138] Philo, *Leg.* 141–2 for Tiberius, 143–7 for Augustus, 156–8 for Augustus' treatment of the Jews, and 159–61 for Tiberius', with Christoforou (2021) for analysis.
[139] *APM* 11.A = *P. Yale* Inv. 1536; *APM* 11.B = *P. Oxy.* 33.
[140] *APM* 11.B.ii.3–9; cf. Musurillo (1954: 205–11). [141] *APM* 11.B.ii.9–13. cf. HA. *Marc.* 1.1.
[142] Cf. Harker (2008: 90–1). [143] Harker (2008: 175–6).

criticism suggests a widespread appeal of this sort of discourse that pushed and pulled at the nature of the emperor and his character.[144] However, such discourse did not necessarily question the legitimacy of the emperorship, or the position in itself, but rather the acceptability of the person who was emperor. The disappointment and open criticism of this literature suggest that it was part of a critique of a hoped ideal and feared reality of the imperial persona, which placed the emperor at the epicentre of mediation between themselves and their enemies, with hope for justice and resignation at a harsh outcome.

A final example concerning justice is the collocation of brigandage and the Roman emperor. It would seem that the proximity of the emperor as a protector and bandits as disturbers of the peace would be contradictory, as they are antithetical figures in society.[145] However, as figures in the imagination, the bandit and the emperor could be seen as counterparts – perhaps even two sides of the same coin.[146] As Gleason put it, 'People enjoyed telling it because such stories were good to think about the legitimacy of imperial power'.[147] An interesting case is the story of Bulla Felix during the reigns of Septimius Severus and Caracalla, which appears in Dio. It recounts the tale of an Italian bandit, who with his six hundred men plundered Italy for a period of two years and, much to the chagrin of the emperors and the army, was able to avoid capture by subterfuge and smarts.[148] Thereafter, Dio provides a few stories that illustrate his point:

---

[144] A further comparison would be the trial scenes of Jesus in the gospels and Paul's trials in the *Acts of the Apostles*. They share similarities with the *acta* in the tradition of exhibiting trials. Of particular importance is Paul's appeal unto Caesar (*Acts* 22.25–27, 25.11–12). The legal and historical problems of making such an appeal were discussed in Sherwin-White (1963: 48–70). That Paul would appeal to Caesar indicates the perception of the supremacy of the emperor. However, see Rowe (2009: 95–102), for the argument of the essential subversiveness of early Christianity and how the proclamation of Christ as King was incongruous with allegiance to the emperor. This suggests a simultaneous habitation of the *imaginaire* between Jesus and the emperor, which is a wrinkle in the perception of the Roman emperor that would require further careful study.

[145] Cf. Jones (2001: 163, 166), for a monumental inscription in which Claudius is commemorated for saving the Lycians from brigandage, amongst other laudations, highlighting the position of emperor as a protector against bandits.

[146] Veyne (1990: 359); cf. Hobsbawm (1972: 56) and Shaw (1984: 51), for the citation of August. *De. civ. D.* 4.4, who argues for the close comparison of *regna* and *latrocinia*. On Bandits generally in the Roman empire, including the historical and more mythical aspects of them, see Grünewald (2004), esp. chaps. 4, 6, and 7, for conflicts with authorities and their status as counterparts.

[147] Gleason (2011: 57).

[148] Dio 77(76).10.1–2; cf. Forsdyke (2012: 39); Grünewald (2004: 110–20); cf. Gleason (2011: 56–60), for her analysis of the Bulla Felix episode, and the inclusion of two other subversive stories in Dio's Severan narrative, namely Dio 75(75).2.4 and 76(75).5, which have to do with Claudius, a masquerading Syrian outlaw's infiltration of Severus' camp, and Numerianus the schoolmaster's precipitous military rise and subsequent retirement, respectively. Like Bulla Felix, they both throw the legitimacy of Severus' principate into relief.

Bulla's seeming omniscience in the movements from Rome towards Brundisium;[149] Bulla masquerading as a governor of his country (πλασάμενος ὡς τῆς πατρίδος ἄρχων), persuading a jail-keeper to let two of his captured brigands escape being thrown to the beasts;[150] and Bulla again pretending to be someone else (ὥσπερ ἄλλος τις ὤν), tricking a centurion to follow him on the false information that he would lead him to the bandit leader. He then proceeded to ambush him, going up to the tribunal to hold a mock trial as a judge (ἐπὶ τὸ βῆμα ἀνέβη σχῆμα ἄρχοντος ἀναλαβών), ordering that the centurion's head be shaved, and that he be sent back with a message to their masters to look after their slaves, so that they do not turn to banditry: ἄγγελλε τοῖς δεσπόταις σου ὅτι τοὺς δούλους ὑμῶν τρέφετε, ἵνα μὴ λῃστεύωσι.[151] These stories about Bulla Felix are tales of reversal, where the authorities are shown to be incompetent, and the bandit leader instead fulfils the role as a protector of justice, literally masquerading as an authority in defiance of the 'real' authority. According to Brent Shaw's analysis of these passages, Bulla Felix is revealed as an anti-emperor and should be seen as a semi-fictitious device, used as a challenge to the legitimacy of the sitting emperor whose power could be questioned.[152] This could certainly be the case, but there are several present tensions that require comment.

The description of Bulla Felix as a foil to the authorities, seeking justice for his companions and freedmen at the expense of the emperor and the military, has led to the analysis of this story as an example of a bandit tale, with questions of its historicity and meaning.[153] The historiographical impetus for such analyses takes its cue from Eric Hobsbawm's book *Bandits*, in which he argues for the existence of 'social banditry' in peasant societies throughout history.[154] However, the problem of the historicity of such a perception and the reality behind what these stories convey formed the basis of the scholarly disagreement with Hobsbawm's thesis.[155] In terms of the study of banditry in the Roman world, these stories form a potential

---

[149] Dio 77(76).10.2–3. [150] Dio 77.10.3.

[151] Dio 77.10.4–5. Cf. George (2011: 397) on the representation of slaves in material culture with shaved heads, with the implication that the centurion was in fact a slave. This conflation is enhanced by the next phrases' explanation of the statement, pointing out that many of Bulla's bandits were freedmen. This has similarities in Epictetus' discussion on freedom at pp. 20–23 and the discussion of asylum on pp. 79–82.

[152] Shaw (1984: 48). [153] Shaw (1984: 46–9); Forsdyke (2012: 39–40, 45).

[154] Hobsbawm (1972: 17): 'The point about social bandits is that they are peasant outlaws whom the lord and the state regard as criminals, but who remain within peasant society, and are considered by their people as heroes, as champions, avengers, fighters for justice, perhaps even leaders of liberation, and in any case as men to be admired, helped and supported.'

[155] Shaw (1984: 4–5, n. 5).

mirror reflecting popular aspirations in the form of the idealised figures that come from an oral context, filtered as they are through the writings of the literate elite.[156] Though mediated in this manner, the tension between the images of emperor and bandit reflects imagined encounters and a way, therefore, to think about the emperor and his power. Stories do not need to be empirically real, as the imagination itself reflects what people thought about the emperor.[157] The reality of banditry in the Roman empire is an important focus of study, but the interest here is on social imagination. In other words, Bulla Felix does not need to be real to have truth value in our understanding of the perception of the Roman emperor that could transcend social boundaries.[158]

For instance, Forsdyke argues that this episode is a case of a slave tale – an example of the hidden transcript of a lower class that saw a world upside down and wished for different power relations.[159] There is a remarkable power to this argument, as Dio's narrative gives the impression of a folk tale: the intrepid bandit's cunning and humorous evasion of the Roman authorities and emperor. However, this cannot be taken in a vacuum or as fully representative of the potential perceptions of the Roman emperor, nor can it reveal a single perspective from one section of society. Instead, it adds to the mosaic of opinion about the emperor and his role in society, which in an alternative implementation of Scott's paradigm would be a simultaneous mixing of different hidden transcripts rather than an attempt to place all as expressions of resistance by the low against the high. Accordingly, there must be a reconciliation between the different strands of discourse about the emperor. As a comparison, the scene in Apuleis' *Metamorphoses*, where, in an endeavour to get aid and free himself from the bandits who stole him, Lucius' attempted exhortation for safety towards the Roman emperor comes out as a donkey's bray,[160] is an amusing episode that perhaps points to a wider theme of importance in this section: that the emperor could be seen as a protector against bandits, which is problematised by the Bulla Felix episode.

However, this should not be seen as inconsistent. Instead, it indicates the existence of a discourse that involved contributions between differing

---

[156] Shaw (1984: 44).   [157] *Pace* Shaw (1984: 44).
[158] On reality, see Shaw (1984: 5), for his discussion of a passage in Galen (Gal. *De Anatomicis Administrationibus* 1.2, where he describes the skeleton of a bandit being left at the side of the road, with the local inhabitants refusing to bury it. Cf. Shaw (1984: 5–6), for his discussion of this passage as an example of the complicated reception of bandits, and 10, n. 25 for a compilation of inscriptions from across the empire on the tombstones of people who were killed by bandits (*interfectus a latronibus*).
[159] Forsdyke (2012: 39–41).   [160] Apul. *Met.* 3.29.

perspectives, allowing for the liminal placement of the emperor between the rule of law and banditry and for him to be interpreted in different ways. This can be observed in the later equation of *regna* with *latrocinia* in Augustine's *De Civitate Dei* in states without justice. In his discussion, Augustine uses an anecdote about Alexander III of Macedon and a pirate to argue that the difference between banditry and kingdoms is one of scale of rapacity and injustice rule. When asked why the pirate made the sea unsafe, the pirate replied: *Quod tibi, inquit, ut orbem terrarum; sed quia <id> ego exiguo navigio facio, latro vocor; quia tu magna classe, imperator* (The same as you do, he said, with the whole world; But because I do it with a tiny ship, I am called a bandit; since you do it with a great fleet, you are an emperor).[161] This negative equation of the political structure of bandit groups and imperial states is striking. It points to the potential of political coercion, economic exploitation, and imperial expansion in both structures that was both intuitive and allowed for a comparison to be made across contexts. It is remarkable, along similar lines, that the *Acta Alexandrinorum* also calls the emperor 'brigand-leaders', such as in the *Acta Appiani*, when Appian calls Commodus a brigand-leader.[162] This is also seen elsewhere in Dio's narrative, in the context of a fragmentary description of the emperor Macrinus' death, in which he invokes the simultaneous distinction and similarity between emperors and bandits and how his fall meant that he would be treated as a robber: δραπετεύσας διὰ τῶν ἐθνῶν ὧν ἦρξε, συλληφθεὶς ὑπὸ τῶν τυχόντων ὥσπερ τις λῃστής (Running away through the provinces which he had commanded, he was arrested by the first person he chanced upon, just like a bandit).[163] In different contexts, then, emperors and bandits are compared and contrasted. To return to the story of Bulla Felix, the last impression of him provided by Dio is a retort of the bandit leader towards the famous jurist and praetorian prefect Papinian: καὶ αὐτὸν ὁ Παπινιανὸς ὁ ἔπαρχος ἀνήρετο 'διὰ τί ἐλῄστευσας;' καὶ αὐτὸς ἀπεκρίνατο 'διὰ τί σὺ ἔπαρχος εἶ; (Papinian the prefect asked, 'Why do you rob?', and he replied: why are you a prefect).[164] The implication of this exchange is similar to Augustine's example of the pirate's reply to Alexander the Great and the *Acta Alexandrinorum*, where brigandry and imperial authority are seen as similar. Thus, there is the spectre of a simultaneously positive or negative

---

[161] August. *De civ. D.* 4.4.
[162] *APM* II.B.iv.7–8 'λῄσταρχος'; For further examples, see Harker (2008: 90, 163).
[163] Dio 79(78).40.4–5.
[164] Dio 77(76).10.7; cf. Champlin (2008: 410–11), on how this can be compared to other stories of similar retorts to authority in ancient and world literature. Cf. Section 4.4.

impression of the Roman emperor from these stories, just as banditry can be seen in a similar paradoxical light.[165]

In the end, the story of Bulla Felix allows us to access a thought-world of the Roman emperor from a wider perspective. It contains concepts of a mixed social background that reveal differing images of the Roman emperor. In terms of justice, this section has attempted to give an impression of this rich variety of vignettes of the emperor's reception. It is remarkable that so many different fears and expectations of the Roman emperor could exist with respect to justice, meaning that he was the topic of discussion and disagreement in different media across social and temporal boundaries. Multivalency as a theme is stressed here, which will remain a focus through different aspects of the dialogue that fashioned the image of the Roman emperorship.

---

[165] Cf. Hobsbawm (1972: 53) for the paradoxical thought that if a bandit is just, then at a certain point he would not be in conflict with a just king, 'since the noble robber is just, he cannot be in real conflict with the fount of justice, whether divine or human. There are a number of versions of the story of conflict and reconciliation between bandit and king.'

CHAPTER 3

The Generosity of the Roman Emperor

3.1 *Benefacta laudare*: Generosity in Roman Imperial Politics

In ceteris vero desideriis hominum obstinatissime tenuit, ne quem sine spe dimitteret; quin et admonentibus domesticis, quasi plura polliceretur quam praestare posset, non oportere ait quemquam a sermone principis tristem discedere; atque etiam recordatus quondam super cenam, quod nihil cuiquam toto die praestitisset, memorabilem illam meritoque laudatam vocem edidit: 'Amici, diem perdidi'.

Indeed, for the remainder of requests he held steadfastly that no one should be sent away without hope. Though admonished by his staff for promising more than he was able to perform, he said it was not right for someone to depart unhappy from a conversation with the *princeps*. Titus even recalled over dinner once that he did not give anything to anyone across a whole day; he produced that memorable and rightly praised maxim: 'Friends, I have lost a day.'[1]

The epigraph about the emperor Titus provides an illuminating impression of the perceived function of the imperial office. The passage connects two closely related vignettes, justice and generosity, revolving around the expectation of favour from the emperor in the granting of requests. Equally important is the corollary that these requests and expectations would not necessarily always be met when Titus' household officials advise him not to promise that which he could not deliver. Such a 'conscious ideology' of generosity underpins the perceptions of the duty of an emperor: to receive and respond favourably to requests.[2]

Euergetism and benefaction are fundamental building blocks of understanding the culture, society, and economics of the Roman empire, in terms of both its imperial superstructure and its tessellated constituent parts, let alone the dynamics of interaction that circulated around the

---

[1] Suet. *Tit.* 8.1.   [2] Millar (1977: 469–70).

Roman emperorship.[3] Such is the impression of a recently published funerary inscription from Pompeii.[4] A couple of points from the inscription present themselves as pertinent here. First is the idea of a currency of cross-imperial interaction, or a vocabulary of benefaction and play that could remain embedded in local custom but also transcend that local context: 'that was so large in scale and magnificent that it could easily be compared to any presentation put on by the most sumptuous colony founded by the city of Rome, since he had four hundred and sixteen gladiators in his gladiatorial training school'.[5] The thrust of the passage seems to be one of comparison, that Pompeii in contrast to other Roman colonies, had the privilege of being amongst the most 'splendid' or 'sophisticated'.[6] The focus on the size of the benefactions is key in this respect as well, given the number of recipients and different occasions of the benefactor's *munera*. The level of competition, thus, transcends context and becomes comparable quantitatively and qualitatively with other such *munera* across the Roman world.[7] The second pertinent point concerns the figure of the Roman emperor, who appears both directly and indirectly in the inscription, as an exemplar, mediator, and model:

> et, cum Caesar omnes familias ultra ducentesimum ab urbe ut abducerent iussisset huic ut Pompeios in patriam suam reduceret permisit . . . propter quae postulante populo, cum universus ordo consentiret ut patronus cooptaretur et IIvir referret, ipse privatus intercessit, dicens non sustinere se civium suorum esse patronum.

> And when Caesar had ordered that they remove all their gladiatorial troupes beyond the two-hundredth milestone from the city, to this man alone he granted permission to bring back (his own gladiatorial troupe) to his home town of Pompeii . . . Because of these deeds, with the people demanding it, when the entire town council agreed that he should be co-opted as a patron and the *duovir* was making the formal proposal, he himself intervened himself as a private citizen, saying that he would not bear the idea that he be a patron of his own fellow citizens.[8]

---

[3] The bibliography is immense. See Veyne (1990) and Zuiderhoek (2009).

[4] First published in Osanna (2018) and then Bodel et al. (2019: 150–2), for the text, translation, and commentary used here.

[5] Bodel et al. (2019: 150), with 161–4 for commentary on the size of the gladiatorial *ludus*: *adeo magnum et splendidum dedit ut cuivis ab urbe lautissimae coloniae conferendum esset, ut pote cum CCCCXVI gladiatores in ludo habuer(it)*; cf. Noreña (2021).

[6] Thanks to Nicholas Purcell for pointing out the relevance of this passage.

[7] Bodel et al. (2019: 160), for this interpretation.

[8] Bodel et al. (2019: 161–2) for translation and commentary.

In this case, the emperor Nero figures directly in the ability of the unnamed benefactor to engage in the politics of euergetism through a special privilege, which exempted him from an imperial order and *senatus consultum* that respectively removed gladiatorial *familiae* from Rome and also banned the holding of gladiatorial *munera* in Pompeii.[9] Thus, we have the dynamics of *benefacta laudare* and *seditiosos compescere* in this context, with the emperor creating a hierarchy of privilege in the removal of gladiatorial troupes and subsequently granting exemptions from those rules. Moreover, such a hierarchy allows the benefactor to underline his exceptionality: the end of the inscription exhibits a form of *recusatio* and *consensus*, which are oft-cited cornerstones of Augustan ideology.[10] Though such an example is unparalleled, the performance here is both local and imperial.[11] The emperor becomes a tool for comparison – a model of civic interaction that is emulated. Loyalty and a watchful imperial eye need not be inferred necessarily.[12] The performance lies in a local and intercommunal context, where the benefactor can mark himself out through a common language of reciprocity. As Noreña articulates on benefactions across the Roman empire: 'Hence, they too had a strong incentive to uphold the idea of the emperor as a model benefactor. The abstract reciprocity that characterized the relationship between imperial benefaction and local honorific practice, in other words, is not just an accident of the surviving evidence. It was a structural feature of the system.'[13] In other words, the language of benefaction and reciprocity was imbued with an imperial vocabulary, with emperors as key words in that vernacular. This does not mean that the emperor was the intended audience but rather that his stated presence was a marker of prestige and status within and between communities.

Such are the dynamics at play in this chapter. The emperor is an instigator of generosity and is expected to fulfil that role. Within the idea of a 'passive' emperor responding to requests is the idea of the emperor as a marker of status, too. This category of 'accessibility' of the emperor and his generosity works directly and indirectly.[14] This idea of an emperor's accessibility forms part of a wider historiographical theme in the study of the Roman empire and the nature of its society, which involves the understanding of the ideology that governed political and social interactions. Vivian Nutton called this the 'beneficial ideology', which was an

---

[9] Bodel et al. (2019: 172–4), with Tac. *Ann.* 14.17.3–4.   [10] See Chapter 1.
[11] Cf. Bodel et al. (2019: 178).   [12] Noreña (2021: 210).   [13] Noreña (2021: 213).
[14] Millar (1977: 271).

intricate social and political contract that ensured peace and prosperity in the Roman empire, bolstered by consensus and guaranteed by the Roman emperor.[15] This argument has had a powerful impact on the study of the Roman empire. There is scholarship on a wide range of topics that involve the competition and exchange of benefits across the empire, from the proclamation of local, civic, or provincial identity through the medium of benefaction to the importance of the emperor within this rubric of imperial benefits.[16]

The purpose of this chapter is to tease apart the expectations of the emperor's generosity through the viewpoint of his subjects. Rather than focussing on rituals of loyalty or the dynamics of the relationship between *plebs* and *princeps* in the city of Rome itself,[17] this chapter is divided as follows. First, I focus on the politics of consensus and acceptance that imbue questions of generosity, which is fundamental to *principes* throughout their lives, and indeed afterwards. Therefore, what follows here is a necessary discussion of the problem of acceptance and nature of acceptance.[18] Second, I discuss the examples of generosity both before and during imperial reigns. Expectations of generosity meant that emperors were in a constant conversation that placed their imagined actions with those of their forebears and successors, which were constantly being reinterpreted and refashioned. Accordingly, this temporal aspect means that discussion of the politics of succession is necessary insofar as it elucidates the importance of potential *principes* to be seen as generous, including examples from those who did not reach sole rule.

3.2   How to Become Emperor: A Digression on the Succession

3.2.1   Legitimacy, 'Acceptance', and the Dynastic Question

As tricky as it is to define the nature and power of the position of emperor, so too is it to describe how the office was passed on from one emperor to the next.[19] Constitutionally, it follows that the emperor received his powers

[15] Nutton (1978: 210–14).

[16] Noreña (2011: 106); Veyne (1976:, esp. 622 and 636); and Veyne (1990: 347). Cf. Price (1984b); cf. Johnston (2017).

[17] Ando (2000: 201), for rituals of loyalty. Cf. Forbis (1996: 40) on the *alimenta*. On the *plebs* and public interaction, see Courrier (2014), Yavetz (1969: 9–37), Veyne (1976: 702–6), Millar (1977: 365–6); cf. Harries (2003: 125–40). On acclamations, see Aldrete (2003: 90–7), Rouèché (1984: 182–6), and Ando (2000: 201–5).

[18] Cf. Hekster (2015), esp. chap. 1, for a full discussion of the display of succession on media across the empire.

[19] Mastrocinque (2011a: 1–3), on the non-hereditary aspect of power.

from the people, which was confirmed by the senate and popular *comitia*, meaning that the senate and people of Rome gave power to a new *princeps* through the performance of consensus.[20] Therefore, it can follow, in an extreme interpretation, that there was no succession in the monarchical sense but rather that the principate died alongside the death of an emperor and was reinstituted once a new *princeps* was confirmed by the political organs of the Roman state.[21] Accordingly, the ideological self-image of the office of emperor was predicated on this idea of recognition, which also included the threat of the violent removal of the *princeps*, making recognition essential to its stability.[22] A concentration on the powers given to a new *princeps* at his accession only illuminates one side of the coin, for the law cannot bestow *auctoritas*.[23] Rather, due weight needs to be afforded to an informal way of expressing constitutional settlements and the importance of more informal arrangements that supplement the legal and political magistracies and duties that are a necessary part of understanding the emperor. The emperor is affirmed informally in constitutional arenas, which is true for *principes* who were introduced into public life in Rome and active participants in the civic rhythms of the city.

To make the argument in this section as clear as possible, I will outline it here. Though the complexities of the succession are manifold, its character is that of a socially affirmed dynasty, which is to say that Romans often turned to dynastic or familial solutions for the handover of power (i.e. that a 'son' by blood or adoption would take the reins), even though that person had to be seen to deserve the emperorship and therefore win over the constituencies of the Roman state. This statement will be fleshed out further in the discussion of Flaig's *Akzeptanz* argument. In short, the political and social aspect of the succession is fundamental.

The complexities of dynastic formation are compounded by several factors, which include the political advancement of future emperors during the reign of another emperor and the place of Roman family planning and law in understanding succession and inheritance. Both factors allowed for several people to be considered *capaces imperii*, to borrow Tacitus' phrase, which is to say, people who were close to the current *princeps*, who held

---

[20] Hammond (1959: 6–8); Veyne (2002: 3). See Section 1.2.2–6, esp. pp. 29–31, for a fuller discussion of the constitutionality of the principate.

[21] *StR* II 844 = *DPR* V 116; Flaig (2010: 277). For the issues of collegiality, see *StR* II 1145–1146 = *DPR* V 459–461. Cf. Weber (1978: 1114–15, 1125).

[22] Cf. Béranger (1953: 72); Flaig (2019: 11). As Flaig argued, the threat of violent removal, which came to fruition under *Usurpationen*, highlighted the importance of this recognition, which he called *Akzeptanz*.

[23] For example, see Suet. *Vesp.* 7.2.

magistracies themselves, and were thus publicly displayed and commemorated as being the future of the state.

The *Senatus Consultum de Pisone Patre* nicely illustrates such complexities in that it stresses the political status and ascendancy of Germanicus Caesar and the importance of the *domus Augusta* as a familial unit that oversaw directing the *res publica*. In the discussion on the inscription of Piso's crimes, the nature of Germanicus' mission seems clear: he was dispatched 'to set in order the state of overseas affairs' (*ad rerum transmarinarum statum componendum missus esset*) by Tiberius through the authority of the senate, which needed the presence of the emperor himself or his sons.[24] Moreover, the *populus Romanus* passed a law stipulating that Germanicus held *maius imperium* over proconsular governors, whilst stating outright that Tiberius' *maius imperium* was greater than that of Germanicus.[25] Thus, we can observe the complex hierarchies in the early principate that incorporated political and social status. Piso's crime was that he neglected both public law and the 'greaterness' of the *domus Augusta* (*neclecta maiestate domus Aug(ustae)*),[26] which thus simultaneously stresses the elevated political positions of both Tiberius and Germanicus through their respective *imperia* underpinned by the institutions and laws of the *res publica*, whilst stressing their family, the *domus Augusta*, as being uniquely elevated in Roman society. An aspect of future stability is also alluded to later in the inscription, when the senate praises Tiberius and exhorts him to turn his attention to Drusus, his remaining son, since 'all hope in the future of the paternal position held on account of the state has been placed in one man'.[27] Though the precarity of the *domus Augusta* is acknowledged, the health of the state and success of the *res publica* are predicated on the future assumption of Tiberius' role.[28] Thus, the family and political institutions sit together, both as fundamental cogs in the stability of the system, and not necessarily in open and uncomfortable antagonism. Though paradoxical, connection to the *domus Augusta* and ascendency through the magistracies of the *res publica* were important criteria for 'acceptance'.[29] As such, considerations of dynastic legitimacy

---

[24] *SCPP* ll. 32–3. See Lott (2012: 142–3). Cf. Dalla Rosa (2021: 204).
[25] *SCPP* ll. 33–6. Cf. Dalla Rosa (2021: 205) and Giradet (2000).
[26] *SCPP* l. 128–9. Lott (2012: 152–3).
[27] *SCPP* l. 33: *omnem spem futuram paternae pro r(e) p(ublica) stationis in uno repos[i]ta<m>*. Cf. Cooley (2019: 76–7).
[28] Lott (2012), for other inscriptions that commemorate the precarity of the *domus*, including the Pisan cenotaphs and the *Tabula Siarensis*.
[29] Cf. Tac. *Hist.* 1.15–16, for the tensions in different familial strategies in selecting new *principes*; Syme (1958: 151–2), for an eloquent paraphrasing of the passage. Cf. Hekster (2015), for a comprehensive

need to take both sides into account: the formal and informal ways political clout was engendered through political and familial strategies.[30]

As pointed out in the *Senatus Consultum de Pisone Patre* (*SCPP*), degrees of unequal 'collegiality', or offices and powers given to potential future emperors, were important methods of stability, which set them apart from other men and magistrates at Rome.[31] Indeed, collegiate association at the apex of the Roman empire seemed to be an important aspect of the 'succession' itself, meaning that emperors would overlap in powers during their reigns.[32] In *Doppelprinzipat und Reichsteilung im Imperium Romanum*, Kornemann compiled statistics on the number of years imperial powers were shared in the time between the start of the principate and the institution of the tetrarchy of Diocletian. His research showed that out of the 311 years of the Roman empire up to that point, 125 years were shared at the apex of power.[33] Therefore, it seems that this method of collegiality was used to ensure dynastic longevity.

However, such an overtly dynastic image of the Roman emperorship was justly challenged by Flaig.[34] He argued provocatively that the word 'legitimacy' itself was inappropriate for describing how the emperor maintained his reign, since it inherently suggested an irrevocable right to rule uncontested.[35] Instead, he moves the question of legitimacy from the person of the emperor to the monarchy itself, for it was the latter that was legitimate and inviolable. As for the emperor, he was devoid of legitimacy by the simple fact that he could lose his right to rule, and therefore his life.[36] Flaig chose the word *Akzeptanz* to describe the process by which an emperor secured his reign. He defines it as follows: '"acceptance" is to be defined as the fact that relevant sectors of a political community support the rule of a specific person by their explicit or implicit consent.'[37] The key phrase is 'relevant sectors', for Flaig argues that in the hierarchy of Roman society, not all sections had political impact on the maintenance of imperial 'acceptance'. For him, these were the senators, the *plebs urbana* at Rome, and the citizen soldiers in the military. Accordingly, it was the beneficial and proper cultivation of the relationship

---

discussion of how familial strategies changed over the course of the principate from the Julio-Claudians onwards.

[30] Cf. Severy (2003).   [31] Hurlet (1997: 541); cf. Hammond (1959: 2–3, 11). Cf. Rowe (2002: 2).

[32] For such overlap and the dynamics of succession as seen through legislation, and for an incisive discussion of Tiberius' accession, see Matthews (2010: 58).

[33] Kornemann (1930: 179–84), esp. 184. In the 262 years between Augustus and Alexander Severus, 106 years were shared. This equates to 40.45 per cent of the time, showing little statistical difference with the third century, which if included drops to 40.19 per cent of the time. Cf. Hurlet (1997: 3).

[34] Flaig (2019).   [35] Flaig (2010: 276).   [36] Flaig (2010: 278–9).   [37] Flaig (2010: 278).

between the emperor and these sectors that ensured that he could maintain 'acceptance' throughout his reign. Flaig also rejects the idea of hereditary succession being important to the acceptance of an emperor, making his paradigm antagonistic to a competing conception of the succession that stresses the dynastic perspective.[38] Such a dynamic seems unmistakable, and indeed euergetism and benefaction seem to be important ways the emperor achieved acceptance. However, more recently, Hekster has argued effectively that stressing familial connectivity was fundamental to the ideology of the principate, its stability, and how it was perceived in contradistinction to Flaig's assertions.[39]

The question then becomes more specific. To what extent did the legitimacy or 'acceptance' of an emperor derive from his familial connections to the imperial dynasty? In other words, can we reconcile the importance of performance to maintaining stability and the importance of bolstering familial connections and displaying those connections to that performance? The legitimacy of a successor was bolstered by the cultivation of heirs within the system, which is a leitmotif that returns throughout the principate with varying degrees of success.[40] However, this could not necessarily always be put into effect. A full treatment of the instability of certain transitional moments in Roman history is impossible here, so the short example of Claudius will have to suffice.[41] Famously, Claudius was disregarded for most of his youth as a contributing member of the *domus Augusta*.[42] According to Suetonius, in a letter to Livia, Augustus had concerns over Claudius' physical ailments and their potential effect on public perceptions of the family and of Claudius himself, particularly when the public was accustomed to deride such things.[43] Therefore, Augustus' suggestion was to keep Claudius away from the limelight by not allowing him into the imperial seat at the circus.[44] Therefore, unlike his other male relatives, such as his brother Germanicus, Claudius was placed in the background.[45] Despite these problems, there is evidence for opinion concerning Claudius prior to him becoming emperor. In particular, during Gaius' principate, Claudius was hailed at spectacles as the uncle of the emperor and brother of Germanicus when he presided.[46] Such acclamations in an open

---

[38] Flaig (2010: 279).   [39] Hekster (2015).

[40] Cf. Hurlet (1997); Hammond (1956, 1959, 1968); cf. Gray (1970: 233–4); cf. Tan (2019); Hekster (2015); Severy (2003).

[41] I have written on such transitional moments more specifically: Christoforou (2017) and Christoforou (2021), esp. 94–103. Cf. Osgood (2011: 29–32) and 32–46, for the aftermath of his succession; Flaig (2019: 249–46).

[42] Tac. *Ann*. 3.18.4.   [43] Suet. *Claud*. 4.2.   [44] Suet. *Claud*. 4.3.

[45] Suet. *Claud*. 5–7, on Claudius' political life.   [46] Suet. *Claud*. 7.

public context suggest the importance of familial connection to political legitimacy, even for one kept away from the limelight.

Such dynamics are seen in the crisis of AD 41 with the assassination of Gaius Caligula. The demise of Gaius was met by deliberation by the senate on what government should be created, whilst the military seized Claudius and hailed him as emperor because of his projected clemency and being of 'ruling stock' (βασιλικοῦ γένους).[47] Accordingly, different sections of Roman society and the state were expressing their opinions on the future of the Roman government, which included the praetorians cohorts, the senate, and the *populus Romanus*.[48] The tapestry of opinions outlined in Josephus' account in his *Jewish Antiquities* is multifaceted and deserves full treatment. However, one scene requires focus that will prove illustrative. The senate and the people are described as being at variance with each other over the direction of the state, with the senate wishing to gain their former 'honour' (ἀξίωμα) and break free from 'servitude' (δουλεία).[49] The *populus Romanus* (ὁ δὲ δῆμος), however, are presented as deliberating on the implications of such a return to senatorial direction, seeing Claudius as a 'refuge' (καταφυγὴν) from civil war, such as that from the time of Pompey and Caesar. Importantly, the people saw the emperors as a 'curb' on the greediness of the senate.[50] According to Josephus, the people preferred the new power structure that was created by having an emperor, for it kept the senate in check and provided the people with safety. Josephus' passage has a strong antagonistic tone: the emperor is portrayed as a foil to the excesses of the senate in the mind of the people.[51] If we follow Wiseman's commentary, there are differences and inconsistencies in the text that suggest Josephus used different sources for the construction of this narrative.[52] Indeed, if the source was Latin, and the words of power used throughout the relevant passage speak to Latin equivalents, the word would have been *frenum*, which translates as a horse's bit but was often used in political contexts to mean the control of power and the restraint of ambition.[53] If this is the case, then the source would emphasise the shortcomings of the senate and contrast it with the wish for protection from the people. This perhaps betrays a Roman *popularis* perspective,

---

[47] Dio 60.1.1–3. Cf. Suet. *Claud.* 10.1–3. For the possibility of the return of the republic, see Lowe (2013).

[48] See Joseph. *AJ*. 19.158–70, 173, 189, 223.

[49] Joseph. *AJ*. 19.227. For ἀξίωμα as honour or *auctoritas*, see Dio 53.18.3, *RGDA* 34.3 in Greek, with 2009 ad loc. Cf. Scott (2019: lxix). For the importance of *auctoritas*, see Section 1.2.3.

[50] Joseph. *AJ*. 19.228: τῶν πλεονεξιῶν αὐτῆς ἐπιστόμισμα τοὺς αὐτοκράτορας εἰδώς.

[51] Cf. Joseph. *AJ*. 19.224 for a similar sentiment expressed amongst the soldiery.

[52] Wiseman (2013: 70, 88).   [53] *TLL* 6.1.1294.19ff. E.g. Ov. *Fast.* 1.532 and Plut. *Galb.* 1

typified by a strong antagonism towards the patricians steeped in republican precedent.[54] The possibility is striking and perhaps points to an understanding that placed relations between the senate, the people, and the emperor within that older framework. Moreover, this passage from Josephus elucidates the variety of potential opinions on the imperial succession, the contested nature of such periods, and the encounter of political deliberation with considerations of dynastic continuity.

Thus, the alteration of Flaig's arguments must consider the place of family in dialogues of 'acceptance'. On the face of it, 'acceptance' and any 'dynastic principle' may seem irreconcilable, but this is not the case.[55] Flaig's argument is based on crisis situations during the history of the Roman principate. His interest lies in usurpation, for he believes that the true character of the regime can be understood in those high-stress situations.[56] Therefore, his paradigm does not necessarily reflect how the succession was secured in peaceful situations; his concern is to see how 'acceptance' was lost rather than how it was gained. Acceptance could be won and lost, despite familial connection, but being a member of the imperial family was a key factor in being included in the conversation.[57] Moreover, having usurpations in monarchic systems of government against the ruling dynasty is not impossible; just because there are challenges does not mean that a dynastic principle did not exist.[58] Despite these objections, Flaig's acceptance hypothesis is essential as it takes into account the impact of the opinions of different constituencies across the empire. An alteration proposed here is to reintroduce a certain degree of importance in dynastic issues, as it helped inform the opinions expressed within the dialogue of 'acceptance'.

Concerning the succession, it seems that a wider population perceived the emperor and his family, or the *domus Augusta*, as a separate entity that derived its legitimacy from its primacy in the Roman world, and thus was an important part of the dialogue.[59] From their perspective, they understood that the legitimacy of a Roman emperor could be defined by his familial ties to the ruling dynasty and interacted with a potential *princeps* on these terms.[60] The volatility of acceptance, though, required interactivity from different members of the *domus Augusta*, which created potential

---

[54] Cf. Wiseman (2019: 14) for analysis of this passage. Cf. Griffin (1991: 27, 32).
[55] Hekster (2001); cf. Hekster (2015: 11); cf. Davenport and Mallan (2014) for a study of Cassius Dio's conception of the ideal imperial succession.
[56] Flaig (2019: 11); cf. Shaw (1984: 34).   [57] Flaig (2010: 275–88).   [58] Hekster (2001: 36).
[59] Cf. Hekster (2015: 177).   [60] Cf. Rowe (2002: 174).

instabilities and expectations of generosity. We now turn to examples of such interactivity and volatility.

3.2.2 Family Matters: The domus Augusta and 'Dynastic' Principles under the Julio-Claudians

A full discussion of familial strategies in the Roman world, such as marriage, adoption, and inheritance, and different familial terms such as *paterfamilias*, *gens*, and *familia* unfortunately cannot be undertaken here.[61] Focus must train on the term *domus* and its flexibility, as it can encapsulate issues at stake in dynastic legitimacy, which in turn created the atmosphere of competing and changing allegiances in the perception of dynastic continuity.

A *domus* was a kinship group that cut across other familial terms in Latin, such as *gens* and *familia*, in that it included relations from both the father's and the mother's lines.[62] It denoted the physical house, the people within it, and the broader kinship groups of the family, including its past and future.[63] *Domus* lacked a strict legal definition and, as such, it cut across lines to include married women *sine manu*, stepbrothers, in-laws, and maternal ancestors, too.[64] Such flexibility translated to the term *domus Augusta*, as seen above in the *SCPP*.[65] The paternal *pro re publica statio* could thus be inherited by those within the *domus*, thus projecting political and dynastic continuity and stability into the future.[66]

At this juncture, we can again stress the familial aspect of the consensus-building rituals that stress unanimity, which we saw with the acclamation of Augustus as *pater patriae* in 2 BC.[67] The fate of the state hinged upon the successful maintenance of the imperial *domus*, and familial terminology was used to describe positions of power and authority. Moreover, the

---

[61] See Christoforou (2016: 39–48) for discussion and bibliography; Smith (2006); Corbier (1994a, 1994b, 1995); Saller (1984); Weaver (1972).

[62] Corbier (1994a: 70); Saller (1984: 342–6).   [63] Saller (1984: 342), for the definition.

[64] Corbier (1994a: 70); cf. Saller (1984: 344): '*Domus* could refer variously to a man's circle of living kin or to his descent group including ancestors and descendants. The extent of the kin encompassed by the *domus*, as by the *familia*, could be greater or lesser, from the whole *gens* to a much narrower circle of relatives. In these respects, *domus* is very much like *familia*, but there is one notable difference: *domus* is an appropriate term for cognate, as well as agnate, kin.'

[65] For a recent overview and analysis of the implementation of the *domus Augusta* and its iterations from Augustus onwards in its projection through inscription, coinage, and portraiture, see Hekster (2015: 162–202), esp. 177: 'The continuous central formulations of imperial descent created a new social structure, in which the elevated position of the imperial household became obvious to all.'

[66] Lott (2012: 9). Cf. Cooley (2019: 76) and Gell. *NA* 15.7.3. Cf. Hekster (2015: 58–109) for the continuation of this theme through the early principate towards the Severans.

[67] Suet. *Aug.* 58.1–2; see pp. 43–45 for analysis.

analogy of the emperor and the position of *pater* suggested the implied relationship between the emperor and the people: one of paternal authority and filial piety.[68] As Dio suggested, the designation itself implies a certain power over all people and a relationship that meant that leaders would love them as children, and they in turn would respect emperors as fathers.[69] Dio also argues that the appellation of *pater* had been one of honour, whereas it developed into giving the emperor *patria potestas* over all people, suggesting a change over time in meaning. Nonetheless, the prevalence of the title throughout our period underlines the importance of familial language in responses to the emperor's role in society. Furthermore, Dio's words suggest a reciprocal relationship based on mutual respect, which of course allows for both successes and failures in such a relationship, as evinced by the rest of Dio's narrative into the third century AD.

Whatever Augustus' intentions were with the *domus* as a way to outline a succession plan, the flexibility of the term *domus Augusta* allowed for varying receptions of who was worthy and thus could be included in that grouping.[70] That said, such flexibility added a sense of uncertainty as to what, or on whom, the proper focus of loyalty should be. That object was in any case a moving target, repeatedly transformed by death and by reversals among the members of the *domus Augusta*.[71] Such flexibility in Roman familial strategies could open the potential for misunderstanding or competing loyalties across the empire.[72] The willingness of different constituencies across the empire to accept and continue to support members of the imperial family, even those who were seemingly out of favour, suggested that the whole household could be subject to adulation, and that acceptance ebbed and flowed according to the varied fortunes of members of the *domus Augusta*.[73]

This is observed by the ambiguity of Ovid's use of the name *Caesar*, which Hardie argues gave the impression that, even though separate individuals were implied, differences were elided to the extent that an

---

[68] Weinstock (1971: 200–1), esp. 204. Cf. Severy (2003: 158–65).

[69] Dio 53.18.3. Saller (1994: 102–32), on *potestas* and *pietas*.   [70] Lott (2012: 5).

[71] Millar (1993: 8); cf. Lott (2012: 15). Such precarity of life in the domus is observed in the *consolatio ad Liviam*, too, esp. ll. 59–72, which talks about the *Caesaris domum* and the pain of losing Drusus, Marcellus, and Agrippa.

[72] Corbier (1994a: 67–8), on the evidence from Carthage and Corinth that talks of a *gens Augusta*, which seems to be a conflation of terms that Corbier calls nonsensical. Carthage: *ILAfr.* 353; Corinth: *Corinth*, 8.2.17. Cf. Christoforou (2021).

[73] Suet. *Aug.* 65, esp. 3, for the calls for Julia the Elder's return. The political and familial intermix here, as it is the *populus Romanus* who calls for her return and it was in the public assembly that Augustus admonishes his daughter.

'unbroken succession' within the family was maintained. This is seen in *Tristia* 2.230: 'and Caesar undertakes war for mighty Caesar' (*bellaque pro magno Caesare Caesar obit*).[74] Another example appears in the context of Tiberius' triumph on 23 October AD 12 (*Pont.* 2.2.67–74):

> tempus adest aptum precibus. valet ille videtque |quas fecit vires, Roma, valere tuas. |incolumis coniunx sua pulvinaria servat,| promovet Ausonium filius imperium. |praeterit ipse suos animo Germanicus annos |nec vigor est Drusi nobilitate minor. |adde nurus neptesque pias natosque nepotum | ceteraque Augustae membra valere domus.

> The present time is right for prayers. That man is well and observes your strength is well, Rome, that strength which he made. His unshaken wife preserves his holy couch. The son advances the empire of the Italians. Germanicus himself outstrips his years in spirit. Drusus' strength is not smaller than his nobility. Add that the daughters-in-law and faithful grand-daughters, the children of grandsons, and the remaining offshoots of the *Domus Augusta* are well.[75]

The family is presented as a collective, alongside the mention of successive generations, with the wish for good health for the whole *domus Augusta*. Moreover, Ovid's descriptions of the imperial family, even if laudatory, are nevertheless vague and transferable; few members get named explicitly, allowing for Ovid to be supple and alter the subject matter as the fortunes of the *domus Augusta* unfolded, which mirrored the flexibility of the *domus* under Augustus.[76] Germanicus and Drusus are the only named members of the family, with familial nouns used instead, such as *coniunx* and *nepos*, with Ov. *Pont.* 4.13.25–33, where Augustus has now died, and his *numen* has transcended to aethereal abodes. Tiberius is mentioned periphrastically as being equal in courage to his father, who takes up the reins of power (*frena . . . imperii*). Germanicus and Drusus are at this point not named but rather called 'youths' (*iuvenes*) who are sure supports for their father. Similarly in this passage, then, save for Livia and Augustus, the members of the *domus* are not mentioned by name, allowing Ovid to be vague and stress the family, which thus can be fudged over, changed, and

---

[74] Hardie (2002: 254–5): 'The ambiguity is a hazard of the imperial fiction that "Caesar = Caesar", power maintained in an unbroken succession through individuals with the same name, and in a sense the same person. In exile poetry Ovid uses repetitions of Caesar to blur the difference between biologically separate individuals of the imperial family, Augustus and Tiberius'; cf. Ov. *Pont.* 2.8.1, 37–8. Cf. Pasco-Pranger (2006: 53–8) on the domus in the Fasti

[75] Cf. Severy (2003: 217); cf. *Inscr. It.* 13.2.17: *Ti. Caesar. triumphavit | ex Illurico.*

[76] For such flexibility, see the fortunes of the *Claudii Nerones*, in the *consolatio ad Liviam*, the *SCPP*, with Vervaet (2020) and Kuttner (1995: 88–9, 143–4) on the Boscoreale cups.

substituted.[77] The example from Ovid, moreover, is observable in different evidence across the empire. Wrinkles in allegiances existed empire-wide, with support for different members of the imperial family (not constricted by gender) contributing to the mosaic of opinion that informed the wider population's view of the emperor, his household, and the question of succession.

Epigraphical evidence points to this. The complicated nature of familial ordering in the imperial family would potentially serve to confuse people across the empire, leading to different responses that would involve inclusions and exclusions in the conception of the *domus*, as well as issues of proper naming. One example comes from a dossier of documents from Sardis that dates from 5 BC to 2 BC. They honour Menogenes, a Sardian aristocrat that went on embassies to Augustus. In the first document (l. 7), he is called the *eldest* of the children of Augustus: ὁ πρεσβύτατος τῶν τοῦ Σεβαστοῦ παίδων. The second document (l. 26), which is Augustus' epistolary response to the Asians and Sardians, corrects this slightly with the *elder* son of two children τοῦ πρεσβυτέρου μου τῶν παίδων.[78] Furthermore, to complement this more restrictive picture is a more inclusive statement for the gratefulness shown to Augustus for the benefactions they received, citing himself and his whole family.[79] Thus, Augustus includes his whole family in the equation. The Sardians seem to respond to the latter of Augustus' statements in the third document (ll. 33–4), which duly includes expressions of joy and goodwill of the city for Gaius and the whole *domus*. Still, they maintain the *eldest* appellation for Gaius in mentioning him as the recipient of the embassy (ll. 30–1: to Gaius Caesar the eldest of his children; πρὸς Γάϊον Καίσαρα | τόν πρεσβύτατον τῶν παίδων), suggesting that their reception of Augustus' *domus* was different from the emperor's.[80]

In Carthage, we see a conflation of Latin terms, where the dedication of a priest, P. Perelius Hedulus, is to *genti Augustae*, using the more restrictive designation *gens*.[81] This is mirrored in another inscription from Corinth: col. I: '*Tiberio* | *Caesari*; col. II: *Ant(oniae)* | *Augu(stae)* | *Genti Augustae*.'[82] Corbier identifies those commemorated as Tiberius Gemellus and

---

[77] Cf. Millar (1993: 12–13, 15–16).

[78] I owe this point to Rowe (2002: 146), who argues that this means Agrippa Postumus is excluded from the equation, meaning the inclusion of Gaius and Lucius.

[79] *EJ* 99 = *IGR* 4.1756 = *I. Sardis* 7.1.8: l. 27: εἴς τε ἐμὲ καὶ τοὺς ἐμοὺς πάντας ἐνδείκνυσθαι. Cf. Lavan (2013: 219–21) and Oliver (1989: n. 217).

[80] Rowe (2002: 145–7).   [81] *ILAfr* 353; Corbier (1994a: 68).

[82] *Corinth* 8.2.17: 'To Tiberius Caesar; To Antonia Augusta, To the *Gens Augusta*.'

Antonia, Augustus' niece, mother of Germanicus and grandmother of Gaius Caligula, who is not part of the *gens Iulia*, if that indeed is what the inscription was meant to allude to.[83] Perhaps this can be explained as a confusion about the appropriate term for the imperial family, and indeed there is evidence from Corinth under Nero for the use of *domus Augusta*, but it shows the scope of confusion as to how and who to commemorate.[84]

Perhaps a more direct attestation of popular opinion can come from the graffiti on the walls of Pompeii. For instance, in the *vestibulum* of the house of Q. Poppaeus Sabinus (Casa del Menandro),[85] where there was a *Lararium* called the *Lares Augustosi*,[86] the outside wall has a graffito about Octavia.[87] This should be read in the context of other graffiti in the area, namely those that favourably mention her erstwhile husband and his new wife, the Pompeian Poppaea.[88] Thus, the existence of this evidence suggests a mosaic of opinion concerning the *domus Augusta*, where well wishes for different, competing members of the imperial family could appear simultaneously.

In conjunction, the oath of allegiance at Paphos on Cyprus takes an interesting view of the *domus* under Tiberius: first, the oath to obey is all-encompassing, which includes 'Tiberius Caesar Augustus, son of Augustus and his whole household' (Τιβέριον Καίσαρα Σεβαστοῦ υὸν Σεβαστὸν σὺν τῶι ἄπαντι αὐτοῦ οἴκωι); second, however, in the proposing of divine honours, the designation is more specific, which includes Tiberius Caesar Augustus, son of Augustus, and 'to the sons of his blood' (υοῖς τε τοῦ αἵματος αὐτοῦ) exclusively.[89] Such ambiguities might be easily explained away, though they do suggest a jaggedness in the reception of the *domus Augusta* and its membership, allowing for different interpretations of who was included and excluded in the rubric to be determined on the ground by the commemorators.[90]

Staying on Cyprus, there is a commemorative inscription of a gymnasiarch, who was also high priest of the imperial cult at Salamis,

---

[83] Corbier (1994a: 68).

[84] Corbier (1994a: 68); *Corinth*, 8.2.68, with Gaius Julius Laconis, which calls him the high priest of the *domus Augusta* (*archieri domus Aug(ustae)*). Cf. *IG*. 3.805 for the title of his priesthood in Greek, which has it as the high priest of the divine *Augusti* and the 'house' of the *Augusti*: Γά· Ἰούλιον Σπαρτια|τικὸν ἀρχιερέα θε|[ῶν] Σεβαστῶν κ[αὶ]|[γέ]νους Σε[β]αστῶν.

[85] Franklin (2001: 109–11).

[86] *CIL* 4.8282. Cf. Franklin (2001: 112); Flower (2017), on *Lares* in general.

[87] *CIL* 4.8277; Franklin (2001: 112): *Octavia Augusti [vale h]abias [pr]opit[–] sa(lutem)*. I wonder if there is a sense of irony with this graffito – a facetious allusion to her demise.

[88] *CIL* 4.1074: *iudiciis Augusti Augustae felicit(er). Vobis salvis felices sumus p[e]rpetuo.* See, in particular, Franklin (2001: 121–2), where there are numerous graffiti concerning Nero and his wife.

[89] Mitford (1960: 75–9); *SEG* 18.578. Cf. Christoforou (2021: 98–9).   [90] Lott (2012: 15).

which in fact is a palimpsest.[91] The first edition was dedicated to Augustus and mentions that the gymnasiarch was a priest for Gaius and Lucius as well. The second edition inscribed on top removed the names of the twins and placed the names of Tiberius' grandchildren, Tiberius Gemellus and Germanicus, instead. This indicates a Salaminian sensitivity to the changing nature of the imperial family, for they changed the names of those who would be the future of the empire once new scions of the *domus* appeared.[92]

The fact that these appear to be statue bases is telling, as erecting statues of the emperor and his family was both a method of marking out status within a local context and a manner in which to observe the reception of the fortunes of the imperial household.[93] An example in comparison can be observed by a group from Thespiae, reconstructed as Julia the Elder with her sons Gaius and Lucius and Agrippa holding Agrippina the Elder in his arms.[94] The attention to detail and suppleness are striking, as the young boys Gaius and Lucius are described as Lucius and Gaius 'Caesar', which suggests their adoption into the *gens Iulia* by Augustus but also within the wider family of their biological father Agrippa, with whom they are presented.[95] In this context, then, we can observe an inclusive understanding of Augustus' family, which commemorates the political reality when Agrippa was ascendant on his second command in the eastern empire, holding *imperium* and *tribunicia potestas*, and points to the future by depicting the next generation of the *domus* as young children.[96] The wider imperial focus should also include the local aspect, as it is the people of Thespiae marking themselves out in commemorating the *domus*. Indeed, the evidence discussed thus far should be read in local political, social, and cultural structures, which might tell us of idiosyncrasies in the systems of advancement within and between those communities.[97] In all senses, we find ourselves squarely in the realm of benefaction and euergetism, where the generosity of the benefactor and community are displayed, and the emperor and his family are found firmly in the language of such interactions.

---

[91] *Salamine XIII* 131a–b = Mitford (1947: 222–3), with Kantiréa (2008: 93–4); *IGR* 3.997. Millar (2002: 309–11), for more evidence across the empire on the attention paid to the imperial household, in particular *IGR* III 137; *OGIS* 532; *ILS* 8781 for an oath of Paphlagonia: καὶ τοῖς τ[έκ]νοις ἐγό[νοις τε] | αὐτοῦ (sc. Augustus).

[92] Cf. Tac. *Ann.* 2.84. Cf. Scott (1930a, 1930b).   [93] Revell (2009: 83).

[94] Rose (1997: 13–14) and cat. 82, 150–1.   [95] Rose (1997: 15); *AE* (1928) 49–50.

[96] Cf. Dio 54.12.4, 19.6, 24.5–7.   [97] Hellström (2020: 165, 176), for evidence from North Africa.

3.3 Exhibiting Generosity through the Next Generation: Heirs and Benefactors

Part of the public presentation of a young male member of the imperial family was the interaction with the people.[98] This involved meeting the people in public spaces, engaging with them by means of gesture or speech, distributing largesse, and giving and attending public shows, such as the circus, theatre, or gladiatorial combat. These public meetings were a place where the people could communicate sentiment and opinion towards the emperor and the men of the imperial family.[99] Therefore, it was a method by which the people could join into the conversation of acceptance, which started early in the life of a potential emperor.

The evidence for this is as follows. In the *Res Gestae*, Augustus lists spectacles that were held not only under his name but also under the names of his sons and his grandsons, suggesting that these deeds and expenses were of importance to his principate: these included fifteen gladiatorial games, three athletic spectacles, and twenty-six beast hunts in the circus, forum, and amphitheatre that he gave in his and his grandsons names.[100] The mention of their 'name' in Latin in the singular (in my name and of my sons and grandsons – *meo nomine aut filorum meorum et nepotum*) is important. These games were under the name of Caesar, or perhaps under the *gens Iulia*. *Nomen* could denote a family group who inherited that name through a *gens*, suggesting that it is used here to denote the imperial collective.[101] Thus, Augustus and his sons are portrayed corporately in front of the *populus Romanus*. This placed Gaius and Lucius, in the role of benefactors, in direct communication with the people, in a medium where popular expression could reach them directly.[102]

Such an image of young *principes* in a public setting is corroborated by other evidence: Augustus is shown with his grandsons at the theatre;[103] he also exhibited Germanicus with his children at a public show.[104] The crowds at the theatre reacted to Gaius and Lucius with cheers and applause.[105] Also,

---

[98] For examples, see Hurlet (1997), Rowe (2002), Hekster (2002: 30–9), and Bowersock (1984: 169–88).

[99] Cf. Millar (1977: 369–75); see Severy (2003) and Vervaet (2020) for more on the importance of 'buttresses for domination' (*subsidia dominationi*) for Augustus.

[100] Aug. *RG*. 22.   [101] Cf. Smith (2006: 15–32) on *gens* and *nomen*.

[102] Veyne (1990: 347); Millar (1965: 369–70).   [103] Suet. *Aug.* 43.5. Cf. Dio 54.27.1 and 55.9.1–2.

[104] Suet. *Aug.* 34.2.

[105] Suet. *Aug* 56.2: that Augustus would be concerned if his sons 'deserved' their acclamation speaks to the world of political contestation in his principate. Cf. Morell et al. (2019); Dio 54.27.1; Dio 55.9.2. Cf. Osgood (2013: 24–5). On the vacillating spectrum of *levitas* and *gravitas* in popularity, see Yavetz (1965) and Yavetz (1969: 97–102).

in the reign of Augustus, Tiberius is seen to have given a banquet and largesse to the people.[106] Drusus (Germanicus and Claudius' father) was named a joint heir (*coheres*) by Augustus in the senate, and when he died Drusus was eulogised by Augustus in front of the people, wishing that future Caesars would be like him, which suggests exemplarity in life and death to be praised and emulated into the future.[107] Drusus presents us with an interesting case, for even though Drusus did not have a direct filial connection with Augustus, he was nevertheless, according to Suetonius, an heir to Augustus' legacy.[108] Such evidence suggests that Drusus could be interpreted as a potential *princeps* and figured as politically prominent with his brother Tiberius in the twenties BC.[109]

Germanicus' popularity reportedly preceded him to the extent that his life was put in danger when he made public appearances.[110] Fortunately, there is papyrological evidence that can shed light on Germanicus' inter-action with a large crowd in public. In *P.Oxy* 2435, there is a scene in Alexandria where Germanicus' speech is interjected repeatedly with laud-atory acclamations from the Alexandrians to the effect of wishing luck, life, and health on him,[111] to the extent that Germanicus had to implore that they refrain from showing approval until he had finished.[112] The vociferous public adulation of Germanicus that has been recorded suggests that a wider population expected that Germanicus was to become emperor in the future, and they were using public occasion to express their acceptance of this possibility.

Tiberius gave largesse to the people on the occasions that his grand-sons, via his adopted son Germanicus and biological son Drusus, came of age, which was also commended by the senate.[113] In conjunction, Nero (the son of Germanicus) is shown at his first entry to the forum to be giving largesse to the *plebs*.[114] The references to the *dies tirocinii* and the first entry to the forum are of interest, and they refer to the start of the educative experience in military and political life for young men.[115] As

---

[106] Suet. *Tib.* 20.1.
[107] Suet. *Claud.* 1.5. Cf. Lott (2012). Cf. *Consolatio ad Liviam* 17–19, 25–7 for Drusus' military exploits.
[108] Corbier (1991: 74).
[109] For more on the prominence of Drusus, see Vervaet (2020: 149–69) and Kuttner (1995: 172–93); cf. Hor. *Carm.* 4.4.27–8.
[110] Suet. *Cal.* 4.1; cf. *P.Oxy* 2435; *EJ* 375.   [111] *P.Oxy.* 2435 recto = *EJ* 379 ll.4–5, 17.
[112] *P.Oxy.* 2435 recto = *EJ* 379 ll.5–9. cf. *EJ* 320, ll. 41–5 = *Sel. Pap.* II, 211, where Germanicus reproaches the Alexandrian crowd for addressing him with ἰσοθέους ἐκφωνήσεις (acclamations equal to the gods) (l. 36).
[113] Suet. *Tib.* 54.1.   [114] Tac. *Ann.* 3.29.1–3.   [115] Cf. Section 3.2.2.

pointed out by Bonner, this *tirocinium*, either *fori* or *militiae*, can be translated as 'recruitment to the forum' or 'recruitment to military life', respectively.[116] This was a year that commenced when the young man assumed his *toga virilis*. As stated by Quintilian, the timing of the *tirocinium* was essential, as if it was done too early they would be ill-equipped and if it was done too late then the fear of public speaking would increase.[117] The key was to experience first-hand the skills of public life, and it was one that was fundamental to the ideology of the early principate, which saw the elevation of the young members of the *domus Augusta* within the political culture of Rome.[118]

Moreover, this has parallels in the title *princeps iuventutis*, a title given to Gaius and Lucius by the *equites*,[119]the point being that this was the beginning of their road to becoming the leaders of the next generation.[120] Indeed, this designation appears on coinage of different denominations, including aurei and denarii that depict on the reverse Gaius and Lucius standing, wearing togas, and holding shields and spears, with PRINC IVVENT appearing as the legend.[121] These coins were produced in large quantities and were geographically widespread, suggesting the importance of this image and their designations for Augustus and the succession.[122] Fascinatingly, the design also appears on lead tokens, which were a sub-monetary currency used at Rome.[123] As Rowan points out, these must have been in response to the coin series struck commemorating their roles as *principes iuventutis*, as the obverse depicts them togate and seated on curule chairs, and the reverse shows the shields and the spears.[124] Such evidence suggests that the images of Gaius and Lucius as leaders of the youth were displayed to different audiences across the Roman empire, and in the case of the tokens the *plebs urbana*, which places into perspective the importance of the interactions between the

---

[116] Bonner (1977: 84–5).   [117] Quint. *Inst.* 12.6.2–3.

[118] Bonner (1977: 85); Quint. *Inst.* 10.5.19; Tac. *Dial.* 34.

[119] Lott (2012: 7); *RG* 14. Vassileiou (1984: 829). See Gartrell (2021: chap. 4), esp. 155–8.

[120] Lott (2012: 8); Ov. *Ars. Am.* 1.194: 'now the leader of the youth, then in the future, of the grown' (*nunc iuvenum princeps, deinde future senum*). Cf. Millar (1988: 18); cf. Tac. *Ann.* 12.41.1 for Nero's advancement, including the title *princeps iuventutis*; cf. Suet. *Ner.* 7.2.

[121] *RIC* I² 205–12.   [122] Rowan (2019: 164).

[123] On tokens and their uses, see Rowan (2020), esp. 251–3. Cf. Russell (2020) for the rich and responsive world of imagery in the Augustan principate, here on the reception of the *corona civica*, Victory and a shield, which all have slight alterations in context, including coinage, altars of the *Lares*, and lamps (figure 2.9: British Museum 1756,0101.618a).

[124] *TURS* 3 (Tokens of the Ancient Mediterranean database, https://coins.warwick.ac.uk/token-types/id/TURS3), argued by Clare Rowan, 'Token Images of the Julio-Claudian Dynasty', The Julio-Claudian Age Seminar, Oxford, 22 January 2019.

imperial family and the Roman people and engagement with political imagery connected to the *domus Augusta*.[125]

Princeps iuventutis is also a title that is not restricted to the Julio-Claudians, as there are many attestations on inscriptions from different eras of the principate, such as Domitian under Titus' reign,[126] Commodus, under his father Marcus Aurelius,[127] Lucius Helvius, Pertinax's son,[128] and Geta, Septimius Severus' son.[129] The passage from childhood to manhood is also commemorated in the Menogenes dossier at Sardis.[130] The first document reports the sending of an embassy from the Asian league and Sardis on the occasion of Gaius' assumption of the *toga virilis*:

Ἐπεὶ Γάϊος Ἰούλιος Καῖσαρ ὁ πρεσβύτατος τῶν τοῦ Σεβαστοῦ παίδων τὴν εὐκταιοτάτην | ἐκ περιπορφύρου λαμπρὰν τῷ παντὶ κό<σ>μῳ ἀνείληφε τήβεννον, ἥδονταί τε πάντες | ἄνθρωποι συνδιεγειρομένας ὁρῶντες τῷ Σεβαστῷ τὰς ὑπὲρ τῶν παίδων εὐχάς, ἥ τε ἡ|μετέρα πόλις ἐπὶ τῇ τοσαύτῃ εὐτυχίᾳ τὴν ἡμέραν τὴν ἐκ παιδὸς ἄνδρα τελησῦσα[ν] | αὐτὸν ἱερὰν ἔκρινεν εἶναι.

Since Gaius Julius Caesar, the eldest of Augustus' children took the *latus clavus* instead of the *toga praetexta*, as desired by the whole world, all the people rejoiced in seeing the rising prayers for Augustus on behalf of his children, and our polis on account of this success decided that the day on which he completed his youth and became a man should be a sacred day.[131]

Thus, the city would commemorate this day, on which wreathes would be worn, sacrifices made, and wishes of welfare for Gaius professed,[132] which would be replicated on the day that they received the news.[133] Further, Gaius' image would be set up in Augustus' temple.[134] Here is evidence of the temporal interest in the lives of the young men of the

[125] Cf. Rowan (2020: 252): 'if small, leaden, circular objects could be used for distributions during a festival or during a banquet or for some other purpose, then it was only the image that communicated to users the object's validity.'

[126] *CIL* 3.12218, from Apa in Galatia. Cf. Hammond (1956: 83).

[127] HA. *Comm.* 2.1–2; cf. *CIL* 8.11928, which has the titles *princeps iuventutis* and *consul designatus*. Cf. Dio 72(71).22(2).1. For evidence of Marcus Aurelius' time as *princeps iuventutis*: Dio 72(71).35.5.

[128] *AE* (1904) 65, from Bostra, Arabia.

[129] *CIL* 8.17727, from Aquae Flavianae in Numidia. It should be noted that Geta's name was chiselled out. However, the line is still legible, with PRINC. IV. at the end of the fifth line. This is compared with another of Septimius at Lauriacum in Noricum (*AE* (1912) 293 = *AE* (1909) 248 = *AE* (2006) 1001 = *ILLPRON* 961), which has the same title restored but less concretely.

[130] Cf. p. 112. For more on Menogenes, and the growth of self-promotion and city euergetism in this period, see Rowe (2002: 145–7).

[131] *EJ* 99 = *IGR* 4.1756 = *I. Sardis* 7.1.8, ll. 7–11.

[132] *EJ* 99 = *IGR* 4.1756 = *I. Sardis* 7.1.8, ll. 11–13   [133] *EJ* 99 = *IGR* 4.1756 = *I. Sardis* 7.1.8, 14–15.

[134] *EJ* 99 = *IGR* 4.1756 = *I. Sardis* 7.1.8, ll. 13–14.

domus Augusta: not only is the felicitous present being commemorated civilly but the hope of the future.

Claudius is seen to exhibit his son Britannicus in front of the soldiers and the people when he was young, in the context of an assembly of soldiers and the plebs at games, at which Claudius would wish for favourable omens with the shouts of the crowd in accompaniment.[135] Such informal political interactivity between people and *princeps* is also reflected in the Trojan games, where Claudius showcased both Britannicus and the recently adopted Nero.[136] In a similar situation, Nero in triumphal dress and Britannicus in the *toga praetexta* appear together at circus games in order to gain the affection of the crowd.[137] Nero is also shown to have given largesse to the people on his coming of age.[138] As such, we see a repeated effort to display young Caesars in front of the Roman people.

Progenies Caesarum in Nerone defecit. As Suetonius so pithily stated, the death of Nero spelt the end of the race of the Caesars.[139] This opened the pool from which an emperor could be made.[140] However, the system of presenting an heir to the soldiers and the people remained a factor beyond the Julio-Claudians, through the second century to the Severan age. For instance, according to the *Historia Augusta*, L. Ceionius Commodus was adopted by Hadrian in AD 136 and was thus named L. Aelius Caesar. The adoption was followed afterwards by circus games and a donative to the troops and people.[141] Similar evidence can be seen for Antoninus Pius in the context of his adoption by Hadrian.[142] Under Marcus Aurelius, Commodus is seen to be giving largesse as part of his move towards adolescence.[143] Septimius Severus bestowed names and titles on his sons Caracalla and Geta,[144] and he gives the troops a donative within the context of Severus' Parthian campaign.[145]

All the above evidence points to a direct interaction between the male members of the imperial family and a wider population in decidedly political arenas with various 'constituencies', suggesting an attentiveness

---

[135] Suet. *Claud.* 27.2. cf. Suet. *Claud.* 43.1, on wanting to give Britannicus the *toga virilis*.

[136] Tac. *Ann.* 11.11.2; cf. Suet. *Ner.* 7.1.   [137] Tac. *Ann.* 12.41.2.

[138] Suet. *Ner.* 7.2; Tac. *Ann.* 12.41.1.   [139] Suet. *Gal.* 1.1.

[140] Plin. *Pan.* 7.6: *Imperaturus omnibus eligi debet ex omnibus*; Syme (1958: 234). Cf. Tac. *Hist.* 1.16.

[141] HA, *Hadr.* 23.12. Cf. HA, *Ael.* 1.2. For the issues concerning the succession of Hadrian, see Barnes (1967 74–9) and Champlin (1976: 79–89). On L. Ceionius Commodus: *PIR2* C 605. Cf. Davenport and Mallan (2014).

[142] HA, *Ant.* 4.9. Cf. Dio 69.20.2–5.   [143] HA, *Comm.* 2.1.

[144] On the nature of Severan succession and the issues therein, see Mastrocinque (2011b) and Hammond (1956: 114–15); cf. HA, *Sev.* 10.3–6.

[145] HA, *Sev.* 16.5.

to their acceptance by current and future Caesars. A familial aspect was accentuated by these meetings and allowed an emperor and potential heirs to cultivate their relationship with the wider population (including the military) in order to bolster the acceptance of their position in the world and to ensure that the succession was tied to the imperial family.[146] These interactions of generosity were an important topic in the understanding of the Roman emperor's role in the world that not only started early before the assumption of his principate but continued thereafter.[147] In all, these activities were complex interactions that tied together the legitimacies of present and future Caesars, intertwining their political legacies. The conversation of acceptance carried out through actions and arenas of generosity was fundamental to the continued legitimacy and future reputation of emperors.

3.4   Generosity As *princeps*

The evidence of generosity indicates that benefaction is an essential component in an emperor's life. However, the forms and distribution of imperial beneficence are a complex problem with several moving parts, in particular because what could be considered as falling under the emperor's generosity is wide-ranging.[148] The essential point to make about the variegated evidence concerns consistency: it all falls under the rubric of the emperor's benefactions and generosity, even with the appreciation of the political, social, economic, and ideological contexts, as argued by Noreña:

> the subjects of a pre-modern empire had difficulty distinguishing between the institutional apparatus of the state and its embodiment in the figure of the emperor, and, even more important, because the ideal of imperial *beneficia* corresponded to a popular *mentalité* and to the desire of the emperor's subjects to imagine that they were ruled by a 'good' sovereign.[149]

---

[146] Cf. Osgood (2013: 34); cf. Rowe (2002: 87–8).   [147] See further Section 3.4.

[148] Veyne (1990: 347–77); cf. Millar (1977) for his discussion of the emperor's benefactions in different arenas: 368–75 (the people at Rome), 401–10 (on the acquisition of city status and the importance of the emperor), 410–34, 447–56 (for the interactions between cities and the emperor for the securing of privileges, maintenance of status, problems of exemptions, monetary contributions for building projects, reconstructions after natural disaster, and the maintenance of temples, priesthoods, and festivals), 477–506 (for grants of citizenships, freedom, cash liberalities, and exemptions from local liturgies).

[149] Noreña (2011: 107), for his discussion of the attribution of all governmental actions to the person of the emperor, citing Veyne (1976: 658–60).

Thus, there is an inevitable conflation of these different forms under the banner of the emperor's generosity, which makes it difficult to tease out the nuances of context. The first example from Dio about Marcus Aurelius will highlight the potential anatomy of discourse about imperial generosity. In the epitome of book 72, different examples of the emperor's generous and financial actions appear in the same chapter, something that is also reflected in other texts.[150] The first vignette is of Marcus' return to Rome and his audience with the people, in which there is an interactive scene where the people shout and gesture the number eight in order to get gold pieces for banquets; Marcus replies and gives them 800 sesterces each.[151] This fits into the theme of the emperor giving out one-off gifts of money, known as *congiaria*, to the people,[152] as well as the equivalent largesse, or *donativum*, to the military.[153] Indeed, the economy and the emperorship seem to be inexorably intertwined, in which lay an expectation that, if there was a shortfall in funds, the money would have to be found at the initiative of the emperor.[154]

The second vignette involves Marcus Aurelius' remission of debts owed to what Dio calls τὸ βασιλικὸν and τὸ δημόσιον, that is, to the *fiscus* and the *aerarium,* the treasuries of the emperor and the state, respectively.[155] The problems of distinction in the organisation and revenue of the government's wealth aside, these distinct bodies of wealth nonetheless exhibit a wavering between public and private, which should not be surprising given the ambiguities of the office of the Roman emperor. Here, the power of the emperor is such that a remission of debts for both were under his jurisdiction, which could only add to the idea of the emperor being the primary benefactor in the government and the primary

[150] See, e.g. Suet. *Aug.* 41–42; Suet. *Tib.* 46–48; Suet. *Cal.* 17–18; Suet. *Claud.* 18–21; Suet. *Vesp.* 17–19; Suet. *Tit.* 8.3–4; HA, *Hadr.* 7.6–12, 10.1, 17.3; HA, *Ant.* 8–9; cf. Ruggiero, *Diz. Epigr.* 'Liberalitas' for the extensive treatment of the different forms of the emperor's liberality, esp. 839 for his discussion on the problem of distinguishing *liberalitas* from *congiaria*, one-off donations to the people, and 875 for the same with *donativi,* similar donations but for the military.
[151] Dio 72(71)32.1–2. Aldrete (2003: 91), on this scene; cf. Dunbabin (2003: 72–102), on public dining and banquets.
[152] Millar (1977: 135–9), for further examples; cf. Ruggiero, *Diz. Epigr.* 'Liberalitas' 837–8 for a discussion on the definitions of *liberalitas* and *congiarium.*
[153] Veyne (1990: 338–41). Some examples: *RG* 15.3; Suet. *Aug.* 101.2; Suet. *Tib.* 48.2; Tac. *Ann.* 12.69.2; Plut. *Galb.* 2.2; Suet. *Dom.* 2.3; HA, *Hadr.* 5.7; HA, *Marc.* 7.9; Hdn. 1.5.1. On donatives to the military and examples, see Campbell (1984: 165–71).
[154] Such is the implication of the vignette in HA, *Marc.* 17.4–5; 21.9, discussed by Shaw (2019: 3–4), with comparative evidence in n. 13: Suet. *Calig.* 58; Dio 59.21, 68.2.2 and 74.5.3–5.
[155] Dio 72(71)32.2. Cf. Millar (1963) on the remit of the imperial *fiscus,* and esp. 41, on the difficulty of distinguishing between public and private in terms of its impact and revenue. Cf. Brunt (1990: 136–63); cf. Millar (1977: 198–9). On the *aerarium,* see Millar (1964b: 33–40).

source of generosity.[156] As such, the emperorship was a lynchpin in the future health of the Roman economy.[157]

The third vignette records Marcus' donations to many cities, in particular a donation to Smyrna for earthquake relief.[158] Importantly, the final phrases of the chapter expose the spectre of refusal in the actions of the Roman emperor:

> ἀφ᾽ οὗπερ καὶ νῦν θαυμάζω τῶν αἰτιωμένων αὐτὸν ὡς οὐ μεγαλόφρονα γενόμενον· τὰ μὲν γὰρ ἄλλα οἰκονομικώτατος ὡς ἀληθῶς ἦν, τῶν δ᾽ ἀναγκαίων ἀναλωμάτων οὐδὲ ἓν ἐξίστατο, καίπερ μήτε τινὰ ἐσπράξει χρημάτων, ὥσπερ εἶπον, λυπῶν, καὶ πλεῖστα ὅσα ἐξ ἀνάγκης ἔξω τῶν ἐγκυκλίων δαπανῶν.[159]

> For this reason, I still wonder at those who accuse him of not being a generous emperor. For on the one hand, in the majority of cases, he was most frugal, which he truly was, but on the other hand he did not once shun necessary expenditures, and although distressed he never levied money from anyone, as I said before, and the majority of such costs by necessity were outside of ordinary expenditures.

Dio is incredulous that Marcus was still, in the third century, being accused of not being generous, offering various examples as evidence to illustrate that the emperor always undertook necessary expenditures, never forcibly exacted money, and also paid above the ordinary expenditures, which were ultimately important parts of the legacy of an emperor and his administrative competence. This elucidates the wide reach of the emperor's potential generosity and the personal discretion in decisions involving the action and refusal of gift-giving, allowing for an equally wide range of potential opinions and interpretations of those actions.[160] So, too, was the case with expectations of relief over the burdens of *munera*, as seen in the *senatus consultum* of AD 177, where praise and criticism sit together in the comments of a priest who complains about the burden that gladiatorial shows put on his estate and praises Marcus Aurelius and Commodus for alleviating the cost of the *munus* through a tax break.[161] It is significant that

---

[156] Cf. Noreña (2011: 107). Cf. Ruggiero, *Diz. Epigr.* 'Liberalitas' 876, on evidence on the remission of debts, including the parallel account of remission under Hadrian in Dio (Dio 69.8.12) and the Hadrianic inscription commemorating the event (*CIL* 6.967 = *ILS* 309).
[157] Cf. Shaw (2019: 4).
[158] Dio 72(71)32.3. Cf. Philostr. *VS* 2.9 (582) for Marcus' tears at Aelius Aristides' lamentation for Smyrna's devastation.
[159] Dio 72(71)32.3.
[160] Cf. Dio 72(71)3.3–4, for the example of an ethical appraisal of Marcus' refusal to give a donative to the troops, exhibiting the necessary characteristics to control the troops.
[161] *CIL* 2.6278 = ILS 5163 ll. 5–9 and 17–18, with Carter (2003: 84–6).

the perception of these actions fell under the ethical rubric of the emperors' generosity, which contributed to his perception and legacy. This may feel like a truism, but it needs to be emphasised as it is a different mode of thinking from a more modern economic approach. As with the concept of justice, here there is expectation and fear with respect to generosity.

To tie this further with understandings of justice, vignettes of generosity feature especially in the *Hadriani sententiae*. As noted, the corpus contains examples of interactions between people of different social standing and the emperor Hadrian.[162] Of note are petitions on financial issues, such as the case of a woman petitioning against her child's guardian for the dereliction of alimentary maintenance payments and the appropriation of the child's *congiarium*. In this case, Hadrian finds against the guardian and orders him to supply some of the maintenance for his ward in order to prevent the death of the child.[163] It indicates a potential mentality that the emperor's indulgence and generosity would safeguard the maintenance of children. Interestingly, it bears close resemblance to a papyrus from near the south coast of the Dead Sea in Arabia. This forms part of the 'Babatha dossier', which contains legal documents on a Jewish woman called Babatha and her attempt to secure maintenance for her son Jesus from his pair of guardians.[164] Of note is the deposition recorded in *P. Yadin* 15, and in particular lines 5–15, where Babatha argues for the dereliction in duty from the guardians and requests the resumption of maintenance payments through the implementation of an *alimenta* scheme. It involves an interest of 1.5 per cent on a security for her property, which is then sequestered as the child's upkeep. The case progresses, with one of the guardians being summoned to the tribunal on the charges that he profited from the orphan's money.[165] It is important to note that this sort of thing could and did occur in the empire, that an illiterate Jewish woman could use legal channels to secure her interests, and that recourse to the Roman government was an option that was exercised, which indicates a knowledge of the intercessory power of the Roman authorities.[166] Thus, the more fictitious *Hadriani sententiae* and the documentary evidence of the Babatha

---

[162] See pp. 86–88. [163] Lewis (1991: 279). *Hadriani sententiae* 11 = 3.1879–1895.

[164] *P. Yadin* 14–15; 'τροφεῖα' (*P. Yadin* 15. l.6) is also used in the Greek version of the *sententia* (*Hadriani sententiae* 11 = 3.1880); cf. Lewis (1991: 279) for the connection. See Grubbs (2002: 250–4) for the papyri of the dossier, selected translations, and analysis of the legal problems, as well as Cotton (1993: 103–7) for the recourse to Roman law and the governor being the recipient of a petition.

[165] *P. Yadin* 15. ll. 5–15 (available online at www.trismegistos.org/text/23494); Grubbs (2002: 252–3) for translation and commentary.

[166] Grubbs (2002: 251); Cotton (1993: 105–7).

dossier converge in theme, even if there is no direct appearance of the emperor in the proceedings.[167]

Furthermore, this evidence touches upon another scheme of imperial generosity, namely the *alimenta* in Italy at the turn of the first century AD.[168] In short, these were fundraising initiatives in order to finance small monthly cash payments for the upkeep of children across Italy. The Veleian inscription of the *alimenta* lists that 245 boys of legitimate birth received 16 sesterces per month, 34 girls of legitimate birth 12 sesterces per month, and a boy and a girl of illegitimate birth 12 and 10 sesterces per month, respectively.[169] They were paid for by the donated interest on a loan given by the government to the landowners.[170] The workings of the loan system, the impact on the economy of Italy, whether or not it reflected agricultural issues, and the debate on their purpose, whether for charitable, eugenic, or ideological reasons, have all interested scholars for generations.[171] However, the rationalisation in the over-explanation of the economics of the *alimenta* may go too far, particularly when other factors outside monetary or demographic gain can help colour decisions. Aspects of honour, gift exchange, and the display of generosity itself must factor into the decision-making behind benefaction.[172] In the end, it is the *reported* aspect of the recipients that is of interest here and what that could potentially tell us of the perception of the emperor with respect to the *alimenta* and generosity in general.

A potential example would be Pliny's description of a similar scheme for children at Rome in the *Panegyricus*. In his discussion of Trajan's generosity, Pliny concentrates specifically on children, and thus the beneficiary of alimentary schemes. The first scene, one where the populace gathers for the reception of a *congiarium*, is worth quoting:

> Adventante congiarii die, observare principis egressum in publicum, insidere vias examina infantium futurusque populus solebat. Labor parentibus erat, ostentare parvulos, impositosque cervicibus adulantia verba blandasque voces edocere.

> On the day of the distribution, a multitude of students, the future *populus*, was accustomed to fill the streets and observe the public appearance of the

---

[167] There is mention of the governor of Arabia, Julius Julianus (*P. Yadin* 14; *P. Yadin* 15, esp. ll. 10–11).

[168] On the explanation of the nature of the system, see Duncan-Jones (1964: 123–4, 145), Duncan-Jones (1974: 288), and Shaw (2019: 13–14).

[169] *CIL* 11.1147 = *ILS* 6675; cf. Veyne (1990: 367).   [170] Duncan-Jones (1974: 288).

[171] For analysis of these issues, see Veyne (1990: 367–7), Duncan-Jones (1974: 291–319), Patterson (1987: 124–44), and esp. Bossu (1989), for a clear description of the scholarship on the *alimenta*. Cf. Woolf (1990: 197–228); Houston (1992); Pagé (2012); Stewart (2019).

[172] Bossu (1989: 382).

princeps. The labour of parents was to display their younglings, to place them on their necks and to teach them flattering words and fawning phrases.[173]

Pliny provides a vivid picture of the customary expectations and fears of the populace at the appearance of the Roman emperor: they place their children on their shoulders and teach them to get the attention of the emperor as he passes by in the hope of receiving favour but with the realisation of probable rejection.[174] It is an acknowledgement that not all requests could be acquiesced to and that it was an issue in perpetuity that the children would learn as they grew and became parents themselves. Pliny switches to Trajan's perspective and both commends his refusal to admit unscheduled requests from the people and Trajan's order for them to be enrolled and admitted officially to see him. The alternative to the spontaneity of generosity in the streets is the image of Roman children being reared through his expense, from the *alimenta* as children to the *stipendia* of the military, thus knowing him as their public parent.[175] The temporal aspect is reiterated by Pliny, who turns to the future to argue for the securement of stability and prosperity and the importance of the emperor in the direction of the *pauperes*:

> Recte, Caesar, quod spem Romani nominis sumptibus tuis suscipis. Nullum est enim magno principe immortalitatemque merituro impendii genus dignius, quam quod erogatur in posteros.

> Rightly, Caesar, do you sustain the hope of the Roman name at your cost. Nothing is in fact more worthy for a great leader, who will deserve immortality, than the type of expense which is paid out to future generations.[176]

The health of the economy and the future of the state come into sharp focus here, where the poor are reliant on the good *princeps* for their upkeep. If the emperor did not embrace his responsibility for their care, he would hasten the fall of the empire and the *res publica*.[177] This negative image is

---

[173] Plin. *Pan.* 26.1.

[174] This passage reveals the spectre of impossibility at meeting all requests and the difficulty of interaction and accessibility in terms of logistics and the emperor's refusal. Cf. Millar (1977: 469).

[175] Plin. *Pan.* 26.3; cf. Woolf (1990: 226) for a comment on the connection of the image of *pater patriae* with the alimentary scheme – the parental concern for children seen directly and as a metaphor for the emperor's generosity in general; cf. Patterson (1987: 127–8) for the argument that the *alimenta* fit into a Trajanic ideology for the replenishment of the military, citing Plin. *Pan.* 28.

[176] Plin. *Pan.* 26.4. The mention of *spes* is of importance, as it opens up a different conversation about the hope for a secure future. For more on the emperor as a transcendent figure, see Chapter 6.1.

[177] Plin. *Pan.* 26.5–7. The Platonic image of a headless *corpus* (sc. *rei publicae*) has abject resonance with times of civil upheaval. Plut. *Galb.* 1 with Ash (1997).

that of the emperor having to be the ultimate *tutor* in the lives of the people, and perhaps their only failsafe. The implication of such a truism is that the emperor's actions had repercussions far down the social scale, meaning that his actions and words mattered to the people. Furthermore, the reciprocal relationship is described in great detail, suggesting the expectations of all sides in such interactions of generosity. One could accuse Pliny of laudatory hyperbole as is the wont in panegyrical literature, yet this idea of the emperor as a safeguard of justice and aid is reflected elsewhere.[178]

One such reflection comes in the form of the Arch of Trajan at Benevento. On the south panel inside the arch's passageway is a scene of Trajan participating in the distribution of the *alimenta*, with similar imagery to the distribution scenes in Pliny's *Panegyric*.[179] On the left, Trajan, wearing military garb and clasping a scroll, is surrounded by lictors with their fasces. In the centre of the panel is a small table with two conically shaped breads. On the right are several representations of children, including two children on the shoulders of men and one being held in the arms of a woman. The scene is more generic than specific, depicting the general act of liberality and exchange.[180] As noted by Torelli, the scene depicts Trajan in a magisterial role in dispensing the *alimenta*, through the representation of the *lex* and the outward display of his *imperium* through his lictors. Moreover, several generations are also illustrated, in the fathers who are shown holding up the *pueri* and the female personifications as *urbes Italiae*, suggesting that the benefaction impacted not only the children themselves but also the previous and subsequent generations. As such, the ideological messaging on the panel is rich and multifaceted and suggests a deep engagement with themes on other media concerning Trajan's political and social outlook.[181] One aspect that is also pertinent in this context is the depiction of a relationship between emperor and citizenry that evinces both specific local contexts and the meaning of an emperor's generosity on a macro level. The emperor as depicted becomes a model benefactor, taking care of citizens of all ages through his liberality and political action. The intermediary levels are also illustrated, with the

---

[178] However, see Bartsch (1994: 148–54) for a different analysis of Pliny's *Panegyricus* as an attempted reconciliation between 'public' and 'hidden' transcripts of the emperor's subjects, using Scott's paradigm to explain Pliny's argument, and an attempt to distance the *Panegyricus* from the view that it is an unproblematic representation of imperial ideology. Cf. Rees (2001).

[179] Cf. Torelli (1997: 167).   [180] Torelli (1997: 145).

[181] Torelli (1997: 170): as Torelli noted, the monument can work as a bolstering of the various messages embedded in the alimentary scheme and its expected outcomes. Cf. *RIC* II Trajan 93, 230, 459–62. Cf. Rodríguez (2021).

depiction of various beneficiaries of the programme, including the cities themselves. On that level, too, Trajan becomes the indirect audience for the benefits of the programme, both in terms of fostering the relationship of euergetism within the Italian communities and as an example to be emulated in the future. In other words, we find ourselves in that vernacular of euergetism where the emperor becomes a marker of status.

Such dynamics are clear when we compare the arch with inscriptions across Italy that commemorate the *alimenta*. They range in location and time period, from the beginning of the scheme in the first years of the first century AD to the early years of the reign of Marcus Aurelius in the 160s, and come from the mountains of Umbria to the coast of Latium.[182] All of them contain similar, but not identical, formulaic dedications to the current emperor or a potential successor, sometimes mentioning the emperor's *liberalitas* and *indulgentia* and then the dedicators (variations of *pueri et puellae alimentari*), save for one from Sestinum in Umbria, in which the recently deceased Antoninus Pius is the dedicatee.[183] The earliest one in the dossier, from Ameria, is set up by public decree and perhaps funded by the municipality, but the majority appear to have been dedicated by the beneficiaries themselves.[184] Thus, there is an impression of a direct line of commemoration between the *pueri et puellae* of the scheme and the emperor. Scholarly debate has been undertaken on the cost of these dedications, which could perhaps reveal the economic situation of the beneficiaries involved in the scheme. In particular, Duncan-Jones and Woolf are diametrically opposed on whether or not they were actually poor, with Duncan-Jones arguing that the low rate of the subsidies meant that they were for the poor and Woolf arguing for a wider range of statuses.[185] However, not all the beneficiaries had to be extremely poor or destitute to the extent that building a statue became unaffordable; it is also dangerous to assume that the *alimenta* were the sole source of subsistence for these children. Decrying the material effectiveness of the *alimenta* should not discount what the act of liberality could mean to the community and society. Indeed, this is where both scholars more or less align in

---

[182] Cf. Woolf (1990: 206) for his discussion of these inscriptions. All dates are AD: *CIL* 11.4351 (Ameria, 101–2); *CIL* 11.5989 = *ILS* 328 (Tifernum Mataurense, 136); *CIL* 11.5956 (Pitinum Mergens, 139); *CIL* 11.5957 (Pitinum Mergens, 149); *CIL* 9.5700 (Cupra Montana, 148–9); *CIL* 11.6002 (Sestinum, 161); *CIL* 14.4003 = *ILS* 6225 (Ficulea, 162); *AE* (2009) 207 (Cereatae Marianae, Hadrianic date: the mention of his third consulship gives a *terminus post quem* of 119, but the inscription is quite fragmentary, with the reconstruction of the word *puellae* being the clue that this is an alimentary dedication); *CIL* 11.5395 = *ILS* 6620 (Asisium – unknown emperor).

[183] *CIL* 11.6002: '*divo | Antonino | Aug(usto) Pio | alimentari(i).*' [184] Woolf (1990: 206).

[185] Duncan-Jones (1974: 301–2) and Woolf (1990: 206–7).

thought.[186] Woolf argues that these inscriptions should be read as part of the reciprocal network of patronage and *beneficia*, thus stressing the ideological aspect of the *alimenta* scheme as a method of symbolic binding of the emperor to the people and communities across the Italian peninsula.[187] Indeed, such an idea works but must be pressed further, particularly if we read euergetism as a model of interactivity not only between emperor and subject but also within the community itself, setting out the *alimentarii* as the future and thus projecting the impact of bene-faction. As such, these relationships were more than a two-way street.[188] The *alimenta* fit into a wider network of the emperor's benefactions that were to resonate into the future, and one in which the recipients took an active role within this performance of reciprocity, thus binding different people from different backgrounds together under the rubric of the emperor's generosity that was not necessarily under his watchful eye.[189] Agency, therefore, is fundamental here.

   To end as we began with the *elogium* of a benefactor from Pompeii and the point about exemplarity, benefaction was meant to resonate through-out society. Relationships of reciprocity were complex and permeated through society; they were also more entangled than simply the 'emperor' as benefactor and 'society' as the recipients. Examples and images of imperial generosity come up as leitmotifs in representations of interactions within society. In the *elogium* from Pompeii, we have already seen how the vocabulary of benefaction transcends context and that comparison was a fundamental way to boast about the exceptional generosity of our benefactor to the town.[190] The next example has to do with bread and therefore belongs to the world of the generous distribution of a foodstuff:

> Et cum munus eius in caritate annonae incidisset, propter quod quadriennio eos pavit, potior ei cura civium suorum fuit quam rei familiaris; nam cum esset denaris quinis modius tritici, coemit et ternis victoriatis populo praes-titit et, ut ad omnes haec liberalitas eius perveniret, viritim populo ad ternos victoriatos per amicos suos panis cocti pondus divisit.

> And since his gladiatorial presentation had coincided with a shortage of grain, on account of which he fed them for four years, his concern for his fellow citizens was stronger than that for his patrimony; for when a *modius* of wheat was valued at five *denarii*, he bought it up and made it available to

---

[186] Duncan-Jones (1974: 302).   [187] Woolf (1990: 226–7).

[188] Woolf (1990: 227–8), for the *alimenta* as theatre.

[189] For the visual representation of the *alimenta* on the Arch of Trajan at Benevento and the ideological significance of its reliefs, see Torelli (1997).

[190] See Section 3.1.

the people for three *victoriati* and, so that this generosity of his should reach everyone, he distributed to the people individually through his own friends a weight of baked bread worth up to three *victoriati*.[191]

Here, then, we see our benefactor distribute bread to people individually, in the form of *baked* bread through his friends, which is a notable detail worth discussing.[192] As noted by Seth Bernard, baked bread being distributed is a first among our extant evidence, at least with respect to the *annona*. Exceptionality aside, the fact that our inscription spells it out for us is important as it illuminates the contours of civic relationships in the form of *amici*. These 'friends' were therefore important conduits in the distribution of a staple foodstuff at a time of a hike in grain prices and thus flesh out the world of benefaction that is more than a two-way relationship.[193]

Who were these friends? They could be bakers themselves, who would process the grain and bake the bread, or perhaps they were supervisors who enforced fair distribution.[194] These seem to be plausible suggestions that give us a vignette of baking and distribution in Pompeii. Indeed, it recalls the depiction of the bread dole in the tablinum of 'House of the Baker', which shows a man dressed in white, who is sitting on an elevated bench surrounded by bread, handing out a loaf to three figures dressed in black.[195] The smallest figure in the lower centre portion of the painting is extending his hands out in seeming jubilation at the gesture. Given that it was found in a rather modest house, interpreting this scene has been puzzling, as it does not seem to belong to an elite citizen of Pompeii, which means that it was not someone running for local political office.[196] It does seem, though, to be a scene of benefaction rather than a transaction. If we add the description of distribution of bread in our *elogium*, perhaps it is one of the benefactor's *amici* who participated in the individual handout of baked bread, which both solves our problem of the modesty of the house *and* gives us a clear sense of the importance of the system of benefaction to different people in society. So, we can trace a relationship of benefaction at Pompeii through a conduit.

[191] Text and translation from Bodel et al. (2019: 150–1).
[192] Bodel et al. (2019: 169), for commentary.
[193] See Bowes (2021: 568–9) for the place of bread in the diets of Pompeians.
[194] For these suggestions, see Bodel et al. (2019: 169).
[195] See Clarke (2003: 260). For the image, see Wikimedia Commons (https://commons.wikimedia.org/wiki/File:Sale_bread_MAN_Napoli_Inv9071_n01.jpg).
[196] See Clarke (2003: 259–61) for interpretations of this scene, including 'the most likely scenario is that he was a bread baker who at a prosperous moment in his life decided to give free bread to the populace'.

The vocabulary of generosity discussed throughout this chapter has commonalities in the gesture shown in the bread dole scene. As Trajan is shown reaching out his hand and giving sustenance to children on the Arch of Benevento and on his coinage that commemorate the alimentary scene, so too we see our man clad in white handing out bread. These scenes of generosity mirror each other; and though they come from different contexts, they both betray a concern for provision and the expectation of generosity, which should be commemorated. That our scene comes from a modest house in Pompeii is in fact crucial, as it suggests that this sort of vignette was important to different sections of society, whether we believe it represents a local magistrate distributing bread or one of those middlemen described in the *elogium*, who was exhibiting pride for his participation in the benefactor's scheme. The language of benefaction therefore resonates through society, which gives us crucial evidence for its importance in the perception of political and social leaders, with the emperor at the top.

These vignettes of imperial generosity leave the impression of an ideological concern for the presentation of the emperor as being 'good'. It is notable that the evidence that points to potential opinions of a wider population on this matter seem to conform to these notions, which presents fears and expectations as part of the discourse about an emperor's generosity.[197] Given that benefaction and euergetism were large social spaces of interaction, we are close to the thought-world of the inhabitants of the Roman empire, as these were spaces for wider participation. It is within these spaces that political legitimacy was rehearsed, tested, and bolstered.

---

[197] Veyne (1990: 295–6); cf. Noreña (2001: 106–7).

CHAPTER 4

Wonder Tales

The topics of conversation about the Roman emperor that have been discussed thus far are ones that figure prominently in historical treatments of the Roman empire, which concern themes of the dispensation of law and justice, the importance of benefaction and euergetism in political and social relationships across the empire, and what each contributes to the historical understanding of the interactions between the emperor and his subjects. These are essential components to understanding the function of the emperor in the Roman world. However, from the transactional end of the ideological spectrum we now move towards the bizarre, counterintuitive, and fictitious end of the spectrum for the remainder of the book. A curiosity about who the emperor was leads to the emperor becoming a curiosity himself. We find ourselves in a thought-world where the emperor could be interpreted as an ambiguous and contradictory figure.

In such a thought-world, the emperor is caught in the middle, which leads to an assertion that he is a liminal figure – caught between polarities of morality, power, and divinity – which makes the understanding of his nature extremely difficult. Such 'doubleness' makes the concept of the emperorship slippery.[1] However, such a revelation is only problematic if one insists on a consistent characterisation of the Roman emperor – that the historical understanding of his actions had to be logical, rational, and neatly delineated. Put in another way, this means that he could be different things to different people, suggesting that perspective mattered and that he could occupy roles that seem illogical and irrational, particularly to a modern observer. This also means that polarised perspectives of the Roman emperor which seem unequivocal are just as valid as hazy perspectives, particularly those that live on and replicate long after the death of an emperor.[2]

---

[1] Cf. Greensmith (2020: 49–51).
[2] For the range of potential afterlives of an emperor, see Malik (2019).

This chapter in particular explores the gaudy side of the emperor, examining the evidence for the emperor's proximity to *mirabilia* and wonder.[3] Perhaps the most important thing to stress here is how the content of these stories is not the most absurd or bizarre component from a modern perspective; rather, it is how normal it seems for the emperor to be a part of miraculous and wondrous stories and that it could be conceived of in the same breath as more realistic and concrete examples of an emperor's duties and actions. His status as emperor meant that there was a cognitive association between him and the wondrous. The emperor was an arbiter and patron of oddity as well as a monster himself. However, this seeming polarity becomes hazier when both characterisations exist simultaneously in discourse. In the end, they both populate the thought-world about what the emperor seemed to be, thus both contributing to his reception.

An interesting example that can act as a bridge between the themes of justice and generosity and tales of wonder is an excerpt from Menander Rhetor. It comes from his *basilikos logos*, a third-century epideictic treatise on how to compose an imperial encomium:[4]

> Καὶ ἐν μὲν τῇ δικαιοσύνῃ τὸ ἥμερον τὸ πρὸς τοὺς ὑπηκόους ἐπαινέσεις, τὴν πρὸς τοὺς δεομένους φιλανθρωπίαν, τὸ εὐπρόσοδον. Οὕτως οὐ μόνον ἐν τοῖς κατὰ τόν πόλεμον ἔργοις ὁ βασιλεὺς ἡμῖν θαυμάσιος, ἀλλὰ καὶ ἐν τοῖς κατ' εἰρήνην θαυμασιώτερος· τίς γὰρ οὐκ ἀγάσαιτο τῶν ἔργων; καὶ προσθήσεις ὅτι καθάπερ οἱ Ἀσκληπιάδαι σώζουσι τοὺς ἀρρωστοῦντας, ἢ καθάπερ τοὺς καταφεύγοντας ἐπὶ τὰ ἄσυλα τεμένη τοῦ κρείττονος ἔστιν ἰδεῖν ῥᾳστώνης τυγχάνοντας (οὐ γὰρ ἀποσπᾶν ἐπιχειροῦμεν οὐδένα) οὕτως ὁ βασιλέως ὄψεσιν ἐντυχὼν τῶν δεινῶν ἀπήλλακται.

> Under 'justice' you should commend mildness towards subjects, humanity towards petitioners, and accessibility. 'Thus not only is the emperor to be admired for his deeds in war, but even more so for his acts in peace. Who would not revere him for his deeds?' You can add that 'just as the sons of Asclepius rescue the sick, just as fugitives obtain security in the inviolate precincts of divine power – for we make no attempt to drag anyone away – so also he who comes into the sight of the emperor is freed from his perils'.[5]

This passage is about the commendation of the emperor for his justice, which involves his gentleness towards subjects, humanity towards the needy, and accessibility. It has references to themes about the perception of the emperor that have already been discussed on expectations placed on

---

[3] Cf. Petsalis-Diomidis (2010: 155).
[4] Men. Rhet. II. 368, translation from Russell and Wilson (1981: 85).　　[5] Men. Rhet. II. 375.8–18.

the emperor. Furthermore, there are parallels to the idea of refuge and asylum, in that a person who comes into the sight of the emperor would be set free from peril.[6] Not only is the emperor admirable, but he is compared to wonder-workers. That this passage appears in a handbook on imperial encomia – laudatory orations on praising the Roman emperor – would perhaps discount it as material of excessive flattery or templates from which further examples of laudation could be embellished.[7] However, such a conclusion would discount the interesting parallels in other evidence. The question is less about the politics of flattery to be spoken in front of the emperor and more about how the language of fiction and wonder was employed to describe the position at all.[8] Even if not literally veracious, that this passage is from the discourse about how one should talk about an emperor is relevant to the theme at hand. Perhaps more importantly, it forms a bridge between a thematic and conceptual divide in both this section and the evidence – between the realistic and the wondrous. The translation by Russell and Wilson renders the second line of the excerpt as 'thus not only is the emperor to be admired for his deeds in war, but even more so for his acts in peace'.[9] The conveyed meaning of the phrase is not incorrect, save perhaps potential latitude of meaning with the word *thaumasios*. This could entail something admirable but also wondrous, extraordinary, and moving towards the absurd. Such a phrase would then imply that the actions and conduct of the emperor were something that could be described as wondrous.

This chapter will be organised as follows: first, there will be a discussion of the appearance of *mirabilia* and paradoxography in ancient literature, as well as connected relevant themes, which involves the problem of locating the wondrous in knowledge and the world; the importance of imperialism and Rome itself as a place to order, collect, and display wonders; and the issues of morality and fiction with respect to the interest in *mirabilia*. Second, there will be a discussion of the relevance of the themes outlined previously in the reception of the Roman emperor, with a particular concentration on previous interpretations of the emperor and his association with *mirabilia*. Third is the discussion of the different evidence that connects the emperor with *mirabilia*, which will consider, respectively, the emperor being a patron and arbiter of wonders and his characterisation as

---

[6] See pp. 79–82 on the emperor's statue as a place of refuge.

[7] Cf. Rees (2002: 25) on excessive flattery in panegyric.

[8] Cf. Men. Rhet. II. 374 on the use of Homeric language as a parallel for an emperor's deeds. Cf. Greensmith (2020: 28–34) on the centrality of Homeric 're-animation' to the Roman world.

[9] Men. Rhet. II. 375; and Russell and Wilson (1981: 89).

a monster himself within various contexts, such as in the arena, triumphal procession, the gardens at Rome, and at court. However, the dichotomy between the two should not be overstressed, as both appear simultaneously in discourse, showing that the line between the emperor as a patron of wonders and a wonder himself was hazy – and that he was seen to take on different guises.

4.1 Paradoxography and Empire: Where *thaumata* and *miracula* Are

First, the nature of *mirabilia* and their appearance in ancient literature. With the campaigns of Alexander the Great and the birth of the Hellenistic successor kingdoms thereafter came a growing curiosity and interest in paradoxographical treatises and literature, which recorded fantastic stories about paradoxical and unbelievable phenomena.[10] The opening up of the world created the tastes for truth and falsity in literature, thus fostering a genre that was pseudo-historical and fantastic.[11] The existence of the genre of paradoxography, and its stories within other forms of literature, shows a curiosity for the wondrous. Further delineations are important before we find the emperor, namely the connection of the wondrous to spatial configuration and the expansion of empire and the problems of credibility and fiction – with closely concomitant issues such as the interest of these stories in the evidence, the moral depravity of such interests, their status as baser forms of curiosity and literature, and thus their 'popular' appeal.

It is difficult to pin down the location of *mirabilia* in the world. It would be simpler to argue that the spatial configuration of such stories could be delineated according to the distant and the near, with the geographically and conceptually 'far' being simultaneously the location of wondrous things. This is no doubt part of the story, but it would be incomplete. Further to the problem of geographical distance are the interactions between the centre and the edges, the celestial and infernal, and the temporal.[12] This tension could be described as the simultaneous distance

---

[10] Schepens and Delcroix (1996: 403–8); Gabba (1981: 52–3); Beagon (2005: 18–20); cf. Schepens and Delcroix (1996: 380–408), for a description of the genre in Greek literature: the organisation of their works, concerns, and arguments for credibility; and for the various appearances of paradoxographical tales in different genres of literature (425–42). Cf. Dench (2005: 283–7), for a brief history on the taste for the strange, from Homer through Alexander the Great and the Hellenistic Age to the displays of the Roman potentates of the late Republic. Cf. Shannon-Henderson (2022) for an excellent introduction to the genre of paradoxography.

[11] Gabba (1981: 53).   [12] Beagon (2007: 21–35), for locations of the wondrous.

and proximity in the concept of the wondrous. In other words, there is a symbiotic relationship between the distant and the adjacent, whether in geographical, spatial, or temporal terms. This is well exemplified by two examples from Plutarch. The first comes in the proemium to his *Life of Theseus*, in which he depicts both a simultaneous curiosity in the edges of the world and the haziness of the enquiry, for reasons of distance (in its different meanings) and the lack of knowledge, allowing for their population with incredible and wondrous things. Whereas geographers might describe faraway places as 'waterless deserts full of beasts, unseen swamps, Scythian cold or a sea made solid', so too are the travels through the *Parallel Lives* to topics far back in the depths of time. As Plutarch articulated on such olden times: 'Those tales over there are monstrous and tragic, where poets and mythographers hold sway, and where there is no trust or surety' (τὰ δ' ἐπέκεινα τερατώδη καὶ τραγικά, ποιηταὶ καὶ μυθογράφοι νέμονται, καὶ οὐκέτ' ἔχει πίστιν οὐδὲ σαφήνειαν).[13] Thus, the temporal distance of Plutarch's subject matter leads him into an apology for his method, moving from the world of reason and basis in historical actions to that of the monstrous, poetical, and mythographical.[14] Furthermore, it seems that geographical and temporal distance are equated here; both are locations where wondrous things exist, suggesting that these different types of distance were conceptually similar. Accordingly, the location of *mirabilia* is faraway in this description yet creating a sense of curiosity in such places.

However, this temporal and spatial distance is radically shortened with the appearance of wondrous phenomena at the centre, exemplified by Rome in the second example from Plutarch. As the nucleus of the empire, Rome was the place where *mirabilia* would be transported and displayed as part of the trappings of imperial expansion.[15] This status of Rome as a locus for curiosities is seen in the Plutarch's second passage, from the treatise *De curiositate* in the *Moralia*, which criticises those who frequent the 'monster-market' (τὴν τῶν τεράτων ἀγορὰν) to gawk at people without calves (ἀκνήμους), with short arms (γαλεάγκωνας), with three eyes (τριοφθάλμους), or with bird heads (στρουθοκεφάλους), in order to find the 'mixed-up shape and monstrous prodigy' (σύμμικτον εἶδος καὶ

[13] Plut. *Thes.* 1.1–3.
[14] Cf. Bowersock (1994: 1–27) for a discussion of such intersections in ancient literature.
[15] Beagon (2007: 29–31) for Rome as the location of the wondrous; cf. Rutledge (2012) for Rome as a place for collecting wonders, intersecting especially with artefacts and art history, and esp. 263–84 for the place of the emperor in this rubric; cf. Clavel-Lévêque (1984), esp. 15–16, for the status of the games at Rome as the arena of social interaction and the space in which the exotic and wondrous were displayed – a sign of Rome's widespread domination of nature and the world.

ἀποφώλιον τέρας).[16] Plutarch's purpose here, then, is to comment on the taste of these *polypragmones* (busybodies), or people who stick their nose into other people's business too readily,[17] whose interest lies not in the beautiful and intellectual but the irregular and deformed, which is catered to by such a market.[18] Thus, the marvels of legend and foreign lands are brought into the centre of the empire, for the tastes and consumption of its inhabitants, meaning that there is an experiential factor in the encounter of the wondrous that problematises its distance and unbelievability.

There are other themes relevant to the wondrous here. For instance, it is important to comment on the Euripides fragment that Plutarch alludes to in this passage. Other than in the *Moralia*, it appears in a different form in his *Life of Theseus*, ending instead with κἀποφώλιον βρέφος ([a] hybrid birth of monstrous shape) rather than the 'marvel' or 'portent' that is referred to with the word *teras*.[19] The word *apophōlion* has been rendered differently in different commentaries, but there is a meaning of 'emptiness' or 'sterility'. Perhaps there is also a reference to the word *phōleia*, which means a bestial life in a hole or a cave.[20] This phrase therefore denotes both a depravity and a uniqueness – not repeated and without offspring – in the teratological. This meaning should be a part of the passage inserted by Plutarch into his description of the monster-market. Moreover, there is also an encounter of the intellectual, mythological, and teratological in Plutarch's choice of phrase. The allusion to Euripides would perhaps be satisfactory to intellectual erudition, but it is important to note that it comes from the context of the description of the Minotaur, an evocation of the mythological, present at the market in Rome.

Citation of this myth recalls an example in Martial's *Liber spectaculorum* and what Coleman called 'Fatal Charades': examples of capital punishment being exacted through the spectacle of mythological re-enactments.[21] In this poem, Martial describes a staged scene of bestiality in the new

---

[16] Plut. *Mor.* 520.C–E. Cf. a discussion of this in Trentin (2011: 197), including the comparison with a passage in Quintilian on the higher price of deformed slaves, also echoing sentiments described in Plutarch, Quint. *Inst.* 2.5.11. The quotation is a fragment from Euripides' *Cretans* (Eur. *Fr.* 472a = 996).

[17] On *polypragmosynē*, see Leigh (2013), esp. 123, on the emperor as *curiosus*.

[18] Cf. Mart. 8.13 for an example of a potential *polypragmōn*, who was left disappointed in his search for an unintelligent slave: *Morio dictus erat: viginiti milibus emi. redde mihi nummos, Gargiliane; sapit* (You said he was a fool: I paid 20 thousand for him. Give me back my money, Gargalianus. He's smart).

[19] Plut. *Thes.* 15.2.

[20] A *TLG* search produced an entry for the word in the *Lexicon* by Photius, a ninth-century patriarch of Constantinople: Photius, *Lexicon* (A-Δ) 2719, which denotes something of little value, uneducated, uncultured, sorry; also monstrous and wild, from dens or caves.

[21] Coleman (1990: 63–4); cf. Bowersock (1994: 8–9); cf. Gunderson (2003: 637).

Colosseum that was a rendition of the mythological scene of Pasiphaë and the bull – the union that bore the Minotaur:

> Iunctam Pasiphaen Dictaeo credite tauro: vidimus, accepit fabula prisca fidem. ne se miretur, Caesar, longaeva vetustas: quidquid Fama canit, praestat harena tibi.

> Believe that Pasiphaë was united with the Dictaean bull. We have seen it, and the ancient tale has credibility. Do not let bygone antiquity marvel at itself, Caesar. Whatever legend sings, the amphitheatre proves it to you.[22]

An ancient tale is rendered a reality in the arena under the direction of the emperor – a story of temporal distance brought close for autopsy and thus made more credible. Such a tale is therefore conceptually similar to the description of Plutarch's monster-market and an interest in *mirabilia*. Furthermore, it suggests a continual play between different worlds. At this point, Caesar himself by implication is to be marvelled at, as is ancient lore. Therefore, 'fact' and 'fiction', 'myth' and 'reality', 'intellectual' and 'baser' pursuits are mixed in the perception of the wondrous.

This wavering is also present in the issues of fiction and morality with respect to *mirabilia*, which problematises certain binaries in historical study. The first one illustrates the problem of the line between fiction and history: there seems to be a haziness between what could be considered truth or fiction and thus what could be included in a work about historical events.[23] Indeed, Plutarch attempted to infuse reason into what he called *to muthōdes*, or the legendary, in the preface to the *Life of Theseus*. Thus, the legendary takes the guise of history, which seems to concede a symbiotic relationship between what was considered true or false rather than arguing that it is an example of the stark polarity between the historical and the legendary, which is something that is reflected in wonder tales. In the end, Plutarch leaves judgement to his audience, praying for considerate and gentle attitudes in receiving his antiquarian enquiries.[24] Thus, the lines between truth and fiction are moveable and require an active and ethical engagement from participants in the conversation, which, put crudely,

---

[22] Mart. *Spect.* 6(5). Allusion to the patronage of the emperor here is key, as Martial places him as the overseer of the re-enaction of myth, meaning that he is the patron of the wondrous. Cf. Coleman (2006: 63) for the resonance of this myth on Pompeian wall paintings.

[23] Cf. Sections 1.1.2–3 and Bowersock (1994: 1–27).

[24] Plut. *Thes.* 1.5. Cf. Schepens and Delcroix (1996: 383) for the concern for credibility, by citing authorities on the subject and autopsy. Cf. Plin. *NH.* 7.8 and Gell. 9.4.3, 13, for similar citations of authority in the discussion of paradoxical stories. Cf. Lucian *Ver. Hist.* 1.1–4 for a playful parody of this dynamic.

makes fiction bear on history and vice versa.[25] As Bowersock suggested: 'For any coherent and persuasive interpretation of the Roman empire it becomes obvious that fiction must be viewed as part of its history.'[26] *Mirabilia* should fall under this understanding.[27]

Uncertainty seems to be incumbent in epistemologies, particularly in the ordering of incredible, ancient, and faraway knowledge that came with imperial expansion. At the beginning of book 7 of the *Natural History*, Pliny discusses that which he does not want to omit from his study of the human animal: the stories about peoples who live far from the sea, which would seem to be *prodigiosa* and *incredibilia* in the views of many.[28] Pliny proceeds to justify his choice by blurring the line between the credible and incredible, arguing that no one believed there were Ethiopians before seeing them and that the power and greatness of nature lack credibility if you only appreciate the part rather than the whole.[29] Within Pliny's universalising rubric of knowledge concerning nature, the possibility of the miraculous becomes more feasible, particularly when the unknown slowly becomes the known. Nonetheless, this argument does not discount the possibility of fiction, and trust must be placed in the authors who transmit these stories, with the ultimate onus remaining on the audience about whether or not to buy into them.[30] A similar dilemma is presented by Aulus Gellius. It describes the story of transit between Greece and Italy, where Gellius happened upon old Greek paradoxography books. He describes them as containing unheard-of, unbelievable stories from ancient authors of some authority.[31] He then states that he includes some of the stories so that the reader would not be ignorant to them, which echoes Pliny's sentiment.[32] Later in the text, Gellius feels disgust at such unworthy writings but at the same time justifies their inclusion with mention of Pliny himself, who he states was a writer of great authority and not only had heard and read but also had known and seen that which he wrote.[33] Therefore, there seems to be a disdainful but keen interest in these tales.

The line of fiction and fact is difficult to delineate, both now and then. Perhaps it is the ambiguity of these stories that is appealing, as they occupy

---

[25] For such an ethical reading, see Chrysanthou (2018).   [26] Bowersock (1994: 12).
[27] Cf. Bowersock (1994: 31–7).
[28] Plin. *NH.* 7.6; cf. Beagon (2005: 116–17): Pliny implies the Mediterranean with it being the centre of the system, meaning populations faraway were exotic in their distance from it.
[29] Plin. *NH.* 7.7.   [30] Plin. *NH.* 7.8.
[31] Gell. 9.4.1–3: *Erant autem isti omnes libri Graeci miraculorum fabularumque pleni, res inauditae, incredulae, scriptores veteres non parvae auctoritatis.*
[32] Gell. 9.5.
[33] Gell. 9.12–13. For further analysis of this text and the paradoxographers Gellius mentions, see Schepens and Delcroix (1996: 410–24).

liminal spaces in the mind.[34] So too with the moral reticence exhibited towards *mirabilia* and the teratological by the discussed thus far: they decry the interest in them but nonetheless engage in the discourse.[35] Then, it perhaps would be too simple to describe it in dichotomous terms: the good and morally upright deriding popular or credulous attitudes towards these stories. Moralising, disgust, and fascination were part of a shared conceptual spectrum in which these stories were understood.[36] This could be a way to explain an apparent dissonance in the evidence – between the derision of *mirabilia* in moral and intellectual terms and the continual appearance of such tales in variant forms of literature, from paradoxographical treatises such as that of Phlegon of Tralles, who was a freedman of the emperor Hadrian, to the biographies and histories of Suetonius, Tacitus, and Dio, of the equestrian and senatorial elite of the empire. It is also useful to acknowledge the existence of a negative moral or intellectual perspective without adopting it as our own, meaning that paradoxical stories, as well as paradoxographical texts, should be part of the historical understanding of the Roman empire. They could be a part of a wider conceptual framework in which these stories circulated, in which credulity and moral judgement were tested. This subjectivity should not be seen as historically unusable or irrelevant, for the stories are a potential window into a common thought-world – one that involved a curiosity about the Roman emperor.

It is therefore important to locate the Roman emperor within this discourse of *mirabilia*. As alluded to in this section, the implication of the growing thirst for wonder knowledge is that it is inexorably tied to the expansion of power. As more of the earth becomes a part of the aegis of the empire, there is a greater interest in attempting to order and compile what may lie at the edges and in between, what Purcell calls a 'conceptual geography' of the world.[37] It therefore binds the peripheries of the mind to the reality of their centre, facilitated by the

---

[34] Cf. Schepens and Delcroix (1996: 448–51) for a discussion on the Romans' interest in *paradoxa*. Cf. Gabba (1981: 57–61).

[35] Cf. Romm (1992: 95); cf. Dench (2005: 288–90).

[36] Murphy (2004: 8), for the argument that Pliny's *Natural History* included such stories in order for the remit of his knowledge collection to be complete (cf. Plin. *NH.* 7.6–8). Note, however, Murphy (2004: 7): 'we know much less about the symbolic culture of antiquity than of today because of the aristocratic bias of the surviving literary sources. The oratory of courts and schools, epic poetry and imperial history imply versions of Roman culture, but they value certain tones and registers and suppress others, embracing tragic and heroic codes while they exclude the banal, the commercial, the technical, and the trivial.' I would argue that interest in paradoxography gives us evidence that transcends this preventative barrier – a potential window into a shared register between divisions in society.

[37] Purcell (1990: 178), and 179 on an emperor 'knowing the minds' of the inhabitants. Cf. Nicolet (1991: 85–8) on imperial expeditions.

route connections laid down by the power of imperial expansion. What is particularly interesting for our purposes is the status of the Roman emperor as the 'traveller' on this journey. Even if vicarious, his patronage means that he is the mediator between the extremes and the orderer and organiser of the world, including the obscure edges.[38] Indeed, a comparative set of materials can be seen in sculpture depicting the Roman emperor as a conqueror on conceptual journeys, which includes the imperial reliefs at the Sebasteion in Aphrodisias, which depict Claudius and Nero subjugating personified representations of Britannia and Armenia respectively.[39] Both figures are depicted as cowering in fear under the emperors, who are displayed in heroic nudity.[40] Thus, from the perspective of the Aphrodisians themselves, imperial expansion is commemorated viscerally and iconographically, showing figuratively the incorporation and ordering of these places into the Roman empire at the direction of the emperor himself.[41] Moreover, as suggested by Davenport, the images of heroism and violence embedded in this monument create many possible readings, which might include an identification with Roman power and Aphrodisias' own elevated position within the hierarchies of Roman order as a free city[42] but also more visceral reminders of the effect of Roman power that turned enemies into subjects and organised them under Roman systems of knowledge and law.[43] As such, the emperor is depicted simultaneously as heroic, mythical, marvellous, and terrifying. The emperor is thus inevitably coloured by these conceptions: wondrous by association and obscured through them. The curiosity included the discourse of the emperor, interested in his own wonder tales and how he seemed – glorious or monstrous as they may have been.

Closely connected to imperial expansion is the collection and display of *mirabilia*, which form part of the intricate negotiation of power.[44] Pliny the Elder's *Natural History* can be read as a cultural artefact of the Roman empire, a compendium that collects universal knowledge as the corollary to

---

[38] Cf. Beagon (2007: 21–3) on extremities in Pliny.
[39] Smith (1987: 115–20) pl. 14. no. 6; pl. 16 no. 7; 90–6, on the monument in general. Smith (2013: 140–1, 145–6).
[40] Davenport (2020: 103–21) for a survey of comparable material, including a relief of Caligula defeating Germania from Koula in Lydia with accompanying inscription (fig. 5.10; *ILS* 8791 = *TAM* 5.1 235 = *IGRR* 4.1279).
[41] On Aphrodisian agency, see Smith (1987: 135–6); cf. Davenport (2020: 107) for context.
[42] Davenport (2020: 110).   [43] Davenport (2020: 111), for this perceptive argument.
[44] Schepens and Delcroix (1996: 450): 'the possession of the unique, of the strange, also had its function within power relations: it could be considered a symbol of domination.'

Rome's vast empire.[45] A part of this argument includes the importance of the emperor's position, which involved the ability to control *mirabilia* as part of his imperial remit:

> The collection, selection, control, and publication or display of knowledge about nature was also an attribute of the emperors' power; emperors were the most authoritative of natural historians, not in the sense of observers or writers about nature, but as arbiters of what was to be regarded as true.[46]

As a qualifier, however, other interpretations of the emperor and *mirabilia* can sit alongside the image of a conqueror and orderer. Connected to this world is a Roman fascination with the strange and deformed, what Dench called the 'freakish'.[47] Dench's interest lies in attempting to describe the Roman fascination with what she terms as 'freakish'.[48] This term includes *mirabilia, prodigia, monstra, ostenta, ludibria,* and *miracula,* all of which accentuate the otherness of such wonders – something that denotes prodigious difference, used to invoke a 'Roman anxiety' for perceived disorder in nature.[49] In this way, then, the emperor's place as a curator of wonder means that he becomes closely associated with such anxieties: 'general connection in Roman thought between freakishness and the person of the emperor includes the idea of the collection and display of freaks, the prominence of freaks within the imperial court, and the emperor himself as freak.'[50] The repeated use of the word 'freak' is appropriate in this sense, as it attempts to view the emperor through a lens of obscurity and difference, coloured by prejudicial conceptions of otherness. Again, the emperor becomes a monstrosity, both as a symbol of empire and its expansion and with regard to the breadth of his *imperium* that he held personally.[51]

The point to stress is complexity in reception. As Dench intimated, the emperor 'muddle(d) "normal" categories and conventions' that exposed the arbitrariness of power, meaning that wonder tales about the emperor were tools to use in order to explain things like tyrannical behaviour and the enormity of his control.[52] However, it would be simplistic to distil these into 'good' or 'bad' vignettes of the Roman emperor, as both coexist and contribute to the reception of the position. Therefore, in the following discussion of the emperor and *mirabilia*, the importance of both in the

---

[45] Murphy (2004: 197–203); cf. Beagon (2005: 23–4, esp. n. 73), for a brief bibliography on these points.
[46] Murphy (2004: 197). Cf. Champlin (2008: 414–15) for a similar argument with respect to Tiberius.
[47] Dench (2005: 280–92), and 281–2, for this term, and esp. n. 167, on its problems.
[48] Cf. Dench (2005: 281–2).   [49] Dench (2005: 282).
[50] Dench (2005: 283); cf. Bowersock (1994: 33) and Garland (1995: 45–58) for similar arguments.
[51] Garland (1995: 50–1).   [52] Dench (2005: 289). Cf. Garland (1995: 45) for a similar argument.

discourse will be stressed rather than attempting to place examples of the emperor (or individual emperors) as a mediator or a *monstrum* into set categories of 'good' or 'bad' emperors. This is not the same as denying the existence of a 'good' or 'bad' interpretation of the emperor but rather is stating that the emperor could seem both good and bad simultaneously.[53] I stress the emperor's doubleness, made so by his proximity to *mirabilia*.[54] The Roman emperor populating these stories could highlight his position in the thought-world of his subjects, suggesting that he could be a patron and arbiter of wonders or monstrous in himself, enhancing both the obscurity and the curiosity of what the emperor was.[55] We are firmly in the world of seeming.

4.2   The Emperor of Wonder at Rome

First is the evidence of the emperor as patron and mediator. Such evidence comes in different forms, including the collection and display of wondrous things from across the world in different contexts, in the presence of the emperor at his court and his own private collection, or in public at the arena or during a triumphal procession, with Rome as a central feature for such displays.[56] The intricacies of the pageantry and the negotiation that are involved in the study of the triumph and the arena are separate topics in their own right, which have both received singular attention and also deserve greater appraisal, and as such differences should not be underestimated. However, it would be impossible to undertake this task of complete differentiation here. The centrality of the Roman emperor indicates that there is a regression toward the mean: his status as patron and mediator in these different contexts allows for similarities to be made, particularly with reference to the emperor himself and the involvement of *mirabilia*. Moreover, the specific concern here is to explore the perception of the interaction between the emperor and the wondrous in our sources across both time and space, rather than a separate historical analysis of any single context, such as a triumph. It is therefore the similarities across these

---

[53] This is like the interpretation of Tacitus' Tiberius in the *Annals*, on which see Christoforou (2022).
[54] Cf. North (1986: 256) for stories percolating around individuals in the late republic.
[55] Cf. Garland (1995: 49–52) on the argument of the Roman emperor's fascination with the monstrous and his power and status making him a monster himself.
[56] For the relevant evidence on this topic, see Beagon (2007: 30–2); Garland (1995: 48–52), and esp. Rutledge (2012: 221–86). For the triumph, see Gagé (1933: 1–43); Versnel (1970), esp. 356–96; McCormick (1986: 11–34); Beard (2003a: 550–2); cf. Edwards (1993: 119); cf. Gunderson (2003). Cf. Nicolet (1991: 45) on Rome and the *oikoumene*.

contexts, rather than their differences, that will be stressed here, as they all show the emperor's proximity to *mirabilia*.

It is best to commence with the triumph, as it can represent the bridging of the conceptual chasm between the imperial centre and the conquered periphery, and indeed between the emperor's more concrete role of conqueror and that of an arbiter of wonder. The triumph is a context in which wonders were brought to Rome from afar, exhibiting Rome's world power, and importantly for the imperial period, the position of the Roman emperor as the triumphant general and patron of the *mirabilia* on display.[57] The Flavian triumph of AD 71, as described in detail by Josephus, was full of displays of riches and wonders and exhibited all at once on that day the greatness of the Roman empire.[58] This included vast quantities of gold, silver, and ivory, which seemed to flow like a river;[59] embroidered cloth and gemstones, with the latter in such great quantity that their previous assumption of their rarity was proven false;[60] statues of the gods made with expensive material for the occasion; and many animals and multitudes of captives as part of the procession, dressed up in such finery as to hide the signs of their torture from view.[61] Additionally, Josephus describes in detail the 'carried stages' or floats, on which re-enactments of the battle scenes in the Jewish War were shown to the spectating public, which also included the representations of fortifications, temples, and natural formations.[62] Furthermore in detail are the descriptions of the spoils of the war, including those from the Temple in Jerusalem.[63] Finally is the description of the imperial family in pomp: μεθ' ἃ Οὐεσπασιανὸς ἤλαυνε πρῶτος καὶ Τίτος εἵπετο, Δομετιανὸς δὲ παρίππευεν, αὐτός τε διαπρεπῶς κεκοσμημένος καὶ τὸν ἵππον παρέχων θέας ἄξιον (after that Vespasian rode first, with Titus following, and Domitian riding alongside, he dressed up magnificently and on his

---

[57] See Beard (2003a: 551–2) and Beard (2007: 123) on the triumph being a physical realisation of Roman imperialism; and Beard (2003b: 37–43) on the triumph as a performance of imperial power at its centre and particularly on examples where the display was 'fake' (see Tac. *Ann.* 2.41.2 for Germanicus, Suet. *Cal.* 47.1 for Gaius, and Tac. *Agr.* 39.1 and Plin. *Pan.* 16.3 for Domitian). Cf. Gunderson (2003) for a similar argument for the fabrication of truth in the Flavian amphitheatre.

[58] Joseph. *BJ.* 7.133.   [59] Joseph. *BJ.* 134.   [60] Joseph. *BJ.* 135.

[61] Joseph. *BJ.* 138. Compare with descriptions of Gaius' triumph in Suetonius and Dio (Suet. *Cal.* 47; Dio 59.25.3–5), which both detail the farcical display of both his spoils and his captives. Cf. Dench (2005: 37–8).

[62] Joseph. *BJ.* 7.139–147: words of viewing and wonderment are used throughout the passage, accentuating the marvellousness of the procession. Cf. Tac. *Ann.* 2.41.2 for a similar, if shorter, parallel.

[63] Joseph. *BJ.* 148–51, which included the golden table, menorah, and the laws of the Jewish people, famously depicted on the inside panel of the Arch of Titus in the Forum. Cf. Beard (2003a: 550–1).

horse, worthy of a spectacle).[64] The Flavians appear as a unit as patrons of the event and conquerors; the ostentatious display of riches and wonders from across the *oikoumene* is directly connected to them, and in turn, they become 'wonders' themselves and a sight to look at. Thus, the specific spoils of the Jewish War along with the display of the vast power and geographical enormity of the Roman empire are combined to prove the clout of Vespasian and his sons, and similarly to Murphy's argument about Pliny's *Natural History*, to help exhibit the emperor as an arbiter of the wonders of the world.[65]

The proximity of the emperor to *mirabilia* is a theme that is observable throughout the history of the early principate. To continue with the Flavians and public display of wonder as a bridge into this material, the aforementioned *Liber spectaculorum* of Martial contains many examples of the vast geography and wonders of the world being collocated at Rome under the emperor, and in this case, the Flavian amphitheatre. In addition to this are descriptions of executions as mythological re-enactments, *venationes*, *naumachiae*, and gladiatorial combats.[66] Accordingly, the nature of the shows and the descriptions are different, but they all fall under the direction of the emperor; he is the equalising factor and patron, and so accordingly is the determining reason for the occurrences in the arena. In poem 3, Martial describes the vast diversity of races and tongues present at Rome, and yet all unite as one in calling him *pater patriae*.[67] In poem 17, an elephant is calmed by the presence of the emperor after its fight with a bull.[68] In poem 33, a doe bows down at the feet of Caesar, and the Molossian hounds that were chasing it cease, a feat attributed to the emperor's divine presence and sacred power.[69] As such, the curious

---

[64] Joseph. *BJ.* 152. Cf. Tac. *Ann.* 2.41.3. Note that both Josephus and Tacitus depict that the family is a spectacle in itself, which conceptually places them in the same category as the other displays in the triumphal procession.

[65] Murphy (2004: 197–201); cf. Beagon (2005: 23–4). Cf. Luke (2010: 77–106), from Suet. *Vesp.* 7, for healing miracles, wonder, and imperial legitimacy; Tac. *Hist.* 4.81–2; Dio 65.8.1–2.

[66] For a list of the relevant examples: Mart. *Spect.* 1–33. I follow the recent numbering as delineated by Coleman in her commentary of the work. See Coleman (2006: xlv–lxiv) for a discussion on the problematic and elusive identification of the 'Caesar' mentioned in the poems, in which she argues for a middle ground, which means mixed composition dates for different epigrams, even if they were collected and published under Domitian. See esp. Coleman (2006: xlvi, n. 92), for the scholarship on the commonly accepted date of AD 80 being the inauguration of the amphitheatre under Titus, and Buttrey (2007: 101–12), who argues strongly for a Domitianic date. However, I agree with Coleman (2006: lxiv) in her argument for Martial's Caesar to be an 'idealised abstraction'. Cf. Welch (2007: 145).

[67] Mart. *Spect.* 3.   [68] Mart. *Spect.* 20.

[69] Mart. *Spect.* 33: *numen habet Caesar: sacra est haec, sacra potestas.*

events that occur in the amphitheatre are explained by the emperor's presence.[70]

Indeed, the occurrence of such *mirabilia* in the presence of the emperor appears in different contexts and sources of the early principate. Natural oddities gravitated towards him, whether they were part of the emperor's entourage at court or gifts from across and outside the empire, and whether they were kept at court or displayed to the public.[71] To start with the first emperor, King Porus sent Augustus an assortment of wonders from India – animals including large snakes, a tortoise, and a partridge and a man who was born without limbs.[72] Pausanias tells us that Augustus took the tusks of the Calydonian boar from Tegea and displayed them at the sanctuary of Dionysus at Rome.[73] Suetonius reports that wondrous animals were also displayed by Augustus in different contexts across Rome.[74] Pliny the Elder states that he displayed two preserved giants called Pusio and Secundilla at the Sallustian Gardens and that Augustus' female relatives kept dwarves in their entourage.[75] On an imperial estate on the Laurentine shore, Aulus Gellius tells us of an imperial slave who bore quintuplets and for whom the princeps, who had promulgated marriage and moral legislation, ordered a monument be set up on the Via Laurentina.[76] The strangeness of the births is coupled with the strangeness of the shore itself – a pleasurable and fertile wilderness full of wondrous beasts, where the procurators kept elephants for the Julio-Claudians.[77]

Such a cornucopia of *mirabilia* surrounding the Roman emperor continues through the reigns of different emperors. Tiberius similarly kept a dwarf as part of a group of court jesters, or *copreae*, as they were called;[78] he also received reports of wonders from across the empire, including the finding of a large skeleton, from which a large tooth was sent to Tiberius

---

[70] Coleman (2006: lxxv), for further examples of the different guises that 'Caesar' is depicted as in the *Liber spectaculorum*. Cf. Coleman (1993: 72–4) for an earlier iteration of this argument.

[71] Cf. Beagon (2007: 30–1), Garland (1995: 48–9), and Dench (2005: 287–8). For a comprehensive look at the emperor and wonders in Pliny's *Natural History*, see Baldwin (1995b).

[72] Strabo 15.1.73.   [73] Paus. 8.46.1, 5.   [74] Suet. *Aug.* 43.3.

[75] Plin. *NH.* 7.75; cf. Suet. *Aug.* 83: note how there is quite a bit of evidence for Augustus' proximity to *mirabilia*, even though Suetonius states he avoided dwarves and cripples. Cf. Dench (2005: 287–8) on the complex and contradictory reception of Augustus' persona and how this translates to a contradictory tradition of him rejecting such oddities as luxuries but having them gravitate towards him regardless. Cf. Harlow and Laurence (2017); cf. Trentin (2011: 202).

[76] Gell. 10.2.2.

[77] *CIL* 6.8583 = *ILS* 1578, with Purcell (1998) for citations and discussion of the wonders of the *litus laurentinum*.

[78] Suet. *Tib.* 61.6. For more on the *copreae*, their name, and the evidence for them, see Beard (2014: 143–4) and Purcell (1999: 182–3), on performers at the court of the emperor and their effect on his perception.

himself to inspect,[79] a report from Lisbon of a cave which had a shell-playing Triton, and another on the existence of Nereids.[80] Gabbara, a giant from Arabia, was brought to the emperor Claudius;[81] and Phlegon of Tralles tells stories about hermaphrodites, including one who had suddenly changed from female to male and was subsequently sent to Claudius and another with a similar change who was kept at Agrippina's country house at Mevania.[82] Moreover, according to Pliny, Claudius is also sent a phoenix,[83] as well as a hippocentaur that had been preserved in honey.[84] Indeed, Claudius himself is depicted as an oddity to be kept at court, as observable in Suetonius' *Claudius*, where is mother calls him a *portentum*,[85] and Augustus is not sure how to deal with him.[86]

Under Nero, Tacitus describes the prodigious and depraved nature of Nero's court, including a deformed man named Vatinius,[87] as well as the opulence of his feasts and banquets, which included birds, beasts, and marine life from distant places.[88] According to Suetonius, there was even a story that Nero kept an Egyptian omnivore that would eat anything given to him.[89] Phlegon reports that a child with four heads was presented to Nero.[90] Furthermore, Pliny states that Nero possessed hermaphrodite mares,[91] and that his wife Poppaea was said to have bathed in the milk of donkeys and also wanted to provide her favourite mules with gold shoes.[92] According to Suetonius, Domitian kept a boy with a small head, dressed in red, at his feet at gladiatorial shows.[93] In Statius, there are descriptions of wondrous food from across the empire, which equates Jupiter's control

---

[79] Phlegon, *Mir.* 13–14; cf. Beagon (2007: 34, n. 64) for other findings of large skeletal remains. Cf. Paus. 8.29.3–4.

[80] Plin. *NH.* 9.9. This passage also contains a report to Augustus from the governor of Gaul on dead Nereids found on the shore.

[81] Plin. *NH.* 7.74.   [82] Phlegon, *Mir.* 6–7.   [83] Plin. *NH.* 10.5.

[84] Plin. *NH.* 7.35. Note that there are reports of two centaurs here, and one with the alleged autopsy of Pliny. Cf. Beagon (2007: 37–8), for the preservation of such wonders, and Phlegon, *Mir.* 34–35, who reports of the centaur being preserved in the imperial storehouses during Hadrian's reign. However, it doesn't seem clear that Phlegon is reporting on the same perseveved centaur.

[85] Suet. *Claud.* 3.2.

[86] Suet. *Claud.* 304. For Claudius' illness, see Levick (1990: 13–14), and esp. 200, n. 7; Osgood (2011: 9), and Valente et al. (2002), for a modern differential diagnosis of both his congenital ailments and his death.

[87] Tac. *Ann.* 15.34.2.

[88] Tac. *Ann.* 15.37: *volucres et feras diversis e terris at animalia maris Oceano abusque petiverat*. For more on Tacitus and this interest in paradoxography, and these cited passages of the *Annals*, see Woodman (1992); cf. Ash (2018) on contemporary literature.

[89] Suet. *Ner.* 37.2.   [90] Phlegon, *Mir.* 20.   [91] Plin. *NH.* 11.262.

[92] Plin. *NH.* 11.238; Plin. *NH.* 33.140; cf. Dio 62.28.1 for both stories; cf. Baldwin (1995b: 74) for the citations.

[93] Suet. *Dom.* 4.2. Cf. Zadorojnyi (2015: 294–5) for this passage as part of his argument that colour forms an interesting tool in the characterisation of the emperor in Suetonius' *Lives*.

over nature with Domitian's.[94] Under Trajan, Phlegon reports a story of a two-headed foetus being born who was then thrown into the Tiber at the behest of the haruspices,[95] as well as reports of a woman in Alexandria giving birth to multiple offspring, with Trajan providing their upkeep.[96] Trajan appears in an anecdote on the power of Zeus/Jupiter Heliopolitanus in Macrobius, before the commencement of Trajan's Parthian campaigns.[97] At the head of a resolutely pious army and on the advice of friends, who were familiar with the god that provides oracular replies, Trajan first tested the trustworthiness of the cult and then consulted with the god on whether or not he would return to Rome after the end of the war (*consuluit an Romam perpetrato bello rediturus esset*).[98] The god then ordered that a centurion's staff, which was found in the dedications of the temple, should be broken, wrapped in a handkerchief, and sent back to Trajan. Trajan died before returning to Rome, and his remains were brought back, which revealed the meaning of the oracle: the fragmentary pieces were his remains, and the staff was a sign of the future.[99] Such a story depicts Trajan as a curious emperor, as a conqueror and epistemologist, expanding Rome's empire and knowledge, and charts those limits in human and divine terms. In the same region and in a similar vein, Pausanias records a story of an emperor, arguably Lucius Verus, who wanted to build a canal for navigation to connect Antioch to the sea. The works revealed the remains of a giant, identified by the oracle at Claros to be that of Orontes from India.[100] This story connects two themes: that of the emperor as an imperial voyager who alters the landscape by the building of thoroughfares and the discoverer and arbiter of wonders. Thus, the parallel themes of imperialism and *mirabilia* are combined under the auspices of the Roman emperor himself.

As final examples to round off the period in question, the *Historia Augusta* gives examples of Elagabalus' famed luxurious tastes and exotic

---

[94] Stat. *Silv.* 1.6.9–27 with Newlands (2002: 240–1).   [95] Phlegon. *Mir.* 25.

[96] Phlegon. *Mir.* 29: 'the emperor Trajan ordered that they be supported from his own funds' (οὓς αὐτοκράτωρ Τραιανὸς ἐκέλευσεν ἐκ τῶν ἰδίων χρημάτων τρέφεσθαι), which mirrors his alimentary scheme.

[97] Macrob. *Sat.* 1.23.14. Many thanks to Nicholas Purcell for pointing this passage out.

[98] Macrob. *Sat.* 1.23.14–16.

[99] Macrob. *Sat.* 1.23.16. Cf. Dio 68.29.1–3: Ἰνδούς τε γὰρ ἐνενόει, καὶ τὰ ἐκείνων πράγματα ἐπολυπραγμόνει (For he had India on his mind, and he was curious about their affairs). Cf. Leigh (2013) for the resonance of meddlesome behaviour (πολυπραγμοσύνη). Trajan died before returning to Rome (Dio 68.33.1–3).

[100] Paus. 8.29.3–4; see Jones (2000) for his identification of the emperor as Lucius Verus and the corroborating evidence, including discussion of the remains of the mythical Orontes and his provenance.

wild animals,[101] and that he enjoyed the company of men with different physical deformities for his amusement.[102] The *Historia Augusta* goes on to describe how Alexander Severus, his successor, disposed of all the *mirabilia* and oddities Elagabalus had accumulated.[103] Notably, he gave them to the public: 'He granted as a present both male and female dwarves, fools, male prostitutes, and all performers and dancers' (*Nanos et nanas et moriones et vocales exsoletos et omnia acroamata et pantomimos populo donavit*).[104] All this evidence shows the Roman emperor in close proximity to the wondrous, which helped shape the nature of the discourse about him and indeed is connected to the public interaction between the people and *princeps* as marvels to be shared. To build upon the theme alluded to in the context of Alexander Severus, the difference in potential interpretation is nicely exhibited by the juxtaposition of the public display of these wonders and their maintenance, hidden away in the court of the emperor. This question of the accessibility of *mirabilia* has been discussed in the evidence from the triumph and games and is a theme that is reflected in the evidence. Martial, Pliny, and Josephus separately admonish Nero for keeping his collection of wonders locked away at the *Domus Aurea*, whilst simultaneously praising Vespasian for doing the opposite, which is part of a moral discourse involving these wonders and how they affect the perception of an emperor.[105] However, as argued, the line between narratives of 'good' and 'bad' is not clearly defined, meaning that the emperor could easily slip into either characterisation, since all this evidence depicts the emperor as having patronised and maintained *mirabilia*, whether in a private collection or as part of a euergetical public display.

In the end, it is interesting that the emperor would be depicted as closely associated with *mirabilia* and that his reception would be affected by this. This gives the impression of the emperor as an inherently complex and ambiguous individual. However, to leave it at that would be similar to concluding that there were binary 'good' or 'bad' understandings of the emperor. Alternatively, there is a flexibility to his reception in that he could be cast into different roles by different people, which all contributed to the discourse about who he was and what he was meant to be. As regards to

---

[101] HA. *Heliogab.* 22–4.   [102] HA. *Heliogab.* 29.3.
[103] HA, *Alex. Sev.* 34.2–4. Cf. Garland (1995: 49–50), Beagon (2007: 32), and Trentin (2011: 203) for this evidence and their analysis.
[104] HA. *Alex. Sev.* 34.2.
[105] Mart. *Spect.* 2; Plin. *NH.* 34.84; 35.120; cf. Joseph. *BJ.* 7.158–160; cf. Darwall-Smith (1996: 58–68) on the *Domus Aurea* and Vespasian's *Templum Pacis*. For more on the function of the *Templum Pacis*, see Noreña (2003: 26–7).

mirabilia, it should be remarkable that the emperor is seen near unbelievable and bizarre things, particularly from a modern perspective. It seems that it was normal for the Roman emperor to be associated with the wondrous. Therefore, there was a cognitive association of the emperor and *mirabilia*, which could be interpreted in moralistic terms (as perhaps either 'good' or 'bad') but not in a way that it was an impossibility. In other words, it was obvious for the emperor to be close to *mirabilia* because he was the emperor.[106] Furthermore, this cognitive association allowed for the emperor to seem as wondrous as the wonders themselves. Hopefully, the following examples will illustrate these points.

4.3   The Emperor As Wonder and Monster

First are the stories of the emperor and marine life. As argued by Purcell, fish were paradoxical and ambiguous, much like the wonders discussed in the previous section, particularly concerning their consumption: 'Eating fish could be as morally ambiguous, therefore, as eating dog, as taxonomically disturbing as a diet of locusts, and as dissonant with the dispositions of Nature as a nice glass of sea-water.'[107] Briefly, there are several axes of ambiguity that concerned the sea and marine life, which included the sea's paradoxical poverty and provision of luxury and that fish could be thought of as inedible yet also an important source of food.[108] Paradoxical and counterintuitive descriptions are features of marine life, *mirabilia*, and indeed the Roman emperorship.

Therefore, it should not be surprising that stories about marine life are similar to stories about wonders and *mirabilia*, and accordingly that the emperor would also be present within this context.[109] Interestingly, the emperor can be portrayed as having a commanding effect on the sea and its

[106] Cf. Garland (1995: 49), Beagon (2007: 31), Murphy (2004: 197), and Dench (2005: 287); cf. Veyne (2002: 19), who cites Fusel de Coulanges on how the emperor was a god because he was emperor. This suggests an interesting parallel to the imperial cult and questions of the emperor's divinity, which could be reconciled with his proximity to these wonders. This will be discussed further in Section 6.3.

[107] Purcell (1995: 132). Cf. Kneebone (2020: 403–4): 'the sea is figured as a realm that may lie geographically or rhetorically within, but that is also morally and epistemologically well beyond, the ordering force of imperial control.'

[108] Purcell (1995: 133–6, 144); cf. Plin. *NH*. 9.104–5, who comments on the inedibility of fish and its potential as a source of luxury and corruption.

[109] See also Purcell (1995: 137) for the citation of Oppian's *Halieutica* (1.56–72), a poem on fishing, which includes a dedication to Marcus Aurelius and Commodus and the imagery of plentiful fish giving themselves willingly to the emperor. Cf. Kneebone (2020: 408–9) for analysis of this passage and the limits of an emperor's power (ὄρχαμος γαίης; the leader of the *earth*), and 396–404, on empire and control at the end of the Antonines in the poem.

inhabitants, which is perhaps a reflection on the perception of his power, significantly in relation to a liminal and feared sea. Pliny tells of a story where a fish jumped out of the water and landed at the feet of Octavian, which was interpreted by seers as testament to his future dominion of the seas.[110] He also provides an anecdote on how a small fish attached itself to the rudder of Gaius' ship on its way back to Antium, preventing its movement.[111] In his section on whales, Pliny provides a story of an encounter between Claudius and a whale that had gotten stuck between a shipwreck and the harbour at Ostia:

> Orca et in portu Ostiensi visa est oppugnata a Claudio principe. Venerat tum exaedificante eo portum, invitata naufragiis tergorum advectorum e Gallia ... Praetendi iussit Caesar plagas multiplices inter ora portus profectusque ipse cum praetorianis cohortibus populo Romano spectaculum praebuit, lanceas congerente milite e navigiis adsultantibus, quorum unum mergi vidimus reflatu beluae oppletum unda.[112]

> A whale was seen in the port of Ostia in a battle with the emperor Claudius. It arrived at that time when he was finishing the port, having been allured by a shipwreck of imported hides from Gaul ... Caesar ordered extensive nets to be stretched out across the entrance of the port, and setting out himself with the praetorian cohorts he offered a spectacle to the Roman people, with spears being showered on the beast by the army from assailing ships, one of which we saw being sunk, having been filled up by a wave from an exhalation of the beast.

It is notable that Claudius is described as having personally led the attack by boat to encounter the 'beast'; as such, the emperor is seen to fight a monster of the sea, bringing into relief the direct association of an emperor with the wondrous. Furthermore, there is a sense of wonder to the proceedings, particularly when Pliny describes it as a *spectaculum*, making it conceptually akin to shows in the arena that were described in the previous section – an aquatic *venatio* of sorts.[113]

There are stories that depict the emperor being presented with a large fish by a fisherman, which includes Suetonius' story of Tiberius being presented with a mullet on Capri,[114] Seneca's anecdote about Tiberius being given a huge mullet, which he promptly sent to be sold,[115] and

---

[110] Plin. *NH*. 9.55.   [111] Plin. *NH*. 32.4.   [112] Plin. *NH*. 9.14–15.

[113] Cf. Coleman (1993: 56), Suet. *Claud*. 21.6, Tac. *Ann*. 12.56, and Dio 61(60).33.3 for evidence of Claudius' staged *naumachia* at the Fucine Lake. Potentially, 'Claudius and the Whale' should be seen within the context of Roman entertainment. See Coleman (1993), esp. 66–7, for evidence of *venationes* with an aquatic element, particularly Mart. *Spect*. 34.3–4.

[114] Suet. *Tib*. 60; cf. Champlin (2008: 408–9, 423–4) for his analysis of this passage.

[115] Sen. *Ep*. 95.42., cf. Suet. *Tib*. 34.1 for Tiberius attempting to regulate the market after three mullets sold for 30,000 sesterces. Cf. Champlin (2008: 423–4).

Juvenal's Fourth Satire, in which a fisherman presents Domitian with a turbot of similarly large proportions, prompting a meeting of the imperial advisors to discuss finding a suitable plate to hold it.[116] The story about Tiberius on Capri will be discussed later in this section, but it is important to tease out the relevant themes that are shared by these stories. First is the size of the fish in question, which is invariably large, and accordingly described with hyperbole, as Juvenal does with his turbot: 'there appeared a wondrous chunk of an Adriatic turbot'.[117] This is comparable to other instances in the poem where the fish is described: in line 45 as a 'monster' (*monstrum*), line 72 for the lacking of a dish big enough for such a fish (*sed derat pisci patinae mensura*), and lines 121 and 127, both instances describing the turbot as a 'beast' (*belua*). Thus, its size and bestial proportions make it strange and paradoxical, a true wonder from the sea. Second is the exorbitant prices that went with fish of such sizes: again, in his fourth satire, Juvenal describes a mullet that was bought for 6,000 *sestertii* by a Crispinus, an elusive member of Domitian's court.[118] Juvenal continues to joke that he could have bought the fisherman for less.[119] Remarkably similar sentiments are articulated by Pliny the Elder, where Asinius Celer bought a mullet for 8,000 *sestertii* in the time of Gaius, and the creeping luxury is described by the exchange rate of three cooks for the price of one fish.[120] These fish are presented as symbols of luxury and depravity. Yet, paradoxically, the concentration is placed on the luxurious aspect of mullet trade, in that they would cost so much, which is starkly juxtaposed to the implied poverty of the fishermen who are depicted in these stories, who seem invariably to give their *monstra* as a gift. Such is the paradox of seafood: produce from destitute areas that required the investment of the wealthy to rear and fish them.[121]

The paradox is taken further in Seneca's anecdote about Tiberius and the mullet. As with the vignettes from Juvenal, Seneca admonishes the buyer for spending 5,000 *sestertii* on the fish yet is not as outraged with the

---

[116] Juv. 4.37–72, esp. 65–72. Cf. Courtney (2013: 168–9).

[117] Juv. 4.39: *incidit Hadriaci spatium admirabile rhombi*; cf. Sen. *Ep.* 95.42 for his description: *Mullum ingentis formae* (a mullet of immense size). Cf. Suet. *Tib.* 60: *grandem mullum*. Cf. Andrews (1949: 186) on the various evidence for the size and price of these specimens.

[118] Juv. 4.14–15. See Baldwin (1979: 109, n. 1) for the discussion on the prosopographical identification of Crispinus as *eques* and praetorian prefect, against which Baldwin argues quite strongly for him being a *scurra* (dandy or jester) at court, with reference to Juv. 4.31. That he is called a *monstrum* at Juv. 4.2 bolsters this point, suggesting that he himself was a wonder himself, as were the *copreae* that were discussed before.

[119] Juv. 4.25–6: *potuit fortasse minoris piscator quam piscis emi* (It was perhaps possible for the fisherman to be bought for less than the fish).

[120] Plin. *NH.* 9.67.　　[121] Purcell (1995: 136).

first individual who had given it to Tiberius as a present, since he thought it 'Caesar worthy'.[122] Thus, such large fish, whilst being monsters and symbols of luxury to be avoided, are simultaneously seen to be obvious gifts for the emperor,[123] which fits nicely into the theme of this section on how such *mirabilia* gravitated to him. The preponderance of this evidence that places the emperor in close proximity with paradoxical marine life suggests that he himself was shaped by that association. In other words, the narratives of luxury and the monstrosities of the deep inevitably coloured the way in which the emperor was perceived.

Second are the stories where the emperor is depicted as a mediator in problems arising with the wondrous.[124] Several anecdotes depict the emperor in a situation that places him in the role of an arbiter in order to settle disputes and give opinions that were meant to prove decisive.[125] As such, they could be associated with legal disputations and dispensations of justice. As argued in the previous section, there is the spectre of hope and fear when it concerns the potential reaction of the emperor in these situations, allowing for the possibility that he could respond either positively or negatively.[126] However, there is a significant difference, given that the subject matter that is being disputed has to do with wondrous objects instead. The 'tale of the unbreakable glass' should be viewed within this rubric, and it appears in different forms and sources.[127] Petronius' version has Trimalchio tell a story of a cup that could not be broken: the inventor goes in front of the emperor to show him his invention, gives a demonstration of its malleability and inability to shatter, but unexpectedly is beheaded on the orders of the emperor so as to keep the knowledge of the invention contained.[128] The alleged reason for this response was the fear that gold would become worthless if such an invention were to hit the market.[129] Pliny the Elder provides a less morbid parallel about flexible

---

[122] Sen. *Ep.* 95.42: *putavit Caesarem dignum.*

[123] On gift-giving to the emperor, see Millar (1977: 139–44).

[124] The closest to a systematic analysis of this sort of material is Champlin (2008) on Tiberius.

[125] Two examples are worth mentioning but unfortunately cannot receive full attention. Both involve Tiberius calling for enquiries and seeking help to solve issues pertaining to the wondrous. These include the story of the tooth mentioned above (Phlegon, *Mir.* 13–14) and the story of the death of Pan being shouted out near the island of Paxoi in the Ionian Sea and consequently being lamented at Palodes on the shore of Epirus (Plut. *Mor.* 419b–d). They are dealt with in Champlin (2008: 422, 414) respectively.

[126] See Section 4.2. Cf. Section 2.3.

[127] Champlin (2008: 411), for the phrase and a discussion of the relevant evidence, to which the following passage is indebted.

[128] Petron. *Sat.* 51.

[129] Petron. *Sat.* 51.6: *quia enim, si scitum esset, aurum pro luto haberemus* (Because if it were to become known, we'd exchange gold for mud). Cf. Ash (2015: 269–71) for an illuminating discussion on the

glass in the time of Tiberius' principate, which resulted in the destruction of the workshop in which it was made, accompanied by similar reasoning for the feared devaluation of precious metals.[130]

In Dio's version of this story, which occurs also under Tiberius, the inventor is rather an architect who also invents a pulley system to repair a portico that had been leaning.[131] Owing to the emperor's jealousy, the man is exiled from the city. However, in the scene in which the inventor pleads for pardon from Tiberius, the tale of the unbreakable glass gets repeated, which bears greater resemblance to Petronius' version with its morbid conclusion.[132] Problems of historicity aside, these tales are historically relevant as they exhibit perceptions of an emperor dealing with wondrous inventions in different ways, accompanied by reasoning for why this was the case.[133] This is also why the story about Vespasian and the mechanical engineer, which tells of another wondrous pulley mechanism that gets suppressed by the emperor so that he could feed the *plebs*, should be seen as similar to the previous stories.[134] Despite the significant differences, the presence of the emperor is a common factor, which suggests that there was a conceptual framework in which the emperor was expected to deal with these situations, whether positively or negatively. To push it slightly further, the desired outcomes of Petronius' and Suetonius' different stories are quite similar, given that they were meant to be protective by keeping the value of gold stable and securing jobs for the *plebs*, but the way this is achieved is different. Such a difference could indeed be explained through a moral discussion of what 'good' or 'bad' emperors do, but it also betrays a cognitive aspect that places the emperor in a position to make these decisions, and in all cases to the detriment of the wondrous invention at hand. It suggests that he is an arbiter and protector, much akin to how he is portrayed with *mirabilia* in general.

In a similar way to how Suetonius organised his *Life of Caligula*, so now we turn to exhibitions of the emperor's monstrosity.[135] As outlined in the

---

moral ambiguity of gold and indeed how this ambiguity is depicted in Tac. *Ann.* 16.1–3, which show's Nero's treasure hunt to find Dido's gold and contains similar themes to what is being discussed in this section.

[130] Plin. *NH.* 36.195. However, Pliny goes on to state that this was of little consequence, since under Nero similarly strong cups called *petrotos* (stony, presumably in reference to their durability) sold for 6,000 sesterces.

[131] Dio 57.21.5–6.   [132] Dio 57.21.7.

[133] Cf. Plin. *NH.* 36.195 for his remark on this matter: 'that is the tale that for some time now more frequently repeated than trustworthy' (*eaque fama crebrior diu quam certior fuit*). Cf. pp. 26–28.

[134] Suet. *Vesp.* 18.

[135] Suet. *Cal.* 22.1. Cf. Gladhill (2012: 315–48) for an exploration of Suetonius' ekphrases of the emperor's body, looking at the lines between biography and sculpture. Gladhill argues that

previous section, the proximity of the emperor to *mirabilia* and the wondrous allowed for the imagination of the Roman emperor to encompass more fantastical and monstrous guises, in which he was the object of wonder and fear.[136] Indeed, Seneca likens a ruler that takes delight in cruelty to a beast.[137]

Thus, the emperor's actions allow him to be conceptually linked to the bestial and accordingly start to be viewed as a beast himself. As a bridge from the previous discussion, the anecdote about Tiberius and the fisherman on Capri provides an interesting case study. As outlined earlier in the section, this story has parallels with others that present a large fish to a monarch, but here, the encounter is unexpected, prompting a gruesome reaction from the emperor:

> In paucis diebus quam Capreas attigit piscatori qui sibi secretum agenti grandem mullum inopinanter obtulerat perfricari eodem pisce faciem iussit, territus quod is a tergo insulae per aspera et devia erepsisset ad se. gratulanti autem inter poenam quod non et lucustam quam praegrandem ceperat obtulisset, lucusta quoque lacerari os imperavit.

> In the early days when Tiberius arrived at Capri, a fisherman appeared unexpectedly at his lair, carrying up to him a large mullet. Tiberius, terrified that he had clambered up from the back of the island to him through the rough and trackless rocks, ordered that his face be scrubbed by that same fish. And though during the punishment the fisherman expressed gratitude that he had not also offered that huge crab that he had caught before, Tiberius also ordered that he be mutilated by the crab.[138]

This has been described as an example of a tradition that depicts Tiberius as a tyrant: dissimulating, grim, and cruel.[139] It is remarkable that an emperor would be depicted as terrified (*territus*) of a fisherman, which calls to mind Fronto's *De eloquentia*, in which the emperor is called to 'frighten the savage' (*feroces territare*),[140] which suggests that it was within the remit of

---

Suetonius inverts the omnipresence and power of the imperial image by using his description to influence his audience's perception of the principate. See Garland (1995: 86–104) and Barton (1994: 95–131) on the status of physiognomy in antiquity.

[136] Garland (1995: 51). Note that this is a similar argument as the one in Section 3.2, in which the nature and power of the Roman emperor were open to ambiguous interpretation, and the spectrum of cruelty and justice and generosity and parsimony could be equally exhibited. Cf. Braund and James (1998), on the depiction of Claudius' monstrosity in Seneca's *Apocolocyntosis*, and in particular Sen. *Apoc.* 5.1–3, which describes Claudius' physical appearance as monstrous.

[137] Sen. *Clem.* 1.25.1; cf. Braund and James (1998: 293); Braund (2009: 367–9), for the juxtaposition of *crudelitas* and *clementia* and particularly on the reference to Alexander of Macedon's savagery.

[138] Suet. *Tib.* 60.

[139] See Syme (1958: 420–30) on the received tradition on Tiberius' characterisation.

[140] Fronto, *De eloquentia* 1.5. See p. 6.

the emperor to be terrifying as well, particularly for those at the edge of society. This indicates a liminality that is shared by both the emperor and the fisherman in that they could be feared.[141] Furthermore, if juxtaposed with the passage from Seneca's *De clementia*, where the cruel ruler becomes a monster by association, so also potentially is Tiberius in Suetonius' vignette when sea creatures are used to torture the fisherman.

A further parallel can be created to compare the potential reactions of the emperor in such situations, and the contours of justice and monstrosity: Vedius Pollio and his man-eating *muraenae*.[142] There is a consistency within the different traditions of this story, which tell of Vedius Pollio's cruelty in his feeding of slaves to morays. The version in Seneca's *De ira* has a slave being punished for breaking a crystal cup by being fed to his eels. As with the slaves who fled to statues of the emperor for asylum, so too does this slave to Augustus, with the result being the destruction of Vedius' cup collection and the filling up of his fishponds.[143] Seneca then gives Augustus' verbal reprimand:

> Fuit Caesari sic castigandus amicus; bene usus est viribus suis: 'E convivio rapi homines imperas et novi generis poenis lancinari? Si calix tuus fractus est, viscera hominis distrahentur? Tantum tibi placebis, ut ibi aliquem duci iubeas, ubi Caesar est?'[144]

> His friend had to be censured as follows by Caesar; he used his powers well: 'Do you order men to be carried away from dinner and be torn to pieces by this new form of punishment? If your cup was broken, will a man's innards be ripped apart? You fancy yourself that much that you would order someone to be carried away even when Caesar is around'?

However, when compared to the story of Tiberius and the fisherman, and the nature of the evidence in terms of imperial justice, the answers to these rhetorical questions could be a 'yes' and indeed perpetuated by Caesar himself. Such was the unpredictability of the potential response by the emperor, which was predicated on the correct use of force, as is reflected in the various stories of fear and expectation in intercession.[145] So too was the

---

[141] Cf. Purcell (1995: 136) for the precarious life of a fisherman, who seems to occupy the edge of society, being more prone to chance and the potential boom or bust of the sea.

[142] On Vedius Pollio's identity, see Syme (1961: 23–30). For the evidence, see Purcell (1995: 141), which are as follows: Sen. *De Ira*, 3.40.2; Sen. *De Clem.* 1.18; Plin. *NH.* 9.77; Dio 54.23.

[143] See pp. 79–82. Compare, however, with the story from Suet. *Aug.* 67.2, where Augustus orders the legs of a trusted slave broken after being bribed. Also, Suet. *Cal.* 32.2, for cutting his slave's hands off and hanging them around his neck for his guests to see. Cf. Trentin (2011: 201–2) for more examples of this sort.

[144] Sen. *De Ira*, 3.40.2.   [145] Gibson (2018: 286–7), on the use of *vis* in Tacitus.

reception of the emperor with respect to wonders, since by his proximity to them in the Roman mindset, he would be coloured by their implications.

The point of this juxtaposition is to highlight how the evidence can reveal different perspectives and that there are always potentially negative characterisations possible with any topics that have been discussed thus far, whether it concerns the public display of *mirabilia* in the arena or a large fish being presented to the emperor at court.[146] An excellent example of the themes explored in this section comes in the form of Dio's description of Commodus' exploits in the arena and of the senatorial acclamation toward Commodus, calling him the first and most fortunate, which fits into a wider theme, and remains observable in the epitome, of Commodus' expectation of constant honouring.[147] However, the reaction of the people at Rome was one of feared anticipation at what the emperor would do:

> τοῦ δὲ δὴ λοιποῦ δήμου πολλοὶ μὲν οὐδὲ ἐσῆλθον ἐς τὸ θέατρον, εἰσὶ δ' οἳ παρακύψαντες ἀπηλλάττοντο τὸ μέν τι αἰσχυνόμενοι τοῖς ποιουμένοις, τὸ δὲ καὶ δεδιότες, ἐπειδὴ λόγος διῆλθεν ὅτι τοξεῦσαί τινας ἐθελήσει ὥσπερ ὁ Ἡρακλῆς τὰς Στυμφαλίδας. καὶ ἐπιστεύθη γε οὗτος ὁ λόγος, ἐπειδή ποτε πάντας τοὺς τῶν ποδῶν ἐν τῇ πόλει ὑπὸ νόσου ἢ καὶ ἑτέρας τινὸς συμφορᾶς ἐστερημένους ἀθροίσας δρακόντων τέ τινα αὐτοῖς εἴδη περὶ τὰ γόνατα περιέπλεξε, καὶ σπόγγους ἀντὶ λίθων βάλλειν δοὺς ἀπέκτεινέ σφας ῥοπάλῳ παίων ὡς γίγαντας.

> As for the rest of the people, the majority did not even enter into the amphitheatre: there were those who departed with a furtive glance; including some who felt shame at what was happening, and others who were also fearful, since rumour had spread that he wanted to shoot with arrows some people just like Heracles had done with the Stymphalian birds. And this story was believed as well, since at that time when Commodus gathered together all those in the city who lost their legs due to illness or other such misfortune and had their knees tied around with some serpent-like appendages; and giving them sponges rather than stones to throw, he executed them with a club smiting them as giants.[148]

There are several themes in this passage that are relevant to the emperor as a monstrosity. As described, the people did not dare enter the arena due to fears that Commodus would re-enact the myth of Hercules and the

---

[146] For Roman arenas and shows as places where social hierarchies and divisions were rehearsed, see Edmondson (1996: 103–4).

[147] Dio 73(72).20.2, for the acclamations of the senators, and 73(72).15.1–6, for the excessive honours given to Commodus. For a discussion on the interesting dynamics of fear, representation, and interchangeability of personal identities in Dio's contemporary books of history, see Gleason (2011), and esp. 33–52 for Commodus' reign.

[148] Dio 73(72).20.2–3.

Stymphalian birds.[149] Myths are restaged in the arena, thus making the wondrous an enacted reality, with the emperor himself at its centre. As outlined in Section 4.1, there is a connection between myth and reality, which is played out in the reported fears of the would-be spectators. What is essential here is the contamination of the emperor in this process: instead of being perceived as a hero, Commodus, the ersatz Hercules, is feared because of the rumour that he would turn his bow and arrow towards the crowd and kill them, like Hercules had the Stymphalian birds.[150] Indeed, there are ambivalences of identity at play throughout the passage, for not only is Commodus an emperor impersonating a deity in the arena but the would-be spectators fear that they too will be perceived as beastly – themselves figures to be feared. Indeed, the reactions of the people to Commodus' exploits in the arena as described by Herodian also point to such ambivalence.[151] Commodus loses favour with the people, as they saw a 'gloomy spectacle' (τότε σκυθρωπὸν εἶδεν ὁ δῆμος θέαμα) and he debased the emperorship due to his appearance in the amphitheatre as a gladiator. The moral judgement in this conversation between people and emperor should not be dismissed; however, it is interesting to compare and contrast the reactions of the crowd to Commodus' exploits. What seems common in their descriptions combines both fascination and disgust, whatever the authorial justifications, suggesting an ambivalent reaction to the emperor. As such, an excellent contrasting image appears in Herodian, where rumour had spread across Italy that in Rome were spectacles that had never before been seen or heard.[152] At first glance, it would seem contradictory to the quoted Dio passage above, but when combined they highlight the fascination and uncertainty in the understanding of the Roman emperor, which elucidates his status as an oddity in of himself.

Furthermore, this is stressed by the subsequent story that Dio provides, which he argues made the potential Stymphalian birds encounter a believable event. Combined with what was described at the beginning of the chapter about the teratological, namely the interest in the 'freakish' or deformed, and the emperor's status as a purveyor of wonders, the spectre of a staged gigantomachy using rounded-up disabled people without legs as

<hr>

[149] Hekster (2002: 120, 146–7). [150] Hekster (2002: 12–13), on the ambiguity of Hercules.
[151] Hdn. 1.14.7–15.7.
[152] Hdn. 1.15.1: 'With the rumours going abroad, people came in from the whole of Italy and the bordering provinces, to marvel at that which they had never before seen or heard' (διαδραμούσης δὲ τῆς φήμης συνέθεον ἔκ τε τῆς Ἰταλίας πάσης καὶ τῶν ὁμόρων ἐθνῶν, θεασόμενοι ἃ μὴ πρότερον μήτε ἑωράκεσαν μήτε ἠκηκόεσαν).

giants (with appendages attached to their knees to make it appear as if they had serpents for legs instead) might not be surprising.[153] Indeed, this same scene is repeated in the *Historia Augusta*, with the manner of their execution the main difference, killed by arrow rather than club.[154] The staged mythical re-enactment becomes a gruesome scene of mass execution, with the emperor at the centre perpetrating the act, meaning that he is the focal point of the display and also that he has muddled his status with his proximity to the mythological and the teratological. In other words, he is feared to be a monster as well.[155]

In his chapter named 'The Roman emperor in his monstrous world', Garland describes the paradoxical nature of the emperor and his power due to his anomalous position, reflected in the monstrosities he patronised, which in turn made him monstrous himself: freakish both in appetite and behaviour, taste and temperament, the emperor was more licentious than Petronius' grossly self-indulgent Trimalchio in satisfying his grotesque whims.[156] However, Garland is not quite there in this description. The continuum of stories that show the emperor in close proximity to *mirabilia* betrays a much more complicated picture, which does not fit so easily into archetypal categories of 'good' and 'bad', with Garland concentrating on the latter. The vignette is more complex: there is the potential that the emperor could be benevolent and monstrous simultaneously. These stories were formed and discussed over time and space, attributed to emperors for many reasons, but all pointing to a larger thought-world about his nature. The stories point to a certain precariousness that would shape the opinion of an emperor during his reign, and indeed after it, and were essential components of the conversation of acceptance. These sorts of stories added to the mystique of the imperial office, obscuring the machinations of the emperor in his court. This is testament to a curiosity about what the emperor seemed to be. They are two sides of the same coin: the vulgarisation of these wondrous

[153] For Commodus' interest in *mirabilia* and the deformed, see HA, *Comm.* 10.4–11.4. Cf. Coleman (1990). This evidence from Dio should be read as a fatal charade. What seems different here is that the 'giants' are the sick and the disabled across the city, which could show both the subversion of this form of execution (hence the fear of the crowd) and the precarious status of the disabled in the Roman world; cf. Garland (1995).

[154] HA, *Comm.* 9.6. Cf. Garland (1995: 51–2); cf. Dio 73(72).21.1–2; Hdn. 1.15.4–5, for further examples of Commodus' exploits in the arena and the consequent reaction.

[155] Compare with Beard (2003b: 39): 'one of the characteristics of monstrous despots is that they *literalize* the metaphors of cultural politics – to disastrous effect.' Thus the line between the performance of ideology and it becoming a reality is thin, also suggesting a similarly thin line between being an emperor and a monster.

[156] Garland (1995: 51).

stories meant that they formed part of what the emperor was in popular discourse, thus colouring the perception of him. This discourse continued throughout his reign and into his legacy, which is an essential theme for the remainder of this book, which will concern making fun of the emperor, or speaking openly to him, the ambiguities of the golden age, and the formation of an imperial afterlife.

CHAPTER 5

Wisdom and Wit: Making Fun of the Emperor

5.1 Public and Hidden Transcripts in Imperial Humour

καί ποτέ τις ἀνὴρ Γαλάτης ἰδὼν αὐτὸν ἐπὶ βήματος ὑψηλοῦ ἐν Διὸς
εἴδει χρηματίζοντα ἐγέλασεν· ὁ δὲ Γάιος ἐκάλεσέ τε αὐτὸν καὶ
ἀνήρετο 'τί σοι δοκῶ εἶναι;' καὶ ὃς ἀπεκρίνατο (ἐρῶ γὰρ αὐτὸ τὸ
λεχθέν) 'ὅτι "μέγα παραλήρημα.' καὶ οὐδὲν μέντοι δεινὸν ἔπαθε·
σκυτοτόμος γὰρ ἦν. οὕτω που ῥᾷον τὰς τῶν τυχόντων ἢ τὰς τῶν
ἐν ἀξιώσει τινὶ ὄντων παρρησίας οἱ τοιοῦτοι φέρουσι.

There was once a certain Gaulish man who laughed when he saw
Gaius on a high pedestal styling himself in the form of Zeus. Gaius
then called him over and asked him: 'What do I look like to you?' to
which he replied (I produce exactly what was said) that he was 'a great
raving lunatic'. And in fact, nothing bad happened to him! For he was
a shoemaker. Thus, I suppose that such humble people who produce
frank speech suffer more lightly in contrast to those who are of
a certain rank.[1]

The anecdote in the epigraph provides a convenient and interesting
transition from the wondrous to interactions between the emperor and
his subjects, particularly concerning themes of jocularity and open
speech. The context of Xiphilinus' epitomised section of Dio concerns
Caligula's pretensions towards the divine, precipitated by a decree that
the emperor should sit on a high platform even in the senate house, so
that he would be elevated and unable to be approached.[2] This physical
separation, as argued by Dio, allowed for Gaius to claim a further divine
separation from his subjects.[3] This was compounded by the display of

---

[1] Dio 59.26.8–9.
[2] Dio 59.26.3, which states that Gaius even wanted a high platform in the senate as well, to prevent
people from approaching him, and even his statues were to be protected under guard.
[3] Dio 59.26.5. Cf. Suet. *Cal.* 22.2–4, esp. Suetonius' first sentence on Gaius moving past the form of the
principate (*species principatus*) and even outstripping the dignity of *principes* and kings towards the
greatness (*maiestas*) of gods.

Gaius in the guise of numerous deities, changing appearance and costume to impersonate Gods such as Zeus, Poseidon, Hercules, Dionysus, Hera, Aphrodite, and Artemis.[4] As with the wonder tales, the emperor's proximity to the mythological and wondrous is being described here, with the emperor being the wonder in question. Concomitant with that, however, is the spectre of negativity and fear in its interpretation, a similar theme to what was described in Chapter 4. The tone of these passages is one of derision and ridicule at the absurdity of Caligula's actions, which culminates in the anecdote of the Gaulish shoemaker near the end of the chapter in Dio. With reference to what Dio had been describing prior, with Caligula on a high step in the guise of Zeus, the Gaulish man let out a laugh.[5] This prompted the emperor to ask the man who he looked to him. The Greek 'τί σοι δοκῶ εἶναι;' is quite loaded with a few interpretations. Perhaps it could be taken as rhetorical, meaning that it was clear that he seemed to be Zeus, making the laugh absurd. Similarly rhetorical is that it could be interpreted as a statement of fact: that it should be clear that he was emperor, with all that is sinister behind that implied.[6] Similarly possible is the straightforward understanding of the question, of what he seemed to be, which brings us to an interesting proposition.

The implication that Gaius' display was open for interpretation and opinion, even if it was not always expressed openly, exposes a dynamic in the perception and critical discussion of the Roman emperor. It finds its parallels in Wintrobe's Dictator's Dilemma, as it is in the interests of the autocratic ruler to obtain this information – something that is a potential interpretation of Gaius' question to the shoemaker.[7] Thoughts and opinions about the Roman emperor would be kept secret unless expressed in different forms, whether openly or more obscurely. Nonetheless, ancient literature is littered with attestations of spoken opinion of these different forms that thus give the impression of how the emperor seemed; and interestingly, it is often exhibited using interactions between individuals or groups from non-elite backgrounds expressing themselves in front of the emperor. This phenomenon is of great interest to this book, as it is a potential window into a thought-world concerning the emperor and

---

[4] Dio 59.26.5–8; cf. Suet. *Cal.* 22.2, where statues of gods from Greece are imported and altered to carry the bust of Gaius.

[5] Cf. Beard (2014: 135).

[6] See Ahl (1984), Rudich (1993), and Rutledge (2001) for the history of potential misfortune if one was not more careful with one's words. For speaking truth to power, see Section 1.1.2.

[7] See Section 1.3.

particularly in this case about the discourses of criticism using humour and joke.[8] Therefore, this section concerns these humorous scenes and jokes. It should be noted that the evidence provided here does not pretend to be exhaustive in that it will catalogue and analyse every attestation of a humorous encounter with the emperor,[9] but it will cover problems and themes that are evoked in these jokes. This includes the problem of 'elite' as opposed to 'popular' discourses; the extent to which such evidence can reveal a 'hidden transcript', or rather concealed opinion being veiled in jocularity; the problem of 'good' and 'bad' characterisations; and what such discourses can tell us about the thought-world concerning the Roman emperor.

Indeed, the example provided in the epigraph can be a good springboard to these themes, which are relevant to this section. Translators have rendered μέγα παραλήρημα as a 'piece of absurdity', which in truth does not convey the full spectrum of its meaning, as it only seems to give a visual aspect: basically that Gaius looked absurd. It seems related to the verb παραληρέω, which means to talk nonsense, or be raving mad, and it seems to give the sense of talking gibberish or engaging in incomprehensible chatter.[10] Perhaps then, alongside a sight that is risible, is the meaning that the Gaulish shoemaker called the emperor crazy. Understandably, the boldness of such a statement directed towards an emperor without consequence required explanation. The argument adopted by Dio once it was determined that nothing bad happened to the man was that it must have been due to his lower station.[11] This sentiment is echoed by Tacitus in the *Annals*, in the context of the popular reaction at Rome to Nero's divorce of Octavia and his subsequent betrothal to Poppaea, which was an active and vociferous support of Octavia: 'hence the frequent and hardly concealed complaints by the public, who have lesser discretion from

[8] This is similar to a 'hidden transcript' in Section 1.1.2, in which 'true' opinions of subordinates in power relationships are obscured but surface intermittently in obscure forms, such as in privy conversations between themselves, and folkish expression, such as fable and song.

[9] See Beard (2014: 128–55) for a discussion of this sort of evidence, Toner (2009: 100–1) for a shorter section on jokes and the emperor, and Laurence and Paterson (1999) for the evidence of the emperor's *dicta*, including those with humour.

[10] Outside of its appearance in Dio, and in Zonaras and Xiphilinus, a *TLG* search gives a majority of examples for the word's use after the tenth century in Byzantine authorship, yet they retain the meaning of 'nonsense' or 'absurdity'. Cf. Winterling (2009: 104–6) on a discussion of ancient views on 'insanity' in his assessment of the strong historiographical impact of the view that Caligula was crazy. Celsus also describes *insania* and how this 'disease' would manifest as incomprehensible chatter, which seems like a relevant parallel to παραλήρημα: Celsus, *Med.* 3.18.1–2.

[11] Beard (2014: 135).

the inferiority of their station and thus have fewer dangers' (*inde crebri questus nec occulti per vulgum, cui minor sapientia ex mediocritate fortunae pauciora pericula sunt*).[12] Thus, both authors overlap to state that, despite the implied danger, neither the shoemaker nor the people at Rome were reprimanded for their outspokenness, meaning that their boldness came from the lack of consequences due to their non-elite backgrounds, or even as Tacitus states, their lack of wisdom and their 'not knowing any better'. This could be interpreted as elite prejudice against the *humiliores* in society, which in turn problematises the historicity and historical relevancy of these attestations.[13]

Such anecdotes reveal the problem of 'elite' and 'popular' perspectives and the issue of historical relevance. Firstly, the existence of several jocular interactions between an individual or group of people from a non-elite background and the emperor is an invaluable source of material, which reveals an aspect of the imagination of the emperor's conduct towards his subjects. However, as Beard rightly stated in her work on laughter in ancient Rome, not all such interactions between the emperor and his subjects would have been humorous.[14] This may seem like a historical truism, but it should be noted that the potential reality of these situations could be unsavoury or violent, as suggested by evidence collated by Yavetz for the *plebs* at Rome during the Julio-Claudian period.[15] That a bold openness in the discussion of the Roman emperor could bring consequences is discussed by Epictetus in his *Discourses* 4.13, which is a treatise about those who are too frank with their own affairs, particularly when one could be tricked into revealing too much. The anecdote Epictetus provides is one of military incognito informants, who were seemingly ubiquitous at Rome, drawing people into their trust and

---

[12] Tac. *Ann.* 14.60.5; cf. Ps.Sen. *Octavia* ll. 273–81, where a chorus of the Roman people appear and give their support to Octavia and her ancestry. There have been numerous debates on various important aspects of the play, such as its date, genre, and political purpose: Kragelund (1982); Flower (1995); Kragelund (2002); Ferri (2003); Boyle (2008). Such uncertainty means that a caveat must be placed with any historical conclusion taken on its context. In essence, it provides us with a literary construction of the people, which is by no means monolithic or straightforward, particularly since there are two choruses, one that favours Octavia (ll. 273–376) and another that favours Poppaea (ll. 877–982), perhaps betraying divided loyalties. See Section 1.1.1 on the *populus Romanus*.

[13] Cf. Morgan (2007: 66) for a comparison in fable of a similar sentiment, namely that the more prominent are in greater danger and that there is 'safety in obscurity': Phaed. 4.6.11–13. Cf. Braund (2009: 224, 243–4) for this sentiment in Seneca, Sen. *Polyb.* 6.4; cf., in general, Sen. *Clem.* 1.7.4, 1.8.1–5.

[14] Beard (2014: 136).

[15] Yavetz (1969: 24–37), on the violent protests of the *plebs* and the consequent reactions of the emperor to them.

thus increasing the potential of being caught saying bad things about Caesar:[16]

> οὕτω καὶ ὑπὸ τῶν στρατιωτῶν ἐν Ῥώμῃ οἱ προπετεῖς λαμβάνονται. παρακεκάθικέ σοι στρατιώτης ἐν σχήματι ἰδιωτικῷ καὶ ἀρξάμενος κακῶς λέγει τὸν Καίσαρα, εἶτα σὺ ὥσπερ ἐνέχυρον παρ᾽ αὐτοῦ λαβὼν τῆς πίστεως τὸ αὐτὸν τῆς λοιδορίας κατῆρχθαι λέγεις καὶ αὐτὸς ὅσα φρονεῖς, εἶτα δεθεὶς ἀπάγῃ.

> In this manner are the reckless also arrested by soldiers in Rome. A solider in civilian clothing sits next to you and starts to speak ill of Caesar, and so you, as a sort of pledge from him taking as a sign of trust his abusive language, say that he started it and you also say all that you think. Afterwards you would be bound up and taken away.[17]

These seizures seem to be indiscriminate. Therefore, there is the spectre of a favourable or unfavourable reaction to frankness of opinion. We are in a similar conceptual space as to what was described throughout Chapter 4, namely that these anecdotes allude to a *mentalité* concerning the emperor, in which expectations and fears of his reactions are negotiated in discourse. This is subtly different from the creation of a historical account that would concentrate on the realities of the potential interactions between emperor and subject – topics that have indeed been discussed in this book and more systematically by Millar.[18] Rather, what we have here is the existence of a shared imagination concerning jokes with, or at the expense of, the emperor. It can provide an account of both jocular and critical discourse about him, which reveals a functional critique on what the emperor was perceived to be, both positively and negatively. Moreover, it reveals a mindset, which was almost a generic expectation, that when you talked about the emperor, you talked in fiction, humour, and riddles.

Similar tensions are observable in the utilisation of a literary perspective. Work in this vein has produced fruitful and thought-provoking analyses of the stock characterisations of the Roman emperor, which uses examples from world literature to explore the different literary guises in which the emperors are portrayed.[19] Moreover, in attempting to construct the perception of the emperor by using this method, the context of the time period within which it was utilised and the people that it characterises

---

[16] Millar (1965: 143), on the dating of the anecdote; cf. Rudich (1993: 286): Suet. *Tit.* 6.1, which has a similar anecdote during Titus' time as praetorian prefect. Cf. Millar (1977: 61–6).
[17] Arr. *Epict. Diss.* 4.13.5.   [18] Millar (1977), esp. 363–549.
[19] Champlin (2008); Jasnow (2015); cf. Edwards (2011); cf. Edwards (2015).

become important for a historical interpretation of the evidence. For instance, to use narratological analysis for the example provided in the epigraph, the Gaulish shoemaker can be interpreted as a 'focalisation', where the author puts words into the mouth of the character in order to put into relief a certain opinion, which can be built upon to help aid our understanding of its historical context. If this was indeed a focalisation, does it then reveal an opinion of the source or the author in question about the emperor Caligula? Is it a device in itself used to engage with a discourse of criticism towards the office of emperor? If so, how representative of a wider thought-world can it be? These questions reveal both the inherent tension and bias present and their tantalising utility. In short, the problematic depictions of non-elite actors in their encounters with the emperor reveal a fascination with this sort of interaction, even if it could be argued that they were used for 'elite' perspectives. As argued, a more *inclusive* understanding of the discourse criticising the Roman emperor allows for different voices to be heard in the rubric. Such an approach not only appreciates the literary context of criticism but also points to a world where it seemed plausible that a shoemaker could and would openly criticise an emperor, suggesting a mental hinterland where such action would be tolerated, despite the inherent dangers, both imagined and real.[20] Put in another way, the jocular and fictional discourse itself becomes the place where emperor critique is possible.[21]

Indeed, the perspective of the 'elite' in terms of *libertas* has received greater attention, particularly in terms of negotiating the right to political free speech in an autocratic environment. Studies seem to concentrate on the understanding of the rhetorical techniques of hiding one's opinion properly, thus being able to claim plausible deniability in the face of claims of derision.[22] Interest also lies in exploring the role that 'free speech' had in the judicial aspect of *maiestas* trials, which have allowed the early principate to be interpreted as an oppressive state that actively sought to suppress the opinions of the elite in Roman society.[23] Material

---

[20] Cf. Section 1.1.2.

[21] Malik (2019: 785–7), with *CIL* 4.8075 = *AE* (1962) 133, where the dynamics of the joke suggest a more local context in Pompeii. In other words, the emperor was not only made fun of but a tool to poke fun at others. Cf. p. 27. Cf. Luraghi (2014: 87): 'the reason why for them (sc. the Greeks) tyrants were so good to think with, in fields ranging from political theory to economy to psychology. With the abolition of cultural and especially political order, the tyrant embodied a dream of unlimited freedom, of boundless possibilities for the individual.'

[22] Ahl (1984); Bartsch (1994); Sluiter and Rosen (2004); Roller (2001).

[23] See Rudich (1993) in particular. For *maiestas*, see Tuori (2016: 127–97), esp. 177–82, and Bauman (1967).

abounds on this topic, which involves the discussion and understanding of terms such as *libertas* and *parrhesia*; the use of figured speech to disguise opinion; and the problem and number of accusations of *maiestas,* and its impact on society. In essence, this chapter attempts to come at the issue of free speech from a different angle. Instead of exploring the definitions of terms and the nuances of *maiestas* in a general sense, it rather analyses a more specific register of evidence by analysing the attestations of jocular interactions between an emperor and individuals or groups of people of a lower station, in order to find a wider perspective on the issue of the freedom of speech and criticising the emperor.[24] Such evidence can be a potential window into a shared thought-world about the emperor. As Beard argues:

> [I]n Roman writing, confrontations between the ruler and individual representatives of the ruled were overwhelmingly delineated, debated, and discursively formulated in terms of laughing and joking. Literary representations, at least, used forms of laughter to facilitate communication across the political hierarchy, allowing a particular form of jocularized conversation to take place between high and low.[25]

Thus, this sort of evidence was part of this discourse of power relations between emperor and subject, potentially revealing a shared critical register of making fun of the emperor, and is an integral part of the historical understanding of the perception of the Roman emperor.

5.2   Collapsing the 'Good' and 'Bad' Emperor Binary

There is also the problem of the categorisation of these stories, particularly concerning the moral designation of a 'good' or a 'bad' emperor. To return to the anecdote about Gaius and the Gaul, the assertion that nothing ill happened to the shoemaker is written with a tone of surprise, with the more believable and expected outcome being the man's execution for such ridicule. There is a disjunct between this anecdote and the impression of Gaius.[26] For instance, there are numerous allusions to his cruelty throughout Suetonius' *Life*, and the constant fear of execution is

---

[24] This is inspired by the work of Scott, discussed pp. 19–20.

[25] Beard (2014: 136); cf. Laurence and Paterson (1999: 188–9) on how this discourse 'crossed class and social lines'. Cf. Webb (2008: 116–38) on masquerade and pantomime and their depictions of role reversals as social interaction.

[26] Dio 59; Suet. *Cal.* 11, 22, esp. 33, on his morbid sense of humour; Philo, *Leg.* esp. 28–31, on the demise of Tiberius Gemellus; 73, on Gaius' cruelty; 119, on Gaius as slave-master, with Christoforou (2021).

presented as a permanent possibility with Gaius.[27] It adds a wrinkle to perceived stereotypes of Caligula's character as a tyrant and a monster if he is seen to be magnanimous towards the Gaulish shoemaker. This suggests the possibility of a spectrum of different opinions that could exist about the emperor, espousing positive, negative, or ambivalent sentiments.[28] That being so, the extent to which archetypes of the Roman emperor could be created becomes more nuanced. In terms of jocularity, the basic characterisation is as follows:

> The basic Roman rule ... was that good and wise rulers made jokes in a benevolent way, never used laughter to humiliate, and tolerated wisecracks at their own expense. Bad rulers and tyrants, on the other hand, would violently suppress even the most innocent banter while using laughter and joking as weapons against their enemies.[29]

With Gaius being seen as a 'bad' emperor, the story in Dio would thus seem incongruous – for it seems that Gaius 'tolerated' a wisecrack, rather than suppressing it unequivocally. Modification is therefore required.

It does not require much digging to find examples that do not fit comfortably with this basic rule. However, being overly critical on the lack of nuance here would miss the point, as the rule which Beard rightly stresses as 'basic' is rather representative of something wider: '[these jokes] point to a bigger truth – a political lesson as much as an urban myth – that laughter helped to characterise both good and bad rulers.'[30] If taken a step further, this 'truth' is representative of a discourse that utilised jokes and laughter as tools to help understand and criticise an emperor. Moreover, there is ambivalence to this discourse: there is a moral aspect of how 'good' or 'bad' emperors respond to jocularity, but the impression is not necessarily binary. As before, there is an unpredictability to the nature of the emperor's reaction, which means that he could respond favourably or unfavourably, with hope for a good outcome accompanied by fear that it could end badly, which is something that is seemingly shared across the

[27] See, for instance, Suet. *Cal.* 32.3, where Caligula's sudden laughter in the company of the consuls was explained by his realisation that he could order their execution immediately – an appropriate parallel, complete with an example of laughter.
[28] Cf. Champlin (2008: 414).
[29] Beard (2014: 130). To be fair to Beard, she does describe the nuance and does stress that this juxtaposition is only a 'basic' rule to understand the characterisation, without putting too much weight on its accuracy. It still provides a pithy statement about the nature of the evidence and how it has been understood. Cf. Trentin (2011: 200) for a similar sentiment.
[30] Beard (2014: 130). Cf. Laurence and Paterson (1999: 193) for a similar interest in the characterisation of emperors through their *dicta*. Cf. Luraghi (2014: 80–8) on the deep ambiguity of the Greek tyrant as trickster and boundary transgressor and the benefits and limits of equating tyrants with tricksters.

received impression of 'good' or 'bad' emperors. Therefore, instead of a polarity, there was a framework in which the emperor is seen as a focal point of laughter and joking, from which moral interpretations could be inferred, all contributing to how the emperor was perceived.[31]

5.3   Laughing with an Elephant and the Dangers of Making Fun of an Emperor

These numerous points and issues are the necessary background for assessing the evidence for making fun of the emperor. A good example is the emperor Vespasian, known for his *civilitas*:[32]

> ἐς δὲ δὴ τἆλλα πάντα κοινὸς καὶ ἰσοδίαιτός σφισιν ἦν. καὶ γὰρ ἔσκωπτε δημοτικῶς καὶ ἀντεσκώπτετο ἡδέως· εἴ τέ τινα γράμματα, οἷα εἴωθεν ἀνώνυμα ἐς τοὺς αὐτοκράτορας, προπηλακισμὸν αὐτῷ φέροντα, ἐξετέθη ποτέ, ἀντεξετίθει τὰ πρόσφορα μηδὲν ταραττόμενος.

> Concerning all other matters, then, he was affable and civil and lived on an equal footing with others. For he also joked in an urbane way and took jokes with pleasure. For if any letters, which were commonly addressed anonymously to emperors, carrying slander against him were ever posted, he would post a suitable response, not at all perturbed.[33]

It is notable that Dio refers to how Vespasian treated his subjects and that he joked on a 'popular' level and would give as good as he got. In particular, the exchanges seem to become heated, if we take the work *propēlakismos* (literally to sling mud) at its meaning as slander, ridicule, and insult. Such 'democratic' imagery of hurling abuse in public settings between the people and the *princeps* suggests not only a more vibrant political vernacular and world in the principate but also simultaneously a discourse that could become acrimonious.[34] The contents of such insults are unknown, but what seems important is how Vespasian was unfazed by them, with Dio providing an extremely interesting context of how such insults were circulated and even how an emperor could respond. The competitive posting suggested that the anonymous slanderers set up their insults in

---

[31] Cf. Laurence and Paterson (1999: 184) for a similar argument on having 'to hang on the emperor's every word', with particular reference to Tiberius' characterisation in Dio 57.1, concerning the emperor's notoriety for being difficult to read and his inconsistency in reaction. Cf. Tac. *Ann.* 1.74.5. for Cn. Piso's remark that he would prefer to follow Tiberius' lead lest he makes the wrong choice.

[32] On *civilitas*, see Wallace-Hadrill (1982a).

[33] Dio 65(66)11.1; cf. Suet. *Vesp.* 13.1, 22–3 on Vespasian's propensity for joking and making fun of himself.

[34] Cf. Makhlaiuk (2020).

written form, giving the image of phrases marked out or painted on walls, with the emperor responding in kind with appropriate retorts.[35] First, this suggests that the form of joking that is alluded to here is not a restrictive category but one that is shared across class and social boundaries and carried out in the public realm.[36] Second, what Dio does not say is also of note, given that it would seem entirely plausible that an emperor would *not* take such insults lightly and instead prosecute perpetrators, evoking the image from Epictetus of the informants eavesdropping and waiting to catch people out. It perfectly encapsulates the nature of fear and expectation when it comes to making fun of an emperor: in how people were able to criticise an emperor, with expectations of how an emperor should respond, and that there was always a lingering danger of the imperial response. In the end, this anecdote gives a tantalising glimpse into the nature of such attestations and how much of these interactions would have been transitory in medium to the extent that they could not survive for posterity.

Nonetheless, there seems to be a public nature to the form and content of these jokes: on the streets, in the arena and theatres, at the baths, at dinner, and in the presence of the emperor himself. One can then perhaps infer that people enjoyed these jokes within the same contexts. This may seem counterintuitive to the seemingly clandestine anonymity of Dio's letters, but these were publicly posted. Indeed, the subsequent example of Vespasian's *civilitas* that Dio uses in the passage is in a public setting. It involves a certain Phoebus, who had rebuked Vespasian during Nero's trip to Greece when Vespasian had seen the emperor's antics and was told to 'go to the crows' (*es korakas*), which could be idiomatically translated as 'go to hell!'. After Vespasian assumed his principate, the new emperor responded to Phoebus in kind, but it was interpreted as wit, since nothing ill happened subsequently to Nero's erstwhile freedman.[37] The phrase is seemingly common and is used as an 'imprecation', as Liddell and Scott state in their entry under κόραξ 'crow', perhaps referring to improper burial and being left out to the ravenous birds. In a search on the *Thesaurus Linguae Graecae*, it appears across the corpus, notably in the

---

[35] For the evidence of graffiti and its content on emperors, see Section 1.3; cf. Franklin (2001: 108), on *CIL* 4.8075, and Malik (2019).

[36] Cf. Laurence and Paterson (1999: 189), who don't cite this particular passage but provide apt analysis: 'Using *dicta* was an excellent way of constructing a persona attractive to all sorts and conditions of people, and of exploring a broader shared culture.' Cf. HA, *Hadr.* 20.1: *In conloquiis etiam humillimorum civilissimus fuit* (In discussions even with the humblest in society, he was most civil).

[37] Dio 65(66).11.2.

comedies of Aristophanes.[38] It also appears once more in Dio in a shorter and more general form, where Phoebus uses the rebuke to dismiss someone who had been refused an audience with Nero.[39] All this shows the morbidity of this sort of humour and how in a different context there could be an unsavoury outcome to the situation.

Furthermore, it should be noted that this sort of joking evokes a certain *urbanitas*, a form of joking that seems conceptually related to the streets and crowds of the city. It is an elusive category that appears intermittently in our sources, which depict humour and knowledge of a lower status.[40] Much like the *mirabilia* and also the dream-book interpretations discussed in Sections 4.1 and 2.3, there is an ambivalent reception of this *urbanitas* – looked down upon yet something to engage and be conversant in.[41] It is interesting that the emperor would be depicted as part of this world as well. This sort of *apologia* is seen in the same book of Dio cited at the beginning of this section about Vespasian's *civilitas*, which records Domitian's habit of impaling flies and an anonymous witty remark about it:

τοῦτο γὰρ εἰ καὶ ἀνάξιον τοῦ τῆς ἱστορίας ὄγκου ἐστίν, ἀλλ' ὅτι γε ἱκανῶς τὸν τρόπον αὐτοῦ ἐνδείκνυται, ἀναγκαίως ἔγραψα, καὶ μάλισθ' ὅτι καὶ μοναρχήσας ὁμοίως αὐτὸ ἐποίει. ὅθεν οὐκ ἀχαρίτως τις εἶπε πρὸς τὸν ἐρωτήσαντα 'τί πράττει Δομιτιανός;' ὅτι 'διάζει τε, καὶ οὐδὲ μυῖα αὐτῷ παρακάθηται.'

Even though this story is unworthy of the weightiness of history, still, since it satisfactorily shows his character, I had to write it down, and especially because he continued to react similarly when he was ruling. Hence, to the question 'How's Domitian doing?', someone said, not with ill-will, 'He's living alone, not even a fly to accompany him.'[42]

As stated by Dio, this anecdote is simultaneously unworthy of history yet absolutely worth recording as relevant to the understanding of Domitian's character. It follows that the content of the anecdote and its jocular medium are also ambivalent in this manner: both unworthy and necessary

---

[38] E.g., Ar. *Ach.* 864; Ar. *Eq.* 1314; Ar. *Nub.* 123, 133. Cf. also Athenaeus' *Deipnosophistae*, for examples of comic fragments: Ath. 1.8e.

[39] Dio 62(63)10.1a: perhaps a different transmission of the same story with Phoebus and Vespasian.

[40] This was discussed in detail by Nicholas Purcell in a presentation entitled '*Vernacula Urbanitas*', which included evidence of such a 'lower-class sense of fun' from the *Natural History*, the antics and discussion at Trimalchio's Dinner in Petronius' *Satyricon*, and particularly Tac. *Hist.* 2.88, and the practical joke gone wrong on the outskirts of Rome, in the context of the Vitellian army camp and the *Nonae Caprotinae*. Cf. Purcell (1996: 810).

[41] Cf. Quint. *Inst.* 6.3.17 on *urbanitas*.

[42] Dio 65(66).9.3–5. Cf. Plin. *Ep.* 4.22 on Domitian's delator Catullus Messalinus being used as a weapon (*telum*). Cf. Suet. *Dom.* 3.1. for the same anecdote 'not even a fly' – *ne muscam quidem*.

at the same time. Just as the emperor could be seen to be close to wondrous things, so too could he be the subject of a joke and an irresistible way to think about absolute power, its effects, and how to respond to it.

However, it should be noted that the tradition is not as neat as Dio's statement at 65(66).11.1, in which Vespasian was accustomed to respond with wit and grace, thus problematising yet again the strict dichotomy of good and bad rulers. Again, in the same source, which is in the historical context of Vespasian's visit to Alexandria during the civil wars of AD 69–70 and his pursuit of the emperorship,[43] the Alexandrians taunted the emperor for increased taxes and Vespasian's pursuit of money:

οἱ δ' οὖν Ἀλεξανδρεῖς διά τε ἐκεῖνα, καὶ ὅτι καὶ τῶν βασιλείων τὸ πλεῖστον ἀπέδοτο, χαλεπῶς φέροντες ἄλλα τε ἐς αὐτὸν ἀπερρίπτουν καὶ ὅτι 'ἓξ ὀβολοὺς προσαιτεῖς', ὥστε καὶ τὸν Οὐεσπασιανὸν καίπερ ἐπιεικέστατον ὄντα χαλεπῆναι, καὶ κελεῦσαι μὲν καὶ τοὺς ἓξ ὀβολοὺς κατ' ἄνδρα ἐσπραχθῆναι, βουλεύσασθαι δὲ καὶ τιμωρίαν αὐτῶν ποιήσασθαι·

Therefore the Alexandrians for those reasons, and also because he sold the majority of the royal palace, rebuked him harshly and uttered other taunts besides, including 'six obols you demand of us!', which made Vespasian angry although he was most moderate, and he ordered that six obols should be exacted from each man, and he deliberated on exacting punishment on them, too.[44]

Here, Vespasian is seen to respond angrily to the shouts of the Alexandrians, resorting to fining them six obols, the amount that they had been chanting, with a view to punishing them further, which was not in line with his expected clemency. To reiterate the publicness of such proceedings, the medium of their discontent was in rhythmical chanting. Indeed, Dio is specific that this aspect is what raised Vespasian's ire, which was the anapaestic rhythm of the chants.[45] It is notable that it is a recitative metre, used in the *parabases* of Attic comedy or the chorus' chant to the audience. This accentuates the image of a collective recitation. This is evidence in support of acclamation and shouts in public towards the emperor being the method with which honours, and indeed grievances, could be expressed to the higher authority.[46] The impact of Vespasian's taxation is being exemplified in Dio by the audible frustrations of the

[43] For a discussion on the chronology of the early years of Vespasian's principate, see Henrichs (1968: 51–4) and Luke (2010). Cf. Sumi (2002: 565) for mimes and impersonations at Roman funerals, esp. Vespasian's.

[44] Dio 65(66).8.4–6.   [45] Dio 65(66).8.4–5.

[46] Cameron (1976: 162–8) on the evidence of these sorts of interaction from the time of Augustus towards late antiquity, and esp. 162: 'From Augustus on it became normal and common for the

Alexandrians, which is an interesting way of expressing and understanding the effects of an emperor's actions, insofar as they were scrutinised in a public verbal reaction. Furthermore, it seems to find corroboration in Suetonius' account with the nickname of *Cybiosactes*, or 'Salt-fish dealer', which the Alexandrians were accustomed to call him after a previous ruler who had been stingy.[47] This evidence seems to contradict Vespasian's image of clemency, on which Suetonius gives a few examples of this and his wit with reference to similar monetary issues.[48]

Moreover, a negative interpretation of Vespasian's conduct is shown by the story of Empona in Plutarch's *Moralia*, in which he recounts a story about the wife of Julius Sabinus, who took part in the Batavian revolt of Julius Civilis in AD 69. The anecdote about Vespasian appears in the context of Plutarch's dialogue concerning love, in which Empona is the *exemplum* of a devoted wife in her steadfast loyalty to her husband in his self-imposed hiding. After a lacuna in Plutarch's text, the story culminates in her execution at the orders of Vespasian, presumably after the couple had been caught.[49] The climax of the story is the provocation of Vespasian (παρώξυνε ὸν Οὐεσπασιανόν) at the woman's brave retort, when she claims she had been happier in the cave than Vespasian had been ruling.[50] Despite the absence of humour, the boldness of Empona is part of this theme of open response towards an emperor, accentuated by her subordinated role as a subject and a woman. This evidence is not meant here to place Vespasian within a category of 'bad' emperors but rather to show that the number and nature of such stories allowed for emperors to be cast in this light and remembered accordingly.[51] Therefore, these anecdotes

    people to make requests of the emperor at the circus and theatre – requests to which he was morally obliged at least to reply.' Cf. Roueché (1984: 182–3); cf. Aldrete (2003: 89–92).

[47] Suet. *Vesp.* 19.2. Cf. Str. 17.1.11 for the nickname belonging to the son-in-law of the Ptolemy 13th. Cf. Ath. 3.118a, in which a fragment of Alexis' *Apeglaukomenos* comedy from the Hellenistic period contains a passage about the price of κύβιον, which seems to be the cured fish referenced in the nickname, and how it cost three obols. What is more interesting is the supposed fluctuation in prices of the salt-fish dealer (here ταριχοπώλης). Perhaps the cry of 'six obols' is related to the selling of fish. For popular epithets given to emperors, see Bruun (2003) and Makhlaiuk (2020). The evocation of fish, and the implication that being such a dealer was dishonest, perhaps should be viewed with other fishy stories that emperors appear in; cf. pp. 149–155.

[48] Suet. *Vesp.* 23.1–3, which includes the various corrupt practices of Vespasian, including a tax on toilets, along with his witty remarks in response, in this case asking his son Titus whether the money reeked.

[49] Plut. *Mor.* 770c–771c.

[50] Plut. *Mor.* 771c: 'for she lived more pleasantly under darkness underground than during his rule' (βεβιωκέναι γὰρ ὑπὸ σκότῳ καὶ κατὰ γῆς ἥδιον ἢ βασιλεύειν ἐκεῖνον). Cf. Ash (2008: 567–8) for further analysis of this passage, its moral implications, and how it differs from Dio's at 65(66).16.2.

[51] For the richness of tradition, see Champlin (2003) and Malik (2019) on Nero.

about jokes and vocal expressions can be vehicles of a thought-world about the Roman emperor, in which his subjects negotiated who the emperor seemed to be. In other words, it was a way to explore and understand the power relationship between ruler and ruled, with humorous or morbid outcomes being two sides of the same coin.

This potentiality is something that has been observable in representations of the interactions between emperor and subject throughout this book. Indeed, many have humorous turns, such as the interaction between Hadrian and the old woman,[52] and the example of Bulla Felix's masquerades that fooled Septimius Severus across Italy.[53] Certain examples are conceptually related to stories with humour, such as the evidence of the 'tale of the unbreakable glass'.[54] The more humorous counterpart involves the emperor Claudius and Titus Vinius before his fame in 69 as one of Galba's advisors. Like the 'tale of the unbreakable glass', this story involves crockery:

> δειπνῶν δὲ παρὰ Κλαυδίῳ Καίσαρι ποτήριον ἀργυροῦν ὑφείλετο· πυθόμενος δὲ ὁ Καῖσαρ τῇ ὑστεραίᾳ πάλιν αὐτὸν ἐπὶ δεῖπνον ἐκάλεσεν, ἐλθόντι δὲ ἐκέλευσεν ἐκείνῳ μηδὲν ἀργυροῦν, ἀλλὰ κεράμια πάντα προσφέρειν καὶ παρατιθέναι τοὺς ὑπηρέτας. τοῦτο μὲν οὖν διὰ τὴν Καίσαρος μετριότητα κωμικωτέραν γενομένην, γέλωτος, οὐκ ὀργῆς ἄξιον ἔδοξεν·

> When dining at Claudius', he stole a silver cup. Caesar, learning about this, on the next day invited him for dinner again and, when he arrived, ordered the slaves to bring out and set before him nothing in silver but everything in ceramic ware. This action seemed to be worthy of laughter rather than anger due to the moderation of Caesar which was more comic.[55]

Claudius' wit was such that he teased the stealer of his silver cup by bringing out earthenware at the next dinner. Plutarch interprets the scene as a joke, attributing his moderation being the reason that this incident seemed worthy of laughter and not anger. *Edoxen* (seemed) is the operative word here, which places the onus on interpretation and perspective, suggesting that the 'joke' could be taken in any way.[56] For instance, Suetonius in his description of Claudius at dinner describes situations where Claudius was the butt of jokes, rather than vice versa.[57]

---

[52] Dio 69.6.3. Cf. pp. 27–28.　　[53] Dio 77(76).10. Cf. pp. 94–96.

[54] Cf. pp. 152–153, with citations and analysis.

[55] Plut. *Galb.* 12.4–5. For analysis of this passage, and particularly Plutarch's characterisation of Claudius in this passage in comparison to images in different authors, see Ash (2008: 560–1).

[56] Cf. Luraghi (2014: 87) on how tyrants cannot be funny. Cf. HA, *Hadr.* 15.13 for hidden laughter behind Hadrian's back.

[57] Suet. *Claud.* 8, which revolved around those present and in particular the *copreae*.

Furthermore, as Ash points out, other authors characterise Claudius differently, particularly with respect to his short temper.[58] Tacitus' version of this cup story is telling in this manner: 'He thereafter defiled himself with a shamefully servile act, as he lifted a golden cup at a feast of Claudius. On the next day Claudius ordered Vinius alone to be served with ceramic ware.'[59] The humorous gloss Plutarch provides in his version is absent from Tacitus' account, which instead focusses on Claudius' anger and Vinius' humiliation in the ups and downs of his career.[60] Thus, tradition affected the reception of an emperor's sense of humour, which reveals in this particular case the different ways a story could be interpreted and also how a joke could be taken seriously or not.

The witty remarks of emperors were important contributing parts of biography and history and reflected that they were 'matters of key importance to those around him', as noted by Laurence and Paterson.[61] Accordingly, these sayings became important ways to think about the emperors in question, were seemingly subject to keen observation, and had implications for the legacy of these emperors as well. The importance of legacy to the reception of the Roman emperor is discussed further in Chapter 6, but it should be stated that many of these *dicta* survive through sources written many years after their dramatic dates. This reflects the longevity of these stories in the imagination about emperors and how they become timeless character sketches, malleable to different contexts, and part of the conversation about what the emperor was and should be.

These different potential interpretations through time make this evidence fascinating, such as the jokes of Augustus that appear in the treasure trove of miscellany that is Macrobius' *Saturnalia*.[62] Analysis of all thirty-one examples would be enjoyable, but a couple will have to suffice. One portrays a petitioner hesitating in his quest to present a request to Augustus, who asks the man if he thought he was giving a coin to an

---

[58] Ash (2008: 560–1), with the examples of Tac. *Ann.* 11.26.2 and Sen. *Apoc.* 6.2.

[59] Tac. *Hist.* 1.48.3: *servili deinceps probro respersus est, tamquam scyphum aureum in convivio Claudii furatus, et Claudius postera die soli omnium Vinio fictilibus ministrari iussit.*

[60] Tacitus' characterisation of the scene as Vinius being disgraced as if a slave reveals an important theme, which Matthew Roller discusses at length the perception of a master–slave relationship and its applicability to understanding the Roman emperor. For Roller, it serves as a vehicle in understanding the meaning of *libertas* and therefore the perspective of the literate elite on the autocracy in which they were living. It should be noted that the master–slave paradigm is conceptually similar to the dominant–subordinate relationship described by Scott, but the differences lie in what parts of society are included in this understanding, on which Roller concentrates on the elite. See Roller (2001: 214–47).

[61] Kuttner (1995: 183–7), quotation from 183–4.   [62] Macrob. *Sat.* 2.4.1–31.

elephant.[63] Similar versions of the story with slight variation appear both in Quintilian and Suetonius as examples of wit, which points to the longevity of this story in particular.[64] However, while Augustus is commended for dispelling the tension, his joke does not hide the elephant in the room. For, given how stressful it must have been to present a petition to an emperor, the metaphor was quite apt. So, by way of this joke, not only is the legacy of Augustus' wit maintained but also a seeming truth about the emperor's presence: one of potential jocularity, present fear and danger, and the potential for such interactions to be replicable and instructive into the future.

Another anecdote from Macrobius highlights a connectivity of genre in these stories – between history, biography, fable, and *mirabilia*. Chapters 29 and 30 both contain stories about talking birds being trained to acclaim Augustus on his victory at Actium with versions of the phrase *ave Caesar victor imperator*. The result is that he buys the birds at the sum of 20,000 sesterces.[65] After Augustus had bought four different birds, the stories end with a poor shoemaker attempting to get into the racket by purchasing a raven to perform a similar deed:

> qui impendio exhaustus saepe ad avem non respondentem dicere solebat, 'opera et impensa periit.' aliquando tamen corvus coepit dicere dictatam salutationem. hac audita dum transit Augustus respondit, 'satis domi salutatorum talium habeo.' superfuit corvo memoria, ut et illa quibus dominum querentem solebat audire subtexeret: 'opera et impensa periit.' ad quod Caesar risit emique avem iussit quanti nullam adhuc emerat.

> The extremely exhausted man was often accustomed to say to the non-responsive bird: 'my effort and money are lost!' After a while the crow started to say the dictated greeting. Hearing the bird as he passed by, Augustus responded. 'I have enough of that sort of greeter at home.' A memory came over the crow, which were the complaints of his master that he was used to hearing, and he added 'my effort and money are lost!' To which Caesar laughed and ordered that the bird be bought, which was as costly as any he had bought up to that point.[66]

Thus, despite Augustus' menagerie of talking birds being full, he accepted yet another at a higher price for the amusement of the bird repeating his owner's frustrations. A charming story no doubt, but there is

---

[63] Macrob. *Sat.* 2.4.3: *putas, inquit, te assem elephanto dare?*.
[64] Quint. *Inst.* 6.3.59; Suet. *Aug.* 53.2.
[65] Macrob. *Sat.* 2.4.29: the second bird got trained to acclaim Antony, the defeated triumvir. Augustus bought this bird also.
[66] Macrob. *Sat.* 2.4.30.

a precariousness to these stories in general, with the potential that the emperor could respond negatively to these requests. It also alludes to a historical phenomenon of expectations of generosity from the emperor, which gives a humorous flair to counterpart examples of the emperor's generosity discussed in Chapter 3.[67] Furthermore, there is a flair of popular imagination in these stories about talking birds, not only in the lowly origins of such fabulous accounts but also in the interesting parallel that appears in Pliny's *Natural History*, in which there was a young raven who flew from its nest at the Temple of Castor and Pollux and was interpreted as a religious bird by the cobbler across the way. It was accustomed daily to greet Tiberius, Drusus, and Germanicus by name before returning to its perch at the cobbler's. Its death by a jealous neighbour prompted the latter's exile from the city and an elaborate funeral for the bird.[68] This story contains similar ingredients to the one in Macrobius, but it importantly suggests an impact on the Roman people, insofar that Pliny notes the esteem of ravens by the people of Rome.[69] Whatever the historicity of Macrobius' anecdote, this corroborating evidence supports the existence of these talking birds in the imagination and stories of the common people. This necessarily extends to the emperor also, as Augustus, Tiberius, Germanicus, and Drusus all appear in the stories as recipients of salutations. Therefore, as Purcell argued, stories, or '*fabulae*', were 'integral to the working of the Roman system' and there was an 'intimate involvement of thousands and thousands of ordinary people in the construction and definition of the image of emperor, his role, and his family'.[70]

This point can perhaps be observed in the genre of fables itself and within the corpus of Phaedrus. As argued by Morgan, it is difficult to define precisely what fables are,[71] but they 'function generally as moral and educational' stories.[72] It has been argued that they also provide opportunities to gain access to a different, more popular perspective, as hidden transcripts that contain opinions of the weak against the strong.[73] Given their timeless appeal and applicability, finding the relevant context for the

---

[67] A parallel story could be the one about Hadrian in the baths giving a soldier a slave so he could rub his back down, with the result of others looking for the same generosity from the emperor at his next visit. HA. *Hadr.* 17.6–7; Cf. Beard (2014: 135–6).

[68] Plin. *NH.* 10.121–124. I owe this reference to Nicholas Purcell's *Vernacula Urbanitas* presentation.

[69] Plin. *NH.* 10.121.

[70] Purcell (1999: 183) analyses the scene in Suet. *Aug.* 70.1 about the 'dinner of the twelve gods' during a famine, with epigrams and lampoons circulating about it.

[71] Morgan (2007: 57–9), on different definitions supplied by antiquity.   [72] Morgan (2007: 60).

[73] Cf. Morgan (2007: 59) on modern scholarship on fable that interprets them as such; cf. Forsdyke (2012).

early empire can be challenging.[74] However, the *oeuvre* of Phaedrus contains fables of direct relevance to the context of the early Roman empire and the emperor in particular.[75] One fable is about the encounter of Tiberius and an *atriensis*, or steward, in which Tiberius reprimands the man for expecting too much for his actions.[76] Tiberius hearkened the steward, who was then expecting some sort of reward: 'Such was the greatness of the leader who said in jest: "you haven't done much and you wasted your effort in vain. Emancipatory slaps sell at a higher price with me."'[77] As Champlin points out, Tiberius' wit and wisdom are highlighted in this passage for posterity, which gives a distinct image of that emperor's legacy with respect to his appearance in Tacitus.[78] However, Champlin uses this passage as an example of how Tiberius' image in the popular imagination was one of a wise old man, which seems to contradict his argument in the article 'Phaedrus the Fabulous' that Phaedrus was not a Greek freedman at all but rather a Roman aristocrat.[79] Indeed, the lampooning of a parasite at court seems to fit into the more general theme of disdain for these characters, which would include freedmen that surrounded the emperor.[80] Thus, there seems to be a logical contradiction at hand here: a genre that conveys a popular mentality yet also betrays seemingly elite Roman concerns. However, there is a solution. First, the form of the story is structurally similar to the jokes that have been discussed throughout this section: the encounter of the emperor with a subordinate, resulting in humour but with the fearful expectation of an unfunny reprimand. Therefore, this fable fits into that thought-world of the emperor which sought to discuss and criticise how the latter dealt with his subjects.

The second part involves the idea of the hidden transcript and the question of the dominant–subordinate relationship. The nature of the

---

[74] Cf. Morgan (2007: 62) on this problem as well.

[75] Henderson (2001: 10). On Phaedrus and his identity, see Champlin (2005).

[76] Phaed. 2.5.1. Phaedrus calls his milieu *ardaliones*, which is a rare word that according to the *TLL* 2.0.481.20 corresponds to the Greek work ἄρδαλος, described in the *LSJ* ὁ μὴ καθαρῶς ζῶν (which has similar unclean connotations to the scatological *copreae*) or ἀρδάλιον, which means water pot, which makes sense given his job of sprinkling water on the hot ground. Nonetheless, there is a negativity to its meaning and should perhaps be seen in the same company as the *scurrae* or parasites of the court.

[77] Phaed. 2.5.21–25: *Tum sic iocata est tanta maiestas ducis:* | *'Non multum egisti et opera nequiquam perit;* | *multo maioris alapae mecum veneunt.'* Cf. Henderson (2001: 10–31) and Champlin (2005: 417) for analysis of this fable.

[78] Champlin (2008: 417, 424–5).   [79] Champlin (2005: 117).

[80] Cf. Plin. *Ep.* 7.29, 8.6, for perspective on Pallas, the freedman of Claudius, and analysis of this evidence from MacLean (2018: 107–11).

position of Roman emperor suggests that his subjects would necessarily experience a subordinated role. The subversive element of the fable remains as it criticises power structures. The final interpretation may be distinctive, and therefore imbued with elite concerns, but the interpretation forms part of a shared conceptualisation of the Roman emperor, suggesting that he was a contested space, open to scrutiny and criticism from his subjects. Thus, instead of stressing a negative characterisation of this evidence as being contaminated with elite concerns, it rather opens up a different, more inclusive mentality, which in turn can provide a different way to conceptualise how the Roman emperor was perceived, including rather than excluding those of an elite milieu as a common topic of conversation. In other words, it is extremely interesting that fable was a shared way to criticise and understand the Roman emperor, which is testament to his impact on the minds of his subjects.

CHAPTER 6

Living in an Age of Gold, or the Emperor As a Temporal Figure

6.1 The Emperor through Time

In an early fifth-century-AD letter addressed to his friend Olympius, Synesius of Cyrene describes the utopian remoteness of the southern extremity of Cyrenaica, praising its culture and rustic lifestyle in comparison to more worldly or better-connected areas of the Mediterranean world. Part of that utopia was the lack of much news or knowledge about the Roman emperor: the tax collectors would come and go, but other than that, not much was known:

> βασιλεὺς δὲ καὶ βασιλέως φίλοι καὶ δαίμονος ὄρχησις, οἷα δὴ συνιόντες ἀκούομεν, ὀνόματά τινα καθάπερ αἱ φλόγες ἐπὶ μέγα τῆς δόξης ἐξαπτόμενα καὶ σβεννύμενα, ταῦτα δεῦρο ἐπιεικῶς σιγᾶται, καὶ σχολὴ ταῖς ἀκοαῖς τοιούτων ἀκροαμάτων. ἐπεὶ καὶ βασιλεὺς ὅτι μὲν ζῇ τις ἀεί, τοῦτ᾽ ἴσως ἐπίστανται σαφῶς (ὑπομιμνήσκονται γὰρ ἅπαν κατ᾽ ἔτος ὑπὸ τῶν ἐκλεγόντων τοὺς φόρους), ὅστις δὲ οὗτός ἐστιν, οὐ μάλα ἔτι τοῦτο σαφῶς· ἀλλ᾽ εἰσί τινες ἐν ἡμῖν οἳ μέχρι καὶ νῦν Ἀγαμέμνονα κρατεῖν ἥγηνται τὸν Ἀτρείδην, τὸν ἐπὶ Τροίαν, τὸν μάλα καλόν τε καὶ ἀγαθόν· τοῦτο γὰρ παιδόθεν ἡμῖν ὡς βασιλικὸν παραδέδοται τοὔνομα.

However, the emperor and the friends of the emperor, and the rhythm of the Gods, of such we hear about when we come together, such names are like flames that shoot up to great renown and are then extinguished. Those matters keep moderately silent here; respite for our ears from such stories. That there is always an emperor who is living is perhaps known for sure (for they are reminded of this every year by those who collect taxes), but who this person is, this is not yet well known for sure. But there are those amongst us who even up to now believe that Agamemnon holds sway, the son of Arteus, who went against Troy, who is very noble and good. For this name from childhood was handed down to us as the name of the king.[1]

---

[1] Synesius of Cyrene, *Letters*, 148.130–143; cf. Birley (1999: ix), for the reference, and Lendon (1997: 267).

There is a fascinating temporality to Synesius' words here. Before this description, the old tradition's permanence in the region is compared to the life and products of other places across the Mediterranean, stressing how unique and pristine life, custom, and produce in Cyrenaica were in contrast to more knowledgeable, luxurious, and worldly places, with their corruption supplied by the sea.[2] The fleeting ignition and extinguishing of the emperor and his favourites and the dance of divine power make such a place outside of time and outside of the human and divine rhythms that govern the rest of the world. The specifics of a certain emperor or his rule are lost to the continuity of time. Such a description is intriguingly similar to the conception of time, or *kairos*, in popular culture in antiquity.[3] Accordingly, time often stood still, only really punctuated with events, rather than a conception of time that moved directionally. This is interestingly similar to what is described by Synesius in the passage: who the emperor was is not *yet* known with any certainty, even if there is some impression that there is *always* an emperor. Much like static time punctuated with events, the existence of Roman power sits outside the experience of life in this place, and the inhabitants are only reminded of its existence when the tax collectors come. The intrigue builds when local knowledge insists in continuity *up to the present* that has Agamemnon as the ruler who holds sway. The call to Homeric authority is striking in the sense of the living and current relevance of Homeric thinking in the Greek world to understand fundamental categories such as power and kingship, which was a way to think critically about encounters with Rome, identity, and one's place in time.[4] The *concept* of an emperor is an accepted phenomenon, but who that may be is open to debate. Moreover, this concept could be understood with epistemologies that are consciously pre-Roman.[5] Of course, it could be stated that Synesius is utilising trope and literary allusion, particularly revolving around bucolic fantasy and the simplicity of a rural and agrarian lifestyle, as well as the Homeric flourish. However, the mention of Agamemnon is striking in the sense of popular conceptuality and perhaps in how he and an emperor could be conflated. Of course, both Agamemnon and various Roman emperors have precarious and often negative portrayals in literature, which suggests that their

---

[2] Synesius of Cyrene, *Letters*, 148.47–52, 59–61, 93–100. For Cyrenaica as a fertile island, and a place of isolation and connectivity, see Horden and Purcell (2000: 65–74).

[3] Morgan (2007: 248–51). Cf. Trédé-Boulmer (2015) for a prolonged study of *kairos* through antiquity.

[4] For such Homeric thinking in the Greek world, see Greensmith (2020) and Kneebone (2020).

[5] Cf. Aristid. *Or.* 26.81–4, for a comparative example of Homeric thinking in descriptions of Roman power.

receptions were slippery and multifaceted. For more specific parallels, in Artemidorus' *Oneirocritica*, a ship-captain dreamt of deliverance from Agamemnon, which resulted in him being excused from his civic duties.[6] Furthermore, Suetonius mentions the accusation raised against a poet who depicted Agamemnon negatively in a tragedy during Tiberius' reign.[7] Such evidence suggests a category of comparison at least, or a conflation between the emperor and the Mycenaean king, which can be pushed back further from Synesius' fifth-century context into the world of Suetonius and Artemidorus, with the latter in particular potentially referring to a similar thought-world that allowed for such elisions to take place.[8] The emperor is a temporal marker throughout this passage who appears both as punctuating events in the calendar (as seen with the tax collectors) and as a way to describe a wider passage of time.

Accordingly, the emperorship is universal and can transcend contexts, including those Synesius describes in this letter; namely, there is an impression that an emperor had always existed and would always exist. It is a hint to a peculiarity about the reception of the emperor: the idea and office of emperor as an entity was an important component to the understanding (and criticism) of the position, which is contrasted with the same process(es) as directed towards individual emperors. In other words, discourse contributed both to the reception of the individual emperor in question and to the idea of the emperor as a whole. It should be stated that this designation is not dichotomous, and that this was not a phenomenon that appeared instantaneously from the time of Augustus, but rather formed and gestated over time and across the early principate and indeed beyond it. There seemed to be fertile ground for discussion of what the emperor was and what he should be, which was continually modified by the discourse of the legacies of past emperors and constantly added to by the actions and words of sitting emperors.

This tradition is a manifestation of the discourse about the Roman emperor that had a temporal aspect. Much of the literary evidence that was discussed in the previous chapters offers posthumous retrospectives on the emperor in question, with more contemporary aspects being far rarer, such as the graffiti on the walls of Pompeii, the various coin issues both

---

[6] Cf. Artem. 5.16, discussed in Section 3.2. See Millar (1977: 499) on the passage and similar gifts of immunity from the emperor.

[7] Cf. Suet. *Tib.* 61.3. Cf. the attestations of Pompey the Great being called Agamemnon in Dio 42.5.5: 'Pompey was thought of beforehand to be the most powerful of the Romans that they called him Agammenon' (Πομπήιος μὲν δὴ κράτιστος πρότερον Ῥωμαίων νομισθείς, ὥστε καὶ Ἀγαμέμνονα αὐτὸν ἐπικαλεῖσθαι). Cf. Plut. *Caes.* 41.2; Plut. *Pomp.* 67.5. Homer was a fundamental mode of thinking in the Roman world.

[8] Cf. pp. 84–86.

imperial and provincial, and perhaps even the inscriptions produced in the
subsequent months or years after the event. With this in mind, the history
being constructed in this book has sought both to describe the discourse
about the emperor in thematic terms, relevant to the hopes and concerns of
his subjects, and to acknowledge how this was conducted *throughout* time.
It is this complex temporality that is the subject of this chapter, which seeks
to explain the appearance of the emperor as a transcendent figure across
time and how this was manifested in the discourse about him, namely
concerning criticism of an emperor's legacy and memory and how it could
have a historical impact.

An illustrative example of an emperor's impact on time comes through the
calendars.[9] Calendars attest to a form of dividing and understanding time,
which could vary across region and era.[10] The advent of dates on the calendar
that concerned the emperor and his family should not be underestimated:
'every few days, another imperial anniversary, another commemoration of
the *princeps* and his family, a positive invasion, a planned and systematic act
of intrusion which has the cumulative effect of recasting what it means to be
Roman.'[11] Given how the rhythms of life permeated out into the provinces
with the proliferation of the cult of emperors, such a statement might be
modified by recasting what is meant to live in the Roman empire, even
though the interfaces of time were complex, allowing for the interlocking of
imperial and local modes of time-keeping.[12] In the Italian *fasti*, each year
birthdays of the imperial family,[13] temple dedications,[14] title conferrals,[15] and

---

[9] Feeney (2007: 184–9); Bultrighini (2021: 84), with bibliography on Caesar's calendar reform; cf.
Stern (2012: 204–28) on the formation and origins of the Julian calendar, and esp. 219–22 for its
political implications. Cf. Hannah (2005), esp. 125–30, for the *horologium* of Augustus and the
effects of calendrical reform.

[10] Morgan (2007: 244): the dating systems could include *AUC* (*ab urbe condita*) from the foundation
of Rome, Olympiads, magisterial, regnal and consular years, and comitial days to festival days; *EJ* 45.
has an edition of compiled calendars. For the compilation, see *Inscr. Ital.* 13.2. Cf. Salzman (1991: 5–
6); cf. Feeney (2007) for the nuances and differences of how the Romans imposed order and
structure on their perceptions of time. Cf. Potter (1994: 137).

[11] Feeney (1992: 5); Feeney (2007: 185), where he cites Horace on how the senate and the people will
commemorate Augustus on the calendar into the ages through inscription and memorial (*Carm.*
4.14.3–5).

[12] Dench (2018: 134–6); Bultrighini (2021: 84–5), on the diffusion of the calendar across the empire. Cf.
Rogers (2012) and Burrell (2004) for examples of how emperors were embedded in commemorable
moments.

[13] *EJ* 51 = *CIL* I, p. 246 = *Inscr. Ital.* 13.2.29, for the *Fasti Pighiani*: *nat(alis) Germanic(i)*. Cf. HA, *Hadr.*,
8.2 and HA. *Pert.* 15.5 on birthday celebrations.

[14] *EJ* 45 = *Inscr. Ital.* 13.2.17: *Concordiae Au[gustae aedis dedicat]a est P(ublio) Dolabella C(aio) Silano
co(n)[s(ulibus)]*. Cf. *EJ* 45 = *Inscr. Ital.* 13.2.22, for the *Fasti Verulani*: *fer(iae) [e]x s(enatus) c(onsulto)
quod eo die aedis | C[o]ncordiae in foro dedic(ata) est*.

[15] For example, the title *pater patriae*: *EJ* 47 = *Inscr. Ital.* 13.2.17: *feriae ex s(enatus) c(onsulto) | quod eo die
Imperator Caesar Augustus pontifex | maximus trib(unicia) potest(ate) XXI co(n)s(ul) XIII | a senatu*

even the assumption of the *toga virilis* of an imperial family member are commemorated, including alongside consular dating.[16] In Asia, at the suggestion of the proconsul Paullus Fabius Maximus, the *koinon* approved that the calendar of the province be reformed to make Augustus' birthday, September 23, the new year. It also brought in the idea of synchronous time, aligning (*synchrēmatizein*) the Greek days with the Roman so that in each city the days would be in line with each other (ὅπως δὲ ἀεὶ ἡ {τε} ἡμέρα στοιχῇ καθ' ἑκάστ|ην πόλιν).[17]

In this context, then, we have a doubleness of Roman and Greek time, with the emperor Augustus as a marker, which stresses both the long continuity of time (ἀεί) in the past as well as in the future and the subsequent permanence of the emperor.[18] Simultaneously, a rupture is created in the reckoning of time for the province of Asia: a new year starts with a new month, called *Kaisar*, to be placed within the framework of the Asian calendar, which is outlined at the end of the inscription (ll. 68–76). The emperor, then, becomes a way in which to understand and organise time that does not supersede other forms of time but rather both engages with and infiltrates those other forms.[19] The emperor became a common denominator between different epistemologies of viewing the world.

Such ubiquity is perhaps best seen in a more mundane context: how regnal years are utilised in documentary papyri for dating purposes. This can include receipts, contracts, census declarations, letters, and birth certificates.[20] Knowledge of regnal years was important to date documents: an innocuous, but far-reaching impact of the coming and going of imperial lives. The banality of such evidence, which might use years of an emperor's

populoque Romano pater patriae | appellatus. Note the enumeration of the titles, which is another method of outlining imperial time.

[16] *EJ* 48 = *Inscr. Ital.* 13.2.17: *Ti(berius) Caesar togam virilem sumpsit Imp(eratore) Caesare VII M(arco) Agrippa | III co(n)s(ulibus)*. Cf. Rüpke (2011: 134); cf. Bultrighini (2021: 85–9) for further examples. On marking the *domus Augusta* in the calendar and calendrical reform, see Ov. *Fast.* 1.709–22 and 3.155–162 with Pasco-Pranger (2006: 64–72, 189–200).

[17] For Paulus Fabius Maximus' letter: *EJ* 98a, ll.20–23 = Sherk, *RDGE* 65A; for the decree of the Koinon: *EJ* 98b. ll. 50–56 = Sherk, *RDGE* 65D. Cf. Bultrighini (2021: 85–7) for analysis and its connection to the imperial cult.

[18] Dench (2018: 134).

[19] Cf. Bultrighini (2021: 89) and Bultrighini and Stern (2021) on the interaction between Roman, Greek, and Jewish forms of timekeeping on a fascinating inscription from Tremetousia, Cyprus (north of Kition and modern Larnaca, just past the UN buffer zone) identified as a horoscope that has a local month name (Tybi), the seventh year of Domitian and the Jewish reckoning of days around the sabbath (*SEG* 20 128), with analysis in Stern (2010).

[20] Cf. *BGU*.1.31; *BGU*.1.50; *BGU* 1.53; *BGU*.1.45; *BGU* 1.110. Other than the *Acta*-related literature, the preponderance of papyri fall under 'dating'-related documents. On the importance of the Roman power and the emperor manifesting themselves on papyri in Egypt (including analysis of the poll tax) and imperial titulature, see de Jong (2003: 243–61).

life to mark down time in documentation about the daily rhythm of life, suggests the emperor is a *basso continuo*. It hints at the pervasiveness of the Roman emperor in the minds and lives of his subjects.

An imperial life punctuates and informs how time is constructed and experienced in a community, in ways which are both profound and banal. It can reflect understandings of how time progresses and how things can seemingly change and remain similar in comparison to different points in the history of the principate, which allows for the conscious comparisons between different emperors across time. Though figures, events, and political arrangements might change with respect to the Roman emperor-ship in the first two centuries AD, there are conscious continuities in the conversations about what the emperor was. Thus, there is another axis with which to consider the emperor: a temporality that is in constant dialogue with the precedents of the past, the appearance of the present, and the projections for the future.[21]

In this chapter, I will discuss the emperor as a temporal figure using familiar markers of time, both for clarity and as a way to anchor the argument of each section into a particular temporal framework. These are 'imperial present', 'imperial past', and 'imperial future'. Each section focusses on a particular aspect of the emperor's temporal reception. By 'present', I stress the importance of current time and the *now*, focussing therefore on the contemporary and current experience of an emperor's rule. Under this category, I include the 'golden age', which is a descriptor for times of plenty and good fortune and a way to elevate an emperor from the past and into the future by making his age exceptional in comparison. By stressing contemporary experience, themes of ephemerality and the precariousness of a golden age will come forth, seen in rituals of preserva-tion and celebration to do with religion and the so-called imperial cult. By 'past', I stress the conscious revisiting and reshaping of the past in Roman culture. I focus particularly on historiography and its ability to nuance and problematise legacies of previous emperors and how looking back into the past can fashion new perspectives for the present and the future. Such memory games mean that an emperor's past is always a fertile ground of interaction, that there were many participants in this conversation, and that whilst the emperor had an outsized voice in this conversation, it was by no means the only or more long-lasting perspective. By 'future', I discuss

---

[21] See Tac. *Ann.* 2.41.3, where Tacitus plays with the temporality of Germanicus by comparing him to the past of his family, the joyous nature of his present situation in the triumphal procession, and the hope/fear of the future embodied by him and his children. Cf. O'Gorman (2000: 55).

the legitimacy of emperors into the future. Building on discussions of 'acceptance' from previous chapters, I argue that future time becomes an important place where an emperor's legitimacy can be tested. Such futurity can be observed in the manifestation of imperial pretenders, who were apparitions of previous emperors who came to test the power of the current emperor, and also in the complex collection of hexameter poems known as the Sibylline Oracles, which are full of layered historicities and apocalyptic futures. The appearance of the emperor in this collection should not be surprising given that he is a symbol of Roman power. More importantly for our purposes, though, his inclusion in apocalyptic visions means that he becomes a marker of future time, a way to map questions of identity and anxiety into the unknown. Through these categories of past, present, and future, the emperor as a temporal figure gives the impression of *timelessness*, though such a point might obscure the nuance of the figure of the emperor through time. Rather, the emperor becomes a marker that can transcend and organise time, which makes him *seem* timeless, but in fact he remains embedded and layered, in constant dialogue with the precedents and examples of the past, the constraints and expectations of the present, and the anxieties and uncertainties of the future.

6.2 An Imperial Present of Gold and Iron

6.2.1 Living in an Age of Gold

περὶ οὗ ἤδη ῥητέον, ἀπὸ χρυσῆς τε βασιλείας ἐς σιδηρᾶν καὶ κατιωμένην τῶν τε πραγμάτων τοῖς τότε Ῥωμαίοις καὶ ἡμῖν νῦν καταπεσούσης τῆς ἱστορίας.

To this topic we must turn immediately: a decline from a kingdom of gold to one of iron and rust, both for the affairs of the Romans then and also now for my history.[22]

Denique quod optimum videri volunt saeculum, aureum appellant.[23] Thus Seneca ends a portion of his 115th letter. It comes within the context of a discussion of the contemporary love of money and care for the superficial.[24] The description of a golden age is here associated with wealth and money and is discussed negatively by Seneca; desire for wealth is

---

[22] Dio 72(71).36.4, trans. adapted from Kemezis (2021: 45).
[23] Sen. *Ep.* 115.13, translation provided later in this paragraph.
[24] Sen. *Ep.* 115.11: *Admirationem nobis parentes auri argentique fecerunt* (Our parents have inculcated us with an admiration for gold and silver).

framed in terms of metal and typifies the moral depravity of the age in question. To him, there is a connection between the use of metal imagery in poetry to describe the gods and the assumption that wealth is the highest attainment for mankind, which culminates in the widest assumption and appellation – the golden age.[25] Seneca is able to bring several themes pertinent to the golden age into his discussion: invocations of divinity when discussing the presence of a golden age,[26] the moral dubiousness of coveting wealth and money, and the seeming ubiquity of using the word *aureus* with passages of time.[27] Indeed, there is a banality to the manner of this statement: 'Finally, that they wish to be seen as the best age, they call golden.'[28] Most importantly for our purposes, though, is the invocation of the golden age to denote *present* time: the golden age returns under the direction of a new emperor, drawing on images of a primordial past to project hope for plenty and prosperity into the future. Such is the conceit of the Cassius Dio epigraph at the start of this section, too: temporal words push us forward, as the narrative must *already* be recounted in order to relay how an age of gold descended to one of iron and rust. The contemporary aspect is fundamental there, both 'then', concerning the affairs of the Romans of that time, and now, for Cassius Dio's history, engaged as he was in the history of his times.[29] Ages of gold and iron, then, become helpful monikers used to evoke images of time as it was experienced.

Such descriptions suggest a certain malleability to the 'Golden Age' and how it can be interpreted differently according to different times and contexts – used by Seneca as a moralistic argument about wealth and by Dio as a shorthand for a transition towards decline. Its broad designation makes it a descriptor that can more comfortably be associated with wider perspectives that transcend a specific context. The contention here follows the argument of this book as a whole: the use of golden age imagery can reveal not only elite concerns and perspectives but also more popular ones, which suggests layered meaning through time. In this way, this particular vignette can be seen as a small-scaled simulacrum of this whole book, as it contains many of the themes that are discussed throughout: the desires of justice, the hope for plenty and generosity, the proximity to the wondrous

[25] Sen. *Ep.* 115.12: Seneca in chapter 13 also quotes Ov. *Met.* 2.1–2, 107–109, which describes the palace and chariot of Sol, both of which are wrought in gold.

[26] On Seneca describing the popular connection between wealth and dedications to the gods: Sen. *Ep.* 115.11.

[27] Cf. Wallace-Hadrill (1982b: 27–8) for more negative interpretations of a 'golden age'.

[28] Cf. Baldry (1952: 90) for the status of this term after the Augustan age as a commonplace and further evidence; cf. *App. Verg. Aetna* 9; cf. Tac. *Dial.* 12.3.

[29] For the negativity of Dio's present, and the fluctuations of the past, see Kemezis (2021), esp. 50.

and miraculous, the closeness of the emperor to those of lower social position, and the jocular discourse involving the emperor, all find parallels within the idea of the 'Golden Age'.[30]

It would be impossible, however, to give this vast topic the full appreciation it deserves. There are numerous aspects of the golden age that could be discussed here, which could include wide-reaching analyses of similar texts and traditions in different contexts, including Greek antiquity and other world cultures, as well as a more specific appraisal of the use of golden age imagery in Augustan literature and art.[31] What follows here is a more specific discussion of a passage of Philo's *Legatio ad Gaium*, in which Philo describes the celebrations following the accession of Gaius to the principate. In other words, the focus here will remain on the ambiguities of golden age imagery and the use of the golden age as a marker of time and a method for comparison.

Before the discussion of Philo's *Legatio*, a couple of preliminary themes should be stated with respect to the golden age and how it relates to understanding the Roman emperor. To reiterate, the 'Golden Age' denotes a time of happy existence, an imaginary utopian world typified by no hard labour, peace, and plentiful abundance that provided for all needs and wants – a time that had existed in a bygone era deep in the mists of time and had certainly vanished from the earth.[32] Though a common image in world literature, the version most familiar in the Greek and Roman world was the metal ages or generations as described by Hesiod in the *Works and Days* (Hes. *Op.* 96–176), which descended in order from gold to iron, through silver and bronze.[33] The outlier heroic age (Hes. *Op.* 156–73) in part resembles the golden age as the heroes now reside in the Isles of the Blessed, free from worry and living in a land of plenty.[34] In this case, then, the potential of return is hinted at, though in a far-off, unattainable utopia. The image of the golden age subsequently resonated through antiquity in different genres with different audiences, ranging from didactic poetry to

---

[30] Cf. Wallace-Hadrill (1982b: 29–32) for the importance of the emperor with the idea of the return of the golden age.

[31] Baldry (1952: 83–92), which explores use of golden age imagery in ancient literature from Hesiod towards the Augustan age; Forsdyke (2012: 53–9), for a comparative approach between Greek evidence and other folk traditions; Versnel (1993a: 89–135), on Kronos and the *Kronia*, 136–227 on the Roman counterpart of Saturn and the Saturnalia, and esp. 192–205 on the Augustan age. For a similar discussion, see Versnel (1993b: 99–122); for more work on Augustan ideology and a new golden age, see Weinstock (1971: 191–6); Zanker (1988: 167–83).

[32] Baldry (1952: 83–4); cf. Wallace-Hadrill (1982b: 20); cf. Versnel (1993a: 192).

[33] For the resonance of ages of plenty, see Forsdyke (2012: 52–9).

[34] See Hes. *Op.* 112 and 170 for the verbatim description of the Golden and Heroic generations: ἀκηδέα θυμὸν ἔχοντες (having a spirit free from care); cf. Luc. *Ver. Hist.* 2.6–28.

old comedy, and seemed to resonate across cultures and speak to audiences irrespective of social class in that it depicted a time of plenty and no labour.[35] Yet with Vergil's fourth *Eclogue*, the idea of the return of a golden age was fostered, pointing to an important novelty of the paradigm in the imperial period: that a golden age *could* be renewed and brought back, that it was closely related to the Roman emperor, and that instead of a time of plenty it was a time of peace, prosperity, and the fruits of labour.[36] In comparison to Hesiod, who makes the Iron Age the current generation which we experience *now* (Hes. *Op.* 176: **νῦν** γὰρ δὴ γένος ἐστὶ σιδήρεον), the now is switched to a return of a golden age and a new age of Saturn.[37] In short, the emperor fulfilled the role as supreme benefactor, ensuring the maintenance of peace and prosperity in the empire, which was framed with the blissful image of the golden age.[38]

Yet there is a deep ambiguity to the golden age. Connected with the ideas of plenty and licence, the golden age was a time when Kronos, or Saturn in the Roman tradition, ruled. As Versnel shows in his study of Kronos and Saturn, and in particular the Saturnalia (a festival of reversal filled with revelry, licentiousness, and the waiving of social norms),[39] there were both attractive and unsavoury aspects to these deities.[40] To elaborate on the myths, rituals, and festivals would unfortunately fall beyond the scope of this section.[41] Nonetheless, the notion of ambiguity is important. As Versnel puts it: 'Though on the one hand generally pictured as a realm of bliss and happiness on the brink of history, it (sc. the golden age) is also described as the amorphous period before human civilisation during which man led a slothful, and indeed beastly life.'[42] Thus the golden age was interpreted as having both positive and negative aspects; it is precisely in this respect that the malleable paradigm can be usefully compared to perceptions of the Roman emperor. As this book endeavours to expose, the Roman emperor

---

[35] Forsdyke (2012: 54–7): 'For the speaker, then, the free and abundant availability of food is closely connected with the idea that there was no need of labor, especially slave labor.' To be read especially with the fragments of comedy preserved in Athenaeus (Ath. 268b–d = Telecleides' *The Amphictyons*, Ath. 267e–f = Crates' *Wild Animals*).

[36] Cf. Smolenaars (1987) for a discussion of the golden age in Vergil.

[37] Vergil *Ecl.* 4.4–10; cf. Aen. 6.792–5. On the fourth *eclogue*, see Du Quesnay (1976) and Miller (2009: 254–6); for Vergil's originality, see Wallace-Hadrill (1982b: 20–2) and Gatz (1967: 87–103).

[38] Versnel (1993a: 195–8), for the importance of the emperor within this paradigm and, in particular, the emperor as a benefactor and being honoured as such by communities across the empire.

[39] Versnel (1993a: 146–8), on the customs and evidence of the Saturnalian festival, and 191, on the anxiety of it lasting longer than it should.

[40] For instance, alongside the revelry associated with the Saturnalia are the gory images of Saturnian cult: Macrob. *Sat.* 1.7.31, cited in Versnel (1993a: 146).

[41] Cf. Versnel (1993a) for a full treatment, esp. 106, for Kronos, and 142–6, for Saturn.

[42] Versnel (1993a: 99).

fulfilled a number of different roles in the minds of his subjects, which were shaped by their hopes and fears – hopes for justice, peace and prosperity and fears of rebuke and reprimand. Accordingly, the connection between the Roman emperor and depictions of the age of Saturn is striking, allowing for the interpretative framework of the golden age, with both its positive and negative aspects, to be applied to the reception of the Roman emperor. Importantly for our purposes, the golden age is made relevant to contemporary society as a way to think about the times in which that society lived.

Indeed, such themes can be seen in the *Hadrianus* in the Montserrat Codex. Dated to the fourth century AD, this codex *miscellaneus* contains many different works in Latin and Greek, including the first and second Catilinarians, a *Psalmus responsorius*, and a list of Greek words, and is thought to be from a context of learning.[43] The *Hadrianus* is a prose text that is difficult to define generically. It has been described as a *narratio* (or *diēgēma*), forming a part of rhetorical exercises (*progymnasmata*).[44] In any case, the *Hadrianus* bears similarity to the *Acta Alexandrinorum* and the *Hadriani sententiae*, in that it seems to portray encounters with the emperor, in this case Hadrian, with the hope for intercession or benefaction.[45] One of the scenes has a delegate from Cologne (*Colonia Agrippinensis*) asking for relief from taxation that had been levied since Vespasian.[46] After Hadrian asked why they had asked for relief from previous emperors, he replied: 'we are petitioning a Saturnian emperor, lord.' Caesar: 'why a Saturnian emperor?' 'Because nature has not yet given us a *princeps* who is content with what he has, and is not interested in the property of others.'[47] What we have, then, is a reference to the golden age in the appellation *Saturnius imperator*, which reveals an aspect about golden age temporality and a reference to an idea of plenty and generosity embedded in its imagery. The implication of this statement, too, is that the golden age had yet to arrive until the reign of Hadrian, placing the coming of a new age at the dramatic date of this story. Flattery notwithstanding, the idea of a constant comparison comes to mind, as the ambassador elevates the present in comparison to the past, with the implication that the age can change and be recast for a new Caesar at the detriment of the old, or vice versa.[48] The expectation of

---

[43] Berg (2018: 9, 14–15).

[44] Berg (2018: 109–11), on the nature of the text, its fictionality and exceptional nature.

[45] Cf. Berg (2018: 27). [46] Berg (2018: 60), ll. 4–7.

[47] Berg (2018: 60), ll. 9–13: '*Saturnium imperatorem petimus, domine.' Caesar: 'Quare Saturnium imperatorem?' 'Quia nondum dederat natura principem qui suo tantum contentus esset, non de alieno.'*

[48] Cf. Suet. *Tib.* 59.1: *Aurea mutasti Saturni saecula, Caesar;* | *Incolumi nam te ferrea semper erunt* (You have changed the golden ages of Saturn, Caesar; for with you being safe, iron shall they always be). Cf. p. 27.

generosity is also enriched here, as the appellation conjures up images of plenty and a lack of suffering where authorities do not exploit people. In this text, then, are images of the fears and expectations in an encounter with a Roman emperor, with golden age imagery as a way of thinking about an emperor's power.

Such images are conjured by Philo Judaeus when he describes the early reign of Gaius. The work describes the encounter of both Alexandrian Greek and Jewish embassies with Gaius within the context of ongoing intercommunity strife in Alexandria in the early first century AD that escalated into a wider conflict concerning the statue in the Temple at Jerusalem.[49] A multifaceted work that defies generic expectations, the *Legatio* is in many parts a prolonged critique and study of the Roman emperorship, through the sharp interrogation of Gaius' character by means of comparison with his predecessors, Augustus and Tiberius, and several historical vignettes that exhibit his conduct throughout his reign.[50] Put another way, Philo engages in temporal thinking through his framework of comparison: by way of his account of events surrounding the Roman emperor and his own embassy to Gaius, he highlights conduct that will become exemplary in the future for others to reflect on and analyse the ethical profile of an emperor.[51]

An example of Philo's invitation to think across time comes in his description of the revelries at the start of Gaius' reign. The joy of the *populus Romanus* and the rest of the Roman empire was palpable, in that their happiness had surpassed that which was felt for all Gaius' predecessors.[52] They thought that they already achieved fulfilment in success (*eutychia*) and prosperity (*eudaimonia*). Accordingly, the outward displays of revelry were everywhere, including civic and religious festivities: sacrifices, festivals, musical contests, horse races, and all sorts of pleasurable experiences for the senses.[53] Thereafter, Philo supplies a series of paradoxes that are worth quoting:

τότε οὐ πλούσιοι πενήτων προύφερον, οὐκ ἔνδοξοι ἀδόξων, οὐ δανεισταὶ χρεωστῶν, οὐ δεσπόται δούλων περιῆσαν, ἰσονομίαν τοῦ καιροῦ διδόντος, ὡς τὸν παρὰ ποιηταῖς ἀναγραφέντα Κρονικὸν βίον μηκέτι νομίζεσθαι

---

[49] For more on this context and the generically similar *Acta Alexandrinorum*, see Harker (2008: 31–4). On the historical context, see Niehoff (2018: 30–1), Gruen (2002: 66–7), Gruen (2012), and Christoforou (2021: 87).

[50] For a summary of the content and themes of the work: Christoforou (2021: 85).

[51] Cf. Christoforou (2021: 88) for the potential of counterfactual futures in Philo, *Leg.* 352; cf. Kosmin (2018: 137–71), and esp. 234 for the late Roman empire and Jacob's Ladder in rabbinical thought.

[52] Philo, *Leg.* 10–11.   [53] Philo, *Leg.* 12 for the full list of activities.

πλάσμα μύθου διά τε τὴν εὐθηνίαν καὶ εὐετηρίαν τό τε ἄλυπον καὶ ἄφοβον
καὶ τὰς πανοικίας ὁμοῦ καὶ πανδήμους μεθ' ἡμέραν τε καὶ νύκτωρ
εὐφροσύνας, αἳ μέχρι μηνῶν ἑπτὰ τῶν πρώτων ἄπαυστοι καὶ συνεχεῖς
ἐγένοντο.

At that time, the rich did not surpass the poor, nor the notable over the
obscure, nor the creditors over the debtors. Masters were not superior to
slaves, that time providing equality before the law, just like the Life of
Kronos as depicted by the poets, no longer thought to be a fashioned story,
due to the prosperity, plenty, lack of pain and fear, and merriment in all
households together and communities day and night, which were continuous and without end for the first seven months.[54]

There are several notable aspects in this passage.[55] Philo describes
a universal phenomenon of rejoicing that spreads across the *oikoumene*,
from the Roman people to the whole of Italy and the European and Asian
provinces.[56] We find ourselves in the familiar world of beneficial ideology
typical of the early principate, based around reciprocal relationships fostered by euergetism and civic life prompted by the accession of a new
emperor.[57] Such a moment prompted revelry in the present and expectations for the future. Here, the hopes and desires of large populations in the
empire are conceptually affected by the emperor.

However, what stands out here is Philo's framing of the scenes of
enjoyment and revelry as a manifestation of a *Kronikos Bios* – a 'Life of
Kronos', which refers to the golden age when Kronos reigned, thus putting
such reactions within a different time frame. The examples that Philo
provides contain all the ingredients of the *Saturnia regna*: happiness,
prosperity, feasting, and the topsy-turvy role reversals between the high
and low, creditors and debtors, masters and slaves. Furthermore, Philo is
not alone in recording the revelry surrounding the accession of Gaius in
this manner, with notable other examples such as Suetonius describing the
happy crowds that met him on Tiberius' funeral train towards Rome[58] and
the utopian metaphors utilised in a decree from Assos.[59] Therefore, there is
evidence for this sort of conceptualisation from separate sources, suggesting that this exceptional 'time' was conceived of in ways analogous to

---

[54] Philo, *Leg.* 10–13.   [55] Cf. Versnel (1993a: 200–1) for his analysis of this passage.
[56] Cf. Christoforou (2021: 103–10).   [57] See Chapter 3.3.   [58] Suet. *Cal.* 13.
[59] *Syll.*3 797 = *IGR* 4.251 = Smallwood, *Gaius*, 33 = *I.Assos* 26, which describes that their hopes had been
answered at Gaius accession, that world's happiness had no limit (οὐδὲν δὲ μέτρον χαρᾶς εὕρηκε ὁ
κόσμος) and that the most pleasant age of men was now present (ὡς ἂν τοῦ | ἡδίστου ἀνθρώποις
αἰῶνος νῦν ἐνεστῶτος). Similarly, it comes in the context of an embassy, here sent on occasion of
Gaius' accession. Cf. *IG* 7.2711 from Acraephia, which has evidence for a Boeotian embassy for like
purposes.

fiction and poetry, as if this manner of description was the way in which to conceptualise the beginning of a promising new reign. Still, Philo's mention of a Life of Kronos is exceptional and thus requires further comment.

As mentioned, 'Golden Age' imagery, which involves descriptions of times when Saturn or Kronos reigned, has a rich history. There are thus many avenues of relevant analysis that could be followed, which could involve a comparative approach exploring the continuities and changes of the imagery from Greek poetry through philosophy towards the Augustan age and beyond, which cannot all be pursued here.[60] Both Wallace-Hadrill and Versnel have separately argued for a more nuanced approach to understanding the golden age, arguing that its reception was more ambiguous than the overtly laudatory tone suggests, which is an important focus of this book.[61] Not only is the Life of Kronos a time of plenty and carelessness; it is also a time of lawlessness and violence, evinced by the familiar myths of Ouranos' castration and Kronos' overthrow at the hands of Zeus. Ambiguity is deeply embedded in ideas concerning the reign of Saturn, connected in times of renewal and transition and embodied by successions between different generations.[62] This potential wavering of opinion brings about the theme of subversiveness and the carnivalesque in representations of the golden age.[63] One particular strand of scholarship since the mid-twentieth century has sought to excavate the remains of popular culture from literature in an attempt to reconstruct a cultural history from below, most famously taking inspiration from Mikhail Bakhtin's *Rabelais and His World*, which studied the subversiveness of the carnival as a festival of reversal.[64] In a similar vein, Scott has argued for a similar reading of these sorts of festivals when studying social dynamics in Southeast Asia and indeed referred to the Saturnalia as an 'authorized ritual occasion when it is possible to break the rules . . . that allow subordinates, momentarily to turn the tables'.[65] Accordingly, a festival of reversal was an arena of direct encounter between the high and the low, where roles could be reversed and traditional power structures could be subverted, and which therefore could reveal popular concerns typically kept hidden under normal

---

[60] Cf. Baldry (1952: 83–92); cf. Forsdyke (2012: 53–9).

[61] Wallace-Hadrill (1982b: 27–32) and Versnel (1993a: 205–10).

[62] For the myths of generational violence, see Hes. *Th.* 154–9; Apollodoros 1.3 and Hes. *Th.* 71–3, 453–506, 851, with Strauss (1993: 159–60). I owe this point to Emma Greensmith

[63] On the 'carnivalesque', see Versnel (1993b: 99–111) and Braund and James (1998: 298–9).

[64] See Forsdyke (2012: 8) and Beard (2014: 60–2) for a discussion of this work and its influence.

[65] Scott (1985: 287, n. 88); cf. Forsdyke (2012: 14–15) on Scott's influence.

circumstances. Thus, we are tantalisingly close to popular sentiments and concepts of the emperor.

At first glance, Philo's summary of the activities is extremely promising. As Versnel argues in his analysis of this passage: 'The *Saturnia Regna* have returned and brought peace, prosperity and justice and, even more emphatically, social equality to the unmatched extent that the masters are not better off than their slaves.'[66] It could follow, then, that Philo's passage is a prime example of subversive opinion – a potential window into the thought-world of a more 'popular' perspective. However, one must be more nuanced in the analysis of this material than simply ascribing it to popular viewpoints willy-nilly.[67] For instance, in a recent criticism of the Bakhtinian approach, Beard has problematised the transposition of the carnivalesque into the ancient world, in particular with regards to the Roman festival of the Saturnalia, arguing that the evidence does not exist for the Bakhtinian carnival or what does survive does not sit well with that paradigm.[68] Moreover, aspects of inversion that were part of such festivals could serve to *reinforce* rather than challenge the status quo, which is a widely accepted way of understanding such reversals.[69]

There are a couple of points that could alleviate these concerns. First, it should be stated that, even if conceptually related, Philo describes the revelry surrounding Gaius' accession as if it were exhibiting the life of Kronos and that it was experienced across the empire for a long period of seven months, rather than the ritualised Saturnalia at Rome. As such, they are in different contexts, allowing for greater spontaneity during the festivities, and perhaps less controlled than the impression of the finite period of the Saturnalia.[70] Second, it is interesting that Philo's interpretation of such events is through an overtly negative lens, which is bolstered by his seemingly incredulous description of the honours paid to Gaius in comparison to his two predecessors, Augustus and Tiberius.[71] Accordingly, there are several potential differing perspectives as described by Philo, which include that of wider revelry at the joyous accession of Gaius and that of his own milieu of the Alexandrian Jewish community, as well as

---

[66] Versnel (1993a: 200).   [67] Cf. Section 1.1.2.

[68] Beard (2014: 63–4), for a short explanation of the festival and that its 'distinctive features' such as 'the gross overconsumption, the emphasis of inversion, on the lower bodily stratum, and even the laughter' are mostly absent from representations of the Saturnalia.

[69] Beard (2014: 62, 64), in which Beard distinguishes between the return of primordial equality stressed in the Saturnalia and the more Bakhtinian reversal of fortune. Cf. Braund (1993: 68).

[70] Cf. Beard (2014: 65), calling it a 'rather prim – or at least paternalistic – occasion'. For a more 'carnivalesque' reading of the Saturnalia in particular, see Versnel (1993a: 146–63).

[71] Philo, *Leg.* 141–51.

a wider Jewish perspective on the desecration of the Temple at Jerusalem.[72] Such disjuncts and inconsistencies should not be troubling but rather point to the richness of responses to the emperor and the different experience of time. Third, the long list of descriptions includes signs of happiness, feasting, 'every kind of pleasure appealing to every sense', and examples of equality between high and low.[73] These experiences fit more comfortably with a carnivalesque interpretation. Therefore, the examples of revelry as described in the above passage could in fact be a window into a wider perspective and particularly one that involves perceptions of an emperor.

Yet does this passage reveal 'popular' concerns about the Roman emperor?[74] Perhaps, but not in a direct, unfiltered manner. The power dynamics in the passage seem to be the most revealing and suggest the existence of the hopes and desires of a wider population across the empire that manifested in reality in direct response to the accession of an emperor. Accordingly, Gaius provides the environment in which social norms are revised and exuberant celebration can occur, which suggests that he was perceived to safeguard the hopes and desires of a wider population across the empire, instead of those few within his milieu. Moreover, that it is a golden age that is conjured suggests its malleability, both in terms of the ambiguities of its reception and in terms of its use as an analogy to describe different periods in imperial time. In the end, the emperor could be thought of as a harbinger of a new golden age, yet there was subjectivity in this interpretation, allowing for nuances and differences in opinion to exist within a similar framework of reference.

The ambiguity of the golden age, with its negative and positive connotations, should inform our views about how the emperor was perceived.[75] Depending on context and perspective, the theme of the golden age could give a more negative impression. Of particular note is Seneca's *Apocolocyntosis*.[76] In this work, Claudius is depicted in the role of the foolish *Saturnalicius princeps*.[77] As Braund and James describe it: 'Claudius' rule is represented as something suited to festival time, but not to the seriousness of everyday political use, hence the horror of

---

[72] On Philo's interpretations of Roman rule, see Barraclough and Haase (1984: 449–52) and Niehoff (2018).

[73] Cf. Versnel (1993a: 200).   [74] Cf. discussion in Sections 1.1.1–1.1.2.

[75] Versnel (1993b: 109–11). See Newlands (2002: 248, 262) with Stat. *Silv.* 4.2 and 1.6.81–4 for Domitian's generosity during the Saturnalia.

[76] See Versnel (1993a: 205–10); Braund and James (1998); Dickison (1977: 634–47).

[77] Sen. *Apoc.* 8.2.

discovering that the monster-emperor was in for a lengthy turn of office.'[78] The perspective of time's movement becomes relative depending on your position in society. This negative interpretation of Claudius' rule is further enriched by his teratological description when he meets Hercules after his death, who was shaken by Claudius' monstrous appearance and a voice more akin to that of a sea-monster than a land animal.[79] This representation connects the Saturnalian context with the world of *mirabilia*, in which Claudius himself is the 'sea-monster' of unknown provenance, which further highlights the absurdity of his status as emperor.[80] Accordingly, this vignette stresses the negativity of this interpretation of a potential golden age gone wrong, giving an impression of the scope of potential interpretations. The issues of authorship and its subsequent audience being within a small circle should not be problematic, as the *Apocolocyntosis* draws upon themes of wide resonance. Indeed, it is interesting that these seemingly 'subversive' descriptions are utilised by Seneca to describe Claudius, which reveals power dynamics that place him and his milieu in a subordinate position, using this satirical medium to reveal a 'hidden transcript' of opinion, even if Seneca is not the typical 'subordinate' imagined.[81] However, this does not necessarily serve to problematise this issue but rather bolsters the present argument that they all form strands of the same wider conversation, with many layers of complexity, which is evidence for a thought-world concerning the emperor from the perspective of his subjects.

In the end, allusions to a golden age and an emperor throughout the period in question should be seen in this subjective and impressionistic light, altered by context, whether positive or negative. It highlights how golden age imagery became a powerful tool in shaping the understanding of what the emperor was and could be, in terms of both hopes and fears.[82] Moreover, the golden age could become temporally narrowing, in that it can be used as a shorthand to supply a set of images to a reign that

---

[78] Braund and James (1998): 298. cf. Sen. *Apoc.* 12.2. cf. Fronto, *Principia Historiae* 20, who advises Lucius Verus on the importance of entertainment within the emperor's duties: *imperium non minus ludicris quam seriis probari atque maiore damno seria, graviore invidia ludicra neglegi.* 'Power is proven not less through public games than through serious affairs. To neglect serious matters does greater damage, but to neglect games provokes more serious ill-will.'

[79] Sen. *Apoc.* 5.3–4.   [80] Cf. p. 150.   [81] Cf. Braund (1993: 67–8).

[82] There are many allusions to the golden age (or its demise) with different emperors throughout our period, helpfully compiled by Gatz (1967: 138–9), which unfortunately cannot receive full treatment. They include Augustus: Verg. *Aen.* 6.792–794; Tiberius: Suet. *Tib.* 59.1; Nero: Sen. *Apoc.* 4.1; Calp. *Ecl.* 1.42 ;1.64; 4.6–7; 4.140. Sen. *Clem.* 2.1.3; Domitian: Mart. 6.3. Antoninus Pius: Aristid. *Or.* 26.106. Marcus Aurelius: Dio 72(71).36.4. Commodus: Dio 73(72).15.6; HA. *Comm.* 14.3 Pescennius Niger: HA *Pesc.* 12. 6; Probus: HA *Prob.* 23.2.

transcends its own context and makes it comparable to other ages. Thus, an emperor could be lifted from his context and utilised as an example, to be either emulated or admonished, in a conversation with a similar vernacular that resonates through time. Accordingly, we can build up a vocabulary of emperor criticism that becomes richer as there are more examples and precedents. However, the version of the golden age as described by Philo was one that stressed the present above all, that is, the emperor was the one to establish a new golden age that would bring prosperity that would be enjoyed *now*. The problem with that image, though, was that prolonging such prosperity depended on the continued health of the emperor himself and his estimation amongst the people. In that sense, Philo accentuates the precariousness of the golden age, a theme that is present in its ambiguous and negative receptions throughout antiquity – never being quite what it seemed and almost always unattainable. What we have with the golden age, then, is an unstable and uncertain present that is seen as golden, reflecting the anxiety and hope placed on the emperor and his rule.

6.2.2   *Devotion, Time, and Imperial Cults*

To continue on the theme of anxiety about the present and the wish to preserve the current peace and prosperity in the empire, we now turn to the phenomenon of *devotiones*.[83] These are related to the *devotiones* of the republican period, which saw either the self-sacrifice of a general or the dedication of an enemy's territory and population to the gods of the underworld.[84] When we move into the principate, there was 'a new phenomenon of people making vows to offer their lives for the well-being of the emperor'.[85] Such self-sacrifice suggests an importance placed on the health and safety of the Roman emperor that is directly proportional to that of the health and safety of the empire. A particularly interesting case comes from Gaius' principate, within the same context of the golden age revelry discussed in the previous section. After the time of celebration, Gaius fell deathly ill, to the extent that there was a precipitous fall from happiness to sorrow, described by Philo in close proximity to the long account of the celebrations following Gaius' accession:

συννοίας τε καὶ κατηφείας πᾶσα οἰκία καὶ πόλις γεγένητο μεστή,
ἰσορρόπῳ λύπῃ τῆς πρὸ μικροῦ χαρᾶς ἀμφικλινοῦς γενομένης. τὰ γὰρ

---

[83] Versnel (1980: 562–77); Versnel (1993a: 219–27).
[84] Versnel (1976), on the complex distinction between these different types of *devotiones*.
[85] Versnel (1993a: 219).

μέρη πάντα τῆς οἰκουμένης αὐτῷ συνενόσησε, βαρυτέρᾳ νόσῳ χρησάμενα
τῆς κατασχούσης Γαίον· ἐκείνη μὲν γὰρ σώματος ἦν αὐτὸ μόνον, ἡ δὲ τῶν
πανταχοῦ πάντων, ψυχικῆς εὐσθενείας, εἰρήνης, ἐλπίδων, μετουσίας καὶ
ἀπολαύσεως ἀγαθῶν.

Every household and city was full of anxiety and despondency, with the
happiness from not long before becoming unseated by an equal measure of
sadness. For all the places of the inhabited world were sick with him,
experiencing a more serious illness than that holding Gaius. For that, in
his case, was only an illness of the body, but theirs was of everything
everywhere, an illness of strength of the soul, peacefulness, hopefulness,
and the participation and enjoyments of all good things.[86]

Such was the empathetic fear for the demise of Gaius.[87] The fluctuating
emotion of the people in this scene contrasts with Philo's call to reason and
measured emotion in the face of uncertainty.[88] Neither Caligula's golden
age nor his sickness last forever, though people across the empire are
described as responding viscerally to the fortunes of the emperor in the
moment. Fears projected into the future will be discussed in the next
section, though the fear in this context seems to concern the potentially
lost future, a lamentation that reflected mourning that was all too
familiar.[89] This context is further enriched by corroborating evidence for
devotiones. In Suetonius' account of this episode, people surrounded the
Palatine, with some vowing to fight as gladiators and others by offering
their lives for his health.[90] Dio offers similar information, but this time
providing the names of those who would give their lives for Gaius.[91]
According to this evidence, anxieties about the health of an emperor
were thus alleviated: by offering up their lives, they would thus ensure the
future of the emperor and, furthermore, ensure that peace and prosperity
would continue in the empire. Moreover, *devotiones* is not restricted to this
context[92] but also seen in more stylised and formal contexts in hundreds of
inscriptions involving the formula *devoti numini maestatique eius*, which are

[86] Philo, *Leg.* 15–16.
[87] Cf. Tac. *Ann.* 2.41, 2.82, and 3.4 for such fear, and outpouring of emotion, in the Roman people over
Gaius' father and mother, Germanicus and Agrippina.
[88] Philo, *Leg.* 1–2; cf. Niehoff (2018: 34–5).
[89] Cf. *CIL* 11.1421, ll. 50–1, on Gaius Caesar, grandson of Augustus, and the *Tabula Siarense* (Lott
2012), esp. ll. 164–5 on the outpouring of grief and the concern to display that feeling into posterity.
[90] Suet. *Cal.* 14.2, for people offering up their lives for the health of Gaius.
[91] Dio 59.8.3: One Publius Afranius Potitus, a member of the plebs, perished, 'not only voluntarily, but
also by oath, promised that he would die if Gaius were saved' (οὐ μόνον ἐθελοντὴς ἀλλὰ καὶ ἔνορκος,
ἄν γε ὁ Γάιος σωθῇ, τελευτήσειν ὑποσχόμενος), cf. Suet. *Cal.* 27.2, where Gaius forces a man who
had vowed to fight as a gladiator to do so after he recovered.
[92] For a collection of this evidence, see Versnel (1980: 565–75).

dedicatory *vota* to the emperors that call for peace and prosperity in the empire, ranging from the time of the Severans through the third century into the late empire.[93] This suggests an active participation in an ideology that saw the emperor as the provider of peace – a potential response within a wider context of possible interpretations of the role of the emperor in the world, which included the emperor as an upholder of justice, a generous benefactor, and a mediator between the known and unknown phenomena in the world. The ubiquity itself suggests a certain banality, too, as if it were commonplace to engage in such action for the health of the emperor in an effort for his life to continue. Such formulaic interactivity, then, suggests a way of viewing the world where the emperors became markers of time, honour, and proxies for the health and identity of the individuals and communities that set up such inscriptions.

The context of *devotiones* brings us to a subject that has largely remained in the background so far in this book, namely the place of the imperial cult and the divinity of the emperor within the discourse of who an emperor was in the *mentalité* of his subjects. I have left this subject until now to explore it in a different way, in contrast to the illuminating scholarly work on the organisation of the imperial cult and, in particular, civic building, competition, and the civic organisation of temples, festivals, and ritual activities across the empire. In line with the conceit of this section, the transactionality of the imperial cult involves not only a dialogue between the human and divine with the emperor as its focus but also one that privileges continued prosperity and peace in the present. In other words, the rhythms of life and ritual are geared towards present relationships in the hope of reciprocal benefits. The bibliography on this topic is immense, with further evidence published and made available for analysis that makes the imperial cult a rich field of study.[94] Not only is the material extensive but the nature of the phenomenon is similarly capacious. As Beard, North, and Price stated in their book *Religions of Rome*, 'there is no such thing as *the* Imperial Cult',[95]

---

[93] Cf. Charlesworth (1937: 22, 31 n. 52) for evidence of this formula and an argument seeing these inscriptions as evidence for vociferous loyalty. For instance, one to Julia Domna, Septimius Severus' wife (*CIL* 2.810) from Cáparra in Lusitania. Cf., though, the arguments of Hellström (2020), which may suggest loyalty alone might not explain such a phenomenon but rather forms part of a language of honour as a marker of privilege and time, which is therefore more about the dedicators than the nominal dedicatees.

[94] For overviews on the bibliography, see Herz (2007, 316), Naylor (2010: 208–15), and McIntyre (2019). Important studies include Price (1984b), Fishwick (1987), Friesen (1993), Harland (2003), Burrell (2004), and Fujii (2013).

[95] Beard, North, and Price (1998: 348). This is provocatively placed at the head of the introduction to McIntyre (2019: 1).

which is to say that the rituals and practices associated with honouring the emperor and his family, and the numerous aspects therefrom such as religious feeling, agency, whether 'local' or 'state-mandated', cannot be easily categorised and defined, as well as the similarities and differences of those practices empire-wide. Thus, any comprehensive treatment of the historiography of the imperial cult in its various forms is impossible here, so I will focus on a couple of preliminary points before discussing the aspect of time in the imperial cult.[96]

Before Price's *Rituals and Power*, the question of emperor worship was treated under the category of political life, thus describing a phenomenon of building political favour, which was poorly clothed as a religious practice.[97] Price problematised this distinction and concentrated on ritual practice and what it means for defining the emperor's position, thus helping bridge the gap between religious practice and political and diplomatic engagement in the Greek east during the imperial period. Though this book remains influential, consensus is hardly secure, not least due to the fact that a comprehensive treatment of the whole phenomenon is yet to be undertaken, with many studies focussing on certain time periods, regions, or cities in order to make the analysis of the material more manageable.[98] What is fundamental to stress, however, about this particular moment in the study of the imperial cult is the appreciation of its polyvalency. To paraphrase Herz, the imperial cult is both a religious and social phenomenon found across the empire, changing in time and space due to local and transregional contexts and also due to the ever-changing concerns of communities, not least fluctuating with the fortunes of the emperor and his family, which ultimately cannot be reduced to a dichotomy of ritual practice and belief (or lack thereof).[99]

Furthermore, this recent work moved towards an appreciation of the 'godly' aspects of emperor worship.[100] This work has fleshed out aspects of the divine around the imperial position, which includes honours received

---

[96] A more comprehensive explanation of the historiography of the 'imperial cult' appears in the literature review articles by Naylor (2010), which is a good summary of work on the imperial cult in Roman history and early Christian studies, and McIntyre (2019), which explores different aspects of the phenomenon.

[97] Nock (1930); cf. Naylor (2010: 209–10).

[98] See Herz (2007: 307–16) for a good survey of different potential avenues of inquiry into the 'imperial cult'.

[99] Herz (2005: 638), summarised and analysed in McIntyre (2019: 2). Cf. pp. 110–114 for examples of changing and competing allegiances manifested through the imperial cult.

[100] Veyne (2002: 19): 'Il n'était pas dieu en vertu de son mérite personnel, il était dieu parce qu'il était empereur.'

in the Greek east, and the meaning of the Latin terms *genius* and *numen*, which appear in contexts of worship.[101] One tension that has been scrutinised is the place of the imperial centre and provincial communities in patronising and expanding the imperial cult, with a concentration on what that means for peer–polity interaction across the Mediterranean, questions of engendering loyalty, and the cultivation of favour.[102] A connected tension lies between local and central initiatives of the imperial cult, which sees the interaction between the imperial centre and cities in tessellated versions of worship, such as different cults of the *theos* Hadrian, and the leagues and *koina*, which gives us another translocal element in the promulgation of the imperial cult.[103] Importantly for us, these league cults did not necessarily overlap with provincial administration, which suggests another organising principle and another arena of interaction and competition between *poleis* in the Roman empire. Moreover, these recent works that appear in the volume *Empire and Religion* by Muñiz, Cortés, and Lozano show a deep interest in discussing the theological component of imperial worship, which includes giving honours to the emperor as a god due to his benefactions.[104] Such work is pushing the boundaries of understanding the imperial cult as a translocal phenomenon (i.e. different versions of emperor worship that are nonetheless recognisable in comparison) and as a set of ideas that casts the emperor's actions as being worthy of worship and cult.

To return to Herz's paradigm, the 'imperial cult' was a polyvalent phenomenon, and thus not a single set of practices. This polyvalency brings us to the question of perception, thinking about emperor worship from the bottom up and how people interacted with the emperor's divine status, a question that I have pursued throughout this book through different topics and concerns about the emperor's position. The evidence discussed in Section 2.2, namely slaves and women going to imperial statues for protection, brings us very close to real-world interactions between people and representations of the Roman emperor.[105] It suggests that this activity had not only a political/legal dimension but also a fundamentally religious one, thus bringing it in line with established

---

[101] Price (1980, 1984a); Scheid (2003: 159–65): 'It was power that could be understood and thought of as the epiphany of a divine power in the hands of a mortal.'
[102] Cf. Harland (2003: 88–9).
[103] See Cortés (2017: 127–8), who discussed the evidence of Hadrian considered as a divinity and on 'supra-civic' imperial cult, see Lozano (2017: 149–176, esp. 169): 'the emperors were gods of harmony and stability, but also divinities of hierarchy and competition.'
[104] See Cortés (2017: 134).
[105] Cf. pp. 76–82; Herz (2007: 311), on the place of statues in those interactions.

scholarship that problematised strict demarcations between politics and religion in the Roman world, though viewing that haziness through a different lens. Much like the vignettes and evidence discussed throughout this book, then, the emperor's divinity is also multivalent, encompassing often paradoxical expectations of the emperor's power and role and thus prompting often incongruous images of how the emperor seemed. Put more forcefully, we should not be surprised to see the emperor cast in godly guises. Given his power and variety of expected roles, what would be surprising is the lack of divine imagery and analogy used to think about and describe the emperor. Pushing this idea further, the semantic range of divine honorifics to the emperor was ambiguous enough to problematise distinctions between human and divine honours, which suggests an ambiguity in how people understood and interacted with imperial representations.[106] In other words, it should not be surprising that statues and images of emperors were regarded numinously, which has very important implications for how we understand the acts of movement towards those representations.

The dynamics of the 'imperial cult', therefore, can be fruitfully observed from different angles. From the perspective of this chapter in particular, the imperial cult can also be a way to perform political, social, and religious identity and how such a performance locates the community within its history and its relationship with Rome.[107] Moreover, given the progress made in scholarship on the imperial cult, the question of agency allows for local concerns and local identity to be drivers in decisions concerning the embedding of an emperor into ritual practices.[108] Put another way, such institutions were a dialogue that allowed people across the empire to embed themselves in an imperial vernacular that was recognisable to other communities as well as to the imperial centre and also to connect their communities at specific times to specific emperors. Such a dialogue transcended temporal contexts, too, as 'imperial cults' could reach back in time to refashion identities and belonging, whilst setting out new identities and markers of distinction in language that placed one within imperial time. An example of such marking comes from the dossier of documents recounting the career of Epaminondas of Acraephia in the early first century AD, who was a prominent participant in the politics of his city

---

[106] Gradel (2002), esp. 234–50.

[107] Cf. Tac. *Ann.* 3.61–3, for an example of cities from the Greek east performing religious identity and historical relationships in the senate, with analysis in Kantiréa (2014).

[108] Russell (2020), for the importance of local knowledge and concerns to the proliferation of altars of the *Lares Augusti* across the *vici* in Rome.

and the *koina*, or leagues, of Greece, an archpriest of the imperial cult, and a commemorated benefactor, whose recorded career in imperial politics spanned an embassy of the Boeotian league at the accession of Gaius in AD 37 to the granting of freedom from taxation to the Greeks by Nero in AD 67.[109] As part of the benefactions to his native city of Acraephia, Epaminondas reconstituted the *agon* of the Ptoia, which was connected to the local sanctuary of Apollo Ptoios and had fallen into abeyance for thirty years.[110] As agonothete, he reformed this contest as that of the Great Ptoia and Caesarea, thus embedding the cult of the Sebastoi into the local practices of Acraephia. Instead of reading such an act only as the performance of loyalty, even though there might be aspects of that due to Epaminondas' prominence in diplomatic life, this act has a local resonance that marks out Epaminondas' piety and euergetism within his community. Epaminondas used the emperors and the imperial cult to mark himself out as exceptional and a 'founder all over again' (l. 58: κτίστης ἄνωθεν). What is striking here for our purposes, then, is how Epaminondas sets himself out in time as a new founder, anchoring himself to the cult of the emperors in the present and into the future.[111]

A further example of this phenomenon comes in the form of a divinity called Quirinus Augustus.[112] In a rural sanctuary near the Chartreuse massif outside Vienne and north of modern Grenoble, there are two altars that are dedicated to this rather obscure deity, including one that bears two names, Coius Modestus and Iulius Macrinus, the first with a Gaulish name and both seemingly without Roman citizenship, and thus it seems the local Allobroges adopted this cult.[113] Quirinus' identity seems enigmatic and disputed, though by the time we reach the Augustan era such polyvalent interpretations yielded to the god's identification with Romulus.[114] What we have then are local initiatives that complicate our understandings of

---

[109]   *IG* 7.2711–13, for the dossier. For his embassy, see *IG* 7.2711.10–12, and his priesthood, see *IG* 7.2713 = *SIG²* 376; *ILS* 8794; Oliver (1989: n. 296).

[110]   *IG* 7.2712.56–8; cf. Oliver (1971).

[111]   Note the future in the next inscription, *IG* 7.2713 = *SIG²* 376; *ILS* 8794; Oliver (1989: n. 296, ll. 27–30): ὁ ἀρχιερεὺς τῶν Σεβαστῶν διὰ βίου καὶ Νέρωνος | Κλαυδίου Καίσαρος Σεβαστοῦ Ἐπαμεινώνδας |ʼΕπαμεινώνδου. Note that in the same inscription, Epaminondas marks Nero out as exceptional amongst his ancestors for the greatness of his benefaction (ll. 45–6.) Note, too, the erasure of the names of Nero and his family from the inscription, though not totally, again suggesting a suppleness to the politics of the present. For commentary, see A. Blanco Pérez, 'Nero and the Freedom of Greece', ERC 'Judaism and Rome' Project website: www.judaism-and-rome.org/nero-and-freedom-greece.

[112]   This discussion is indebted to Johnston (2017: 190–3).   [113]   *CIL* 12.2201 and *CIL* 12.2202.

[114]   Johnston (2017: 191–2). Cf. *AE* (1999) 1828 for a third-century AD inscription from Bir Mshriqah in Tunisia, which has the same epithet 'Augustus' and is called *deus pater* and *genius municipii*. Temporal games of identity and (re)foundation are found here, too.

local and Roman identities about power and foundation myths and the embedding of complex aetiologies that not only mediated versions of a Roman or local past but also engaged with the present and the future in the god's association with the emperor and therefore Roman power.[115] In this case, the emperor becomes a fundamental part of the vocabulary in the negotiation of identity through time and in different contexts.

More specifically, what this section has hopefully shown, through the examples of the golden age, *devotiones*, and the imperial cult, is that the emperor was conceived of in terms that were related to divine matters and more specifically to expectations of the present.[116] In this case, what was at stake here were concepts and strategies that served as ways to understand and secure current peace and prosperity, which also exhibit anxieties about an uncertain future, in which the health of the emperor and the concomitant prosperity of the *oikoumene* were inextricably linked but not guaranteed. Such was the precariousness of the imperial present that depended on the participation of the wider population to acknowledge and confirm the prosperity of the times. We now turn to the subjectivity of remembering imperial reigns and the fickleness of looking into the past.

6.3   Imperial Past: Memory, History, and Remembering the Roman Emperor

6.3.1   The Fear of Oblivion

Incohavit, cum in Germania militaret, somnio monitus: adstitit ei quiescenti Drusi Neronis effigies, qui Germaniae latissime victor ibi periit; commendabat memoriam suam orabatque, ut se ab iniuria oblivionis adsereret.

He commenced the work when he was serving in Germany, warned by a dream. Stood before him while he was resting was the ghost of Drusus Nero, who had been victorious far and wide in Germany where he died. He entrusted his memory to him and prayed that Pliny would protect him from the injustice of being forgotten.[117]

In a letter to Baebius Macer, Pliny the Younger describes his uncle's literary achievements, including the inspiration for the writing of his German Wars.[118] Pliny describes a dream that his uncle had when he was on duty

---

[115] Cf. Johnston (2017: 192–3), with Tac. *Hist.* 4.58.
[116] Indeed, Versnel (1993b: 219) argues that the *devotiones* were rituals as part of the emperor cult.
[117] Plin. *Ep.* 3.5.4, cited in Flower (2006: 3).   [118] Henderson (2002), for Pliny's studiousness.

in Germany, which inspired him to write his history of the German wars: in it, Drusus, father of Germanicus and Claudius and brother of Tiberius, appeared in dream, exhorting Pliny to praise his memory and save him from obscurity.[119] It was Drusus' *effigies*, or indeed his image or representation, that appears to Pliny, including within its semantic range a common word for the portrait or likeness of the emperor, itself imbued with a care and record for posterity. Layers of piety and attentiveness to posterity are at play in this letter. In a virtuoso performance on studiousness, Pliny writes a mini-biography and bibliography of his uncle throughout the rest of the letter, showing how prolific a writer he was. Not only does this reflect on Pliny the Elder's encyclopaedic knowledge; it also reflects well on his nephew, who is preserving his uncle's memory by talking about his books. Concerning memory, Pliny also highlights his uncle's attentiveness to the memory of others. Not only did he write the *Life of Pomponius Secundus*, a figure known to have been more famous for his poems than his military exploits, as a duty (*munus*) to preserve Pomponius' memory; he also wrote the *Bella Germaniae* after seeing Drusus the Elder in a dream.[120] Here, the fear of oblivion weighs heavily; so even if this account was about the German wars more generally, nonetheless it was conceived for the preservation of the deeds of exemplary individuals. Indeed, the fragment we *do* have has Agrippina welcoming the troops over the Rhine after exorcising the ghosts surrounding the *Clades Variana*.[121] Therefore, such a history seems geared towards the biographical and the exemplarity of individuals, reaching into the past in order to preserve such material for posterity.

This example is an emotive and evocative illustration of the culture of commemoration at Rome.[122] As Flower has articulated: 'Roman memory (*memoria*) was designed precisely in opposition to the vast oblivion into which most of the past was conceived as having already receded. Such an

---

[119] On the dates of Pliny's military service at Rome, see Syme (1969: 205–8), with three separate posts between the years AD 46–58, with the interval between the second and third being four years. His nephew is vague enough that it could have happened at any point during his time in Germany. However, it seems to be more politically expedient to have an earlier date for this dream, to his service before the death of Claudius in 54, using the opportunity to praise the memory of the emperor's father. I owe this point to Nicholas Purcell. Cf. Hekster (2015: 49–50, n. 24) for coin types under Claudius that stress the paternal bond between him and Drusus and in particular the stress on his German campaigns, making it a ripe situation for Pliny. See Hekster (2015: 56–7) for the resurrection of Drusus coin types under Vespasian, for a new paternal–filial context for the success of Pliny's history.

[120] Tac. *Ann.* 12.28.2. Cf. *consolatio ad Liviam* ll. 365–8, esp. l. 367 for the weight of Drusus on memory: *pars erit historiae totoque legetur in aevo* (it will be a part of history, and will be read in every age).

[121] Tac. *Ann.* 1.69.2.   [122] Cf. Flower (2006: 2–4). Cf. Marincola (1997: 47–8).

attitude was a product of a world in which life was often short and unpredictable.'[123] Within this context, Pliny the Elder is inspired by unresolved memories of the past, urged on by effigies of a broken branch of the imperial family and to preserve and enhance the fallen for posterity's sake.[124] Therefore, this passage is a window into perceptions of memory, as it shows strategies of commemoration that the Romans used to combat oblivion. From this passage alone, it is notable that the clout of a great man is worth cultivating and that a method for doing this is the writing of history.

There are several potential avenues to explore Roman strategies of memory, which is a complex and variegated topic.[125] As summarised by Flower, memory was:

> symbolic space, a power and definitive marker of elite status, (which) stretched across the various visual and textual media and between the generations to ensure the survival and continuity of the community and of the particular culture of its political families . . . The politics of the present were expressed in terms of a narrative of the past, by those who had or claimed the authority to shape and to pass on that narrative.[126]

Accordingly, the commemoration of the past was a complex tapestry, which was passed on and added to with each successive generation through different media, which includes monument, text, and ritual.[127] In terms of commemorating and remembering in the Roman world, which would include the emperor, these memory games could range from architectural monuments such as tombs and mausolea, to texts such as honorific inscriptions, funeral speeches, and historical works, and to ritualistic activity such as the funeral trains involving the procession of ancestral masks and the performance of mimes impersonating Caesar, the consecration of a recently deceased emperor, and the civic and provincial rituals involving the imperial cult.[128]

---

[123] Flower (2006: 3).

[124] Cf. Tac. *Ann.* 1.33.2 on his popularity. For more on Drusus, see Vervaet (2020) and Kuttner (1995: 178–9).

[125] For surveys on memory in Roman history, see Galinsky (2014, 2015b); Galinsky and Lapatin (2016). Cf. Nora (1989) for an introduction to his category of *lieux de mémoire* that takes its cue from Walter Benjamin's *Theses on the philosophy of history* (Benjamin 1999), a fundamental component of memory studies in modern historiography more widely.

[126] Flower (2006: 276). Cf. Veyne (1988: 8–9) on a similar argument in the construction of historiography.

[127] Flower (2006).

[128] For monuments, see Davies (2010: 13–48); see Flower (2006: 115–256) on the strategies of memory in the early imperial period, particularly to do with *damnatio memoriae*; on the *imagines*, funeral processions, and *laudationes*, see Flower (1996: 16, 223–55; 91–126 and 128). On the consecration of

Added to these various methods is the aspect of negative memory, most famously known under the modern term *damnatio memoriae*, which is the damnation of an individual's legacy through various ways, such as the mutilation of their portraits and images, the removal of their *imago* from their family's ancestral masks, and the erasure of their name from inscriptions.[129] Such a variety of responses to death and memory suggests a constant dynamic of reinterpreting and reshaping the past, to be enacted in visceral moments of deposing and defacing statutes and inscriptions, and the revision of historical memory through historiography and literature into the future.[130] Such processes of commemoration and damnation are never static and are exhibited by statues that are reworked to resemble current emperors, which fits into the attentive responsiveness to the ebbs and flows of political life.[131] Indeed, a letter by Marcus Aurelius and Lucius Verus to Ulpius Eurycles in Ephesus, which has instructions to preserve the silver images of their predecessors and not to alter them or smelt them down, suggests the mutability and recycling of such examples.[132] Another example of the marble head of Vespasian from Carthage, now housed in the British Museum, is a case in point. Carved to exhibit realism, Vespasian is shown with wrinkles and a double chin. The unevenness at the back of the neck shows substantial reworking, suggesting the removal of long hair, and has inconsistencies in hairstyle and disproportionate ears.[133] Narratives of commemoration and damnation are not static either. Indeed, the curious anecdote about a statue of Domitian on the *clivus Capitolinus* points to such resonance.[134] Procopius

---

the emperor, see Price (1987) and Bickerman (1973). On mimes, see Sumi (2002). On the imperial cult in general, see Price (1984b), Fishwick (1987), Gradel (2002), and McIntyre (2019).

[129] For a clear general discussion and different methods of defacing or altering portraits, see Huet (2004). For a complete recent appraisal, see Stewart (2003: 267–78) and Flower (2006), esp. 132–8 on the memory games of the *SCPP*. For the mutilation of portraits, see Varner (2004), esp. 2–9 for his general discussion of *damnatio*. Cf. Calomino (2016: 12–14) for a comprehensive list of ancient sanctions against emperors. For the provincial politics and the unsystematic dynamics of divinisation or damnation, see Cauwenberghe (2008).

[130] Reinterpretation of the meaning of public statues and their deposition has recently become a heated topic ('George Floyd protests: The statues being defaced', BBC News, 10 June 2020: www .bbc.co.uk/news/world-52963352); cf. Calomino (2016: 1), who chose Saddam Hussein as a modern parallel, one which resonates with me having lived in Kuwait through and between both Gulf wars.

[131] See Calomino (2016) for a full account of the different strategies of commemoration and damnation. Cf. Varner (2004: 52–66). Cf. pp. 104–114 for responses to the fortunes of the *domus Augusta*, and Rose (1997), for such reworking and resemblances in Julio-Claudian statuary.

[132] Oliver (1989: no. 170, ll. 11–20).

[133] Calomino (2016: 66, fig. 19), for picture and description. The bust was displayed as the final piece at the recent exhibition *Nero: the man behind the myth*, at the British Museum, 27 May 2021 to 24 October 2021.

[134] Procop. *Anecdota* 8.13–21.

recounts an apocryphal story of Domitian's body, which had been hacked to bits at his deposition.[135] Domitia Longina, showing piety to her husband, took the mangled body and sewed it up, commissioning sculptors to reproduce a faithful representation in bronze that preserved the signs of mutilation, so that she might leave an account for posterity of the butchery.[136] That Procopius claimed to have seen the statue himself even in his day (ἐς τόδε τοῦ χρόνου) and argued that it resembled Justinian suggests the resonance of tarnished memory with accompanying moralising anecdotes that could speak to different contexts and indeed, in this case, a different emperor.[137] Such interactions with statues, then, means that the emperor's images were places where memory was made that resonated into the future: all the examples discussed here show active reworking of both the material and its memory, as well as the potential for recasting (both literally and figuratively) the meaning and reading of such images as time moves forward. In other words, the act of looking into the past in different temporal contexts can alter the reception of an image or subject. All this reveals the vast potential for different methods of commemoration and how subjective the production of memory could become.

Accordingly, there are numerous avenues that could be taken to provide a comprehensive account of Roman memory and the treatment of an emperor's legacy. The remainder of this section will be devoted to the discussion of the contribution of historiography to an emperor's legacy, looking at the part of history in the production of memory.[138] The act of looking into the past through historiography makes it a compelling field of activity, where the legacy of an emperor was fought over. This contested space becomes a crucial topic for study in this book, not least due to the material used throughout. It takes further inspiration from the phenomenon of the universality of the emperor, as described in Section 6.1, with the peculiar effect it had on the construction and shaping of historical narrative, as hinted by Pelling: 'Given the power now exercised by one man who dominated the world, the line between imperial biography and history was always likely to be a thin one.'[139] Put

---

[135] Suet. *Dom.* 17.3.   [136] Procop. *Anecdota* 8.18.

[137] Kristensen (2013: 244–5), for an analysis of the interaction with spoliated statues in late antiquity; cf. Stewart (2003: 275).

[138] Cf. Sailor (2008: 9). See more recently Steffensen (2018), esp. 25–6.

[139] Pelling (1997: 418); cf. Marincola (1997: 30–1) for his analysis on historiography's reaction to one-man rule. Cf. Feeney (2007: 190–3) on the emperor's effect on historical time, *fasti*, and the writing of annalistic history.

another way, the principate fostered comparisons that moved past genre and specific context, making emperors look the same.

Returning to the excerpt from Pliny about his inspiration for writing a history of the German wars, there seems to be an impact to history which is meant to resonate in the context of its publication and subsequent reception. This idea of history being able to contribute to the discourse of how the emperor seemed gives the medium power in how an emperor was understood. History itself was a part of the reception of the emperor that placed him in a more passive role, as he was not necessarily able to control and shape his narrative or legacy fully, since that conversation continues decades or even centuries after his death. Such is the concern of engaging in memorialisation, and the emperor himself becomes a historian, so to speak, in his own attempt to add perspectives to the narrative of his reign through monumentality, whether written or iconographic.[140]

The inspiration for this argument comes from the first third of an early twenty-first-century book about early modern scholarship and its pitfalls titled *The Limits of History* by Constantin Fasolt. Fasolt writes about the successes and pitfalls of modern historical writing, particularly concerning the purpose of writing history and the generic expectations of this pursuit. He argues that history is going through an existential crisis brought about by what he describes as the strict adherence to the tenets of history: first, that 'the past is gone forever'; second, 'to understand the meaning of a text, you must first put it in the context of its time and place'; and third, 'you cannot tell where you are going unless you know where you are coming from'.[141] Accordingly, historians strive to look back at the past and provide an accurate account of that time and context in the past, which has the danger of being lost to oblivion, either by attempting to excise received bias from the historian's period or by expressing acknowledgement of that bias, in order to give the most accurate and unadulterated account of the truth.

In short, Fasolt problematises this premise by arguing that the writing of history was an inherently *political* act, which is to say that there is inherent bias in every pursuit of historical knowledge. In fact, he goes further by arguing that history in its very structure has political implications, insofar as it involves the act of looking into the past and

---

[140] For such a conceit, see Nicolet (1991: chap. 1), on the *Res Gestae Divi Augusti*.

[141] Fasolt (2004: ix); cf. Walter Benjamin's essay in fragments *On the concept of history*, in Benjamin (1999: 253–64).

interpreting it for its utility in the present and future.[142] The following quotation is a telling paradigm of his viewpoint:

> History only appears to be a form of knowledge about the past. In truth history serves to confirm a line between now and then that is not given in reality. The complementary relationship between history, politics, and nature ... goes deeper than mere agreement on dividing respective spheres of influence ... The prohibition on anachronism? It merely seems to be a principle of method by which historians secure the adequacy of their interpretation. In truth the prohibition on anachronism defines the purposes for which the discipline of history exists: to divide the reality of time into past and present. History enlists the desire for knowledge about the past to meet a deeper need: the need for power and independence, the need to have done with the past and to be rid of things that cannot be forgotten.[143]

Fasolt's iconoclastic approach to historical thought directs its blows towards the process and writing of modern historiography and its expectations. His point about the relation of history to politics, and its lack of innocence in reaching into the past in order to understand it, has resonance in how the Romans approached their own past. We find ourselves in a more familiar world of ancient historiography that was more openly political and more comfortable with the performance of curating the past for different purposes.[144]

An important point of departure is the notion that ancient historians were involved in politics and indeed their experience counted in favour of their authority as historians.[145] Thus, they had political lives; Dio and Tacitus both held consular rank as part of the senatorial elite, Suetonius was an *ab epistulis* in Hadrian's court, and Plutarch was involved in local politics in his native Chaeronea and Boeotia and maintained ties with philhellene Romans. Even Herodian, whose political career has been challenging to reconstruct from his work, writes a history about the emperor and politics, whatever he meant by his statement in 1.2.5: 'I had a personal share in some of these events during my imperial and public service' (ἔστι δ' ὧν καὶ πείρᾳ μετέσχον ἐν βασιλικαῖς ἢ δημοσίαις ὑπηρεσίαις γενόμενος).[146]

---

[142] Fasolt (2004: 3–45).   [143] Fasolt (2004: 13).

[144] Cf. Cic. *ad Fam.* 5.12 for the politics of historiography.

[145] Marincola (1997: 133–48), and esp. 143–4 for historians writing under the Roman empire; Sailor (2008: 7–8): 'In justifying his historiographical activity, a historian often used in his favor his own political experience, which established his right to speak knowledgeably about the events he was reporting. Writing history was then a lot like politics, in that the practitioners of each were, at least in theory, to be drawn from the same pool.'

[146] Hdn. 1.2.5, cf. Kemezis (2014: 307): 'While it is true that claiming to have political experience was a standard authority-building technique for ancient historians generally, Herodian's version of that claim is deliberately, even parodically, generic and unverifiable.'

Moreover, the self-professed goals of ancient historians feel much more profound than those of their modern counterparts. Ancient historiography argues for its utility in the present and future for subsequent audiences, seen again in Pliny's quotation in the epigraph of this section. Of course, there are different approaches and opinions in antiquity on what this constitutes,[147] but the aspect that is pertinent here is the goal of permanence: that history pretends to be something to withstand the ages – to be reinterpreted accordingly in the future.[148] In our period, this concern is also reflected in what Pliny tells Tacitus about the ravages of memory and time and his expectation that they would stand that test.[149] *Reverentia Posterorum* – the respect for posterity – is coupled with a hope for future recognition, helped by their own care for posterity. There is thus a personal and emotive context to their pursuits, with the hope that they themselves may be remembered also. This sentiment is well-articulated by Sailor:

> [A] history stands on a continuum with lyric poetry and encyclopaedias, with tombs and public architecture, with priestly duties and triumphal processions, with cultivated dress and comportment. The function of a history is to be a writer's public *monumentum* both present and posthumous, to attract good repute and weight to his name – in short, to be a 'big deal' and to make him a 'big deal' as well.[150]

As such, historiography and the emperorship occupy similar places in the landscape of time and memory; the emperor, too, engages in exemplarity and monumentality that are set to stand the test of time.

Thus, the claim to be effectively immortal through their actions, including their writing, is perhaps something to take seriously.[151] In this sense, there seems to be a competitiveness in the field of memory, which is all the more contentious with the existence of a supreme figure such as the emperor within that rubric. As I have argued throughout this book, there was a great importance placed on how the emperor seemed. Historiography contributed to the wider reception of an emperor, fashioning authoritative views for posterity. Historiography, then, was an arena in which the emperor's deeds and actions could be scrutinised in great detail.[152] Such antagonism suggests

---

[147] For a discussion on the call to history, see Marincola (1997: 34–62).

[148] Cf. the *locus classicus* for the care for posterity in historiography: Thuc. 1.22.4.

[149] Plin. *Ep.* 9.14.　　[150] Sailor (2008: 9).　　[151] Cf. Section 6.1 on timelessness.

[152] For an excellent discussion concerning the potential reception of history by the regime, see Sailor (2008: 252–9), on the ways that Tacitus' *Annals* could have been received. Cf. Syme (1958: 499): 'No emperor could approve of a work like the *Annales* of Cornelius Tacitus', from his arguments that it was filled with criticisms against Hadrian (492–503), which even if not fully convincing to a modern reader (see Sailor 2008: 256) nonetheless allows for the possibility that it could have been interpreted as criticism. Cf. Turpin (2008: 399).

a certain 'unsafeness' to the composition of history: perhaps it was dangerous in the sense that criticisms towards any emperor could be interpreted as slights to a contemporary one, but this is not to argue the existence of authorial intent to resist the emperor explicitly or to question the legitimacy of the principate systemically, nor the thought that Rome was a police state akin to an Orwellian dystopia, suggesting that everyone was in danger of fatal repercussion.[153] Instead, the idea should be framed differently, in the sense of the contestation of the historical legacy of the Roman emperor and the important role that historiography had in that conversation. In other words, there was always an inherent risk in thus criticising the emperor, but it was an important contributing part of the discourse of what the emperor was and what he should be. So, 'safe' is a euphemism that sterilises history and thus makes it seem inconsequential to the context in which it was written, and to what it could mean for subsequent audiences.

I will focus on selected passages to further illustrate the themes discussed so far, which includes one from Dio and two from Tacitus, from both the *Annals* and the *Histories*. To start with Dio, much of the later books of his *Roman History* survive in epitome and excerpt, truncated versions of the narratives of the contemporary Severan world that he himself witnessed. Despite the difficulties of the texts, there is much that one can glean from them, as shown by Gleason in her article on the identity crises exhibited in Dio's contemporary narrative, through images of impersonation and masquerade.[154] She shows the interesting work that can be done with the anecdotal material that abounds in those books, which have been essential in understanding the perception of the Roman emperor, as utilised in previous sections of this book.[155] One in particular includes a description of Dio's inspiration for writing his history, which comes at the point in the narrative at the end of Commodus' life and the beginning of the civil wars leading to Septimius Severus' principate:

> βιβλίον τι περὶ τῶν ὀνειράτων καὶ τῶν σημείων δι' ὧν ὁ Σεουῆρος τὴν αὐτοκράτορα ἀρχὴν ἤλπισε, γράψας ἐδημοσίευσα· καὶ αὐτῷ καὶ ἐκεῖνος πεμφθέντι παρ' ἐμοῦ ἐντυχὼν πολλά μοι καὶ καλὰ ἀντεπέστειλε. ταῦτ' οὖν ἐγὼ τὰ γράμματα πρὸς ἑσπέραν ἤδη λαβὼν κατέδαρθον, καί μοι καθεύδοντι προσέταξε τὸ δαιμόνιον ἱστορίαν γράφειν. καὶ οὕτω δὴ

---

[153] Cf. Giusti (2016) on how dark it might be.

[154] Gleason (2011). For recent work on Dio and the principate, see Davenport and Mallan (2021) and particularly Chris Mallan's chapter on Dio's contemporaries, which unfortunately has not been taken fully into account, as it was published near the completion of this manuscript.

[155] See pp. 94–98 and 156–158 for analyses of passages of Dio's contemporary books, in particular Dio 77(76).10, on Bulla Felix, and Dio 73(72)20.2–3, on Commodus in the arena.

ταῦτα περὶ ὧν νῦν καθίσταμαι ἔγραψα ... καὶ καλὰς ἐλπίδας περὶ τοῦ
μέλλοντος χρόνου διδοῦσάν μοι ὡς ὑπολειψομένου τὴν ἱστορίαν καὶ
οὐδαμῶς ἀμαυρώσοντος, ἐπίσκοπον τῆς τοῦ βίου διαγωγῆς, ὡς ἔοικεν,
εἴληχα, καὶ διὰ τοῦτο αὐτῇ ἀνάκειμαι.

I wrote and published a book concerning dreams and signs, which gave
Severus hope for imperial power; and he, after reading the copy I sent him,
wrote me a long and complimentary acknowledgement. I received these
letters around night-time, having already gone to sleep, and during my sleep
the divine sprit ordered me to write history. Thus it was that I came to write
these matters which I am at present concerned with ... She (sc. Fortune)
gives me fair hope about the future, which will permit my history to survive
and in no way become obscure; she, it seems, has fallen to my lot as guardian
of the course of my life, and therefore I have dedicated myself to her.[156]

There are several points that deserve comment here. The nature of the
times was such that it was substance of history, which is alluded to by the
mention of civil strife at the beginning. However, it is interesting that Dio's
first stated experience in erudition and publishing was for a book on
dreams and portents, which adds an interesting wrinkle to what could be
seen as acceptable themes for the writing of history.[157] That this was a field
of interest and erudition should not come as a surprise when compared to
contemporaries; Artemidorus and Aelius Aristides are notable examples of
those who thought and wrote about dreams and their interpretations.[158]
Within this context, both Dio's penchant for dream interpretation and the
fact that he received his inspiration via a dream would suggest a certain
seriousness placed on the power of dreams on the imagination and,
importantly for this context, their interpretative power in explaining
political events and phenomena in the world that concerns the Roman
emperor.[159]
Moreover, this material was important in the very relevant sense of
omina imperii, or the portents for the future power of a potential emperor,
and signs (including dreams) litter the narratives of historians of the
period, which include an interesting case of Dio mentioning Vespasian's
dream of receiving a tooth from Nero which directly reflects a dream
interpretation of Artemidorus of receiving teeth from a king, or when
Suetonius recounts a dream where scales appeared to Vespasian that had

---

[156] Dio 73(72).23.1–5, translation adapted from Cary's Loeb edition.
[157] Cf. pp. 134–139 on *mirabilia* in the understanding the past.
[158] On Artemidorus and dream interpretation in antiquity, see Price (1986: 3–37); on Aristides,
Artemidorus, and the medical context for dream interpretation, see Israelowich (2012: 71–86).
For more on dreams, see pp. 83–85.
[159] Cf. a more sceptical interpretation of this scene in Marincola (1997: 50–1).

Claudius and Nero on one side and Vespasian, Titus, and Domitian on the other in equal balance, reflective of the span of their respective dynasties. [160] The similarity of this evidence suggests a shared framework of understanding, which transcended genre and which, in this particular case, utilises dream interpretation to make sense of the transition from one emperor to the next. Indeed, Dio's supposed role in providing encouragement to Severus can show the political nature of this material and how it could elicit serious consequences. Therefore, Dio used his work as a historical agent to affect change for the future, which affects not only his own clout but that of Severus as well.

The evocation of *to daimonion* in his inspiration deserves comment, too, even though it would be impossible to discuss the intricate detail of the religiosity here. In my opinion, it exhibits the lofty claims of historiography as something that should be undertaken as a calling or obligation, with the end product being preserved for posterity and having divine sanction. Thus, there is a universality of history being there to stand the test of time and provide accounts of importance for the future. It is also interesting that Severus is mentioned as having read Dio's book approvingly, given its favourable prognostication for his future emperorship. In a Fasoltian sense, Dio seems entirely comfortable with the political implications and purposes of his work (both the dream interpretations and the greater history), given that it concerned the direction of the state and the person of the emperor. Indeed, this emperor-centric conception of historical writing is observed further in an earlier section of book 73, which comes in the context of Commodus' exploits as a gladiator in the arena and describes the necessity of including all the details for the memory of those in the future who may find importance in it. [161] Even with the apology for the nature of the account, it was deemed relevant for the presence of the emperor and the sensory experience of the exhibition. It is even further bolstered by Dio's treatment of Severus in later books, which exhibits him unfavourably in many ways and suggests the power of historical writing in the interpretation of an emperor's life and how open-ended that interpretation could be. [162] Essentially, Dio reveals part of the process of the construction of history and also how the passage of time could alter the interpretation of that history: at first, it would include *omina* that were favourable to the potential emperor and thus receive his personal

---

[160] Dio 65(66).1.3; Artem. 4.31; Suet. *Vesp.* 25; cf. p. 84.

[161] Dio 73(72).18.3–4. Cf. Gleason (2011: 45–6).

[162] For a discussion of his treatment by Dio, see Gleason (2011: 52–60).

approbation; but it could also include less savoury aspects of an emperor's conduct, allowing posterity to interpret and reinterpret his legacy outside of the power of the *princeps* to alter it. It shows that the promise and legacy of Severus' reign remained contested and open for scrutiny, which opens up the reigns of other emperors to similar criticism.

Tacitus also provides an illuminating case of the political nature of emperor history. There are many potential passages from his *oeuvre* that could come under scrutiny with this in mind, but two particularly compelling examples will be included here, *Histories* 1.1 and *Annals* 1.9–10, the latter of which involves the discussion of Augustus' legacy in the aftermath of his death. Sailor's lengthy treatment of the preface to the *Histories* is of particular note, as it attempts to dissect the problems raised by Tacitus in his short history of historiography and its apparent decline, whilst simultaneously elevating his subject as worthy of record. Tacitus shows the difficulty of writing history, his own lack of bias, and a *recusatio* for not extending his history beyond the end of Domitian's principate.[163] Accordingly, Tacitus highlights the importance of political history to posterity and the dangers of writing it under the power of an emperor:[164]

> Mihi Galba Otho Vitellius nec beneficio nec iniuria cogniti. dignitatem nostram a Vespasiano inchoatam, a Tito auctam, a Domitiano longius provectam non abnuerim: sed incorruptam fidem professis neque amore quisquam et sine odio dicendus est. quod si vita suppeditet, principatum divi Nervae et imperium Traiani, uberiorem securioremque materiam, senectuti seposui, rara temporum felicitate ubi sentire quae velis et quae sentias dicere licet.

> Galba, Otho and Vitellius were not known to me, either through favour or injury. I shall not deny that my political esteem was fostered by Vespasian, was increased by Titus, and for a long time was advanced by Domitian. Yet for those who avow incorruptible trustworthiness, any person must be spoken of without either overt affection or hatred. If my life would last, I have assigned the principate of the divine Nerva and reign of Trajan more copious and safe material, in the rare good fortune of our times where it is allowed to feel what you wish and say what you feel.[165]

Thus, Tacitus attempts to accentuate his closeness to the conduct of politics in the age, whilst also absolving himself of any implication of unfair bias, either negative or positive, towards any emperor in particular.[166] Any negative connotations that it could evoke are

---

[163] Sailor (2008: 121–60).   [164] Tac. *Hist.* 1.1.   [165] Tac. *Hist.* 1.1.3–4.
[166] Sailor (2008: 152); Marincola (1997: 144).

downplayed, as Pelling argues: 'his political experience and the insight he will have gained … builds his authority with his readers even as it may arouse their suspicions.'[167] As such, despite the difficulties, Tacitus' subject is one of great importance: *cura posteritatis*; posterity was a stated goal, and so he deals with this material for later generations. To evoke Pelling yet again, Tacitus' use of his personal voice in this preface, and his involvement of the reader (*facile averseris*), invites his audience to be critical in their reading of his history, as they had been wont to do, regardless of assurances of fairness and non-bias.[168] This puts into relief his final line of the passage, on the felicity of his own times, opening it up also to scrutiny on whether or not they can (actually) say what they feel.

The point made about Tacitus' historiography can be pressed further. Tacitus elevates the importance and impact of his histories in competition with the emperor since he is asserting his independence in thought and historical enquiry. With his apparent deferential refusal to engage first in a history of the civil war and the Flavian dynasty and then in a history of Nerva and Trajan due to *temporum felicitate*, Tacitus means to assert his impartiality to the felicitous age in which he writes.[169] This refusal allows for what is not included, namely the accounts of those reigns, to be placed under similar scrutiny to those of previous emperors and in particular allows for the silence about Augustus' reign to reflect his silence on Nerva and Trajan and perhaps even on how this would reflect on Hadrian later. Accordingly, Tacitus creates a power struggle over the production of historical memory for future generations. As Sailor puts it, Tacitus' preface 'makes a strong declaration of authorial control and of authenticity: *Histories* is not really Trajan's version of the past rendered in Tacitus' words, but, rather, emphatically the creation and property of the historian himself.'[170] Historiography of the emperorship was a contested space, over which an emperor did not have full control, despite his enormous power and resources to fashion narratives in word, iconography, and monument.

Such a view is reflected in Tacitus' treatment of Augustus' death. As Tacitus describes it, in the immediate context of Augustus' funeral there was much talk about his principate and legacy: *multus hinc ipso de Augusto sermo*.[171] The talk included trivialities and both positive and negative remembrances: from the coincidence of dying in the same room in Nola as his father Octavius, the number of offices he had held, his conduct during the civil wars, the security and peace in the empire, and the

---

[167] Pelling (2009: 149).   [168] Pelling (2009: 150), on Tac. *Hist.* 1.1.2.   [169] Sailor (2008: 157).
[170] Sailor (2008: 160). Cf. Turpin (2008: 399).   [171] Tac. *Ann.* 1.9.1.

adornment of Rome itself to the bribery, proscriptions and betrayals, periods of war and conflict, his desire for divine honours, and the vicissitudes of his family.[172] Indeed, the final point about Tiberius is telling of the subjectivity of opinion:

> ne Tiberium quidem caritate aut rei publicae cura successorem adscitum, sed, quoniam adrogantiam saevitiamque eius introspexerit, comparatione deterrima sibi gloriam quaesivisse.

> Not even was Tiberius adopted as a successor out of affection or a care for the *res publica*, but, since he recognised the arrogance and cruelty of Tiberius, Augustus sought glory for himself through comparison to the worst.[173]

Thus, Tacitus gives agency to those present in the aftermath of Augustus' death to give their own variant perspectives on the memorable deeds of the deceased emperor, and thus allows his readers to decide for themselves in their own contexts what the Augustan past means. Furthermore, Tacitus gives Augustus an imagined perspective also, with his hope that he would seem better than his successor. Whether or not this was true is immaterial, as it serves to add further patterns in the formation of Augustus' memory. Tacitus is playing with time here, giving the impression of numerous voices adding to the tradition of Augustus' legacy, through the present time of Tacitus' context of criticising Rome's first emperor, providing this tradition and his treatment of it for posterity's sake. Accordingly, the formation and reception of an emperor's memory and legacy are not a static, monolithic phenomenon but constantly changing according to context and interpretation.

However, we return to the question of precariousness, discussed at the start of this section with Pliny, which involves the *active* concern of Romans to preserve memory. One of my contentions in this section is that the Roman emperor only constitutes *a* voice in the preservation of memory, even though it was a loud and resonant one. In an Ozymandian sense, the Roman emperor can also engage in authorship, which involved writing and setting up monuments to stand the test and ravages of time and oblivion.[174] Indeed, a manifestation of Augustus' famous *auctoritas* can be seen in Suetonius' description of the *Forum Augustum*:

> Proximum a dis immortalibus honorem memoriae ducum praestitit, qui imperium p. R. ex minimo maximum reddidissent. Itaque et opera cuiusque

---

[172] Tac. *Ann.* 1.9–10.

[173] Tac. *Ann.* 1.10.7. Cf. Tac. *Hist.* 2.47.2, for Otho's concern on how future generations would remember him.

[174] Cf. de Angelis (2021: 19–20) on the *Forum Augustum* and its reception in antiquity.

manentibus titulis restituit et statuas omnium triumphali effigie in utraque fori sui porticu dedicavit, professus et edicto: commentum id se, ut ad illorum vitam velut ad exemplar et ipse, dum viveret, et insequentium aetatium principes exigerentur a civibus.

Next to the immortal Gods he honoured the memory of the leaders who had raised the power of the Roman people from obscurity to greatness. Accordingly, he restored the works of each man with their original inscriptions, and in the two colonnades of his forum dedicated statues of all of them in triumphal garb, also declaring by edict: 'I have contrived this to lead the citizens to require me, while I live, and the *principes* of later times as well, to attain the standard set by those worthies of old.'[175]

Enclosing the Temple of Mars Ultor, the *Forum Augustum* (*RGDA* 21) had a particular interpretation of Roman history that culminated in Augustus himself: statues of *summi uiri* and members of the *gens Iulia*, with the centre being a statue of Augustus in a triumphal chariot in front of the temple itself. Much can be, and should be, said about this space, but there is the sense of both the biographical and the historical here, curated by Augustus and underlined as being exemplary for the future. Indeed, the Forum was intended to be and used as a place of civic life, which Dio outlines carefully to include the *deductio in forum* for youths coming of age, the starting point of *profectiones* for military commanders, the place of senatorial votes for the granting of triumphs, the dedications of the sceptre and wreaths to Mars Ultor after the celebration of the triumph, and even the driving of nails into the columns of the Temple of Mars Ultor at the conclusion of their terms.[176] Accordingly, the *Forum Augustum* was a vibrant political and civic arena, where the historical motifs displayed through the statuary interacted with the contemporary activity of military commanders and boys entering manhood, thus serving didactic purposes, inspiring the political and military leaders of the present and future to live up to Rome's illustrious past. As noted by de Angelis, the role of the forum 'points to the generative dimension inherent within the prescriptions of the *lex templi*: the decoration of the forum was not conceived as frozen and immutable; quite to the contrary, it was explicitly open to the future and intended to organically grow over time.'[177] Such was the dynamic that was fostered, which resembles the

---

[175] Suet. Aug. adapted from the Loeb translation.
[176] Dio 55.10.2–5. Cf. Severy (2003: 175–6) and de Angelis (2021: 25) for analysis. Cf. *LTUR* II, 289–95. For such political reading with Ov. *Fast.* 5.551–8, see Pasco-Pranger (2006: 49–50).
[177] de Angelis (2021: 25).

conversational and interactive nature of historiography that reaches through time.

However, the issue with the conversational nature of such spaces means that messages could be taken up or disregarded. To take an illustrative example of this dynamic conversation, let us focus on the status of the triumph from Augustus onwards. In a recent article on the 'end of the triumph' under Augustus, Flower has argued compellingly for an 'Augustan' interpretation of the conferral of triumphal honours, moving towards a system of refusal and the conferral of the *ornamenta triumphalia* instead.[178] In short, Flower argues that Augustus did not necessarily intend for the triumph to be the *sole* preserve of the imperial family, as it would become in the future, but rather that the Forum itself was the culmination of the triumph in Roman history with Augustus at the pinnacle.[179] Such arguments suggest a wider story behind the development of the triumph during the Augustan era and bring into relief how restrictive we should be in interpreting the statues of the triumphal generals in the Forum and the messages in their depiction.[180] Accordingly, the inscription included in Suetonius would change its meaning depending on context, and the knowledge that future *principes* would in fact triumph in the future, despite the *auctoritas* of Augustus. This is all to say that Augustus only remained one authorial voice, open to interpretation, and that his legacy could be refashioned and reinterpreted as we move through history.

In the end, historical discourse contributed to and could shape an emperor's legacy, adding to a larger discourse of who the emperor was and who he should be that had numerous participants across time. The act of reaching into the past and reshaping it in different contexts evinces the dynamic and precarious nature of memory games. It was a constant process of negotiation that projected examples from the past in order to discuss and map the anxieties of the present. Owing to this process, the shape and understanding of an emperor's legacy are also dynamic, prone to revisions and alterations. He is a constant topic of conversation that must be remembered both positively and negatively for posterity's sake. Connected to this consideration is how historiography depicts conversation amongst people, particularly in attempts to come to terms with the fluctuating fortunes of emperors.

---

[178] Flower (2020: 13); Lange (2019).   [179] Flower (2020: 13).
[180] Compare with the iconography celebrating Tiberius' triumph on the Boscoreale Cups (*BR* II), with Kuttner (1995: 143, 148).

6.3.2   The Fickleness of Fortune

In a summary of the historiographical tradition about the Roman *plebs*, Yavetz used a small section of Tacitus' *Annals* to sum up his view that the stock characterisation of the people was overtly negative: 'Hence the rulers could not rely on the people's affections, these being fleeting and unblest: *brevis et infaustos populi Romani amores.*'[181] What Yavetz wanted to stress was the opposite: that the love of the Roman people was not fleeting and that they in fact remembered their allegiances.[182] However, there is an alternative reading to Tacitus' text. In the context of the chapter, Tacitus was discussing the scene of Germanicus' triumph and had just informed the reader of the people's public devotion towards Marcellus and Drusus. This had been disadvantageous to their longevity, suggesting that their popularity was their demise: 'but there lurked underneath a hidden fear that popular devotion was in no way advantageous to Drusus, his father, and that his uncle Marcellus was taken away in youth from the burning attention of the plebs.'[183] Therefore, the statement about the brief and unfortunate devotions of the Roman people has another meaning; they were short and unfortunate because of the short lives of their favourites, rather than them being fickle. The innate fear for the future of their favourites bubbles to the surface here, and perhaps hope that misfortune would not come to pass, revealing a potential manner of thinking about the success or demise of an emperor as perceived by his subjects: present anxieties and concerns that take examples from the past to reflect on what might happen in the future.

Germanicus, like many figures in Tacitus' *Annals*, is enigmatic. His significance does not adhere to a strict chronology, as he is simultaneously a relic of the past and a symbol of the future – a histrionic and unstable character whose impulsive behaviour creates further problems.[184] As such, his characterisation seems anachronistic: Germanicus cut an attractive figure but was not of his time, unsuited to the brutal world of the principate. This status made him an interesting model to think about, allowing

---

[181] Yavetz (1969: 4–5): Yavetz was quoting Tac. *Ann.* 2.41.3. The use of the religious word *infaustus* is striking, for it points to the potential role of bad luck and fortune in the demise of these favourites. It is even more striking in the fact that this term and synonyms such as *felix* and *fortunatus* are found with the positive antonym *faustus* when describing the future of the emperors. It seems that it is with this language that the hope of the future was described. Cf. Noreña (2011: 136–8).

[182] Yavetz (1965: 101).

[183] Tac. *Ann.* 2.41.3: *sed suberat occulta formido reputantibus haud prosperum in Druso patre eius favorem vulgi, avunculum eiusdem Marcellum flagrantibus plebis studiis intra iuventam ereptum.*

[184] Pelling (1993: 77–8); O'Gorman (2000: 46). Cf. Ross (1973: 215–20) for the histrionic and unheroic reading of Germanicus.

his example to be transposed to other times, particularly about what *might
have been*, since his life was cut short. This anachronistic quality, which
O'Gorman describes as a 'continual movement between retrospection
and ... anticipation', is present in the quoted passage of Tacitus and
seems to be a feature of Tacitus' historiography.[185] The scene of
Germanicus and his children is focalised through the onlookers, who
now see not only the present triumphal parade but the past and future
appearing simultaneously *in situ*.[186] The first line *augebat visus*, which has
been translated as 'sight ... intensified', suggests a keen and broadened
interpretation that points to a revelation, namely of the hope for the future
embodied in Germanicus and his family. However, the antithesis comes
immediately after, with an *occulta formido* – a hidden dread existing within
the mind of the spectator: that his past kin, his father Drusus, and his uncle
Marcellus, had not been so fortunate and had met early demises. The fear is
accentuated by a common denominator: *favorem vulgi* and *flagrantibus
plebis studiis* – popular favour, popular zeal, or perhaps even just popularity. With that being the case, different scenarios are acted out: one where
the hopes of the spectators are realised and Germanicus and his kin will
take the reins of empire and another where the *brevis et infaustos amores* of
the people meant the doom and demise of the family.

Tacitus' point may reflect the range of potential perceptions and emo-
tions from a wider perspective, which could be informed by popular
morality.[187] The striking allusion here concerns fortune, brought in by
calling the loves of the Roman people 'unfortunate' (*infausti*). *Fortuna* is
a slippery concept, and there are different, seemingly contradictory ways to
approach this idea in antiquity.[188] Scholarship has largely created two
broad concepts of Fortune: one that emphasises the good aspect, that
there was a 'force of a benevolent goddess' that brought good luck, and
another that was unpredictable, fickle, and often brought bad luck, connected to the Greek concept of *tyche*.[189] From this understanding of
fortune, it is an unknowable force that affected good and bad alike, with
no consideration of merit. The allusion to this world of understanding is
what Tacitus has focalised through the people in *Annals* 2.41.3: the people
fear their love was unlucky and that it will lead to an unpropitious future.
This opens a potential window into a popular mentality, informing

---

[185] O'Gorman (2000): 55.   [186] O'Gorman (2000): 55.   [187] Morgan (2007).
[188] Morgan (2007: 33, 77, 111–13, 134–5, 161–2, 165, 242–3).
[189] Noreña (2011: 136); Kajanto (1981: 525–7). Cf. Section 6.3.1 on Dio's inspiration from *Tyche*. Cf.
Isid. *Etym.* 8.11.94.

perceptions of the future of an imperial favourite, which in turn could also inform how they perceive the emperor.

This uncertainty is exploited in Tacitus' narrative to accentuate the antagonism within the imperial family, including the exploration of problematic relationships between a sitting emperor and another imperial family member or between two potential heirs to the emperorship. This is an important theme that runs throughout the *Annals*, which elevates the fear of chaos from the perspective of the people.[190] The people are also cast in the role of an antagonist – exhibited as vociferously taking the side of one over the other, something which would seem to have consequences for the development of the narrative. The antagonism between Tiberius and Germanicus is outlined early, where Tiberius is shown to have quickly seized power after Augustus' death, with the fear that Germanicus, his son by adoption, would take the initiative and become emperor himself.[191] One of the reasons that Tacitus provides for Germanicus' ability to assume the role of emperor is his favour with the people. It also becomes a primary reason for there to be animosity between them, for we have the juxtaposition between a popular potential emperor within whom the hopes of the wider population lie and a dissimulating emperor who preferred to remain distant and aloof.[192] Therefore, Tacitus uses the people to signify that all is not well in the *domus Augusta*, through the note that the memory of Drusus, Germanicus' father, was great amongst the Roman people and that favour and hope (*spes*) rested in Germanicus.[193]

The disquiet signified by the people returns when Germanicus appears in front of them at his triumphal procession in *Annals* 2.41 quoted at the start of this section. There is a fear that Germanicus would meet an early end and that the potential for him to become emperor would diminish. The fear would come true and their despair justified at his death. Even upon his demise, the antagonism is accentuated by the cries of the people, who organised themselves into the tribes of the Roman people at his funeral.[194] The atmosphere in the city is one of deep mourning, which culminates in the people shouting that the state had fallen and that there was no hope left. This is the manifestation of the fear that was hidden in the triumphal scene of *Annals* 2.41.3: that a favourite had now met an early and unpropitious end. However, *augebat visus* is implied again; the object of

---

[190] See, e.g., Tac. *Ann.* 3.31.1.   [191] Tac. *Ann.* 1.3.5, 1.7.5–6.   [192] Tac. *Ann.* 1.76.4, 1.54.2.
[193] Tac. *Ann.* 1.33.1–2.
[194] Tac. *Ann.* 3.4; the fact that the people are presented in their tribes is fascinating: it was a state affair, so they came organised in their official capacity, which is mirrored in the senatorial inscriptions from the era. Cf. *Tabula Siarensis* b. II 155 cf. Lott (2012: 94–5).

laudation has now shifted from Germanicus to Agrippina. Similar to the triumphal procession, Agrippina is now the timeless figure: someone that represents the glorious past of her ancestry and the hope for the future – that she and her progeny (and for that matter Germanicus') may outlive their opponents.[195] Such were the dynamics of imperial politics that rested on the hope for the future and the precarity of life. The words used here, *decus patriae*, the honour of her country, *solum Augusti sanguinem*, the only one with Augustan blood, and *unicum antiquitatis specimen*, the sole example of ancient (morally better) times, all highlight an interest in the past, one that was made present by the existence of Agrippina and projected into the future through the prayer for her and her children. As such, this branch of the *domus Augusta* is representing different aspects of time simultaneously.[196] The rift between Tiberius and Germanicus widens even in death, and the people of Rome are thus presented as one-sided, in favour of Germanicus and his kin, to the detriment of Tiberius.[197] The Roman people are used as a lens through which dynastic history is presented: the devotion of past exploits of imperial favourites, experiences of the present, and the hope for future success.[198]

Tacitus' historiography is complex and qualified; his opinions and thoughts on the republic and empire are brought out by the comparison between Tiberius and Germanicus, and it is but one comparison and theme that runs throughout the *Annals*.[199] As Pelling has argued, Germanicus is not a simple foil for Tiberius but rather an alternative future and someone who would have been *princeps* if things had gone another way.[200] Yet this does not mean that the assessment of Germanicus is overtly favourable, for he is seen 'rather as he [Tacitus] regards the past, particularly the republican past: nostalgically attractive, brilliant, the sort of thing it is good to write about; but out of keeping with the real needs of the modern world.'[201] Accordingly, Tacitus adds layers to his counterfactual suggestions, exploring both positive and negative connotations of

---

[195] Cf. Flower (2010: 138–43) on her afterlife.

[196] Cf. pp. 104–114. This may point to the different conceptions of the imperial family and, in this case, one that stresses blood relations, rather than looser concepts of kinship; Smith (2006: 33).

[197] Cf. Tac. *Ann.* 2.84. This passage is quite arresting, as it juxtaposes the reported joy of Tiberius to have twins entering his house, including the allusion to fortune in his words, and the people's pain that Drusus' gain would be Germanicus' demise. It's a zero-sum game, and the people come out on one side or the other.

[198] The reality, though, of Tiberius' and Germanicus' reception is more complex; see Ross (1973) and Champlin (2008), with Section 4.3.

[199] Pelling (1993: 59–85), esp. 78.   [200] Pelling (1993: 68). Cf. Ross (1973: 214).

[201] Pelling (1993: 77–8). Cf. Tac. *Ann.* 4.32–3.

timelines that were never to be – timelines which were not necessarily more positive or preferable.[202]

These themes continue in the later books of the *Annals*. Similar scenes are constructed: exposure of the young men of the imperial family in public, in the context of which the people are shown to be taking sides, with an interest in the past, present, and future of the *domus* Augusta.[203] It is within this sort of scene, in the context of Claudius' Secular Games, that Britannicus and L. Domitius Ahenobarbus are shown in the 'Trojan' game.[204] Within the bustle of this scene, Tacitus brings the reader to concentrate on the juxtaposition between Britannicus and the future Nero: Tacitus has told not only that the future of the empire lies in Nero but also that the *favor plebis* was on his side, and from this early date.[205] This is compounded further in the next chapter: truthfully, the bias of the people persisted from the memory of Germanicus, whose last remaining male offspring he was.[206] The reader is reminded of Germanicus and his popularity in the past, which is now being transferred to his last remaining scion, Nero. Again, this is visually accentuated with their appearance at more circus entertainments, in the context of Nero's assumption of the *toga virilis*, where the appearance of Nero in triumphal garb and Britannicus in the *toga praetexta* posited alternative fortunes for both in the minds of the people.[207] From the opposite appearance of Britannicus and Nero, the people are shown to be making assumptions about the future, to the presumed detriment of Britannicus. In other words, a potential rift is accentuated by the projected thoughts of the spectating public; they are cast in the middle of dynastic politics.[208]

Tacitus layers the past, present, and future in his history, making his readers reflect on the pasts and backgrounds of his characters, their appearance in narrative, and their fates to come, both in his work and in history more generally. Tacitus also uses the perspective of the people, the collective of the *populus Romanus* at Rome, in different ways to accentuate both the rifts in the imperial family and indeed how uncertain the future was for

---

[202] Cf. O'Gorman (2006) for Tacitus' interest in the counterfactual in his work. Cf. Ross (1973: 210–11) for a more nuanced appreciation of Tacitus' Germanicus.

[203] Cf. pp. 104–120.

[204] Cf. Weinstock (1971: 191–7). Cf. Zanker (1988: 167). On the *Ludi Saeculares* more generally, see the *OCD* 'Saecular Games' entry by Dunning: https://doi.org/10.1093/acrefore/9780199381135.013.5781.

[205] Tac. *Ann.* 11.11.2.

[206] Tac. *Ann.* 11.12.1: *verum inclinatio populi supererat ex memoria Germanici, cuius illa reliqua suboles virilis.*

[207] Tac. *Ann.* 12.41.1.   [208] Cf. Rogers (1955).

emperors and their kin: vicissitudes of fear and fortune move on as time continues, transferring to new situations and new characters. Tacitus gives the impression that this uncertainty was in full view of the emperor's subjects, toying with the future stability and prosperity of the empire. Yet, however fruitful the scrutiny of one source may be, does this translate to perceptions of the future and the fear of the untimely demise of imperial favourites? How are imperial futures imagined and described, and how are emperors' legitimacies contested?

6.4   Imperial Futures: Impersonations, Resurrections, and the Afterlife of an Emperor

During the principate of Commodus, one Maternus, who was an ex-soldier turned bandit, ravaged Gaul and Italy with his band of criminals, attacking cities, freeing prisoners from their cells, and burning settlements.[209] The story as told by Herodian continues to reveal Maternus' grander designs, which were to overrun Italy also and challenge the emperor's legitimacy. His plan was to attack Rome, which would take place in the spring festival of the *Hilaria* dedicated to the goddess Cybele, in which disguises and masquerades were a prominent part of the festivities.[210] Maternus hoped that with his disguise as a praetorian he could infiltrate the guards in the procession and thus cut down Commodus at the opportune moment.[211] However, he was betrayed and ultimately executed:

> ἀλλὰ προδοσίας γενομένης διά τινων τῶν σὺν αὐτῷ προκατελθόντων εἰς τὴν πόλιν καὶ τὴν ἐπιβουλὴν κατειπόντων (φθόνος γὰρ αὐτοὺς ἐς τοῦτο παρώξυνεν, εἰ δὴ ἔμελλον ἀντὶ λῃστοῦ δεσπότην ἕξειν καὶ βασιλέα), πρὶν ἐλθεῖν τὴν ἑορτὴν αὐτός τε ὁ Μάτερνος συλληφθεὶς τὴν κεφαλὴν ἀπετμήθη, καὶ οἱ συνωμόται ἀξίας ὑπέσχον δίκας. ὁ δὲ Κόμοδος θύσας τε τῇ θεῷ καὶ χαριστήρια ὁμολογήσας τὴν ἑορτὴν ἐπετέλει, παρέπεμπέ τε τὴν θεὸν χαίρων. καὶ σωτήρια τοῦ βασιλέως ὁ δῆμος μετὰ τῆς ἑορτῆς ἐπανηγύριζεν.

> But Maternus was betrayed by some of his men, who went ahead to Rome and revealed the plot. (It was jealousy that drove them to it – the prospect of having an emperor in place of a robber chief.) Before the day of the festival, Maternus was arrested and beheaded, while his fellow-conspirators received the punishments they deserved. Commodus sacrificed to the goddess and conceded a public thanksgiving before completing the festival and joining in

---

[209] Hdn. 1.10.1–3. On Maternus, problems of authenticity and fiction, and connections to themes of banditry, see Grünewald (2004: 120–36).

[210] Hdn. 1.10.5.   [211] Hdn. 1.10.6.

the rejoicing and procession of the goddess. During the festival, the people had a public celebration for the safety of the emperor.[212]

As with other stories of bandits, which were discussed in Chapter 2, Maternus could be interpreted as a foil to Commodus, appearing to challenge the legitimacy of his rule. Moreover, the context of the *Hilaria*, which incorporates elements of a festival of reversal, accentuates a link between a bandit and an emperor as opposite sides of the same coin, in which bandits could become emperors and vice versa.[213] We find ourselves in the familiar world of role reversals and humour: spaces that are in-between various categories, including humour and seriousness, justice and lawlessness, performance and real life, and the heroic and the monstrous. All such ambiguities are common ingredients in descriptions about the emperor's role in society that have been outlined throughout this book thus far, including the Saturnalian role reversal discussed in this chapter.[214]

This story also brings up the question of being an impostor vying for power. In this scene, Maternus has designs on becoming emperor himself and uses a disguise in order to achieve this goal. However, in this confrontation, he fails; as Herodian describes, his true identity is revealed. This is accentuated by the actions of Commodus and the people in consequence to Maternus' attempts, with sacrifices to the gods and thanksgiving for the safety of the emperor. Such public celebrations thus bring us back to the world of apotropaic ritual, conceptually linked to *devotiones*. Nonetheless, it is also an episode where Commodus' principate is challenged, leading to an evaluation of his principate before its reaffirmation.

Within this rubric of imposters and impersonators is the evidence of the appearance of false emperors or members of the imperial family, which litter the histories and biographies of emperors.[215] Like the story of Maternus, these appearances share similar characteristics: such stories involve an individual who invariably is of lower status who is found to either resemble or be impersonating a deceased emperor or member of the

---

[212] Hdn. 1.10.7, translation from the Loeb edition.

[213] For analysis of this episode, see Shaw (1984: 45–6). For masquerades and humour, see Webb (2008: 118–20).

[214] See Section 6.2.1.

[215] Impersonators: Agrippa Postumus (Tac. *Ann.* 39–40, Dio 57.16.3–4); Drusus, son of Germanicus (Tac. *Ann.* 5.10); Nero (Tac. *Hist.* 1.2.1, 2.8–9. Suet. Ner. 57; Dio 63(64).9.3, 66.19.3b). Cf. Potter (1994: 109). On false Neros, see Bowersock (1987: 308–11). For discussion on Nero's appearance in Talmudic legend, see Bastomsky (1969) and, in general, Pappano (1937: 385–92), with Malik (2019: 16–78) on Nero in the biblical tradition. Cf. Gleason (2011) on impersonation in general. Cf. the joke of Macrobius (Macrob. *Sat.* 2.4.20), where a young man who looks like Augustus gets an audience with the emperor. Cf. Grünewald (2004: 137–54) on this topic.

imperial family in a region at a suitable distance from the sitting emperor. As time wears on, rumour spreads of the resurrection of this formerly deceased individual, who escapes notice and evades authority until his luck runs out, when he invariably is executed.

The story of Clemens fits the pattern of these stories, in this version about a slave of Agrippa Postumus who had impersonated his deceased master before being caught.[216] In Tacitus' version, Clemens, who is presented as cunning and crafty, goes to the isle of Planasia where Agrippa was being held.[217] After finding that he had been killed, he vanishes to improve his resemblance to his master.[218] Thereafter, rumour spread, allowing for the cultivation of the story that Agrippa was in fact not dead but alive.[219] Accordingly, the story allows Tacitus to put Tiberius' legitimacy into relief, exposing a familiar theme in the Tiberian hexad of the brooding, sinister, and untrusting emperor.[220] Furthermore, Tacitus also accentuates the popularity of the imposter Agrippa, stating that a rumour had spread out across Italy that Agrippa had survived by gift of the gods, resulting in crowds gathering in Ostia, and also in Rome itself, secretly rejoicing at the news.[221] Such an anecdote affects the perception and legacy of Tiberius and Agrippa in multiple dimensions. In the context of the past, the impression Tacitus gives is that not only is the legacy of Agrippa Postumus (as a potential emperor) being cultivated but so too is the acceptance of Tiberius' principate, suggesting that Tiberius could lose it.[222] In the context of constructing history, Tacitus is adding to the edifice of Tiberius' legacy, which Champlin has shown was rich and variegated.[223] It culminates in the encounter between the imposter and Tiberius himself, where the emperor asks how the slave had become Agrippa, to which the slave replied 'the same way you became Caesar'.[224] The bold joke is similar to those discussed in Section 5.1, in that a person of lower status has the audacity to speak openly in front of an emperor. In that context, as in this one, the joke is used as a method of criticism, in this case to suggest that Tiberius himself was an impostor too. Such anecdotes were ways of criticising an emperor and appear as challenges to an emperor's legitimacy, particularly in a developing discourse that might preserve several versions

---

[216] Tac. *Ann.* 2.39–40; Dio. 57.16.3–4.   [217] Tac. *Ann.* 2.39.1.   [218] Tac. *Ann.* 2.39.2.
[219] Tac. *Ann.* 2.39.3–40.1.   [220] Tac. *Ann.* 2.40.1–3.   [221] Tac. *Ann.* 2.40.1.
[222] Cf. discussion of similar issues in Section 6.3.2 with Tacitus' treatment of Germanicus and Tiberius.
[223] Champlin (2008). For more on the images of Tiberius and his tradition, see pp. 26–27.
[224] Tac. *Ann.* 2.40.3.

of an anecdote, which reflects not only a rich contemporary conversation but also a rich conversation that deals in exemplarity for posterity.[225]

Indeed, this joke is an element that is shared by both Tacitus' and Dio's versions, to similar effect:

> κἀν τῷ αὐτῷ ἔτει Κλήμης τις, δοῦλός τε τοῦ Ἀγρίππου γεγονὼς καί πῃ καὶ προσεοικὼς αὐτῷ, ἐπλάσατο αὐτὸς ἐκεῖνος εἶναι, καὶ ἐς τὴν Γαλατίαν ἐλθὼν πολλοὺς μὲν ἐνταῦθα πολλοὺς δὲ καὶ ἐν τῇ Ἰταλίᾳ ὕστερον προσεποιήσατο, καὶ τέλος καὶ ἐπὶ τὴν Ῥώμην ὥρμησεν ὡς καὶ τὴν παππῴαν μοναρχίαν ἀποληψόμενος. ταραττομένων τε οὖν ἐπὶ τούτῳ τῶν ἐν τῷ ἄστει, καὶ συχνῶν αὐτῷ προστιθεμένων, ὁ Τιβέριος σοφίᾳ αὐτὸν διά τινων ὡς καὶ τὰ ἐκείνου φρονούντων ἐχειρώσατο, καὶ μετὰ τοῦτο βασανίσας ἵνα τι περὶ τῶν συνεγνωκότων αὐτῷ μάθῃ, ἔπειτ᾽ ἐπειδὴ μηδὲν ἐξελάλησεν, ἐπύθετο αὐτοῦ ʻπῶς Ἀγρίππας ἐγένου;ʼ καὶ ὃς ἀπεκρίνατο ὅτι ʻοὕτως ὡς καὶ σὺ Καῖσαρ.ʼ

> And in the same year, a certain Clemens, who had been a slave of Agrippa and resembled him to a certain extent, pretended to be Agrippa himself. He went to Gaul and won many to his cause there and many later in Italy, and finally he marched upon Rome with the avowed intention of recovering the sole rule of his grandfather. The population in the city became excited at this, and quite a few joined his cause; but Tiberius got him into his hands through his wisdom with the aid of some persons who pretended to sympathise with the upstart. He thereupon tortured him, in order to learn something about his fellow-conspirators. When he did not give up any information, he asked him: ʻHow did you become Agrippa?ʼ And he replied: ʻIn the same way you became Caesar.ʼ[226]

Both versions of the story contain very similar elements, which suggests a similar source. The difference lies of course in the characterisation of Tiberius, as in Tacitus' account the impression of that emperor is more negative.[227] However, this distinctiveness bolsters the arguments made in Section 1.1.3 about the nature of anecdotes and their usefulness for historians.[228] Here, we see the same story in different iterations, which ultimately give differing perspectives on Tiberius' conduct and which would ultimately affect the development of his legacy, which by the time of Dio was in its second century. Again, the richness of difference in the tradition is a feature of the emperor, whose legacy could change in his

---

[225] Cf. Joseph. *AJ.* 17.331–336, who uses his smarts to outwit a false Alexander, which shows how such impersonators could reflect on the abilities of an emperor.

[226] Dio. 57.16.3–4, translation Loeb edition, modified.

[227] Furthermore, the joke included at the end bears resemblance to the encounter of Papinian and Bulla Felix at Dio 77(76).10.7, cited on p. 97.

[228] See pp. 24–27.

afterlife. For instance, Clemens' characterisation is less cunning and Tiberius is the one who gets the credit for his 'wisdom', whereas in Tacitus' version, it is Sallustius Crispus who was responsible for the arrest of Clemens.[229] Whichever was true, it suggests differing traditions on Tiberius' character. In comparison to the general themes of this book, this adds to the strong impression of a continual imperial discourse, in which an emperor's deeds and actions are scrutinised and, in this case, his legacy is discussed and reformed.

An enigmatic collection and source for such impressions of the Roman emperor comes in the form of the *Sibylline Oracles*, the prophetic hexameter poems with a deep and varied tradition that straddles several worlds and traditions.[230] They are a variegated collection of eschatological futures and historical events that transcend different epistemic boundaries, imbued with Jewish, Christian, Greek, and Roman ways of describing the world.[231] This collection of Homeric hexameter verses comprises sixteen books of various compositional dates, with some, including the Fifth Sibyl that is included in this discussion, a composite poem with various interpolated verses.[232] The oracles generally engage with myth and history from different contexts, whilst keeping an eye on the narrative future of its prophecies, which of course are invariably in the past for the reader. As such, events always will have happened in the eye of the Sibyl, thus performing her ultimate poetic, religious, and mantic authority writ large.[233]

For our purposes here, the temporal authority of the Sibyl in the relevant oracles, in our discussion the Fourth and the Fifth, and that of the emperor engage in combative interaction with each other, which is perhaps a more belligerent version of the memory games that have been the subject of this chapter thus far.[234] One common point of interest has been the use of the Roman emperor as a temporal marker. Indeed, scholars have attempted to use the mention of emperors in these poems to securely date their compositional dates. The temporality of the Sibylline Oracles is extremely

---

[229] Tac. *Ann.* 2.40.2.
[230] Potter (1990: 95–6), on the dates and extant collections; cf. Potter (1994: 71–5) and Lightfoot (2007). See more recently Greensmith (2022).
[231] See Gruen's entry in the *OCD* 'Sibylline Oracles': https://doi.org/10.1093/acrefore/9780199381135.013.8134.
[232] Jones (2011: 213–15).
[233] For the complexity of the poetics in the Sibylline Oracles, see Greensmith (2022), to which my argument here is indebted.
[234] Cf. Potter (1994: 137–45), esp. 140–1 on the broad impressions about the emperor in the oracles and the argument for them not being as subversive as assumed.

complex, as the poem invites comparison through time between different authorities. Without wading into the debate on dating, perilous for both the individual oracles and the collection as a whole, I want to stress that the appearance of the emperor only partly gives us an *impression* of historical time, which is part of the authoritative positing of the Sibyl as a manner of grounding prophetic visions. Instead, the appearance of the emperor can function as markers for future time to come as well as an engagement with historical events, which means that the emperor was used as a way to question the legitimacy of Roman power and indeed the emperor himself. Connected to the problem of dating is the problem of subject matter in the collection: summarising the Sibylline oracles as a whole evades simple categorisation or explanation, given that the collection contains different subjects and historical moments that exist together *in situ* extrapolated across several centuries.[235]

Accordingly, a full appreciation of the total collection is impossible here, so I will concentrate on a couple of pertinent examples from the Fourth and Fifth Sibyl.[236] A short precis of both poems will suffice. The Fourth Sibyl positions herself as God's seer, in contrast to Apollo's,[237] and then moves towards a historical explanation of various kingdoms of Near Eastern history, culminating in the coming of Rome and the destruction of the Temple at Jerusalem.[238] As noted by Gruen, the Fourth Sibyl has 'a clear historical sense' as the poem engages with several notable historical events, including the end of the Hellenistic kingdoms at the Rise of Rome and the eruption of Vesuvius in AD 79.[239] The Fifth Sibyl is far more composite and temporally slippery, as it seems to contain allusions from vastly different contexts, including predictions of destruction wrought against Rome and Egypt, with a remarkable interest in Egypt as a focus for animosity, and a list of successive Roman rulers culminating in Hadrian through to Marcus Aurelius.[240] Indeed, the appearance of the emperor, and in particular Nero, shows an interest in the complex temporality that

---

[235] Lightfoot (2007); Potter (1994); Jones (2011).

[236] For summaries of these poems, see Jones (2011: 210–12).

[237] *Orac. Sib.* 4.4–7, with Gruen (2020: 191–2).

[238] *Orac. Sib.* 4.115–16: ἥξει καὶ Σολύμοισι κακὴ πολέμοιο θύελλα Ἰταλόθεν, νηὸν δὲ θεοῦ μέγαν ἐξαλαπάξει.

[239] Gruen (2020); *Orac. Sib.* 4.102–14: οὐδὲ Μακηδονίης ἔσται κράτος· ἀλλ᾽ ἀπὸ δυσμῶν Ἰταλὸς ἀνθήσει πόλεμος μέγας, ᾧ ὕπο κόσμος λατρεύσει δούλειον ἔχων ζυγὸν Ἰταλίδῃσιν. 130–4: ἀλλ᾽ ὁπόταν χθονίης ἀπὸ ῥωγάδος Ἰταλίδος γῆς πυρσὸς ἀποστραφθεὶς εἰς οὐρανὸν εὐρὺν ἵκηται.

[240] Cf. Jones (2011), who argues that after the mention of Hadrian at *Orac. Sib.* 5.46–8, the mention of Marcus Aurelius and his predecessors at line 51 feels tacked on. Cf. Gruen (2020: 196–7) for the Fifth Sibylline oracle as a hodge-podge.

has been the subject of this chapter and indeed precisely reflects how the emperor could be used both as a marker of time and as a way to think through Roman power.

Concentrating on Nero and starting with the Fourth Sibyl, the last Julio-Claudian is an enigmatic figure who doubles as a monster of enormous vice and depravity and as a reckoner who will come from the east to bring destruction to Rome.[241] Nero flees to the east (4.119–124), with the spectre of a later return bringing war to the west.[242] In many ways, this image of Nero is familiar, as it alludes to the phenomenon of pretender emperors appearing and challenging the power of the sitting emperor, seen with the impersonators Clemens and Maternus discussed in this section.[243] However, as noted by Gruen, Nero's vengeance was more indiscriminate than directed solely at Rome, meaning that a reading of resistance in this text is problematic:

> The Sibyl hardly served as vehicle for Jewish response, let alone resistance, to Roman authority. If Vesuvius and Nero were the instruments of divine wrath, they had already done their worst in the past. The future apocalypse will burn the entire earth and destroy the whole of mankind.[244]

Gruen is correct to note the problems of reading a too straightforward transcript of Jewish resistance to Rome in the aftermath of the destruction of the Temple in AD 70 and the subsequent revolts in the second century AD. The Fourth Sibyl, for instance, includes Antioch, Cyprus, Caria, and the lands watered by the Maeander as victims of God's wrath to come – hardly making Rome the focus of future destruction.[245] However, what is missed in this analysis is an acknowledgement that it will be *Roman* power that will ultimately bring the demise of both Rome and the lands across its empire, as it is the return of Nero that will bring war. How should we read apocalyptic imaginings of the end coming in the form of a monstrous Roman emperor in the future? Perhaps this image might be read as manifested retributive justice. In that case, we find ourselves in a similar ideological world to Fronto's, where the emperor's duties are to suppress the rebellious and cow the proud (*feroces territare*), or even the negative world of justice being meted out to the emperor's subjects.[246] Perhaps also it might reflect a component of the thought-world of resistance against

---

[241] On Nero's rich afterlife, both from the Sibyl and otherwise, see Gruen (2014, 2020); Malik (2020).

[242] *Orac. Sib.* 4.137–139: ἐς δὲ δύσιν τότε νεῖκος ἐγειρομένου πολέμοιο ἥξει καὶ Ῥώμης ὁ φυγάς, μέγα ἔγχος ἀείρας, Εὐφρήτην διαβὰς πολλαῖς ἅμα μυριάδεσσιν.

[243] Bowersock (1987: 308–11).   [244] Gruen (2020: 202).   [245] *Orac. Sib.* 4.140–49.

[246] Cf. pp. 6–8 and 86–98.

Rome, namely that the future cannot even be imagined without reference to Roman might – here embodied by the most common symbol of that power, the emperor himself – even if that future will bring Rome's ultimate demise. Such an argument rests on the pervasiveness of Roman ideology and power throughout their world. Put another way, people who suffered under the yoke of Rome, who we might expect to imagine resistance and life away from Rome, could not think of themselves outside of Roman power.[247]

This theme of Neronian revenge is mirrored in the Fifth Sibyl, which tells that the 'cunning man who murdered his mother' will seize the whole world and rule all. This is a strikingly ambiguous image, both destructive and benevolent images come forth in this description of Nero's future role.[248] Again, we find ourselves in the world of Fronto discussed at the start of Chapter 1. Moreover, both temporal and geographical wavering are present here. The mention of the Euphrates and the 'ends of the earth' evoke the themes of wonder and empire, with the emperor being the mediator between near and far, here evoked in a destructive and eschatological sense, associating Nero with the wondrous that we saw before with the emperor as an arbiter of wonder and as a monster himself.[249] Moreover, he is a trigger for a challenging of the world order, a conceptualisation that the emperor is a key component in the differences between periods of time and a testament to anxieties being mapped on both the rise and fall of emperors and their evolving legacies into the future. With this in mind, the *Sibylline Oracles* serve as an example of the scope of an imperial future, which is in constant dialogue with the past and the present of the empire.

In the end, the appearance of false pretenders and emperors coming back from the dead to the emperorship in ancient literature serves as an interesting example of a thought-world concerning the Roman emperor. These stories contain many of the elements that were present in previous discussions of this book, most broadly a manifestation of the conversation of acceptance, in which an emperor was criticised. It shows the precariousness of his position, meaning that he had to contend with unfavourable opinion and the chance of usurpation. It also shows the nature of the critical discourse, which was complex and vibrant, with seemingly

---

[247] This is the effect of epistemicide, where imperial epistemologies become embedded in the epistemologies of conquered peoples. Cf. Padilla Peralta (2020).

[248] *Orac. Sib.* 5.362–365: καὶ ἐπίκλοπος ἐν δολότητι ἥξει δ' ἐν περάτων γαίης μητροκτόνος ἀνὴρ φεύγων ἠδὲ νόῳ ὀξύστομα μερμηρίζων, ὃς πᾶσαν γαῖαν καθελεῖ καὶ πάντα κρατήσει πάντων τ' ἀνθρώπων φρονιμώτερα πάντα νοήσει . . .

[249] Cf. pp. 142–159.

numerous contributors and participants, indicating the impact of the emperor on the imagination. Moreover, as I have pressed in this chapter, this discourse made the emperor a temporal figure, where the emperor might appear timeless as a figure to organise and describe time, but also reveals an emperor in time, in constant dialogue with the precedents and examples of the past, the constraints and expectations of the present, and the anxieties and uncertainties of the future. The axes of potential analyses are manifold.

Coda
The Worlds of the Roman Emperor

The goal of this book was to construct an alternative approach to the Roman emperor. The conceit was to take a subjective view, which strives to reconstruct how the emperor seemed from the perspective of the inhabitants of the Roman empire. This approach, though, moves away from overt biographical approaches to emperors, which dominate ancient and modern historiography alike. The point here is less to find out what people thought about, say, Tiberius or Pertinax, as individual emperors and more about how their examples contributed to the discourse about the emperor more widely: What were the expectations placed on the emperor? What were the duties that he was expected to fulfil? How did people talk about him?

The themes of this book can be split into five takeaways. First, the Roman emperor as a figure was inherently ambiguous. He was caught between different impressions and ideas, which included his position of absolute power that was mediated through Roman law and political culture, his absolution from the laws but the expectation that he would live according to them, and the expectations and fears placed upon him from the moral exemplarity and tyrannical actions of his forebears. Second, the Roman emperor was meant to be seen as accessible and criticisable, which creates a rich discourse about who he was and what he was meant to be. These perceptions, whether fictional or not, were crucial to forming a picture of his role and contributed to an emperor's legitimacy and acceptance. Third, the tension in this reception led to contradictory and wacky stories in our transcript, which reveal the spectrum of thought and imagination about our emperors, with historicity put firmly to the side. Fiction about the emperor is not a bug in our historical record that must be explained away. Rather, it is a feature – a feature of the discourse that used stories, fables, and allegories to understand and criticise the position. Instead of worrying about which of these stories are true or false or how we can reconcile negative stories with an overtly positive view of a single emperor (or vice versa), the

233

truth value of these stories lies in their place in the thought-world of the Roman emperorship. The point is to distinguish between what people thought and who the emperor actually was.

Fourth, such a thought-world makes the Roman emperor a crucial figure to think *with*. His power made the emperor a mediator: within the legal sphere as a judge, a benefactor who gave generously and was a model to emulate, and a supreme commander who could curate the marvellous for the enjoyment of the Roman people. The emperor was a figure that could be the butt of jokes, and it was crucial that he was seen to take them. The emperor was also seen as a god; his power was understood and commemorated through divine worship, which was described as golden ages of peace and prosperity reborn. And the emperor was a temporal figure, who was in constant dialogue with the past and future of his position. Such considerations encompassed the banal, in that the emperor was a unit of measurement in terms of regnal years, and the impactful, in that the emperor had to contend with apocalyptical versions of himself that came to challenge his authority.

Fifth, I stress the emperor (or emperorship) as a category of enquiry, a theme that should be studied in its own right, and a position that transcends the personalities of specific emperors[1] – not in the sense that personality does not matter but rather that those personalities contribute to a wider discourse of how the emperor seemed. Such was the success of *The Emperor in the Roman World*, where Millar took the Roman emperor as a category and office that needed to be considered together. My innovation is to underline how anecdotes and a wide range of evidence all form fundamental data for understanding the emperor as he was perceived. Such an idea can transcend context and make the Roman emperor a comparative tool with which to assess different forms of autocracy in world history.[2]

As a final note that stresses that the emperor is a figure to think with, I turn to political philosophy and comparative history. The examples I discuss from Agamben and Hegel isolate both the ambiguity incumbent within the emperorship, respectively the lines between the human and the divine, and the relationship of the emperor with politics and law. Agamben was struck by the religious and judicial category of *homo sacer*, a man who was a bare life, left outside a community for death and irredeemable by law or religious custom,[3] and the ritual of the imperial apotheosis. The emperor

---

[1] Kahane (2022: 33), for Achilles as an embodied theme in Homer.   [2] Cf. Duindam (2016: 4–5).
[3] Festus s.v. *sacer homo*. Cf. Fowler (1911: 60–1).

becomes a cornerstone of Agamben's discussion of sovereignty and a way to understand the concept of the sacred life.[4] The main point of interest concerns the 'double' funeral, which involved the interment of the emperor's body in a mausoleum and the burning of a likeness after the fact, which was described in detail by Herodian.[5] For Agamben, this meant that the emperor had within himself competing natures that had to be treated differently:

> Thus it is as if the emperor had in himself not two bodies but rather two lives inside one single body: a natural life and a sacred life. The latter, regardless of the regular funeral rite, survives the former and can only ascend to the heavens and be deified after the *funus imaginarium*.[6]

Agamben finds a deep commonality in understanding categories that stood in between different worlds: here, the tension between life and death, a *homo sacer* occupying that liminal point in between, and an emperor who contained different forms of life within his person.[7] Starting from here, the paradox of the Roman emperor as a historical phenomenon is distilled into its simplest form: the existence of a tension of various statuses within the body of the emperor himself, filled with the hopes, fears, and expectations of his subjects. The emperor was a person and a symbol all contained in one. This designation engages with complex issues of religious, legal, and political statuses in the Roman world and in so doing connects the Roman emperor to these categories of understanding that involve the ambiguities of status that the emperor himself embodied: above and under the laws, the same and greater power enjoyed by his position with different magistracies, and a position between the human and divine. The emperor is a way to think about divinity and death.

Agamben seems to refer to Kantorowicz's famous designation of the king's two bodies, though the dichotomy of the political body and the natural body is not as clear-cut in the Roman case.[8] The efficacy of the 'king's two bodies' for the Roman emperor, however, is not what is at stake here. Rather, it is what both Agamben and Kantorowicz noticed: the Roman emperor was a form of autocracy that encountered the issue of permanence and ephemerality in its existence. The distinction between the

---

[4] For more on the development of sacrality at Rome, see Evêque (2018: 37–48).
[5] Hdn. 4.2. Cf. *OLD* 4 s.v. *consecratio*.
[6] Agamben (1998: 100–2, sec. 5.6). Cf. Kantorowicz (1997: 427) for his discussion of the passage in Herodian.
[7] Evêque (2018: 23); cf. Evêque (2018: 28–32) for the ambivalence of the terminology.
[8] Kantorowicz (1997: 314–16). Cf. Section 1.2.1.

political and the natural body of the Roman emperor was almost non-existent and hard to distinguish, which gave the emperorship a quality of 'doubleness'. In other words, the person and the 'office' were connected closely, which manifested most visibly in the question of the imperial succession, the volatility of dynastic continuity in imperial Rome, and the jagged and often contradictory transcript of an emperor's actions in his life.[9] The meaning of being the 'emperor' would change and develop depending on its holder and thus be connected to him and his memory in the future but also be recast and reinterpreted with each subsequent holder. This makes the Roman emperorship dynamic, confusing, and difficult to theorise, with contradictions and ambiguities incumbent in the position.

Indeed, this dynamic interpretation of the Roman emperor was appreciated by Hegel, who saw a dialectical tension contained within the position, which was both the harbinger of fundamental legal and political change and yet seemingly did not change anything at all, and noticed the paradoxical nature of the emperorship. In *The Philosophy of History*, Hegel describes the emperor as follows:

> The first thing to be remarked respecting the imperial rule is that the Roman government was so abstracted from interest, that the great transition to that rule hardly changed anything in the constitution. The popular assemblies alone were unsuited to the new state of things, and disappeared. The emperor was *princeps senatus*, Censor, Consul, Tribune: he united all their nominally continuing offices in himself; and the military power – here the most essentially important – was exclusively in his hands. The constitution was an utterly unsubstantial form, from which all vitality, consequently all might and power, had departed.[10]

Though partly schematic in discussion, Hegel's points here are of interest to Roman historians. He noticed the tension between the pageantry of political institutions and magistracies and the concentration of power into one figure, with a Tacitean flourish.[11] Hegel provides a statement that might be applicable to the study of the *res publica* in many periods of Roman history, that the constitution itself was ineffable and did not necessarily line up with the existence of an absolute monarch within its framework.[12] Generally, Hegel's

---

[9] For the complexity of dynastic succession at Rome, see Hekster (2015).   [10] Hegel (2004: 314).

[11] Tac. *Ann.* 1.2: *munia senatus magistratuum legum in se trahere* ([Augustus] took for himself the duties of the senate, magistrates and laws).

[12] Flower (2010), esp. 9–17, for important definitions of the term *res publica* and its fluidity. Straumann (2016); Hodgson (2017), with Suet. *Iul.* 77: *nihil esse rem publicam, appellationem modo sine corpore ac specie* (The *res publica* is nothing save a name without body or form).

interest was to see Rome as the 'interval' in a political development from the Greek *polis* towards early modern European monarchies, in terms of political philosophy, the Roman interest in the relationship between the coercive power of the state and the function of law, and the momentous advent of Christianity in the development of the individual and subjectivity.[13] In this schema, the position of 'Caesar' itself becomes interstitial, an appreciation of the inherent tensions and contradictions.[14]

Such contradictions and ambiguities as underlined in philosophy were the focus of this book throughout, which collected a diverse array of evidence to rebuild the ideology of the Roman emperorship from the perspectives of his subjects. The roles the emperor had to fulfil, and the 'doubleness' of his perception, in turn created the expectation that an exceptional person should occupy it. Such a mentality created a world in which the emperor was a crucial force in its functioning, which was underpinned by his exceptional actions and the worship he received due to those actions. Rather than making him more inviolable, however, it allowed for further scrutiny. Perhaps Gaius' words to the Jewish embassy should be taken more seriously when he claimed that the whole world acknowledged him as a god.[15] In the end, both the idea that Gaius was viewed as a god and the countering perspective that he was not were part of the conversation that resonated into the future. We should be mindful to take seriously, but not too seriously, the outlandish claims made about the emperor in antiquity. These stories are the substance of what the emperor seemed to be.

---

[13] Cf. Desmond (2020: 104–5): 'Ultimately, the dualism issues forth in the proto-constitutional monarchy of the Empire, that fostered legal equality and a proto-conscience, within the framework of a vast, alienating, but lawful Leviathan. Aristocratic republic or proto-monarchy: Hegel struggles to name a *single* constitution to express the Roman political spirit in its long evolution.'

[14] Desmond (2020: 106), on Hegel's argument that the principate was a 'proto-constitutional monarchy'.

[15] Philo, *Leg.* 353. Cf. Tac. *Ann.* 3.36.2; cf. Philostr. *VA.* 1.15, for comparable passing mention of the godliness of the emperor.

References

Abbott, F. F. and Johnson, A. C. 1926. *Municipal administration in the Roman empire*. Princeton, NJ.

Abdy, R. and Harling, N. 2005. 'Two important new Roman coins', *Numismatic Chronicle* 165, 175–8.

Agamben, G. 1998. *Homo sacer: sovereign power and bare life*. Stanford, CA.

Ahl, F. 1984. 'The art of safe criticism in Greece and Rome', *American Journal of Philology* 105, 174–208.

Aldrete, G. S. 2003. *Gestures and acclamations in ancient Rome*. Baltimore, MD.

Alexander, L. (ed.) 1991. *Images of empire*. Sheffield.

Alföldy, G. 1985. *The social history of Rome*. London.

Ando, C. 1999. 'Was Rome a polis?', *Classical Antiquity* 18, 5–34.

Ando, C. 2000. *Imperial ideology and provincial loyalty in the Roman empire*. Berkeley, CA.

Ando, C. 2013. 'The origins and import of republican constitutionalism', *Cardozo Law Review* 34, 917.

Andrews, A. C. 1949. 'The Roman craze for surmullets', *The Classical Weekly* 42, 186–8.

Arce, J. and González Fernández, J. (eds.) 1988. *Estudios sobre la 'Tabula Siarensis'*. Madrid.

Armstrong, D. 1986. 'Stylistics and the date of Calpurnius Siculus', *Philologus* 130, 113–36.

Arnason, J. P. and Raaflaub, K. A. (eds.) 2010. *The Roman empire in context: historical and comparative perspectives*. Malden, MA, and Oxford.

Ash, R. 1997. 'Severed heads: individual portraits and irrational forces in Plutarch's *Galba* and *Otho*', in J. Mossman (ed.) *Plutarch and his intellectual world*. Swansea: 189–214.

Ash, R. 1999. *Ordering anarchy: armies and leaders in Tacitus' Histories*. London.

Ash, R. 2008. 'Standing in the shadows: Plutarch and the emperors in the *Lives* and *Moralia*', in A. Nikolaides (ed.) *The unity of Plutarch's work*. Berlin: 557–75.

Ash, R. 2015. 'At the end of the rainbow: Nero and Dido's gold (Tacitus *Annals* 16.1–3),' in R. Ash, J. Mossman, and F. B. Titchener (eds.) *Fame and infamy: essays for Christopher Pelling on characterization in Greek and Roman biography and historiography*. Oxford: 269–84.

Ash, R. 2018. 'Paradoxography and marvels in post-Domitianic literature: "an extraordinary affair; even in the hearing!"', in A. König and C. Whitton (eds.) *Roman literature under Nerva, Trajan and Hadrian: literary interactions, AD 96–138*. Cambridge: 126–45.

Ash, R., Mossman, J., and Titchener, F. B. (eds.) 2015. *Fame and infamy: essays for Christopher Pelling on characterization in Greek and Roman biography and historiography*. Oxford.

Back, K. W. 1988. 'Metaphors for public opinion in literature', *Public Opinion Quarterly* 52, 278–88.

Baldry, H. C. 1952. 'Who invented the golden age?', *Classical Quarterly* 2, 83–92.

Baldwin, B. 1979. 'Juvenal's Crispinus', *Acta Classica* 22, 109–14.

Baldwin, B. 1995a. 'Better late than early: reflections on the date of Calpurnius Siculus', *ICS* 20, 157–67.

Baldwin, B. 1995b. 'Roman emperors in the Elder Pliny', *Scholia: Studies in Classical Antiquity* 4, 56–78.

Balsdon, J. P. V. D. 1960. '*Auctoritas, dignitas, otium*', *Classical Quarterly* 10, 43–50.

Balmaceda, C. (ed.) 2020. *Libertas and res publica in the Roman republic: ideas of freedom and Roman politics*. Leiden.

Barnes, T. D. 1967. 'Hadrian and Lucius Verus', *Journal of Roman Studies* 57, 65–79.

Barraclough, R. and Haase, W. 1984. 'Philos's politics: Roman rule and Hellenistic Judaism', *ANRW* 2.21.1, 417–553.

Barry, W. D. 2008. 'Exposure, mutilation, and riot: violence at the *Scalae Gemoniae* in early imperial Rome', *G&R* 55, 222–46.

Bartlett, R. 2020. *Blood royal: dynastic politics in medieval Europe*. Cambridge.

Barton, T. 1994. *Power and knowledge: astrology, physiognomics, and medicine under the Roman empire*. Ann Arbor, MI.

Bartsch, S. 1994. *Actors in the audience: theatricality and doublespeak from Nero to Hadrian*. Cambridge, MA, and London.

Bastomsky, S. J. 1969. 'The Emperor Nero in Talmudic legend', *The Jewish Quarterly Review* 59, 321–5.

Bauman, R. A. 1967. *The crimen maiestatis in the Roman republic and Augustan principate*. Johannesburg.

Bauman, R. A. 1974. *Impietas in principem: a study of treason against the Roman emperor with special reference to the first century A.D.* Munich.

Beagon, M. (ed.) 2005. *The Elder Pliny on the human animal: Natural History book 7*. Oxford.

Beagon, M. 2007. 'Situating nature's wonders in Pliny's *Natural History*', in E Bispham and G. Rowe (eds.) *Vita vigilia est: essays in honour of Barbara Levick*. London: 19–40.

Beard, M. 2003a. 'The triumph of Flavius Josephus', in A. J. Boyle and W. J. Dominik (eds.) *Flavian Rome: culture, image, text*. Leiden: 543–58.

Beard, M. 2003b. 'The triumph of the absurd: Roman street theatre', in C. Edwards and G. Woolf (eds.) *Rome the cosmopolis*. Cambridge: 21–43.

Beard, M. 2007. *The Roman triumph*. Cambridge, MA, and London.

Beard, M. 2008. *Pompeii: the life of a Roman town*. London.

Beard, M. 2014. *Laughter in ancient Rome: on joking, tickling, and cracking up*. Berkeley, CA.

Beard, M. 2020. 'How to be an emperor: re-reading Fergus Millar's *The Emperor in the Roman World*', *The Times Literary Supplement*, 24 July. www.the-tls.co.uk/articles/how-to-be-a-roman-emperor-essay-mary-beard/.

Beard, M., North, J., and Price, S. R. F. 1998. *Religions of Rome*. Cambridge.

Bénabou, M. 1976. *La résistance africaine à la romanisation*. Paris.

Benjamin, W. 1999. *Illuminations*. London.

Benson, L. 1967. 'An approach to the scientific study of past public opinion', *Public Opinion Quarterly* 31, 522–67.

Béranger, J. 1953. *Recherches sur l'aspect idéologique du principat*. Basel.

Béranger, J. 1973. *Principatus: études de notions et d'histoire politiques dans l'Antiquité gréco-romaine*. Geneva.

Berg, T. 2018. *L'Hadrianus de Montserrat (P. Monts. Roca III, inv. 162–165): édition, traduction et analyse contextuelle d'un récit latin conservé sur papyrus*. Liège.

Berger, A. 1953. 'Encyclopedic dictionary of Roman law', *Transactions of the American Philological Association* 43, 333–808.

Bergmann, B. A. and Kondoleon, C. (eds.) 1999. *The art of ancient spectacle*. Washington, DC, and New Haven, CT.

Bickerman, E. J. 1973. 'Consecratio', in W. D. Boer and E. J. Bickerman (eds.) *Le culte des souverains dans l'Empire Romain: sept exposés suivis de discussions*. Geneva: 3–25.

Birley, A. 1999. *Septimius Severus: the African emperor*. London.

Bispham, E and Rowe. G. (eds.) 2007. *Vita vigilia est: essays in honour of Barbara Levick*. London.

Bodel, J. 2016. 'Status dissonance and status dissidents in the equestrian order', in A. B. Kuhn (ed.) *Social status and prestige in the Graeco-Roman world*. Stuttgart: 29–44.

Bodel, J., Bendlin, A., Bernard, S., Bruun, C., and Edmondson, J. 2019. 'Notes on the *elogium* of a benefactor at Pompeii' *Journal of Roman Archaeology* 32, 148–82.

Boer, W. D. and Bickerman, E. J. (eds.) 1973. *Le culte des souverains dans l'Empire Romain: sept exposés suivis de discussions*. Geneva.

Bonner, S. F. 1977. *Education in ancient Rome: from the elder Cato to the younger Pliny*. London.

Bonte, P. (ed.) 1994. *Épouser au plus proche: inceste, prohibitions et stratégies matrimoniales autour de la Méditerranée*. Paris.

Bossu, C. 1989. 'L'objectif de l'institution alimentaire: essai d'évaluation' *Latomus* 48, 372–82.

Bowersock, G. 1984. 'Augustus and the East: the problem of the succession', in F. Millar and E. Segal (eds.) *Caesar Augustus: seven aspects*. Oxford: 169–88.

Bowersock, G. 1987. 'The mechanics of subversion in the Roman provinces', in A. Giovannini and K. A. Raaflaub (eds.) *Opposition et résistances à l'Empire d'Auguste à Trajan: neuf exposés suivis de discussions*. Geneva: 291–320.

Bowersock, G. 1994. *Fiction as history: Nero to Julian*. Berkeley and London.

Bowes, K. 2021. 'Tracking consumption at Pompeii: the graffiti lists', *Journal of Roman Archaeology* 34, 552–84.

Boyle, A. J. (ed.) 2008. *Octavia: attributed to Seneca*. Oxford.

Boyle, A. J. and Dominik, W. J. (eds.) 2003. *Flavian Rome: culture, image, text*. Leiden.

Bradley, K. and Cartledge, P. (eds.) 2011. *The Cambridge world history of slavery, vol. 1: the ancient Mediterranean world*. Cambridge.

Braund, S. M. 1993. 'Paradigms of power: Roman emperors in Roman satire', in K. Cameron (ed.) *Humour and history*. Oxford: 56–69.

Braund, S. M. (ed.) 2009. *Seneca: De clementia: text, translation and commentary*. Oxford.

Braund, S. M. and James, P. 1998. '*Quasi Homo*: distortion and contortion in Seneca's "Apocolocyntosis"', *Arethusa* 31, 285–311.

Brelich, A. (ed.) 1980. *Perennitas: studi in onore di Angelo Brelich*. Rome.

Brouwer, R. 2015. 'Ulpian's appeal to nature: Roman law as universal law', *The Legal History Review* 83, 60–76.

Brunt, P. 1977. '*Lex de imperio Vespasiani*', *Journal of Roman Studies* 67, 95–116.

Brunt, P. 1990. *Roman imperial themes*. Oxford.

Bruun, C. 2003. 'Roman emperors in popular jargon: searching for contemporary nicknames (I)', in L. de Blois, P. Erdkamp, O. Hekster, G. de Kleijn, and S. Mols (eds.) *The representation and perception of Roman imperial power*. Amsterdam: 69–98.

Bultrighini, I. 2021. 'Calendars of the Greek east under Rome', in S. Stern (ed.) *Calendars in the making: the origins of calendars from the Roman empire to the later Middle Ages*. Leiden: 80–128.

Bultrighini, I. and Stern, S. 2021. 'The seven-day week in the Roman empire: origins, standardization, and diffusion', in S. Stern (ed.) *Calendars in the making: the origins of calendars from the Roman empire to the later Middle Ages*. Leiden: 10–79.

Buongiorno, P. 2012. 'Idee vecchie e nuove in tema di *Lex de Imperio Vespasiani*', *Athenaeum* 100, 513–28.

Burke, P. 1978. *Popular culture in early modern Europe*. London.

Burrell, B. 2004. *Neokoroi: Greek cities and Roman emperors*. Leiden.

Buti, I. 1982. 'La "cognitio extra ordinem": da Augusto a Diocleziano,' *ANRW* II.14, 29–59.

Buttrey, T.V. 2007 'Domitian, the rhinoceros, and the date of Martial's "Liber de Spectaculis"', *Journal of Roman Studies* 97, 101–12.

Caballos Rufino, A. 2021. '*Un Senadoconsulto del Año 14 d. C. en un epígrafe Bético*', *Zeitschrift für Papyrologie und Epigraphik* 219, 305–26.

Calomino, D. 2016. *Defacing the past: damnation and desecration in imperial Rome*. London.

Cameron, A. 1976. *Circus factions: blues and greens at Rome and Byzantium.* Oxford.

Cameron, K. (ed.) 1993. *Humour and history.* Oxford.

Campbell, J. B. 1984. *The emperor and the Roman army, 31 BC–AD 235.* Oxford.

Cannadine, D. and Price, S. R. F. (eds.) 1987. *Rituals of royalty: power and ceremonial in traditional societies.* Cambridge.

Carter, M. 2003. 'Gladiatorial ranking and the "*SC de Pretiis Gladiatorum Minuendis*" (*CIL* II 6278 = *ILS* 5163)', *Phoenix* 57, 83–114.

Cauwenberghe, C. H.-V. 2008. '"Bons" et "Mauvais" empereurs en Achaïe au Premier Siècle de Notre Ère', in A. D. Rizakis and F. Camia (eds.) *Pathways to power: civic elites in the eastern part of the Roman Empire.* Athens: 161–79.

Cébeillac-Gervasoni, M. and Lamoine, L. (eds.) 2003. *Les élites et leurs facettes: les élites locales dans le monde hellénistique et romain.* Rome.

Champlin, E. 1976. 'Hadrian's heir', *Zeitschrift für Papyrologie und Epigraphik* 21, 79–89.

Champlin, E. 1978. 'The life and times of Calpurnius Siculus', *Journal of Roman Studies* 68, 95–110.

Champlin, E. 1986. 'History and the date of Calpurnius Siculus', *Philologus* 130, 104–12.

Champlin, E. 2003. *Nero.* Cambridge, MA, and London.

Champlin, E. 2005. 'Phaedrus the Fabulous', *Journal of Roman Studies* 95, 97–123.

Champlin, E. 2008. 'Tiberius the wise', *Historia* 57, 408–25.

Champlin, E. 2012. 'Seianus Augustus', *Chiron* 42, 361–88.

Champlin, E. 2015a. 'Mallonia', *Histos* 9, 220–30.

Champlin, E. 2015b. 'The richest man in Spain', *Zeitschrift für Papyrologie und Epigraphik* 198, 277–95.

Charlesworth, M. P. 1937. *The virtues of a Roman emperor: propaganda and the creation of belief.* London.

Charlesworth, M. P. 1939. 'The refusal of divine honours, an Augustan formula', *Papers of the British School at Rome* 15, 1–10.

Christoforou, P. 2016. 'Living in an age of gold: being a subject of the Roman emperor.' Unpublished DPhil thesis, University of Oxford.

Christoforou, P. 2017. '"If he is worthy": interactions between crowds and emperors in Plutarch and Tacitus' accounts of AD 69', *Rosetta* 21, 1–16.

Christoforou, P. 2021. '"An indication of truly imperial manners": the Roman emperor in Philo's *Legatio ad Gaium*', *Historia* 70, 83–115.

Christoforou, P. 2022. '*qualem diem Tiberius induisset*: Tiberius' absences on Capri as an inspiration for wonder and uncertainty', in J. McNamara and V. E. Pagán (eds.) *Tacitus' wonders: empire and paradox in ancient Rome.* London: 197–220.

Chrysanthou, C. S. 2018. *Plutarch's parallel lives: narrative technique and moral judgement.* Berlin.

Clarke, J. R. 2003. *Art in the lives of ordinary Romans: visual representation and non-elite viewers in Italy, 100 BC–AD 315.* Berkeley, CA.

Classen, C. J. 1991. 'Virtutes imperatoriae', *Arctos: Acta Philologica Fennica* 25, 17–39.

Clavel-Lévêque, M. 1984. *L'empire en jeux: espace symbolique et pratique sociale dans le monde romain.* Paris.

Coarelli, F. 2001. 'Les *Saepta* et la technique du vote à Rome de la fin de la République à Auguste', *Pallas* 55, 37–51.

Coleman, K. 1990. 'Fatal charades: Roman executions staged as mythological enactments', *Journal of Roman Studies* 80, 44–73.

Coleman, K. M. 1993. 'Launching into history: aquatic displays in the early empire', *Journal of Roman Studies* 83, 48–74.

Coleman, K. M. (ed.) 2006. *M. Valerii Martialis Liber spectaculorum: introduction, translation and commentary.* Oxford.

Cooley, A. (ed.) 2009. *Res gestae divi Augusti: text, translation, and commentary.* Cambridge.

Cooley, A. 2019. 'From the Augustan Principate to the invention of the age of Augustus', *Journal of Roman Studies* 109, 71–87.

Corbier, M. 1991. 'Divorce and adoption as Roman familial strategies (le divorce et l'adoption "en plus")', in B. Rawson (ed.) *Marriage, divorce, and children in ancient Rome.* Oxford: 47–78.

Corbier, M. 1994a. 'À propos de la *Tabula Siarensis*: le Sénat, Germanicus et la *domus Augusta*', in J. González Fernández (ed.) *Roma y las provincias: realidad administrativa e ideología imperial.* Madrid: 39–85.

Corbier, M. 1994b. 'La maison des Césars', in P. Bonte (ed.) *Épouser au plus proche: inceste, prohibitions et stratégies matrimoniales autour de la Méditerranée.* Paris: 213–91.

Corbier, M. 1995. 'Male power and legitimacy through women: the *Domus Augusta* under the Julio-Claudians', in R. Hawley and B. Levick (eds.) *Women in antiquity: new assessments.* London: 178–93.

Cornwell, H. 2017. Pax *and the politics of peace: republic to principate.* Oxford.

Cortés Copete, J. M. 2017. 'Hadrian among the Gods', in Muñiz Grijalvo, E., Cortés Copete, J. M., and Lozano Gomez, F. (eds.) *Empire and religion: religious change in Greek cities under Roman rule.* Leiden: 112–36.

Cotton, H. 1993. 'The guardianship of Jesus Son of Babatha: Roman and local law in the province of Arabia', *Journal of Roman Studies* 83, 94–108.

Courrier, C. 2014. *La plèbe de Rome et sa culture (fin du IIe siècle av. J.-C. – fin du siècle ap. J.-C.* Rome.

Courtney, E. (ed.) 2013. *A commentary on the satires of Juvenal.* Berkeley, CA.

Cowan, E. 2019. 'Hopes and aspirations: *res publica, leges et iura,* and alternatives at Rome', in K. Morrell, J. Osgood, and K. Welch (eds.) *The alternative Augustan age.* Oxford: 27–45

Czajkowski, K., Eckhardt, B. and Strothmann, M. (eds.) 2020. *Law in the Roman provinces.* Oxford.

Dalla Rosa, A. 2021. 'The *provincia* of Augustus, or how to reconcile Cassius Dio's vision of the principate, Augustus' own public image and early imperial institutional practices', in A. Díaz Fernández (ed.) *Provinces and provincial command in republican Rome: genesis, development and governance.* Zaragoza: 191–216.

Darwall-Smith, R. 1996. *Emperors and architecture: a study of Flavian Rome.* Brussels.

Davenport, C. 2019. *A history of the Roman equestrian order.* Cambridge.

Davenport, C. 2020. 'Roman emperors, conquest, and violence: images from the eastern provinces', in A. Russell and M. Hellström (eds.) *The social dynamics of Roman imperial imagery.* Cambridge: 100–27.

Davenport, C. 2021. 'News, rumour, and the political culture of the Roman imperial monarchy in the Roman history', in C. Davenport and C. Mallan (eds.) *Emperors and political culture in Cassius Dio's Roman history.* Cambridge: 52–73.

Davenport, C. and Mallan, C. 2014. 'Hadrian's adoption speech in Cassius Dio's *Roman History* and the problems of imperial succession', *American Journal of Philology* 135, 637–68.

Davenport, C. and Mallan, C. (eds.) 2021. *Emperors and political culture in Cassius Dio's Roman history.* Cambridge.

Davies, P. J. E. 2010. *Death and the emperor: Roman imperial funerary monuments from Augustus to Marcus Aurelius.* Austin, TX.

de Angelis, F. 2021a. 'Decoration and attention in the forum of Augustus: the agency of ancient imagery between ritual and routine', in A. Haug and M. T. Lauritsen (eds.) *Principles of decoration in the Roman world.* Berlin: 15–32.

de Angelis, F. (ed.) 2021b. *Emperors in images, architecture, and ritual.* Boston, MA.

de Blois, L. (ed.) 2001. *Administration, prosopography and appointment policies in the Roman empire.* Leiden.

de Blois, L., Erdkamp, P., Hekster, O. de Kleijn, G., and Mols, S. (eds.) 2003. *The representation and perception of Roman imperial power.* Amsterdam.

de Coulanges, F. 1891. *Histoire des institutions politiques de l'ancienne France: la Gaule romaine.* Paris.

de Jong, J. 2003. 'Representation and perception of Roman imperial power in Greek papyrus texts from A D 238', in L. de Blois, P. Erdkamp, O. Hekster, G. de Kleijn, and S. Mols (eds.) *The representation and perception of Roman imperial power.* Amsterdam: 269–81.

de Pury-Gysel, A. 2017. *Die Goldbüste des Septimius Severus: Gold-und Silberbüsten römischer Kaiser.* Basel and Frankfurt.

de Pury-Gysel, A. 2019. 'The gold bust (*imago*) of Septimius Severus from Didymoteicho (Plotinopolis)', *Journal of Roman Archaeology* 32, 313–28.

de Ste. Croix, G. E. M. 1981. *The class struggle in the ancient Greek world: from the archaic age to the Arab conquests.* London.

Dench, E. 2005. *Romulus' asylum: Roman identities from the age of Alexander to the age of Hadrian.* Oxford.

Dench, E. 2018. *Empire and political cultures in the Roman world.* Cambridge.

Desmond, W. D. 2020. *Hegel's antiquity.* Oxford.

Díaz Fernández, A. (ed.) 2021. *Provinces and provincial command in republican Rome: genesis, development and governance.* Zaragoza.

Dickey, E. 2001. 'Kypie, ΔΕΣΠΟΤΑ, Domine Greek politeness in the Roman empire', *Journal of Hellenic Studies* 121, 1–11.

Dickey, E. 2012. *The colloquia of the hermeneumata pseudodositheana*. Cambridge.

Dickison, S. K. 1977. 'Claudius: *Saturnalicius princeps*', *Latomus* 36, 634–47.

Dmitriev, S. 2005. *City government in Hellenistic and Roman Asia minor*. Oxford.

Dolganov, A. 2018. 'Empire of law: legal culture and imperial rule in the Roman province of Egypt'. Unpublished PhD Dissertation, Princeton.

Döpp, S. (ed.) 1993. *Karnevaleske Phänomene in antiken und nachantiken Kulturen und Literaturen*. Trier.

Drinkwater, J. F. 2013. 'Nero Caesar and the half-baked principate', in A. G. G. Gibson (ed.) *The Julio-Claudian succession: reality and perception of the "Augustan model"*. Leiden: 155–73.

Drinkwater, J. F. 2019. *Nero: emperor and court*. Cambridge.

Drogula, F. K. 2007. '*Imperium, potestas*, and the *pomerium* in the Roman Republic', *Historia* 56, 419–52.

du Plessis, P., Ando, C., and Tuori, K. (eds.) 2016. *The Oxford handbook of Roman law and society*. Oxford.

du Quesnay, I. M. L. M. 1976. 'Vergil's fourth Eclogue', *Liverpool Latin Seminar* 1, 25–99.

Duindam, J. F. J. 2016. *Dynasties: a global history of power, 1300–1800*. Cambridge.

Dunbabin, K. M. D. 2003. *The Roman banquet: images of conviviality*. Cambridge.

Duncan-Jones, R. 1964. 'The purpose and organisation of the *alimenta*', *Papers of the British School at Rome* 32, 123–46.

Duncan-Jones, R. 1974. *The economy of the Roman empire: quantitative studies*. Cambridge.

Eck, W., Schneider, D. L., and Takács, S. A. 2003. *The age of Augustus*. Malden, MA, and Oxford.

Edmonson, J. C. 1996. 'Dynamic arenas: gladiatorial presentations in the city of Rome and the construction of Roman society during the early empire', in W. J. Slater (ed.) *Roman theater and society: E. Togo Salmon papers I*. Ann Arbor: 69–112.

Edwards, C. 1993. *The politics of immorality in ancient Rome*. Cambridge.

Edwards, C. and Woolf, G. (eds.) 2003. *Rome the cosmopolis*. Cambridge.

Edwards, M. J. and Swain, S. (eds.) 1997. *Portraits: biographical representation in the Greek and Latin literature of the Roman Empire*. Oxford.

Edwards, R. 2011. 'Tacitus, Tiberius and Capri', *Latomus* 70, 1047–57.

Edwards, R. 2015. 'Caesar telling tales: Phaedrus and Tiberius', *Rheinisches Museum* 158, 167–84.

Elkins, N. T. 2017. '*Aequitas* and *Iustitia* on the coinage of Nerva: a case of visual panegyric', *Numismatic Chronicle* 177, 93–106.

Evêque, R. 2018. 'Chronique d'un mort-vivant: mise en altérité et devenir de l'*homo sacer* romain', *Droit et cultures: Revue internationale interdisciplinaire* 76, 31–83.

Ewald, B. C. and Noreña, C. F. (eds.) 2010. *The emperor and Rome: space, representation, and ritual*. Cambridge.

Fasolt, C. 2004. *The limits of history*. Chicago and London.

Fears, J. R. 1981. 'The cult of virtues and Roman imperial ideology', *ANRW* II.17.2: 828–948.

Feeney, D. 2007. *Caesar's calendar: ancient time and the beginnings of history*. Berkeley, CA.

Feeney, D. C. 1992. '*Si licet et fas est*: Ovid's *Fasti* and the problem of free speech under the principate', in A. Powell (ed.) *Roman poetry and propaganda in the age of Augustus*. London: 1–25.

Feig Vishnia, R. 2012. *Roman elections in the age of Cicero: society, government, and voting*. New York.

Ferri, R. 2003. *Octavia: a play attributed to Seneca*. Cambridge.

Fiori, R. 1996. *Homo sacer: dinamica politico-costituzionale di una sanzione giuridico-religiosa*. Naples.

Fishwick, D. 1987–2005. *The imperial cult in the Latin West: studies in the ruler cult of the western provinces of the Roman empire*. 4 vols. Leiden.

Flach, D. 1976. '*Destinatio* und *nominatio* im frühen Prinzipat', Chiron 6, 193–204.

Flaig, E. 2010. 'How the Emperor Nero lost acceptance in Rome', in B. C. Ewald and C. F. Noreña (eds.) *The emperor and Rome: space, representation, and ritual*. Cambridge: 275–88.

Flaig, E. 2011. 'The transition from republic to principate: loss of legitimacy, revolution, and acceptance', in J. P. Arnason and K. A. Raaflaub (eds.) *The Roman empire in context: historical and comparative perspectives*. Malden, MA, and Oxford: 67–84.

Flaig, E. 2019. *Den Kaiser herausfordern: die Usurpation im Römischen Reich*. 2nd ed. Frankfurt.

Flower, H. I. 1995. '*Fabulae Praetextae* in context: when were plays on contemporary subjects performed in Republican Rome?', *Classical Quarterly* 45, 170–90.

Flower, H. I. 1996. *Ancestor masks and aristocratic power in Roman culture*. Oxford.

Flower, H. I. 2006. *The art of forgetting: disgrace and oblivion in Roman political culture*. Chapel Hill, NC, and London.

Flower, H. I. 2010. *Roman republics*. Princeton, NJ.

Flower, H. I. 2017. *The dancing lares and the serpent in the garden: religion at the Roman street corner*. Princeton, NJ.

Flower, H. I. 2020. 'Augustus, Tiberius, and the end of the Roman triumph', *Classical Antiquity* 39, 1–28.

Forbis, E. 1996. *Municipal virtues in the Roman empire: the evidence of Italian honorary inscriptions*. Stuttgart.

Forsdyke, S. 2012. *Slaves tell tales: and other episodes in the politics of popular culture in ancient Greece*. Princeton, NJ.

Fowler, W. W. 1911. 'The original meaning of the word *sacer*', *Journal of Roman Studies* 1, 57–63.

Franklin, J. L. 2001. *Pompeis difficile est: studies in the political life of imperial Pompeii*. Ann Arbor, MI.

Freudenburg, K. 2014. '*Recusatio* as political theatre: Horace's letter to Augustus', *Journal of Roman Studies* 104, 105–32.

Friesen, S. J. 1993. *Twice Neokoros: Ephesus, Asia, and the cult of the Flavian imperial family*. Leiden.

Fujii, T. 2013. *Imperial cult and imperial representation in Roman Cyprus*. Stuttgart.

Furedi, F. 2013. *Authority: a sociological history*. Cambridge.

Gabba, E. 1981. 'True history and false history in classical antiquity', *Journal of Roman Studies* 71, 50–62.

Gagé, J. 1933. 'La théologie de la 18 dminist impériale', *Revue historique* 171, 1–43.

Gale, M. and Scourfield, J. H. D. (eds.) 2018. *Texts and violence in the Roman world*. Cambridge.

Galinsky, K. (ed.) 2014. *Memoria Romana: memory in Rome and Rome in memory*. Ann Arbor, MI.

Galinsky, K. 2015a. 'Augustus' *Auctoritas* and *Res Gestae* 34.3', *Hermes* 143, 244–9.

Galinsky, K. 2015b. *Memory in ancient Rome and early Christianity*. Oxford.

Galinsky, K. and Lapatin, K. (eds.) 2016. *Cultural memories in the Roman empire*. Los Angeles, CA.

Garland, R. 1995. *The eye of the beholder: deformity and disability in the Graeco-Roman world*. London.

Garnsey, P. and Whittaker, C. R. (eds.) 1978. *Imperialism in the ancient world*. Cambridge.

Gartrell, A. 2021. *The cult of Castor and Pollux in ancient Rome*. Cambridge.

Gatz, B. 1967. *Weltalter, goldene Zeit and sinnverwandte Vorstellungen*. Hildesheim.

George, M. 2011. 'Roman slavery and Roman material culture', in K. Bradley and P. Cartledge (eds.) *The Cambridge world history of slavery, vol. 1: the ancient Mediterranean world*. Cambridge: 385–413.

Gibson, A. G. G. (ed.) 2013. *The Julio-Claudian succession: reality and perception of the "Augustan model"*. Leiden.

Gibson, B. J. 2018. 'Tacitus and the language of violence', in M. Gale and J. H. D. Scourfield (eds.) *Texts and violence in the Roman world*. Cambridge: 269–85.

Gil, J. and Torallas Tovar, S. (eds.) 2010. *Hadrianus. P.Monts. Roca III*. Barcelona.

Giovannini, A. and Raaflaub, K. A. (eds.) 1987. *Opposition et résistances à l'Empire d'Auguste à Trajan: neuf exposés suivis de discussions*. Geneva.

Giradet, K. M. 2000. '"*Imperium maius*": politische und verfassungsrechtliche Aspekte. Versuch einer Klärung', in F. Millar and A. Giovannini (eds.) *La révolution romaine après Ronald Syme: bilans et perspectives*. Geneva: 167–236.

Giusti, E. 2016. 'Did somebody say Augustan totalitarianism? Duncan Kennedy's "reflections," Hannah Arendt's *Origins*, and the continental divide over Virgil's *Aeneid*,' *Dictynna: revue de poétique latine* 13. https://doi.org/10.4000/dictynna.1282.

Gladhill, B. 2012. 'The emperor's no clothes: Suetonius and the dynamics of corporeal ecphrasis', *Classical Antiquity* 31, 315–48.

Gleason, M. 2011. 'Identity theft: doubles and masquerades in Cassius Dio's contemporary history', *Classical Antiquity* 30, 33–86.

González Fernández, J. (ed.) 1994. *Roma y las provincias: realidad 20 dministrative e ideología imperial*. Madrid.

Gradel, I. 2002. *Emperor worship and Roman religion.* Oxford.

Gray, E. W. 1970. 'The *Imperium* of M. Agrippa: a note on P. Colon. Inv. Nr. 4701', *Zeitschrift für Papyrologie und Epigraphik* 6, 227–38.

Greensmith, E. 2018. 'When Homer quotes Callimachus: allusive poetics in the proem of the *Posthomerica*', *Classical Quarterly* 68, 257–74.

Greensmith, E. 2020. *The resurrection of Homer in imperial Greek epic: Quintus Smyrnaeus' Posthomerica and the poetics of impersonation.* Cambridge.

Greensmith, E. 2021. 'Beginning at the end in imperial Greek epic', *Arethusa* 54, 379-97.

Greensmith, E. 2022. 'The wrath of the sibyl: Homeric reception and contested identities in the Sibylline Oracles 3', in J. König and N. Wiater (eds.) *Late Hellenistic Greek literature in dialogue.* Cambridge: 178–201.

Griffin, M. T. 1991. 'Urbs Roma, plebs and princeps', in L. Alexander (ed.) *Images of empire.* Sheffield: 19–46.

Grubbs, J. E. (ed.) 2002. *Women and the law in the Roman empire: a sourcebook on marriage, divorce and widowhood.* London.

Gruen, E. S. 1974. *The last generation of the Roman republic.* Berkeley, CA.

Gruen, E. S. 2002. *Diaspora: Jews amidst Greeks and Romans.* Cambridge, MA, and London.

Gruen, E. S. 2012. 'Caligula, the imperial cult, and Philo's *Legatio*', *Studia Philonica Annual*, 24, 135–47.

Gruen, E .S. 2014. 'Nero in the Sibylline Oracles', *Scripta Classica Israelica* 33, 87-98.

Gruen, E. S. 2020. 'The Sibylline Oracles and resistance to Rome', in J. J. Price and K. Berthelot (eds.) *The future of Rome: Roman, Greek, Jewish and Christian visions.* Cambridge: 189–205.

Grünewald, T. 2004. *Bandits in the Roman empire: myth and reality.* London.

Gunderson, E. 2003. 'The Flavian Amphitheatre: all the world as stage', in A. J. Boyle and W. J. Dominik (eds.) *Flavian Rome: culture, image, text.* Leiden: 637–58.

Gygax, M. D. and Zuiderhoek, A. (eds.) 2021. *Benefactors and the polis: the public gift in the Greek cities from the Homeric world to late antiquity.* Cambridge.

Habermas, J. 1989. *The structural transformation of the public sphere: an inquiry into a category of bourgeois society.* Cambridge, MA.

Hall, U. 1998. '"*Species libertatis*": voting procedure in the late Roman republic', *Bulletin of the Institute of Classical Studies* 42, 15–30.

Hammond, M. 1956. 'The transmission of powers of the Roman emperor from the death of Nero in AD 68 to that of Severus Alexander in AD 235', *Memoirs of the American Academy in Rome*, 24, 63–133.

Hammond, M. 1959. *The Antonine monarchy.* Rome.

Hammond, M. 1968. *The Augustan principate in theory and practice during the Julio-Claudian period.* New York.

Hannah, R. 2005. *Greek and Roman calendars: constructions of time in the classical world.* London.

Hardie, P. R. 2002. *Ovid's poetics of illusion.* Cambridge.

Harker, A. 2008. *Loyalty and dissidence in Roman Egypt: the case of the Acta Alexandrinorum*. Cambridge.

Harland, P. A. 2003. 'Imperial cults within local cultural life: associations in Roman Asia', *AHB* 17, 85–107.

Harlow, M. and Laurence, R. 2017. '*Augustus senex*: old age and the remaking of the Principate', *Greece & Rome* 64, 115–31.

Harries, J. 2003. '*Favor Populi*: pagans, Christians and public entertainment in late antique Italy', in K. Lomas and T. Cornell (eds.) *Bread and circuses: euergetism and municipal patronage in Roman Italy*. London: 125–41.

Harris, E. H. and Canevaro, M. (eds.) 2015. *The Oxford handbook of ancient Greek law*. Oxford.

Haug, A. and Lauritsen, M. T. (eds.) 2021. *Principles of decoration in the Roman world*. Berlin.

Hauken, T. 1998. *Petition and response: an epigraphic study of petitions to Roman emperors, 181–249*. Bergen.

Hawley, R. and Levick, B. (eds.) 1995. *Women in antiquity: new assessments*. London.

Hazirlayanlar, Y., Takmer, B., Arca, E. N. A., and Özdil, N. G. (eds.) 2016. *Vir Doctus Anatolicus: studies in memory of Sencer Sahin*. Istanbul.

Hegel, G. W. F. 2004. *Lectures on the philosophy of history*. Trans. J. Sibtree. Mineola, NY.

Hekster, O. 2001. 'All in the family: the appointment of emperors designate in the second century AD', in L. de Blois (ed.) *Administration, prosopography and appointment policies in the Roman empire*. Leiden: 35–49.

Hekster, O. 2002. *Commodus: an emperor at the crossroads*. Amsterdam.

Hekster, O. 2015. *Emperors and ancestors: Roman rulers and the constraints of tradition*. Oxford.

Hekster, O. 2017. 'Identifying tradition: Augustus and the constraint of formulating sole rule', *Politica Antica* 7, 47–60.

Hekster, O. 2020. 'Imperial justice? The absence of images of Roman emperors in a legal role', *Classical Quarterly* 70, 247–60.

Hekster, O. 2023. *Caesar rules: the emperor in the changing Roman world (c. 50 BC–AD 565)*. Cambridge.

Hellström, M. 2020. 'Local aspirations and statues of emperors in North Africa', in A. Russell and M. Hellström (eds.) *The social dynamics of Roman imperial imagery*. Cambridge: 159–79.

Hellström, M. and Russell, A. 2020. 'Introduction', in A. Russell and M. Hellström (eds.) *The social dynamics of Roman imperial imagery*. Cambridge: 1–24.

Henderson, J. 2001. *Telling tales on Caesar: Roman stories from Phaedrus*. Oxford.

Henderson, J. 2002. 'Knowing someone through their books: Pliny on Uncle Pliny ("Epistles" 3.5)', *Classical Philology* 97, 256–84.

Henrichs, A. 1968. 'Vespasian's visit to Alexandria', *Zeitschrift für Papyrologie und Epigraphik* 3, 51–80.

Herklotz, F. 2007. *Prinzeps und Pharao: der Kult des Augustus in Ägypten*. Frankfurt.

Herz, P. 2005. 'Caesar and God: recent publications on Roman imperial cult', *Journal of Roman Archaeology* 18, 638–48.

Herz, P. 2007. 'Emperors: caring for the empire and their successors', in J. Rüpke (ed.) *A companion to Roman religion*. Oxford: 304–16.

Herz, Z. 2020. 'Precedential reasoning and dynastic self-fashioning in the rescripts of Severus Alexander', *Historia* 69, 103–25.

Hobsbawm, E. J. 1972. *Bandits*. Harmondsworth.

Hodgson, L. 2017. *Res publica and the Roman republic: 'without body or form'*. Oxford.

Hölkeskamp, K.-J. 2010. *Reconstructing the Roman republic: an ancient political culture and modern research*. Princeton, NJ.

Honoré, T. 1994. *Emperors and lawyers*. Oxford.

Hopkins, K. 1978a. *Conquerors and slaves*. Cambridge.

Hopkins, K. 1978b. 'Rules of evidence', *Journal of Roman Studies* 68, 178–86.

Horden, P. and Purcell, N. 2000. *The corrupting sea: a study of Mediterranean history*. Oxford.

Horsfall, N. 1997. 'Criteria for the dating of Calpurnius Siculus', *Rivista di filologia e di istruzione classica* 125, 166–95.

Horsfall, N. 2003. *The culture of the Roman plebs*. London.

Houston, G. W. 1992. 'What uses might Roman farmers have made of the loans they received in the Alimenta program', *Rivista Storica dell'Antichità* 22, 97–105.

Howgego, C. J. 2005. 'Coinage and identity in the Roman provinces', in C. J. Howgego, V. Heuchert, and A. Burnett (eds.) *Coinage and identity in the Roman provinces*. Oxford: 1–17.

Howgego, C. J., Heuchert, V., and Burnett, A. (eds.) 2005. *Coinage and identity in the Roman provinces*. Oxford.

Huet, V. 2004. 'Images et *damnatio memoriae*', *Cahiers du Centre Gustave Glotz* 15, 237–53.

Hurlet, F. 1997. *Les collègues du prince sous Auguste et Tibère: de la légalité républicaine à la légitimité dynastique*. Rome.

Hurlet, F. 2001. 'Les auspices d'Octavien/Auguste', *Cahiers du Centre Gustave Glotz*, 12, 155–80.

Hurlet, F. 2020. 'The *Auctoritas* and *Libertas* of Augustus: metamorphosis of the Roman *Res Publica*', in C. Balmaceda, (ed.) *Libertas and res publica in the Roman republic: ideas of freedom and Roman politics*. Leiden: 170–88.

Hurlet, F. and Mineo, B. (eds.) 2009. *Le principat d'Auguste: réalités et représentations du pouvoir autour de la* res publica restituta. Rennes.

Israelowich, I. 2012. *Society, medicine and religion in the sacred tales of Aelius Aristides*. Leiden.

Jacques, F., Scheid, J., and Lepelley, C. 1990. *Rome et l'intégration de l'Empire: 44 av. J.-C.-260 apr. J.-C*. Paris.

Jasnow, B. 2015. 'Germanicus, Nero and the Incognito King in Tacitus' Annals 2.13 and 13.25', *Classical Journal* 110, 313–31.

Jehne, M. 1995. *Demokratie in Rom? die Rolle des Volkes in der Politik der römischen Republik*. Stuttgart.

Johnston, A. C. 2017. *The sons of Remus: identity in Roman Gaul and Spain.* Cambridge, MA.

Jones, C. 2000. 'The emperor and the giant', *Classical Philology* 95, 476–81.

Jones, C. P. 2001. 'The Claudian Monument at Patara', *Zeitschrift für Papyrologie und Epigraphik* 137, 161–8.

Jones, K. R. 2011. *Jewish reactions to the destruction of Jerusalem in A.D. 70: apocalypses and related pseudepigrapha.* Leiden and Boston, MA.

Jördens, A. 2020. '*Aequmm et iustum*: on dealing with the law in the province of Egypt', in K. Czajkowski, B. Eckhardt, and M. Strothmann (eds.) *Law in the Roman provinces.* Oxford: 19–31.

Kahane, A. 2022. 'Homer and ancient narrative time', *Classical Antiquity* 41, 1–50.

Kajanto, I. 1981. 'Fortuna', *ANRW*, II.17.1, 502–58.

Kaldellis, A. 2015. *The Byzantine republic: people and power in New Rome.* Cambridge, MA.

Kantiréa, M. 2008. 'Le culte impérial à Chypre: relecture des documents épigraphiques' *Zeitschrift für Papyrologie und Epigraphik* 167, 91–112.

Kantiréa, M. 2014. 'Reconstituer l'histoire grecque sous l'Empire: à propos de l'asile au temps de Tibère (Tacite, *Annales* 3, 60–64 et 4, 14, 1–2)', *Latomus* 73, 415–38.

Kantor, G. 2013. 'Law in Roman Phrygia: rules and jurisdictions', in P. Thonemann (ed.) *Roman Phrygia: culture and society.* Cambridge: 143–67.

Kantor, G. 2015. 'Greek law under the Romans', in E. H. Harris and M. Canevaro (eds.) *The Oxford handbook of ancient Greek law.* Oxford: 1–25.

Kantor, G. 2020. 'Navigating Roman law and local privileges in Pontus-Bithynia', in K. Czajkowski, B. Eckhardt, and M. Strothmann (eds.) *Law in the Roman provinces.* Oxford: 185–209.

Kantorowicz, E. H. 1997. *The king's two bodies.* Princeton, NJ.

Kaster, R. A. 2016. *Studies on the text of Suetonius' De uita Caesarum.* Oxford.

Kelly, G. 2013a. 'Pliny and Symmachus', *Arethusa* 46, 261–87.

Kelly, G. 2013b. 'The political crisis of AD 375–376', *Chiron* 43, 357–410.

Kemezis, A. M. 2014. *Greek narratives of the Roman empire under the Severans: Cassius Dio, Philostratus and Herodian.* Cambridge.

Kemezis, A. M. 2021. '*Vox populi, vox mea*? Information, evaluation and public opinion in Dio's account of the principate', in C. Davenport and C. Mallan (eds.) *Emperors and political culture in Cassius Dio's Roman history.* Cambridge: 33–51.

Kneebone, E. 2020. *Oppian's* Halieutica: *charting a didactic epic.* Cambridge.

Kokkinos, N. 1993. *The Herodian dynasty: origins, role in society and eclipse (2nd century BC to 2nd century AD).* Sheffield.

König, A., Langlands, R., and Uden, J. (eds.) 2020. *Literature and culture in the Roman empire 96–235: cross-cultural interactions.* Cambridge.

König, A. and Whitton, C. (eds.) 2018. *Roman literature under Nerva, Trajan and Hadrian: literary interactions, AD 96–138.* Cambridge.

König, J. and Wiater, N. (eds.) 2022. *Late Hellenistic Greek literature in dialogue.* Cambridge.

Kornemann, E. 1930. *Doppelprinzipat und Reichsteilung im Imperium Romanum.* Leipzig and Berlin.

Kosmin, P. J. 2018. *Time and its adversaries in the Seleucid empire.* Cambridge, MA, and London.

Kragelund, P. 1982. *Prophecy, populism, and propaganda in the Octavia.* Copenhagen.

Kragelund, P. 2002. 'Historical drama in ancient Rome: republican flourishing and imperial decline', *Symbolae Osloenses* 77, 5–51.

Kristensen, T. M. 2013. *Making and breaking the Gods: Christian responses to pagan sculpture in late antiquity.* Aarhus.

Kröss, K. 2017. *Die politische Rolle der stadtrömischen Plebs in der Kaiserzeit.* Leiden.

Kruse, M. 2019. *The politics of Roman memory: from the fall of the Western empire to the age of Justinian.* Philadelphia, PA.

Kugelmeier, C. 2019. 'The interaction between 'history' and 'story' in Roman historiography: the rhetorical construction of the historical image of Nero', *Church, Communication and Culture* 4, 255–65.

Kuhn, A. B. (ed.) 2016. *Social status and prestige in the Graeco-Roman world.* Stuttgart.

Kuhn, C. T. (ed.) 2012a. *Politische Kommunikation und öffentliche Meinung in der antiken Welt.* Stuttgart.

Kuhn, C. T. 2012b. 'Politische Kommunikation und Öffentliche Meinung in der Antike Welt: Einleitende Bemerkungen', in C. T. Kuhn (ed.) *Politische Kommunikation und öffentliche Meinung in der antiken Welt.* Stuttgart: 11–30.

Kurke, L. 2011. *Aesopic conversations: popular tradition, cultural dialogue, and the invention of Greek prose.* Princeton, NJ and Oxford.

Kuttner, A. L. 1995. *Dynasty and empire in the age of Augustus: the case of the Boscoreale Cups.* Berkeley, CA, and Oxford.

Lange, C. H. 2019. 'For Rome or for Augustus? Triumphs beyond the imperial family in the post-civil-war period', in K. Morrell, J. Osgood, and K. Welch (eds.) *The alternative Augustan age.* Oxford: 113–29.

Laurence, R. and Paterson, J. 1999. 'Power and laughter: imperial dicta', *Papers of the British School at Rome* 67, 183–97.

Lauro, M. G. (ed.) 1998. *Castelporziano III: campagne di scavo e restauro 1987–1991.* Rome.

Lavan, M. 2013. *Slaves to Rome: paradigms of empire in Roman culture.* Cambridge.

Lavan, M. 2016. 'The spread of Roman citizenship, 14–212 CE: quantification in the face of high uncertainty', *Past & Present* 230, 3–46.

Lavan, M. 2018. 'Pliny *Epistles* 10 and imperial correspondence: the empire of letters', in A. König and C. Whitton (eds.) *Roman literature under Nerva, Trajan and Hadrian: literary interactions, AD 96–138.* Cambridge: 280–301.

Lavan, M. 2019. 'The army and the spread of Roman citizenship', *Journal of Roman Studies* 109, 17–69.

Lavan, M. 2020. 'Beyond Romans and others: identities in the long second century', in König, A., Langlands, R., and Uden, J. (eds.) *Literature and culture in the Roman empire 96–235: cross-cultural interactions.* Cambridge: 37–57.

Leigh, M. 2013. *From* polypragmon *to* curiosus*: ancient concepts of curious and meddlesome behaviour.* Oxford.

Lendon, J. E. 1997. *Empire of honour: the art of government in the Roman world.* Oxford.

Lenski, N. 2016. *Constantine and the cities: imperial authority and civic politics.* Philadelphia, PA.

Leon, D. W. 2021. *Arrian the historian: writing the Greek past in the Roman empire.* Austin, TX.

Levick, B. 1967. 'Imperial control of the elections under the early principate: *commendatio, suffragatio,* and nominatio', *Historia* 16, 207–30.

Levick, B. 1975. 'Primus, Murena, and "Fides": notes on Cassius Dio LIV.3', *Greece & Rome* 22, 156–63.

Levick, B. 1990. *Claudius.* London.

Levick, B. 1999. *Tiberius the politician.* London.

Levick, B. 2010. *Augustus: image and substance.* Harlow.

Levick, B. 2013. 'In the Phrygian mode: a region seen from without', in P. Thonemann, (ed.) *Roman Phrygia: culture and society.* Cambridge: 41–54.

Lewis, N. 1991. 'Hadriani Sententiae', *Greek, Roman and Byzantine Studies* 32, 267–80.

Lewis, N. and Reinhold, M. 1990. *Roman Civilization* II. New York, 3rd ed.

Lightfoot, J. L. 2007. *The Sibylline Oracles: with introduction, translation, and commentary on the first and second books.* Oxford.

Lintott, A. 1993. Imperium Romanum: *politics and administration.* London.

Lobur, J. A. 2008. *Consensus, concordia, and the formation of Roman imperial ideology.* New York and London.

Lomas, K. and Cornell, T. (eds.) 2003. *Bread and circuses: euergetism and municipal patronage in Roman Italy.* London.

Long, A. A. 2002. *Epictetus: a Stoic and Socratic guide to life.* Oxford.

Lott, J. B. 2012. *Death and dynasty in early imperial Rome: key sources, with text, translation, and commentary.* Cambridge.

Lowe, K. 2013. 'Memoriae Eximere: AD 41 and the survival of republicanism under the principate', in A. Powell (ed.) *Hindsight in Greek and Roman history.* Swansea: 201–21.

Lozano, F. 2017. 'Emperor worship and Greek leagues: the organization of supra-civic imperial cult in the Roman East', in E. Muñiz Grijalvo, J. M. Cortés Copete, and F. Lozano Gomez (eds.) *Empire and religion: religious change in Greek cities under Roman rule.* Leiden: 149–76.

Luce, T. J. and Woodman, A. J. (eds.) 1993. *Tacitus and the Tacitean tradition.* Princeton, NJ.

Luke, T. S. 2010. 'A healing touch for empire: Vespasian's wonders in Domitianic Rome', *Greece & Rome* 57, 77–106.

Luraghi, N. 2014. 'The cunning tyrant: the cultural logic of a narrative pattern,' in A. Moreno and R. Thomas (eds.) *The cunning tyrant: the cultural logic of a narrative pattern.* Oxford: 67–92.

MacLean, R. 2018. *Freed slaves and Roman imperial culture: social integration and the transformation of values.* Cambridge.

MacMullen, R. 1966. *Enemies of the Roman order: treason, unrest, and alienation in the Empire*. Cambridge, MA, and London.

Madsen, J. M. 2016. 'Criticising the benefactors: the Severans and the return of dynastic rule', in J. M. Madsen and C. H. Lange (eds.). *Cassius Dio: Greek intellectual and Roman politician*. Leiden: 136–58.

Madsen, J. M. and Lange, C. H. (eds.). 2016. *Cassius Dio: Greek intellectual and Roman politician*. Leiden.

Magdelain, A. 1947. *Auctoritas principis*. Paris.

Magdelain, A. 1990. 'De l'"auctoritas partum" à l'"auctoritas senatus"', *Publications de l'École Française de Rome* 133, 385–403.

Makhlaiuk, A. 2020. 'Emperors' nicknames and Roman political humour' *Klio* 102, 202–35.

Malik, S. 2019. '*Cvcvta ab rationibvs neronis avgvsti*: a joke at Nero's expense', *Classical Quarterly* 69, 783–92.

Malik, S. 2020. *The Nero-Antichrist*. Cambridge.

Mantovani, D. 2008 '"*Leges et iura p (opuli) R (omani) restituit*": principe e diritto in un aureo di Ottaviano' *Athenaeum* 96, 5–54.

Marastoni, S., Mastrocinque, A., and Poletti, B. (eds.) 2011. *Hereditas, adoptio e potere politico in Roma antica*. Rome.

Marincola, J. 1997. *Authority and tradition in ancient historiography*. Cambridge.

Martin, B. 1996. 'Calpurnius Siculus 'New' *Aurea Aetas*', *Acta Classica* 39, 17-38.

Mastrocinque, A. 2011a. 'L'Eredità come Strumento di Legittimazione di Diritti Politici. Introduzione al Problema', in S. Marastoni, A. Mastrocinque, and B. Poletti (eds.) *Hereditas, adoptio e potere politico in Roma antica*. Rome: 1–14.

Mastrocinque, A. 2011b. 'L'Eredità Politica al Tempo dei Severi', in S. Marastoni, A. Mastrocinque, and B. Poletti (eds.) *Hereditas, adoptio e potere politico in Roma antica*. Rome: 71–83.

Matthews, J. 2010. *Roman perspectives: studies in political and cultural history, from the first to the fifth century*. Swansea.

Mattingly, D. J. 2011. *Imperialism, power, and identity: experiencing the Roman empire*. Princeton, NJ.

Mayer, R. 1980. 'Calpurnius Siculus: technique and date', *Journal of Roman Studies* 70, 175–6.

McCormick, M. 1986. *Eternal victory: triumphal rulership in late antiquity, Byzantium, and the early medieval West*. Cambridge and Paris.

McIntyre, G. 2019. 'Imperial cult', *Brill Research Perspectives in Ancient History* 2, 1–88.

McNamara, J. and Pagán, V. E. (eds.) 2022. *Tacitus' wonders: empire and paradox in ancient Rome*. London.

Millar, F. 1963. 'The fiscus in the first two centuries', *Journal of Roman Studies* 53, 29–42.

Millar, F. 1964a. *A study of Cassius Dio*. Oxford.

Millar, F. 1964b. 'The Aerarium and its officials under the empire', *Journal of Roman Studies* 54, 33–40.

Millar, F. 1965. 'Epictetus and the imperial court', *Journal of Roman Studies* 55, 141–8.

Millar, F. 1977. *The emperor in the Roman world (31 B.C.–A.D. 337)*. London.

Millar, F. 1988. 'Imperial ideology in the *Tabula Siarensis*', in J. Arce and J. González Fernández (eds.) *Estudios sobre la 'Tabula Siarensis'*. Madrid: 11–19.

Millar, F. 1993. 'Ovid and the *domus Augusta*: Rome seen from Tomoi', *Journal of Roman Studies* 83, 1–17.

Millar, F. 1998. *The crowd in Rome in the late Republic*. Ann Arbor, MI.

Millar, F. 2002. *Rome, the Greek world, and the East: the Roman republic and the Augustan revolution*. Chapel Hill, NC; London.

Millar, F. and Giovannini, A. (eds.) 2000. *La révolution romaine après Ronald Syme: bilans et perspectives*. Geneva.

Millar, F. and Segal, E. (eds.) 1984. *Caesar Augustus: seven aspects*. Oxford.

Miller, J. F. 2009. *Apollo, Augustus, and the poets*. Cambridge.

Mitchell, L. 2013. *The heroic rulers of Archaic and classical Greece*. London and New York.

Mitchell, S. 1993. *Anatolia: land, men, and Gods in Asia Minor*. 2 vols. Oxford.

Mitchell, S. 2016. 'ΕΡΜΗΝΕΙΑ: the Greek translations of the *sacrae litterae* on official hospitality (AD 204)', in Y. Hazirlayanlar, B. Takmer, E. N. A. Arca, and N. G. Özdil (eds.) *Vir Doctus Anatolicus: studies in memory of Sencer Sahin*. Istanbul: 635–9.

Mitford, T. B. 1947. 'Some published inscriptions of Roman date from Cyprus', *Annual of the British School at Athens* 42, 201–30.

Mitford, T. B. 1960. 'A Cypriot oath of allegiance to Tiberius', *Journal of Roman Studies* 50, 75–9.

Morgan, T. 2007. *Popular morality in the early Roman Empire*. Cambridge.

Morgan, T. 2015. *Roman faith and Christian faith:* pistis *and* fides *in the early Roman empire and early churches*. Oxford.

Moreno, A. and Thomas, R. (eds.) 2014. *The cunning tyrant: the cultural logic of a narrative pattern*. Oxford.

Morrell, K., Osgood, J., and Welch, K. (eds.) 2019. *The alternative Augustan age*. Oxford.

Morstein-Marx, R. 2004. *Mass oratory and political power in the late Roman republic*. Cambridge.

Morstein-Marx, R. 2021. *Julius Caesar and the Roman people*. Cambridge.

Mossman, J. (ed.) 1997. *Plutarch and his intellectual world*. Swansea.

Mouritsen, H. 2017. *Politics in the Roman republic*. Cambridge.

Muñiz Grijalvo, E., Cortés Copete, J. M., and Lozano Gomez, F. (eds.) 2017. *Empire and religion: religious change in Greek cities under Roman rule*. Leiden.

Murphy, T. M. 2004. *Pliny the Elder's Natural history: the empire in the encyclopedia*. Oxford and New York.

Murray, O. 1971. '*Peri basileias*: studies in the justification of monarchic power in the Hellenistic world.' Unpublished DPhil thesis, University of Oxford.

Musurillo, H. 1954. *The acts of the pagan martyrs: Acta Alexandrinorum*. Oxford.

Naylor, M. 2010. 'The Roman imperial cult and revelation', *Currents in Biblical Research* 8, 207–39.

Newlands, C. 2002. *Statius' Silvae and the poetics of empire*. Cambridge.

Nikolaides, A. (ed.) 2008. *The unity of Plutarch's work*. Berlin.

Nicolet, C. 1980. *The world of the citizen in republican Rome*. London.

Nicolet, C. 1991. *Space, geography, and politics in the early Roman empire*. Ann Arbor, MI.

Niehoff, M. 2018. *Philo of Alexandria: an intellectual biography*. New Haven, CT.

Nock, A. D. 1930. 'Σύνναος θεός', *Harvard Studies in Classical Philology* 41, 1–62.

Nollé, J. 1989. 'Hans von Aulock, Münzen und Städte Phrygiens 2', *Bonner Jahrbücher* 189, 657–60.

Nora, P. 1989. 'Between memory and history: les lieux de mémoire', *Representations* 26, 7–24.

Noreña, C. 2021. 'Emperors, benefaction and honorific practice in the Roman imperial Greek polis', in M. D. Gygax and A. Zuiderhoek (eds.) *Benefactors and the polis: the public gift in the Greek cities from the Homeric world to late antiquity*. Cambridge: 201–21.

Noreña, C. F. 2001. 'The communication of the emperor's virtues', *Journal of Roman Studies* 91, 146–68.

Noreña, C. F. 2003. 'Medium and message in Vespasian's *Templum Pacis*', *Memoirs of the American Academy in Rome* 48, 25–43.

Noreña, C. F. 2007. 'The social economy of Pliny's correspondence with Trajan', *American Journal of Philology* 135, 239–77.

Noreña, C. F. 2011. *Imperial ideals in the Roman West: representation, circulation, power*. Cambridge.

North, J. A. 1986. 'Religion and politics, from Republic to principate', *Journal of Roman Studies* 76, 251–8.

Nutton, V. 1978. 'The beneficial ideology', in P. Garnsey and C. R. Whittaker (eds.) *Imperialism in the ancient world*. Cambridge: 209–21.

O'Gorman, E. 2000. *Irony and misreading in the Annals of Tacitus*. Cambridge.

O'Gorman, E. 2006. 'Alternate empires: Tacitus's virtual history of the Pisonian principate', *Arethusa* 39, 281–301.

Oliver, J. H. 1971. 'Epaminondas of Acraephia', *Greek, Roman and Byzantine Studies* 12, 221–37.

Oliver, J. H. 1989. *Greek constitutions of early Roman emperors from inscriptions and papyri*. Philadelphia, PA.

Omissi, A. 2018. *Emperors and usurpers in the later Roman empire: civil war, panegyric, and the construction of legitimacy*. Oxford.

Osanna, M. 2018. 'Games, banquets, handouts, and the population of Pompeii as deduced from a new tomb inscription', *Journal of Roman Archaeology* 31, 310–22.

Osgood, J. 2011. *Claudius Caesar: image and power in the early Roman empire*. Cambridge.

Osgood, J. 2013. 'Suetonius and the accession to Augustus', in A. G. G. Gibson (ed.) *The Julio-Claudian succession: reality and perception of the "Augustan model"*. Leiden: 19–40.

Padilla Peralta, D. 2020. 'Epistemicde: the Roman case', *Classica: Revista Brasileira de Estudos Classicos* 33, 151–86.

Pagé, M.-M. 2012. *Empereurs et aristocrates bienfaiteurs: autour de l'inauguration des alimenta dans le monde municipal italien (fin Iᵉʳ siècle – début IVᵉ siècle)*. Quebec.

Pappano, A. E. 1937. 'The false Neros', *Classical Journal* 32, 385–92.

Pani, M. 1997. *La politica in Roman antica. Cultura e prassi*. Bari.

Pasco-Pranger, M. 2006. *Founding the year: Ovid's Fasti and the poetics of the Roman calendar*. Leiden.

Patterson, J. R. 1987. 'Crisis: what crisis? Rural change and urban development in imperial Appennine Italy', *Papers of the British School at Rome* 55, 115–46.

Pecere, O. and Stramaglia, A. (eds.) 1996. *La letteratura di consumo nel mondo greco-latino*. Cassino.

Pelling, C. 1983. 'Cassius Dio und Augustus. Philologische Untersuchungen zu den Büchern 45–56 des Dionischen Geschichtswerkes', *Gnomon* 53, 221–6.

Pelling, C. 1993. 'Tacitus and Germanicus', in T. J. Luce and A. J. Woodman (eds.) *Tacitus and the Tacitean tradition*. Princeton, NJ: 59–85.

Pelling, C. 1997. 'Biographical history? Cassius Dio on the early principate', in M. J. Edwards and S. Swain (eds.) *Portraits: biographical representation in the Greek and Latin literature of the Roman Empire*. Oxford: 197–213.

Pelling, C. 2009. 'Tacitus' personal voice', in A. J. Woodman (ed.) *The Cambridge companion to Tacitus*. Cambridge: 147–67.

Petsalis-Diomidis, A. 2010. *Truly beyond wonders: Aelius Aristides and the cult of Asklepios*. Oxford.

Plisecka, A. 2019. 'Material aspects of Severan legislation in the light of documentary papyri', in C. Ritter-Schmalz and R. Schwitter (eds.) *Antike Texte und ihre Materialität: Alltägliche Präsenz, mediale Semantik, literarische Reflexion*. Berlin: 287–308.

Potter, D. S. 1990. *Prophecy and history in the crisis of the Roman empire: a historical commentary on the Thirteenth Sibylline Oracle*. Oxford.

Potter, D. S. 1994. *Prophets and emperors: human and divine authority from Augustus to Theodosius*. Cambridge, MA, and London.

Powell, A. (ed.) 1992. *Roman poetry and propaganda in the age of Augustus*. London.

Powell, A. (ed.) 2013. *Hindsight in Greek and Roman history*. Swansea.

Price, J. J. and Berthelot, K. (eds.) 2020. *The future of Rome: Roman, Greek, Jewish and Christian visions*. Cambridge.

Price, S. R. F. 1980. 'Between man and god: sacrifice in the Roman imperial cult', *Journal of Roman Studies* 70, 28–43.

Price, S. R. F. 1984a. 'Gods and emperors: the Greek language of the Roman imperial cult', *Journal of Hellenic Studies* 104, 79–95.

Price, S. R. F. 1984b. *Rituals and power: the Roman imperial cult in Asia Minor*. Cambridge.

Price, S. R. F. 1986. 'The future of dreams: from Freud to Artemidorus', *Past & Present*, 113, 3–37.

Price, S. R. F. 1987. 'From noble funerals to divine cult: the consecration of Roman emperors', in D. Cannadine and S. R. F. Price (eds.) *Rituals of royalty: power and ceremonial in traditional societies*. Cambridge: 56–105.

Purcell, N. 1990. 'Maps, lists, money, order and power', *Journal of Roman Studies* 80, 178–82.

Purcell, N. 1994. 'The city of Rome and the *plebs urbana* in the late Republic', *CAH²* 9, 644–88.

Purcell, N. 1995. 'Eating fish: the paradoxes of seafood', in J. Wilkins, M. Dobson, and D. Harvey (eds.) *Food in antiquity.* Exeter: 132–50.

Purcell, N. 1996. 'Rome and its development under Augustus and his successors', *CAH²* 10: 782–811.

Purcell, N. 1998. 'Alla scoperta di una costa residenziale romana: il *litus Laurentinum* e l'archeologia dell'otium', in M. G. Lauro (ed.) *Castelporziano III: campagne di scavo e restauro 1987–1991.* Rome: 11–32.

Purcell, N. 1999. 'Does Caesar mime?', in B. A. Bergmann and C. Kondoleon (eds.) *The art of ancient spectacle.* Washington, DC, and New Haven, CT: 181–93.

Raaflaub, K., Toher, M., and Bowersock, G. (eds.) 1990. *Between republic and empire: interpretations of Augustus and his principate.* Berkeley, CA, and London.

Radice, B. 1968. 'Pliny and the *Panegyricus*', *Greece & Rome* 15, 166–72.

Rafferty, D. 2021. 'Rural voters in roman elections', *Transactions of the American Philological Association* 151, 127–53.

Rawson, B. (ed.) 1991. *Marriage, divorce, and children in ancient Rome.* Oxford.

Rees, R. 2001. 'To be and not to be: Pliny's paradoxical Trajan', *Bulletin of the Institute of Classical Studies* 45, 149–68.

Rees, R. 2002. *Layers of loyalty in Latin panegyric,* AD *289–307.* Oxford.

Revell, L. 2009. *Roman imperialism and local identities.* Cambridge.

Rich, J. 2012 'Making the emergency permanent: *auctoritas, potestas* and the evolution of the principate of Augustus', in Y. Rivière (ed.) *Des réformes augustéennes.* Rome: 37–121.

Rich, J. W. and Williams, J. H. C. 1999. '*Leges et Ivra PR Restitvit*: a new aureus of Octavian and the settlement of 28–27 BC', *Numismatic Chronicle* 159, 169-213.

Ritter-Schmalz, C. and Schwitter, R. (eds.) 2019. *Antike Texte und ihre Materialität: Alltägliche Präsenx, mediale Semantik, literarische Reflexion.* Berlin.

Rivière, Y. (ed.) 2012. *Des réformes augustéennes.* Rome.

Rizakis, A. D. and Camia, F. (eds.) 2008. *Pathways to power: civic elites in the eastern part of the Roman Empire.* Athens.

Rodríguez, G. 2021. 'New observations on the three arches of Benevento', in F. de Angelis (ed.) *Emperors in images, architecture, and ritual.* Boston, MA: 61–78.

Rogers, G. M. 1991. *The sacred identity of Ephesos: foundation myths of a Roman city.* London.

Rogers, G. M. 2012. *The mysteries of Artemis of Ephesos: cult, polis, and change in the Graeco-Roman world.* New Haven, CT, and London.

Rogers, R. S. 1955. 'Heirs and rivals to Nero', *Transactions of the American Philological Association* 86, 190–212.

Roller, M. 2001. *Constructing autocracy: aristocrats and emperors in Julio-Claudian Rome.* Princeton, NJ.

Roller, M. 2018. *Models from the past in Roman culture: a world of* exempla. Cambridge.

Romm, J. S. 1992. *The edges of the earth in ancient thought: geography, exploration, and fiction.* Princeton, NJ.

Rose, C. B. 1997. *Dynastic commemoration and imperial portraiture in the Julio-Claudian period.* Cambridge.

Rosenblitt, A. 2016. 'Hostile politics: Sallust and the rhetoric of popular champions in the Late Republic', *American Journal of Philology* 137, 655–88.

Rosillo-López, C. 2017. *Public opinion and politics in the late Roman Republic.* Cambridge.

Ross, D. O. 1973. 'The Tacitean Germanicus', *Yale Classical Studies* 23, 209–27.

Roueché, C. 1984. 'Acclamations in the later Roman empire: new evidence from Aphrodisias', *Journal of Roman Studies* 74, 181–99.

Rowan, C. 2019. *From Caesar to Augustus (c. 49* BC–AD *14): using coins as sources.* Cambridge.

Rowan, C. 2020. 'The imperial image in media of mechanical reproduction', in A. Russell and M. Hellström (eds.) *The social dynamics of Roman imperial imagery.* Cambridge: 247–74.

Rowe, C. K. 2009. *World upside down: reading Acts in the Graeco-Roman age.* Oxford.

Rowe, G. 2002. *Princes and political cultures: the new Tiberian senatorial decrees.* Ann Arbor, MI.

Rowe, G. 2013. 'Reconsidering the *auctoritas* of Augustus', *Journal of Roman Studies* 103, 1–15.

Rudich, V. 1993. *Political dissidence under Nero: the price of dissimulation.* London.

Rüfner, T. 2016. 'Imperial *cognitio* process', in P. du Plessis, C. Ando, and K. Tuori (eds.). *The Oxford handbook of Roman law and society.* Oxford: 257–69.

Rüpke, J. (ed.) 2007. *A companion to Roman religion.* Oxford.

Rüpke, J. 2011. *The Roman calendar from Numa to Constantine: time, history, and the fasti.* Oxford.

Russell, A. 2016. *The politics of public space in Republican Rome.* Cambridge.

Russell, A. 2019. 'Inventing the imperial Senate', in K. Morrell, J. Osgood, and K. Welch (eds.) *The alternative Augustan age.* Oxford: 325–42.

Russell, A. 2020. 'The altars of the *Lares Augusti*: a view from the streets of Augustan iconography', in A. Russell and M. Hellström (eds.) *The social dynamics of Roman imperial imagery.* Cambridge: 25–51.

Russell, A. and Hellström, M. (eds.) 2020. *The social dynamics of Roman imperial imagery.* Cambridge.

Russell, D. A. and Wilson, N. G. (eds.) 1981. *Menander Rhetor: a commentary.* Oxford.

Rutledge, S. 2001. *Imperial inquisitions: prosecutors and informants from Tiberius to Domitian.* London.

Rutledge, S. 2012. *Ancient Rome as a museum: power, identity, and the culture of collecting.* Oxford.

Ryberg, I. S. 1966. '*Clupeus Virtutis*', in L. Wallach (ed.) *The classical tradition: literary and historical studies in honor of Harry Caplan*. Ithaca, NY: 232–8.

Sailor, D. 2008. *Writing and empire in Tacitus*. Cambridge.

Saller, R. P. 1980. 'Anecdotes as historical evidence for the principate', *Greece & Rome* 27, 69–83.

Saller, R. P. 1984. '"Familia, Domus", and the Roman conception of the family', *Phoenix* 38, 336–55.

Saller, R. P. 1994. *Patriarchy, property and death in the Roman family*. Cambridge.

Salzman, M. R. 1991. *On Roman time: the codex-calendar of 354 and the rhythms of urban life in late antiquity*. Berkeley, CA.

Schäfer, T. 1989. *Imperii insignia: Sella curulis und Fasce: zur Repräsentation römischer Magistrate*. Mainz.

Scheid, J. 2003. *An introduction to Roman religion*. Bloomington, IN.

Schepens, G. and Delcroix, K. 1996. 'Ancient paradoxography: origin, evolution, production and reception', in O. Pecere and A. Stramaglia (eds.) *La letteratura di consumo nel mondo greco-latino*. Cassino: 373–460.

Schulz, F. 1945. 'Bracton on kingship', *The English Historical Review* 60, 136–76.

Scott, A. G. 2019. 'Cassius Dio and the Augustan settlement', *Histos* 13, lxvi–lxx.

Scott, J. C. 1985. *Weapons of the weak: everyday forms of peasant resistance*. New Haven, CT, and London.

Scott, J. C. 1990. *Domination and the arts of resistance: hidden transcripts*. New Haven, CT, and London.

Scott, K. 1930a. 'Drusus, nicknamed "Castor"', *Classical Philology* 25, 155–61.

Scott, K. 1930b. 'The Dioscuri and the imperial cult', *Classical Philology* 25, 379–80.

Severy, B. 2003. *Augustus and the family at the birth of the Roman empire*. New York and London.

Shannon-Henderson, K. 2022. 'Tacitus and paradoxography', in J. McNamara and V. E. Pagán (eds.) *Tacitus' wonders: empire and paradox in ancient Rome*. London: 17–51.

Shaw, B. D. 1982. 'Social science and ancient history: Keith Hopkins *In Partibus Infidelium*', *Helios* 9, 17–57.

Shaw, B. D. 1984. 'Bandits in the Roman empire', *Past & Present* 105, 3–52.

Shaw, B. D. 2019. 'Did the Romans have a future?', *Journal of Roman Studies* 109, 1–26.

Sherwin-White, A. N. 1963. *Roman society and Roman law in the New Testament*. Oxford.

Slater, W. J. (ed.) 1996. *Roman theater and society: E. Togo Salmon papers I*. Ann Arbor, MI.

Sluiter, I. and Rosen, R. M. 2004. *Free speech in classical antiquity*. Leiden.

Smith, C. J. 2006. *The Roman clan: the gens from ancient ideology to modern anthropology*. Cambridge.

Smith, R. R. R. 1987. 'The imperial reliefs from the Sebasteion at Aphrodisias', *Journal of Roman Studies* 77, 88–138.

Smith, R. R. R. 2013. *The marble reliefs from the Julio-Claudian Sebasteion*. Mainz.

Smolenaars, J. J. L. 1987. 'Labour in the golden age: a unifying theme in Vergil's poems', *Mnemosyne* 40, 391–405.

Sogno, C. 2006. *Q. Aurelius Symmachus: a political biography*. Ann Arbor, MI.

Stacey, P. 2014. 'The Princely Republic', *Journal of Roman Studies* 104, 133–154.

Starr, C. G. 1949. 'Epictetus and the tyrant', *Classical Philology* 44, 20–29.

Steffensen, N. 2018. *Nachdenken über Rom: literarische Konstruktionen der römischen Geschichte in der Formierungsphase des Principats*. Stuttgart.

Stern, S. 2010. 'A "Jewish" birth record, Sambat-, and the Calendar of Salamis', *Zeitschrift für Papyrologie und Epigraphik* 172, 105–14.

Stern, S. 2012. *Calendars in antiquity: empires, states, and societies*. Oxford.

Stern, S. (ed.) 2021. *Calendars in the making: the origins of calendars from the Roman empire to the later Middle Ages*. Leiden.

Stewart, C. 2019. 'Fractional arithmetic in the *Tabula Alimentaria* of Veleia', *Journal of Roman Studies* 109, 89–102.

Stewart, P. 2003. *Statues in Roman society: representation and response*. Oxford.

Straumann, B. 2016. *Crisis and constitutionalism: Roman political thought from the fall of the republic to the age of revolution*. Oxford.

Strauss, B. S. 1993. *Fathers and sons in Athens: ideology and society in the era of the Peloponnesian War*. London.

Sumi, G. S. 2002. 'Impersonating the dead: mimes at Roman funerals' *American Journal of Philology* 123, 559–85.

Syme, R. 1939. *The Roman revolution*. Oxford.

Syme, R. 1958. *Tacitus*. Oxford.

Syme, R. 1961. 'Who was Vedius Pollio?', *Journal of Roman Studies* 51, 23–30.

Syme, R. 1969. 'Pliny the procurator', *Harvard Studies in Classical Philology* 73, 201–36.

Syme, R. 1980. 'Biographers of the Caesars', *Museum Helveticum* 37, 104–28.

Tan, J. 2019. 'How do you solve a problem like Marcus Agrippa?', in K. Morrell, J. Osgood, and K. Welch (eds.) *The alternative Augustan age*. Oxford: 182–98.

Thom, J. 2009. 'Justice in the Sermon on the Mount: an Aristotelian reading', *Novum Testamentum* 51, 314–38.

Thonemann, P. (ed.) 2013. *Roman Phrygia: culture and society*. Cambridge.

Thonemann, P. 2020. *An ancient dream manual: Artemidorus' The Interpretation of Dreams*. Oxford.

Toner, J. P. 2009. *Popular culture in ancient Rome*. Cambridge.

Torelli, M. 1997. '"*Ex his castra, ex his tribus replebuntur*": the Marble Panegyric on the Arch of Trajan at Beneventum', *Studies in the History of Art*, 49, 144–77.

Townend, G. B. 1980. 'Calpurnius Siculus and the *Munus Neronis*', *Journal of Roman Studies* 70, 166–74.

Trédé-Boulmer, M. 2015. *Kairos: l'à-propos et l'occasion: le mot et la notion, d'Homère à la fin du IVᵉ siècle*. Paris.

Trentin, L. 2011. 'Deformity in the Roman imperial court', *Greece & Rome* 58, 195–208.

Tuori, K. 2016. *The emperor of law: the emergence of Roman imperial adjudication*. Oxford.

Turpin, W. 2008. 'Tacitus, Stoic *exempla*, and the *praecipuum munus annalium*', *Classical Antiquity* 27, 359–404.

Valente, W. A., Talbert, R. J. A, Hallett, J. P., and Mackowiak, P. A. 2002 'Caveat cenans', *The American Journal of Medicine* 112, 392–8.

Varner, E. R. 2004. *Mutilation and transformation:* damnatio memoriae *and Roman imperial portraiture*. Leiden and Boston, MA.

Vassileiou, A. 1984. 'Caius ou Lucius Caesar proclamé princeps iuuentutis par l'ordre équestre', in H. Walter (ed.) *Hommages à Lucien Lerat*. Paris: 827–40.

Versnel, H. S. 1970. *Triumphus: an inquiry into the origin, development and meaning of the Roman triumph*. Leiden.

Versnel, H. S. 1976. 'Two types of Roman *devotio*', *Mnemosyne* 29, 365–410.

Versnel, H. S. 1980. 'Destruction, *devotio* and despair in a situation of anomy: the mourning of Germanicus in triple perspective', in A. Brelich (ed.) *Perennitas: studi in onore di Angelo Brelich*. Rome: 541–618.

Versnel, H. S. 1993a. *Inconsistencies in Greek and Roman religion: transition and reversal in myth and ritual*. Leiden and New York.

Versnel, H. S. 1993b. 'Two carnivalesque princes: Augustus and Claudius and the ambiguity of Saturnalian imagery', in S. Döpp, (ed.) *Karnevaleske Phänomene in antiken und nachantiken Kulturen und Literaturen*. Trier: 99–122.

Vervaet, F. J. 2014. *The high command in the Roman republic: the principle of the* summum imperium auspiciumque *from 509 to 19 BCE*. Stuttgart.

Vervaet, F. J. 2020. '*Subsidia dominationi*: the early careers of Tiberius Claudius Nero and Nero Claudius Drusus revisited' *Klio* 102, 121–201.

Veyne, P. 1976. *Le pain et le cirque: sociologie historique d'un pluralisme politique*. Paris.

Veyne, P. 1988. *Did the Greeks believe in their myths? An essay on the constitutive imagination*. Chicago.

Veyne, P. 1990. *Bread and circuses: historical sociology and political pluralism*. London.

Veyne, P. 2002. 'Qu'était-ce qu'un empereur romain', *Diogène* 199, 3–25.

Wallace-Hadrill, A. 1981a. 'Galba's *aequitas*', *Numismatic Chronicle* 141, 20–39.

Wallace-Hadrill, A. 1981b. 'The emperor and his virtues', *Historia* 30, 298–323.

Wallace-Hadrill, A. 1982a. '*Civilis princeps*: between citizen and king', *Journal of Roman Studies* 72, 32–48.

Wallace-Hadrill, A. 1982b. 'The golden age and sin in Augustan ideology', *Past & Present* 95, 19–36.

Wallach, L. (ed.) 1966. *The classical tradition: literary and historical studies in honor of Harry Caplan*. Ithaca, NY.

Walter, H. (ed.) 1984. *Hommages à Lucien Lerat*. Paris.

Weaver, P. R. C. 1972. *Familia Caesaris: a social study of the emperor's freedmen and slaves*. Cambridge.

Webb, R. 2008. *Demons and dancers: performance in late antiquity*. Cambridge, MA, and London.

Weber, M. 1978. *Economy and society: an outline of interpretive sociology*. Berkeley, CA.

Weinstock, S. 1971. *Divus Julius*. Oxford.

Welch, K. E. 2007. *The Roman amphitheatre: from its origins to the Colosseum*. New York and Cambridge.

Whitton, C. 2015. 'Pliny's progress: on a troublesome Domitianic career', *Chiron* 45, 1–22.

Wilkins, J., Dobson, M., and Harvey, D. (eds.) 1995. *Food in antiquity*. Exeter.

Winterling, A. 2009. *Politics and society in imperial Rome*. Chichester.

Wintrobe, R. 1998. *The political economy of dictatorship*. Cambridge.

Wirszubski, C. 1950. *Libertas as a political idea at Rome during the late Republic and early principate*. Cambridge.

Wiseman, T. P. 1982 'Calpurnius Siculus and the Claudian Civil War', *Journal of Roman Studies*, 72, 57–67.

Wiseman, T. P. 2009. *Remembering the Roman people: essays on late-Republican politics and literature*. Oxford.

Wiseman, T. P. (ed.) 2013. *The death of Caligula: Josephus Ant. Jud. xix 1–273*. Liverpool.

Wiseman, T. P. 2019. *The house of Augustus: a historical detective story*. Princeton, NJ.

Wolf, J. G. 2011. *Die Lex Irnitana: ein römisches Stadtrecht aus Spanien: lateinisch und deutsch*. Darmstadt.

Woodman, A. J. 1992. 'Nero's alien capital: Tacitus as paradoxographer (*Annals* 15.36–7)', in A. J. Woodman and J. G. F. Powell (eds.) *Author and audience in Latin literature*. Cambridge: 173–88.

Woodman, A. J. 1998. *Tacitus reviewed*. Oxford.

Woodman, A. J. 2004. *Tacitus: The Annals. Translated, with introduction and notes*. Indianapolis.

Woodman, A. J. (ed.) 2009. *The Cambridge companion to Tacitus*. Cambridge.

Woodman, A. J. and Powell, J. G. F. (eds.) 1992. *Author and audience in Latin literature*. Cambridge.

Woolf, G. 1990. 'Food, poverty and patronage: the significance of the epigraphy of the Roman alimentary schemes in early imperial Italy', *Papers of the British School at Rome* 58, 197–228.

Woolf, G. 2015. 'Pliny/Trajan and the poetics of empire', *Classical Philology* 110, 132–51.

Wytzes, J. 1977. *Der letzte Kampf des Heidentums in Rom*. Leiden.

Yakobson, A. 1992. '*Petitio et largitio*: popular participation in the centuriate assembly of the late republic', *Journal of Roman Studies* 82, 32–52.

Yakobson, A. 2010. 'Traditional political culture and the people's role in the Roman republic' *Historia* 59, 282–302.

Yavetz, Z. 1965. '*Levitas popularis*', *Atene & Roma* 10, 99–110.

Yavetz, Z. 1969. *Plebs and princeps*. Oxford.

Yavetz, Z. 1990. 'The personality of Augustus: reflections on Syme's Roman revolution' in K. Raaflaub, M. Toher, and G. Bowersock (eds.) *Between republic and empire: interpretations of Augustus and his principate*. Berkeley, CA, and London: 21–41.

Zadorojnyi, A. V. 2015. 'Colour in Suetonius' *Lives of the Caesars*', in R. Ash, J. Mossman, and F. B. Titchener (eds.) *Fame and infamy: essays for Christopher Pelling on characterization in Greek and Roman biography and historiography.* Oxford: 286–98.

Zanker, P. 1987. *Augustus und die Macht der Bilder.* Munich.

Zanker, P. 1988. *The power of images in the age of Augustus.* Ann Arbor, MI.

Zuiderhoek, A. 2009. *The politics of munificence in the Roman empire: citizens, elites and benefactors in Asia Minor.* Cambridge.

Index

acceptance, 102–9
accessibility, 14, 16
   see also proximity
accountability, 13, 52, 57
Acta Alexandrinorum, 88–9, 93–4, 97
   Acta Appiani, 93, 97
   Acta Hermaisci, and Trajan, 91
   Acta Isidori, 89–91, 93
adjudication, 48–9
Aelius Caesar, L., 119
aequitas coinage, 68–70
afterlife, 228
Agamben, G., 234–5
Agamemnon, 85, 179–81
Agrippa Postumus (Agrippa Julius Caesar),
      225n215, 226–8
Agrippina the Elder, 14–15
Alexander III of Macedon, 97
Alexander Severus (M. Aurelius Severus
      Alexander), 78–9
Alexandria, 88, 89–93
   coinage, 69
   and Germanicus, 116
   and Vespasian, 171–2, 193–4
Alföldy, Geza, 16
alimenta scheme, 123–8
amici (friends), 129–30
amphitheatre, Flavian, 144–5
Ando, C., 54–6, 74n50
anecdotes, 24–8
Annia Rufilla, 81–3
annulment edicts, 37, 42
Antoninus Pius, 79–81, 127
Aphrodisias, Sebasteion, 140
Appian (gymnasiarch), 93
Apuleis, *Metamorphoses*, 96
Arch of Trajan (Benevento), 126–7, 130
Arrian, on statue of Hadrian, 75–6
Artemidorus, *Oneirocritica*, 83–5, 181
Ash, R., 174
Assos decree, 191

asylum, 72–3, 79–83
auctoritas, 29–30, 36–41
Augustine, *De Civitate Dei*, 97
Augustus, 6
   auctoritas, 29–30, 36–41
   benefaction, 115
   death of, 215–16
   divine image of, 72
   and the *domus Augusta*, 109–14
   fish story, 150
   leges et iura coin, 41–3
   as a monster, 155–6
   and natural oddities, 145–6
   and *pater patriae*, 43–5
   triumphal procession, 218
   wit of, 174–5
Aurelius Antonius, M., *see* Caracalla
Aurelius, Marcus
   in *Acta Appiani*, 93
   generosity of, 121–2, 127
   images of, 74
   letter from Fronto, 6
   letter to Ulpius Eurycles, 206
Aurelius Severus Alexander, M., *see* Alexander
      Severus

Babatha dossier, 123–4
Bakhtin, Mikhail, *Rabelais and His World*, 192–3
banditry, 94–8
Beard, Mary, 32, 163, 166, 167n29, 193
   Religions of Rome, 198
benefaction, 99–102, 115–20
Benevento, Arch of Trajan, 126–7
Bernard, Seth, 129
binary, good/bad, 166–8
birds
   Stymphalian, 156–7
   talking, 175–6
Bonner, S. F., 117
Bowersock, G., 138
bread, 126, 128–30

brigandage, 94–8
Britannicus (Tiberius Claudius Caesar
    Britannicus), 119, 223
Brunt, P., 53–4
Bulla Felix, 94–8

Caesar (term), 110–12
calendars, 182–3
Caligula *see* Gaius
Callistratus, 80–1, 82
Calpurnius Piso, Gn., 104
Calpurnius Siculus, 1, 2
canals, 147
Caracalla (Marcus Aurelius Antonius), 119
    Digest on *maiestas*, 77
Cassius Dio *see* Dio (Cassius)
Cervidius Scaevola, Q., *Regulae*, 76–7
Cestius, Gaius, 82–3
Champlin, Edward, 26–7, 177
charismatic authority, 4
Charlesworth, M. P., 9
Chrysippus, *On Laws*, 51–2
Chrysippus of Corinth, dream interpretation, 84
Cicero, on living according to law, 57
civilitas, 168–71
Claudius Drusus, Nero (Drusus the Elder), 116,
    204, 219, 220, 221, 225n215
Claudius Marcellus, Marcus, 219–20
Claudius (Tiberius Claudius Caesar Augustus
    Germanicus), 53, 89–91, 93, 106–7, 119
    crockery story, 173–4
    depiction on the Sebasteion in
        Aphrodisias, 140
    as monstrous, 194–5
    natural oddities, 146
    Secular Games, 223
    whale story, 150
Clemens, 226–8
cognitio extra ordinem, 62–3
coins/coinage
    leges et iura, 41–3
    and *princeps iuventutis*, 117–18
    and virtues depicted on, 67–71
collegiality, 105
commemoration, 204–7
Commodus, 93, 97, 118
    generosity, 119
    as gladiator, 213
    and Maternus, 224–5
    as monstrosity, 156–8
communication role, 7, 10, 34
comparability, 1
consensus, 101–9
    see also consent
consent, 4, 10, 38–9, 42–8

constitutionality, 33–5
    auctoritas, 36–41
    expectations, 43–8
    and the law, 48–58
    leges et iura coin, 41–3
Cooley, Alison, 30–1
Corbier, M., 112–13
Cortés Copete, J.M., 200
cult, imperial, 72–3
Cyprus, oath of allegiance to Tiberius, 113
Cyrenaica, 179–80

damnatio memoriae, 206–7
Davenport, C., 140
de Angelis, F., 217
de plano, 49–50
de Pury-Gysel, A., 72, 73
Dench, E., 141
devotion/*devotiones*, 196–203
'Dictator's Dilemma', 60–1, 161
Digest, 76, 77, 79–80, 88
dikaiosynē, 65, 69–71
Dio (Cassius), 50–3
    on banditry, 94–5, 97
    and Clemens, 227–8
    on Commodus, 156–8
    on the *Forum Augustum*, 217
    on Gaius/Caligula, 160–2, 165, 197
    on the Golden Age, 185n22, 186
    on *maiestas*, 78
    on Marcus Aurelius, 121–2
    on *pater patriae*, 110
    political life, 209
    and politics in writing history, 211–14
    tale of the inventor, 153
    on Vespasian, 168–72
display, of *mirabilia*, 140–5, 148
distance, and wonder tales, 134–7
divinity
    and Gaius/Caligula, 160–2, 237
    imperial cult, 196–203
Domitian
    commemoration of, 206–7
    and the Flavian triumph of AD 71, 143–4
    and flies, 170
    and natural oddities, 146
Domitius Ahenobarbus, L., *see* Nero (Nero
        Claudius Caesar)
domus Augusta, 15, 44, 109–14, 221–3
    and Piso, 104–5
domus (defined), 109
doubleness, x, 44–5, 236, 237
    and tales of wonder, 131, 142
    and time, 183
dreams, 83–5, 203–4, 212–13

Drusus the Elder *see* Claudius Drusus, Nero
Drusus Julius Caesar (Drusus the Younger), 82,
    104, 111, 116, 176
Duncan-Jones, R., 127–8

economy, 121–2, 124, 125
Elagabalus, 78–9, 147–8
elites/non-elites, 12, 18–19, 23–4, 83
    and humour, 161–6
Empona, 172
Ennius, L., 77
Epaminondas of Acraephia, 201–2
Epictetus
    Discourses, 163–4
    On Freedom, 20–3
euergetism, 99–101, 127, 191
Euphrates, 231
Euripides, 136

Fabius Maximus, Paullus, 183
fairness, 68–70
Fasolt, Constantin, *The Limits of History*, 208–9
festivals
    Hilaria, 224
    Saturnalia, 188
fictionality, 24–8
fish, 149–52
Flaig, E., 13, 61, 105–6, 108
Flavians
    amphitheatre, 144–5
    triumph of AD 71, 143–4
flies, and Domitian, 170
Flower, H.I.204–5, 218
focalisation, 165
food distribution scheme, *alimenta*, 123–8
formal/informal, 14, 37–8, 66–7, 105
Forsdyke, S., 96
Fortuna, 220–1
forum, 116–17
Forum Augustum, 216–18
freakishness, 141, 157–8
freedom, Epictetus on, 20–1
friends (*amici*), 129–30
Fronto, 7
    de eloquentia, 90, 154
    imperial images, 74
    letter to Marcus Aurelius, 6
future *see* imperial future

Gaius (Caligula), 106–7, 115, 190–4
    and fish tale, 150
    and the Gaulish shoemaker, 160–2, 165, 166–7
    illness of, 196–7
    and the Jewish delegation, 91–2, 237
Galinsky, K., 40

Garland, R., 158
Gellius, Aulus, tales of wonder, 138, 145
generosity
    heirs and benefaction, 115–20
    in politics, 99–102
    as princeps, 120–30
    in succession, 102–9
        Domus Augusta, 109–14
Germanicus (Germanicus Iulius Caesar), 14–15,
    104, 115–16
    and the *Domus Augusta*, 111–12
    incognito, 61
    and the talking bird, 176
    triumph, 219–23
Germanicus (grandson of Tiberius), 114
Geta (Publius Septimius Geta), 118, 119
giants, 145–6
glass, unbreakable, 152–3
Gleason, M., 94, 211
'go to the crows', 169–70
Golden Age, 184, 185–96
graffiti, 17–18, 113
Griffin, Miriam, 14
Gruen, E. S., 229–30

Habermas, J., 17
Hadrian
    generosity, 119
    and the *Hadriani Sententiae*, 86–8
    and the old woman anecdote, 27–8
    personality traits of, 25
    statue of, 75–6
    and taxation, 189–90
Hadriani Sententiae, 86–8, 123–4
Hadrianus (Montserrat Codex), 189–90
Hardie, P. R., 110–11
Harker, A., 93
Hegel, G. W. F., *The Philosophy of History*, 236–7
heirs, 115–20
Hekster, O., 67–9, 106
    Emperors and Ancestors, 9–10
Hellström, M., 73, 75
Helvius, Lucius, 118
Herodian, 235
    on Maternus, 224–5
    political life, 209–10
Herz, P., 199
Hesiod, *Works and Days*, 187
hidden transcripts, 20, 160–6, 177–9
hierarchy, social, 16, 23
Historia Augusta
    on Commodus, *maiestas*, 78
    on Elagabalus, 147–8
    maiestas, 78–9
    on Hadrian, 25

historiography, 207–18
Hobsbawm, Eric, *Bandits*, 95
Hopkins, Keith, 32–3, 80
humour
    dangers of making fun of the emperor, 168–78
    emperors as good or bad, 166–8
    political, 17–18
    public/hidden transcripts, 160–6

imperial cult, 196–203
imperial future, 184–5, 224–32
imperial past, 184, 203–19
imperial present, 184, 185–96
    and imperial cult, 196–203
imperium, and Augustus, 36–40
impersonations/imposters of emperors, 225–6,
        231–2
    Clemens, 226–8
    Maternus, 224–5
informal *see* formal/informal
Isidorus (gymnasiarch), 89–90, 93
Iulia Agrippina *see* Agrippina the Elder
iustitia coinage, 68

Jewish people, 193–4, 230
    and fictional accounts of justice, 88–93
    and the Jewish War, 143–4
Josephus, and the Flavian triumph of AD 71,
        143–4
Julius Caesar, Agrippa *see* Agrippa Postumus
        (Agrippa Julius Caesar)
Julius Caesar, Gaius, 115
    as *princeps iuventutis*, 117–19
justice, 62–5
    and coinage, 67–71
    fictional accounts of, 83–98
    and images, 71–3
    in statuary, 73–83
    and tales of wonder, 132
    and virtues, 65–7
    see also mediators
Justinian, *Institute*, 57
Juvenal, 151

Kantorowicz, E. H., 235
Kronos, 188, 191–2
Kuhn, Christina, 17

Laurence, R., 174
law, 48–58
league cults, 200
leges et iura coin, 41–3
legibus vivere (to live according to the laws), 57–8
legitimacy, 105–9
Lex de Imperio Vespasiani, 53–8

Lex Iulia Maiestatis, 76
Life of Caracalla, on maiestas, 78
Life of Kronos, 191–3
liminality, 1–2, 3, 5
live according to the law, 57–8
Lozano Gomez, F., 200
Lucius Caesar, 115
    as *princeps iuventutis*, 117–18

Macrobius
    Saturnalia, Augustus, 174–5
    on Trajan, 147
maiestas, 76–9, 165–6
Malik, S., 17–18
Marcellus *see* Claudius Marcellus, Marcus
marine life, 149–52
Mars Ultor (temple), 217
Martial, *Liber Spectaculorum*, 136–7, 144
Maternus, 224–5
mediators, 16, 28, 142–3, 152–3
memory, 204–19
Menander Rhetor, 132
Menogenes, 112
Millar, Fergus, 11, 27–8, 31–3, 34
    The Emperor in the Roman World, 234
Minotaur, 136–7
mints, imperial, 68–9
mirabilia see wonder tales
Mitchell, S., 70
Modestinus, 88
Mommsen, Theodor, 29, 38
monsters
    Claudius as, 194–5
    fish as, 151–2
monstrosity, emperors', 153–9
morality, *mirabilia*, 139, 149
Morgan, T., 176–7
munera, 100–1, 122–3
Muñiz Grijalvo, E., 200

natural law, 51–2, 57
natural oddities, 145–9
negative memory, 206–7
Nero (Nero Claudius Caesar), 119, 223
    depiction on the Sebasteion in
        Aphrodisias, 140
    divorce, 162–3
    and natural oddities, 146, 148
    in the *Sibylline Oracles*, 229–31
Nikon, 85
Noreña, C. F., 65–6, 101, 120
North, J., *Religions of Rome*, 198

Octavia, 162–3
Octavian *see* Augustus

oddities, natural, 145–7
O'Gorman, E., 220
Ovid, 53
  use of term Caesar, 110–12

Papinian (prefect), 97
paradoxography, 134–42
parricide, 87–8
Pasiphaë, 137
past *see* imperial past
pater patriae, and Augustus, 43–5, 109–10
Paterson, J., 174
patrons, 142–9
Pausanias
  on Augustus, 145
  on canal, 147
Pelling, C., 52, 207, 215
Petronius, unbreakable glass tale, 152
Phaedrus, 176–7
Philo Judaeus
  Legatio ad Gaium, 91–3, 190–4
    celebrations following accession of Gaius/
      Caligula, 187
    on illness of Gaius/Caligula, 196–7
Phlegon of Tralles, 146, 147
Phoebus, 169–70
plebs, 12, 13–16
Pliny the Elder
  as historian, 203–5
  Natural History, 140–1
    bird story, 176
    fish tales, 150, 151
    paradoxography, 138, 146
    unbreakable glass tale, 152–3
  on tales of wonder, 145
Pliny the Younger
  effigy of Trajan, 72
  on memory and time, 210
  Panegyricus, 46–7, 58
  on Pliny the Elder, 203–4
  on Trajan's food distribution scheme, 124–6
Plisecka, A., 49
Plutarch
  De curiositate, 135–6
  Galba
    on Claudius' crockery, 173–4
    maiestas, 78
  Life of Theseus, 135, 136, 137
  Moralia, Empona, 172
  political life, 209
poison, 17–18
political act, history as, 208–9
Pompeii
  and benefaction, 100–1
  graffiti, 113

'House of the Baker', 129–30
Pomponius Secundus, P., 204
populus Romanus see Roman people
portraits, statuary, 73–83
potestas, 37–40
power of the emperor, 28–31
  see also *auctoritas*; *imperium*; *potestas*
power relationships, 19–23
precariousness, and the Golden Age, 184, 196,
    203, 216–19
present *see* imperial present
Price, S. R. F.
  Religions of Rome, 198
  Rituals and Power, 199
princeps iuventutis, 117–19
principate/'Principate', and Augustus, 30–1, 37–9
Procopius, on Domitian, 206–7
proscription, 40–1
proximity to the emperor, 16–16
Prymnessos (Phrygia), coins, 69–71
public opinion, 8–11
  anecdotal evidence, 24–8
  and the *populus Romanus*, 11–16
  transcripts, 17–23
public transcripts, 19
Purcell, N., 26, 139, 149, 176

Quintilian
  on the *tirocinium*, 117
  on the wit of Augustus, 175
Quirinus Augustus, 202–3

reciprocity, 46, 101, 128, 191, 198
regnal years, 183–4
Res Gestae Divi Augusti, 29–30
  and *auctoritas*, 40
  benefaction, 115
  consent, 45
  and *pater patriae*, 43–4
resurrection, 226, 231–2
reversal, festivals of, 188, 191, 192–3, 225
role of the emperor, Fronto on, 6
roles, 6–8, 31–2, 58–61
  see also generosity; justice; mediators
Roman people (*populus Romanus*), 11–16, 107–8,
    223–4
Rowan, C., 117
Rowe, G., 30, 40
Russell, A., 44–5, 73, 75

Sailor, D., 210, 214, 215
Saller, R. P., 25–6
Sallustius Crispus, 228
Salt-fish dealer, in Suetonius, 172
saltus Burutianus, 86

sanctuary *see* asylum
Sardis, and Menogenes, 112
Saturn/*Saturnalia* (festival), 188–96
Saturnalia (festival), 188, 192–3, 195, 225
Scaevola *see* Cervidius Scaevola, Q.
Scott, J. C., 19–20, 23–4, 60
Sebasteion (Aphrodisias), 140
Senatus consultum de Pisone patre (SCPP),
   30–1, 104
Seneca, 53
   on an emperor's monstrosity, 154
   Apocolocyntosis, 194–5
   De clementia, 155
   De ira, 155–6
   Golden Age, 185–6
   mullet story, 150, 151–2
Septimius Geta, P., *see* Geta
Septimius Severus
   Digest on *maiestas*, 77
   Dio on, 213–14
   generosity of, 119
   gold bust, 71–2
settlements
   Augustan, 35
      auctoritas, 36–41
      and the *leges et iura* coin, 41–3
Shaw, Brent, 95–6
shoemaker, and Caligula, 160–2, 165, 166–7
Sibylline Oracles, 185
Sibylline Oracles, 228–31
slaves/slavery
   and asylum, 79–83
   De ira (Seneca), 155–6
   On Freedom (Epictetus), 20–1
   and Vedius Pollio, 155
Smyrna, and earthquake relief, 122
speech acts, 7, 10, 34
statio, 30–1
Statius, on wondrous food, 146–7
statues, 73–83
   Domitian, 206–7
   family group in Thespiae, 114
status dissonance, 22–3
Stewart, C., 73–4
Stymphalian birds, 156–7
succession, and acceptance, 102–9
Suetonius
   and Agamemnon, 181
   on Claudius, 106–7, 146
      at dinner, 173
   on the *Forum Augustum*, 216–17
   on Gaius/Caligula, 191, 197
   Life, on Caligula, 166–7
   on *maiestas*, 78
   mullet story, 150

   on natural oddities kept by emperors, 146–7
   on Nero, 119
   on *pater patriae*, 44–5
   political life, 209
   Salt-fish dealer, 172
   Tiberius and the fisherman in Capri,
      154–5
   on Vespasian's dream, 212–13
   on the wit of Augustus, 175
   on wondrous animals displayed
      by Augustus, 145
Symmachus, Quintus Aurelius, 47–8
Synesius of Cyrene, 179–80, 181

Tacitus
   on Agrippina the Elder, 15
   on Anna Rufilla, 81–2
   asylum, 72
   on Augustus' death, 215–16
   and bust of Caesar, 72
   on Claudius at dinner, 174
   on Clemens, 226–7
   on Germanicus, 219–23
   on Nero and Octavia's divorce, 162–3
   political life, 209
   and politics in history, 214–16
Thespiae, statue group, 114
Thonemann, Peter, 83–4
Tiberius Gemellus (grandson of Tiberius), 114
Tiberius Julius Caesar Augustus, 104–5
   anecdotal evidence, 26–7
   and benefaction, 116
   case against L. Ennius, 77
   and Clemens, 226–8
   fish stories, 150–2
   and the fisherman on Capri, 154–5
   and *maiestas*, 78
   and natural oddities, 145–6
   oath of allegiance at Paphos, 113
   in *Ovid*, 111
   and *statio*, 30–1
   and the steward fable, 177
   as successor of Augustus, 216
   and the talking bird, 176
time/timelessness, 1, 179–85
   devotion and imperial cult, 196–203
tirocinium, 117
Titus, 99
toga virilis, 117, 118–19, 183
Torelli, M., 126
Trajan, 46–7, 72, 91, 124–7, 130
transcripts (defined), 20
tribunals, 49–50
triumphal processions, 142–4, 218
Tuori, K., 63

uirtutis coinage, 68–70
Ulpian
  on asylum, 79–80
  on consent, 39
  on law and the emperor, 49–50
Ulpius Eurycles, 206
unbreakable glass tale, 152–3
uncertainty principle, xi
urbanitas, 170
usurpation, 108

Vaga (Africa) inscription, 86
Varro Murena, 40
Vedius Pollio, 155
Velleius Paterculus, 30
Venuleius Saturninus, *De iudiciis publiciis*,
  77
Versnel, H. S., 188, 192, 193
Verus, Lucius, 147
  letter to Ulpius Eurycles, 206
Vespasian
  dangers of making fun of, 168–72
  dreams, 212–13
  and the Flavian triumph of AD 71, 143–4

Lex de Imperio Vespasiani, 53–8
  marble head, 206
  and the mechanical engineer, 153
Veyne, Paul, *Bread and Circuses*, 17–18
Vinius, Titus, 173–4
virtues, 65–8
volatility, 4

Wallace-Hadrill, A., 65, 192
Weber, M., 4
whales, and Claudius, 150
Wintrobe, R., and the 'Dictator's Dilemma',
  60, 161
Wiseman, T. P., 107
wit, of the emperor, 170, 174–5
wonder tales, 131–4, 231
  paradoxography, 134–42
  and Rome, 142–9
  as wonder and monster, 149–59
Woolf, G., 127–8

Xiphilinus, 160

Yavetz, Z., 24, 163, 219